Learning OpenStack Networking (Neutron)

Second Edition

Wield the power of OpenStack Neutron networking
to bring network infrastructure and capabilities to
your cloud

James Denton

[PACKT] open source *
PUBLISHING   community experience distilled

BIRMINGHAM - MUMBAI

Learning OpenStack Networking (Neutron)
Second Edition

Copyright © 2015 Packt Publishing

First published: October 2014

Second edition: November 2015

Production reference: 1251115

Published by Packt Publishing Ltd.
Livery Place
35 Livery Street
Birmingham B3 2PB, UK.

ISBN 978-1-78528-772-5

www.packtpub.com

Credits

Author
James Denton

Reviewers
Will Foster
Mostafa A. Hamid
Kevin Jackson

Commissioning Editor
Kartikey Pandey

Acquisition Editor
Reshma Raman

Content Development Editor
Shweta Pant

Technical Editor
Humera Shaikh

Copy Editors
Shruti Iyer
Karuna Narayanan

Project Coordinator
Shipra Chawhan

Proofreader
Safis Editing

Indexer
Mariammal Chettiyar

Production Coordinator
Conidon Miranda

Cover Work
Conidon Miranda

About the Author

James Denton lives with his beautiful wife, Amanda, and son, Wyatt, in San Antonio, Texas. He is an experienced IT professional with extensive experience in application networking technologies and OpenStack Networking. James is a principal architect at Rackspace and currently supports OpenStack Networking for customers of the Rackspace Private Cloud product. He can be found on Twitter as @jimmdenton and on Freenode IRC as busterswt.

I'd like to thank my wife, Amanda, for providing encouragement and patience throughout the writing of this book and its predecessor. I would also like to thank my team and managers at Rackspace for reviewing many rough drafts and providing excellent feedback.

Without NASA, Rackspace, and the ever-growing OpenStack community, the opportunity to write this book would not have been possible. I would like to extend thanks to everyone involved, in the past and present, in making OpenStack what it is today.

About the Reviewers

Will Foster is originally from Raleigh, North Carolina. He attended The Citadel, The Military College of South Carolina, in 1996, where he pursued a degree in English. Will was a performing member of The Summerall Guards, an elite close-order Prussian drill unit, as well as a cadet officer within Tango Company, class of 2000. He also holds a degree in technical writing from Appalachian State University and is a Red Hat Certified Engineer.

Since 2000, Will has worked as a UNIX/Linux systems administrator involved in mission-critical customer-facing production business environments. A lifelong skateboard enthusiast, he had a brief stint as a snowboarding instructor during the years 2000-2001.

Will has worked at Red Hat since 2007 as a senior systems administrator / DevOps engineer managing enterprise IT storage and core infrastructure. Currently, he works in the OpenStack deployment team. His team designs, architects, and builds labs and infrastructure to test and vet real-world customer deployments and cloud scenarios. They also collaborate with the upstream development community and partners to improve and build upon the OpenStack platform.

Will currently resides in Dublin, Ireland, and in his free time, he performs stand-up comedy, travels, and blogs at `http://hobo.house`. Will can be found on Twitter as `@sadsfae`.

Mostafa A. Hamid is an information systems engineer from Potsdam, The State University of New York (SUNY). He has completed certifications such as CISSP, CEH, and LPIC as well as in IBM RUP architecture. Besides these, Mostafa is also certified in JavaScript, PHP, Backbone.js, Java, and XML from Potsdam. He has a bachelor's degree from Modern Academy for Computer Science and Management Technology.

Mostafa has worked with Hilton Worldwide as an internet support engineer, with United Systems as a technical support engineer, and with Media Plans as an IT manager/architect. He has also worked with MOIS as an IT manager/teacher and is currently working as a software developer at Wassaq.

Mostafa has also reviewed *OpenStack Essentials, Packt Publishing*.

> I would like to thank Manon Niazi, the Deutschlander I met in college; my family; and Shipra Chawhan, the project coordinator. Of course, much thanks go to the author, James Denton.

Kevin Jackson is married and has three children. He is an experienced IT professional working with business and enterprises of all sizes at Rackspace as a principal OpenStack engineer. Kevin has been working with OpenStack since early 2011 and has extensive experience of various flavors of Linux, Unix, and hosting environments. Kevin can be found on twitter @itarchitectkev.

Kevin authored the first edition, and coauthored the second and recently published third editions of the *OpenStack Cloud Computing Cookbook* by Packt Publishing. Kevin also co-authored the OpenStack Foundation's *OpenStack Architecture Design Guide* during a 5-day book sprint in California.

www.PacktPub.com

Support files, eBooks, discount offers, and more

For support files and downloads related to your book, please visit www.PacktPub.com.

Did you know that Packt offers eBook versions of every book published, with PDF and ePub files available? You can upgrade to the eBook version at www.PacktPub.com and as a print book customer, you are entitled to a discount on the eBook copy. Get in touch with us at service@packtpub.com for more details.

At www.PacktPub.com, you can also read a collection of free technical articles, sign up for a range of free newsletters and receive exclusive discounts and offers on Packt books and eBooks.

https://www2.packtpub.com/books/subscription/packtlib

Do you need instant solutions to your IT questions? PacktLib is Packt's online digital book library. Here, you can search, access, and read Packt's entire library of books.

Why subscribe?

- Fully searchable across every book published by Packt
- Copy and paste, print, and bookmark content
- On demand and accessible via a web browser

Free access for Packt account holders

If you have an account with Packt at www.PacktPub.com, you can use this to access PacktLib today and view 9 entirely free books. Simply use your login credentials for immediate access.

Table of Contents

Preface

In the fall of 2015, the OpenStack Foundation released the 12th version of OpenStack, code-named Liberty, to the public. Since its introduction as an open source project in 2010 by NASA and Rackspace, OpenStack has undergone significant improvements in its features and functionality and has matured into production-ready cloud software that powers workloads of all sizes throughout the world.

In 2012, the Folsom release of OpenStack introduced a standalone networking component, known then as Quantum. Now known as Neutron, the networking component of OpenStack provides cloud operators and users with an API to create and manage networks in the cloud. Neutron's extensible framework allows for third-party plugins and additional network services, such as load balancers, firewalls, and virtual private networks, to be deployed and managed.

As an architect and operator of hundreds of OpenStack-based private clouds since 2012, I have seen much of what OpenStack has to offer in terms of networking capabilities, and I have condensed what I feel are its most valuable and production-ready features to date into this book. Throughout this book, we will take a look at a few common network and service architectures and lay a foundation for deploying and managing OpenStack Networking, which will help you develop and sharpen your skills as an OpenStack cloud operator.

What this book covers

Chapter 1, Preparing the Network for OpenStack, provides an introduction to OpenStack Networking, including supported networking technologies and examples of how to architect the physical network to support an OpenStack cloud.

Chapter 2, Installing OpenStack, provides instructions to install the core components of the Kilo release of OpenStack on the Ubuntu 14.04 LTS operating system.

Chapter 3, Installing Neutron, explains how to install the Neutron networking components of OpenStack. We will also cover the internal architecture of Neutron, including the use of agents and plugins to orchestrate network connectivity.

Chapter 4, Building a Virtual Switching Infrastructure, helps you to install and configure the ML2 plugin to support both the LinuxBridge and Open vSwitch drivers and agents. We will also cover the architectural differences between the LinuxBridge and Open vSwitch drivers and agents and how they connect instances to the network.

Chapter 5, Creating Networks with Neutron, walks you through creating networks and subnets in the cloud, booting and attaching instances to networks, and exploring the process of obtaining DHCP leases and metadata.

Chapter 6, Managing Security Groups, examines the use of iptables to secure instance traffic at the compute node and walks you through creating and managing security groups and associated rules.

Chapter 7, Creating Standalone Routers with Neutron, walks you through creating standalone virtual routers and attaching them to networks, applying floating IPs to instances, and following the flow of traffic through a router to an instance.

Chapter 8, Router Redundancy Using VRRP, explores Virtual Routing Redundancy Protocol and its use in providing highly-available virtual routers.

Chapter 9, Distributed Virtual Routers, walks you through creating and managing virtual routers that are distributed across multiple nodes.

Chapter 10, Load Balancing Traffic to Instances, explores the fundamental components of a load balancer in Neutron, including virtual IPs, pools, pool members, and monitors, and walks you through creating and integrating a virtual load balancer into the network.

Chapter 11, Firewall as a Service, covers the creation and management of virtual firewalls, their associated policies and rules, and the integration of virtual firewalls in the network.

Chapter 12, Virtual Private Network as a Service, examines the fundamental concepts of IPSec-based virtual private networks and walks you through configuring and managing VPN connections that connect tenant networks to remote networks.

Appendix A, Additional Neutron Commands, briefly covers additional Neutron functionality that is outside the scope of this book, including commands related to Cisco 1000V, VMware NSX, and more.

Appendix B, Virtualizing the Environment, describes the process of deploying OpenStack across multiple virtual machines using VirtualBox virtualization software in case physical servers are not available to the reader. Examples are limited to VirtualBox 5 on Mac OS but can be adapted to other operating systems and releases if necessary.

What you need for this book

This book assumes a moderate level of networking experience, including experience with Linux networking configurations as well as physical switch and router configurations. While this book walks the reader through a basic installation of OpenStack, little time is spent on services other than Neutron. Therefore, it is important that the reader has a basic understanding of OpenStack and its general configuration prior to configuring OpenStack Networking.

In this book, the following is required:

* Operating system:

    Ubuntu 14.04 LTS

The following software is needed:

* OpenStack Kilo (2015.1)

Internet connectivity is required to install OpenStack packages and to make use of the example architectures in the book. While virtualization software, such as VirtualBox or VMware, can be used to simulate servers and the network infrastructure, this book assumes that OpenStack is installed on physical hardware and that a physical network infrastructure is in place.

Major OpenStack releases occur every six months, and after the M- or N-release, Kilo repositories may no longer be available. In the event that the OpenStack installation procedure documented in this book no longer functions properly, refer to the installation guide at docs.openstack.org for instructions on installing the latest version of OpenStack.

Who this book is for

This book is geared towards OpenStack cloud administrators or operators with a novice to intermediate level of experience in managing OpenStack-based clouds who are looking to build or enhance their cloud using the networking service known as Neutron. By laying down a basic installation of OpenStack based on the installation guide found at `docs.openstack.org`, the reader should be able to follow the examples laid out in the book to obtain a functional understanding of the various components of OpenStack Networking using open-source reference architectures.

Conventions

In this book, you will find a number of text styles that distinguish between different kinds of information. Here are some examples of these styles and an explanation of their meaning.

Code words in text, database table names, folder names, filenames, file extensions, pathnames, dummy URLs, user input, and Twitter handles are shown as follows: "The `OPENSTACK_KEYSTONE_DEFAULT_ROLE` setting in the `/etc/openstack-dashboard/local_settings.py` file must also be modified before the dashboard can be used."

A block of code is set as follows:

```
[DEFAULT]
...
my_ip = 10.254.254.101
vncserver_proxyclient_address = 10.254.254.101
vnc_enabled = True
vncserver_listen = 0.0.0.0
novncproxy_base_url = http://controller01:6080/vnc_auto.html
```

When we wish to draw your attention to a particular part of a code block, the relevant lines or items are set in bold:

```
nova boot --flavor <FLAVOR_ID> --image <IMAGE_ID> \
--nic net-id=<NETWORK_ID> --security-group <SECURITY_GROUP_ID> \
INSTANCE_NAME
```

Any command-line input or output is written as follows:

```
# service nova-api restart
# service nova-cert restart
# service nova-consoleauth restart
# service nova-scheduler restart
# service nova-conductor restart
# service nova-novncproxy restart
```

New terms and **important words** are shown in bold. Words that you see on the screen, for example, in menus or dialog boxes, appear in the text like this: "Looking at the following screenshot, the **System Information** panel provides the user with information about the environment, including **Services** and **Compute Services**."

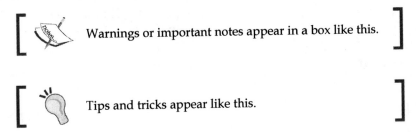

Warnings or important notes appear in a box like this.

Tips and tricks appear like this.

Reader feedback

Feedback from our readers is always welcome. Let us know what you think about this book—what you liked or disliked. Reader feedback is important for us as it helps us develop titles that you will really get the most out of.

To send us general feedback, simply e-mail feedback@packtpub.com, and mention the book's title in the subject of your message.

If there is a topic that you have expertise in and you are interested in either writing or contributing to a book, see our author guide at www.packtpub.com/authors.

Customer support

Now that you are the proud owner of a Packt book, we have a number of things to help you to get the most from your purchase.

Downloading the example code

You can download the example code files from your account at `http://www.packtpub.com` for all the Packt Publishing books you have purchased. If you purchased this book elsewhere, you can visit `http://www.packtpub.com/support` and register to have the files e-mailed directly to you.

Downloading the color images of this book

We also provide you with a PDF file that has color images of the screenshots/diagrams used in this book. The color images will help you better understand the changes in the output. You can download this file from: `https://www.packtpub.com/sites/default/files/downloads/7225OS_Graphics.pdf`.

Errata

Although we have taken every care to ensure the accuracy of our content, mistakes do happen. If you find a mistake in one of our books—maybe a mistake in the text or the code—we would be grateful if you could report this to us. By doing so, you can save other readers from frustration and help us improve subsequent versions of this book. If you find any errata, please report them by visiting `http://www.packtpub.com/submit-errata`, selecting your book, clicking on the **Errata Submission Form** link, and entering the details of your errata. Once your errata are verified, your submission will be accepted and the errata will be uploaded to our website or added to any list of existing errata under the Errata section of that title.

To view the previously submitted errata, go to `https://www.packtpub.com/books/content/support` and enter the name of the book in the search field. The required information will appear under the **Errata** section.

Piracy

Piracy of copyrighted material on the Internet is an ongoing problem across all media. At Packt, we take the protection of our copyright and licenses very seriously. If you come across any illegal copies of our works in any form on the Internet, please provide us with the location address or website name immediately so that we can pursue a remedy.

Please contact us at copyright@packtpub.com with a link to the suspected pirated material.

We appreciate your help in protecting our authors and our ability to bring you valuable content.

Questions

If you have a problem with any aspect of this book, you can contact us at questions@packtpub.com, and we will do our best to address the problem.

1
Preparing the Network for OpenStack

In today's data centers, networks are composed of more devices than ever before. Servers, switches, routers, storage systems, and security appliances now exist as virtual machines and virtual network appliances. These devices place a large strain on traditional network management systems, as they are unable to provide a scalable, automated approach to managing next-generation networks. Users now expect more control and flexibility of the infrastructure with quicker provisioning, all of which OpenStack promises to deliver.

This chapter will introduce many features that OpenStack Networking provides as well as various network architectures supported by OpenStack.

What is OpenStack Networking?

OpenStack Networking is a pluggable, scalable, and API-driven system to manage networks and IP addresses in an OpenStack-based cloud. Like other core OpenStack components, OpenStack Networking can be used by administrators and users to increase the value and maximize the utilization of existing data center resources.

Neutron, the code name of OpenStack Networking, is a standalone service that can be installed independently of other OpenStack services such as Nova (compute service), Glance (image service), Keystone (identity service), Cinder (block storage), and Horizon (dashboard). OpenStack Networking services can be split among multiple hosts to provide resiliency and redundancy, or they can be configured to operate on a single node.

OpenStack Networking exposes an application programmable interface, or API, to users and passes requests to the configured network plugins for additional processing. Users are able to define network connectivity in the cloud, and cloud operators are allowed to leverage different networking technologies to enhance and power the cloud.

Like many other OpenStack services, Neutron requires access to a database for persistent storage of the network configuration.

Features of OpenStack Networking

OpenStack Networking includes many technologies one would find in a data center, including switching, routing, load balancing, firewalling, and virtual private networks. These features can be configured to leverage open source or commercial software, and provide a cloud operator with all the tools necessary to build a functional and self-contained cloud. OpenStack Networking also provides a framework for third-party vendors to build on and enhance the capabilities of the cloud.

Switching

A **virtual switch** is defined as a software application that connects virtual machines to virtual networks at layer 2, or the data-link layer, of the OSI model. Neutron supports multiple virtual switching platforms, including Linux bridges provided by the `bridge` kernel module and Open vSwitch. Open vSwitch, also known as OVS, is an open source virtual switch that supports standard management interfaces and protocols, including NetFlow, SPAN, RSPAN, LACP, and 802.1q VLAN tagging. However, many of these features are not exposed to the user through the OpenStack API. In addition to VLAN tagging, users can build overlay networks in software using L2-in-L3 tunneling protocols, such as GRE or VXLAN. Open vSwitch can be used to facilitate communication between instances and devices outside the control of OpenStack, which include hardware switches, network firewalls, storage devices, dedicated servers, and more. Additional information on the use of Linux bridges and Open vSwitch as switching platforms for OpenStack can be found in *Chapter 4, Building a Virtual Switching Infrastructure*.

Routing

OpenStack Networking provides routing and NAT capabilities through the use of IP forwarding, iptables, and network namespaces. Inside a network namespace, we can find sockets, bound ports, and interfaces that were created in the namespace. Each network namespace has its own routing table, interfaces, and iptables processes that provide filtering and network address translation. By leveraging network namespaces to separate networks, there is no concern of overlapping subnets between networks created by tenants. Configuring a router within Neutron enables instances to interact and communicate with outside networks or other networks in the cloud. Router namespaces are also leveraged by the advanced networking services **Firewall as a Service** and **Virtual Private Network as a Service**, which will be discussed later in this book. More information on routing within OpenStack can be found in *Chapter 7, Creating Standalone Routers with Neutron*; *Chapter 8, Router Redundancy Using VRRP*; and *Chapter 9, Distributed Virtual Routers*.

Load balancing

First introduced in the Grizzly release of OpenStack, **Load Balancing as a Service**, also known as **LBaaS**, provides users with the ability to distribute client requests across multiple instances or servers. Users can create monitors, set connection limits, and apply persistence profiles to traffic traversing a virtual load balancer. The Kilo release of OpenStack introduced version 2 of the LBaaS API in an experimental status. The v2 API is a vast improvement over version 1, and by the Liberty release, it should be stable. OpenStack Networking is equipped with a plugin for LBaaS that utilizes HAProxy in the open source reference implementation. More information on the use of load balancers within Neutron can be found in *Chapter 10, Load Balancing Traffic to Instances*.

Firewalling

In the current release of OpenStack, there are two methods of providing security to instances: security groups and firewalls. When using security groups, instances are placed into groups that share common functionality and rule sets. Iptables rules are configured on compute nodes and filter traffic in and out of Linux bridges connected to each instance. In a reference implementation, when using virtual firewalls provided by **Firewall as a Service**, also known as **FWaaS**, security is handled at the edge of the network on a Neutron router rather than at the compute node. Through the Liberty release of OpenStack, the FWaaS API remains in an experimental status with no guaranteed backward compatibility in future releases. More information on securing instances can be found in *Chapter 6, Managing Security Groups*, and *Chapter 11, Firewall as a Service*.

Virtual private networks

A **virtual private network**, or **VPN**, extends a private network across a public network such as the Internet. A VPN enables a computer to send and receive data across public networks as if it were directly connected to the private network. Neutron provides a set of APIs to allow users to create IPSec-based VPN tunnels from Neutron routers to remote gateways when using the open source reference implementation. More information on creating and managing virtual private networks can be found in *Chapter 12, Virtual Private Network as a Service*.

Network functions virtualization

Network functions virtualization, or **NFV**, is a network architecture concept that proposes using traditional virtualization techniques to replace standalone network appliances used for various network functions. These functions include intrusion detection, caching, gateways, WAN accelerators, firewalls, and more. Support for NFV within OpenStack is growing, but requires a major shift in the current design model to support features such as VLAN trunking directly to virtualized instances, unaddressed interfaces, and others that may be required by network devices. In Juno, support for **SR-IOV**, also known as **single root I/O virtualization**, was introduced. Using SR-IOV, instances are no longer required to use para-virtualized drivers or to be connected to virtual bridges within the host. Instead, the instance is attached to an SR-IOV port that is associated with a **virtual function** (**VF**) in the NIC, allowing the instance to access the NIC hardware directly. Explaining how to configure support for SR-IOV is outside the scope of this book, but more information can be found on the OpenStack Wiki at https://wiki.openstack.org/.

Preparing the physical infrastructure

When architecting the network, it is important to first determine how the cloud will be used. Is a highly scalable environment with multiple levels of network, hardware, and service redundancy required? Or, are your needs less complex, requiring nothing more than a sandbox for application development, with little concern given to the resiliency of the network or compute platform? Are all of the advanced networking features that OpenStack Networking has to offer in terms of routing, firewalling, and load balancing required? Or, are you looking to leverage existing physical hardware in the data center to accomplish those tasks?

OpenStack Networking can serve many roles within different clouds but is better at some technologies than others. The purpose of the cloud itself, along with security requirements and available hardware, will play a big part in determining the architecture of the network and OpenStack's role in the network.

The official OpenStack website (www.openstack.org) provides reference architectures for OpenStack clouds leveraging Neutron networking that involves a combination of one or more of the following nodes:

- Controller node
- Network node
- Compute node

Before the installation of OpenStack can begin, the physical network infrastructure must be configured to support the networks needed for an operational cloud. In the following diagram, I have highlighted the area of responsibility for the network administrator:

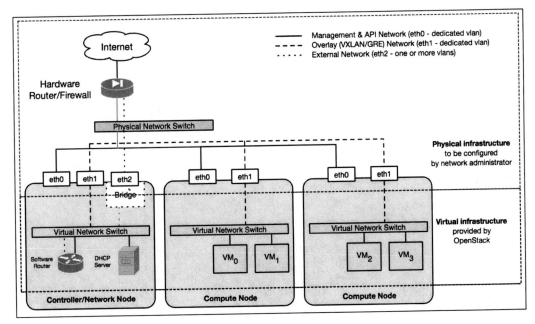

Figure 1.1

The physical network infrastructure must be configured to support OpenStack Networking, which can include a dedicated management interface, a network dedicated to overlay network traffic, and one or more networks that provide external connectivity to instances. As shown in the preceding diagram, the configuration of interfaces and networks represented in the top half of the diagram are the responsibility of the network or system administrator. These responsibilities include the configuration of physical switches, firewalls, or routers as well as interfaces on the servers themselves. The bottom half of the diagram represents interfaces and devices such as virtual switches and virtual machines that will be configured automatically by OpenStack.

In the next few chapters, I will define networks and VLANs that will be used throughout the book to demonstrate the various components of OpenStack Networking. Generic information on the configuration of switch ports, routers, or firewalls can be found in the upcoming chapters as well.

Types of network traffic

The reference architecture for OpenStack Networking defines at least four distinct types of traffic that will be seen on the network:

- Management
- API
- External
- Guest

Although I have taken the liberty of splitting out the network traffic into dedicated interfaces in this book, it is not necessary to do so to create an operational OpenStack cloud. In fact, many administrators and distributions choose to collapse multiple traffic types onto single or bonded interfaces using VLAN tagging. Depending on the chosen deployment model, the administrator may spread networking services across multiple nodes or collapse them onto a single node. The security requirements of the enterprise deploying the cloud will often dictate how the cloud is built. The various network and service configurations will be discussed in the upcoming sections.

Management network

The **management network**, also referred to as the internal network in some distributions, is used for internal communication between hosts for services such as the messaging service and database service. All hosts will communicate with each other over this network. In many cases, this same interface may be used to facilitate Glance image transfers between hosts or some other bandwidth-intensive traffic. The management network can be configured as an isolated network on a dedicated interface or combined with another network, as described in the following section.

API network

The **API network** is used to expose OpenStack APIs to users of the cloud and services within the cloud. Endpoint addresses for services, such as Keystone, Neutron, Glance, and Horizon, are procured from the API network.

It is a common practice to utilize a single interface and IP address for API endpoints and management access to the host itself over SSH. A diagram of this configuration is provided later in this chapter.

It is recommended, though not required, that you physically separate management and API traffic from other traffic types, such as storage traffic, to avoid issues with network congestion that may affect operational stability.

External network

An **external network** provides Neutron routers with network access. Once a router has been configured and attached to the external network, the network becomes the source of floating IP addresses for instances and other network resources. IP addresses in an external network are expected to be routable and reachable by clients on a corporate network or the Internet.

Guest network

The **guest network** is a network dedicated to instance traffic. Options for guest networks include local networks restricted to a particular node, flat or VLAN-tagged networks, or virtual overlay networks made possible with GRE or VXLAN encapsulation. For more information on guest networks, refer to *Chapter 5, Creating Networks with Neutron*.

The physical interfaces used for external and guest networks can be dedicated interfaces or ones that are shared with other types of traffic. Each approach has its benefits and drawbacks, and they are described in more detail later in the chapter.

Physical server connections

The number of interfaces needed per host is dependent on the purpose of the cloud, the security and performance requirements of the organization, and the availability of hardware.

A single interface per server that results in a combined control and data plane is all that is needed for a fully operational OpenStack cloud. Many organizations choose to deploy their cloud this way, especially when port density is at a premium. Collapsed networking may also be used when the environment is simply used for testing, or network failure at the node level is a non-impacting event. It is my recommendation, however, that you split control and data traffic across multiple interfaces whenever possible.

Single interface

For hosts using a single interface, all traffic to and from instances as well as internal OpenStack, SSH management, and API traffic traverse the same interface. This configuration can result in severe performance degradation, as a guest can create a denial of service attack against its host by consuming all available bandwidth.

The following diagram demonstrates the use of a single physical interface for all traffic when using the Open vSwitch driver. On the controller node, a single interface is connected to a bridge and handles external, guest, management, and API service traffic. On the compute node, a single interface handles guest and management traffic:

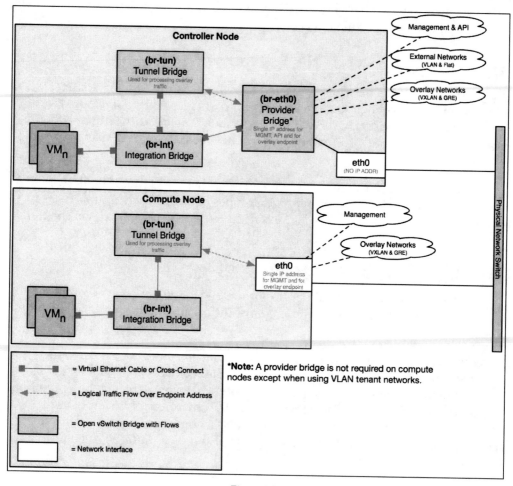

Figure 1.2

In the preceding diagram, all OpenStack service and management traffic traverses the same physical interface as guest traffic.

Multiple interfaces

To reduce the likelihood of guest network bandwidth consumption impacting management traffic and to maintain a more robust security posture, segregation of traffic between multiple physical interfaces is recommended. At a minimum, two interfaces should be used: one that serves as a dedicated interface for management and API traffic and another that serves as a dedicated interface for external and guest traffic. Additional interfaces can be used to further segregate traffic. The following diagram demonstrates traffic split across two physical interfaces when using the Open vSwitch driver:

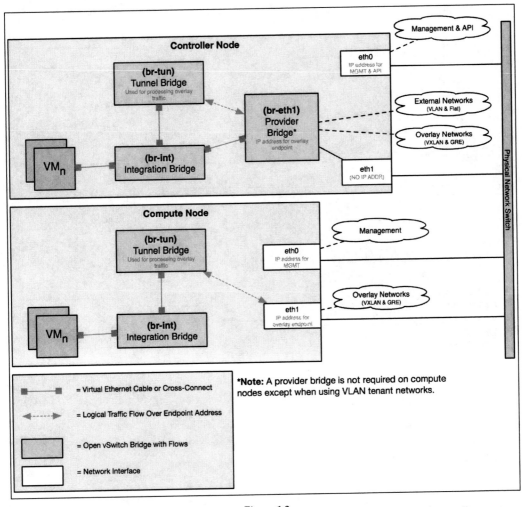

Figure 1.3

In the preceding diagram, a dedicated physical interface on the controller node handles OpenStack API and management traffic. Another interface is connected to a bridge that handles external and overlay traffic to and from Neutron routers and other network resources. On the compute node, a dedicated physical interface is used for management traffic and another for overlay traffic to and from instances.

In this book, the environment will be built using three interfaces: one for management and API traffic, one for external or VLAN tenant network traffic, and another for overlay network traffic:

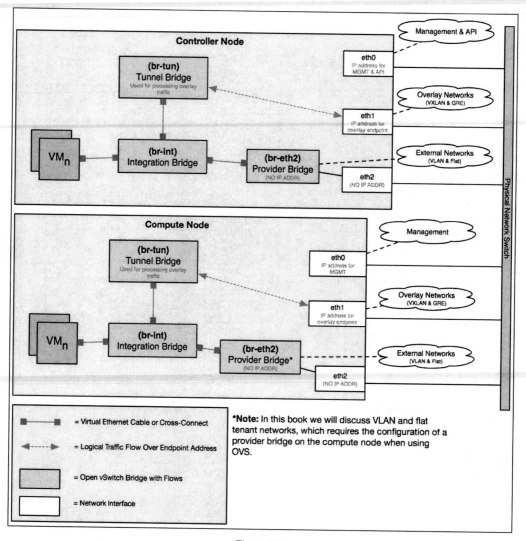

Figure 1.4

In the preceding diagram, a dedicated interface on the controller node handles OpenStack API and management traffic. Another dedicated interface handles overlay traffic, and another is connected to a bridge that handles external traffic. On the compute node, a dedicated interface is used for management traffic, another dedicated interface handles overlay traffic, and another is connected to a bridge that handles VLAN traffic when VLAN tenant networks are in use.

Bonding

NIC bonding offers users the ability to multiply available bandwidth by aggregating links. Two or more physical interfaces can be combined to create a single virtual interface, or bond, which can then be placed in a bridge or used as a regular interface. The technology used to accomplish this is known as IEEE 802.1ad **Link Aggregation Control Protocol**, or **LACP**. The physical switching infrastructure must be capable of supporting this type of bond. Legacy switching devices required the multiple links of a bond to be connected to the same switch. Modern devices support technology such as vPC and MLAG. They allow links of a bond to be connected to two switches, providing hardware redundancy between switches while allowing users the full bandwidth of the bond in normal operating conditions, with no changes to the server configuration necessary.

In addition to aggregating interfaces, bonding can also refer to the ability to create redundant links in an active/passive manner. Both links are simultaneously cabled to a switch or pair of switches, but only one interface is active at any given time. Both types of bonds can be created within the operating system when the appropriate kernel module is installed. Bonding can be configured in Open vSwitch if desired, but is outside the scope of OpenStack and this book.

Bonding interfaces can be an inexpensive way to provide hardware-level network redundancy to the cloud infrastructure. If you are interested in configuring NIC bonding on your hosts, refer to the Ubuntu bonding page at `https://help.ubuntu.com/community/UbuntuBonding`.

 Bonding configurations vary greatly between Linux distributions. Refer to the respective documentation of your Linux distribution for assistance in configuring bonding.

Separating services across nodes

Like other OpenStack services, cloud operators can split OpenStack Networking services across multiple nodes. Small deployments may use a single node to host all services, including networking, compute, database, and messaging. Others might find benefit in using a dedicated compute node and a dedicated network node to handle guest traffic routed through software routers and to offload Neutron DHCP and metadata services. The following sections describe a few common service deployment models.

Using a single controller node

In an environment consisting of a single controller and one or more compute nodes, the controller will likely handle all networking services and other OpenStack services, while the compute nodes strictly provide compute resources.

The following diagram demonstrates a controller node hosting all OpenStack management and networking services where the Neutron layer 3 agent is not utilized. Two physical interfaces are used to separate management and instance network traffic:

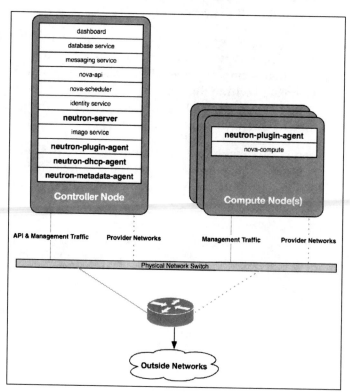

Figure 1.5

The preceding diagram reflects the use of a single combined controller/network node and one or more compute nodes, with Neutron providing only layer 2 connectivity between instances and external gateway devices. An external router is needed to handle routing between network segments.

The following diagram demonstrates a controller node hosting all OpenStack management and networking services, including the Neutron L3 agent. Three physical interfaces are used to provide separate control and data planes:

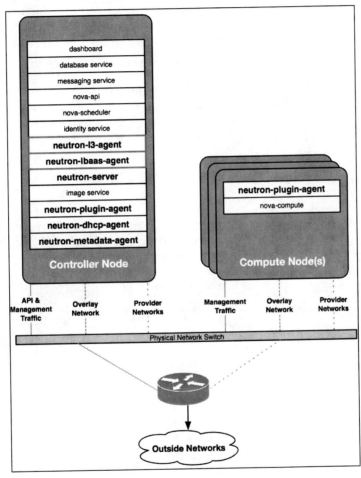

Figure 1.6

The preceding diagram reflects the use of a single combined controller/network node and one or more compute nodes in a network configuration that utilizes the Neutron L3 agent. Software routers created with Neutron reside on the controller node and handle routing between connected tenant networks and external provider networks.

The environment built out in this book will be composed of a single controller node running all OpenStack network services and two compute nodes running Nova compute services.

Using a dedicated network node

A network node is dedicated to handling most or all the OpenStack Networking services, including the L3 agent, DHCP agent, metadata agent, and more. The use of a dedicated network node provides additional security and resilience, as the controller node will be at less risk of network and resource saturation. Some Neutron services, such as the L3 and DHCP agents and the Neutron API service, can be scaled out across multiple nodes for redundancy and increased performance.

The following diagram demonstrates a network node hosting all OpenStack Networking services, including the Neutron L3, DHCP, metadata, and LBaaS agents. The Neutron API service, however, remains installed on the controller node. Three physical interfaces are used where necessary to provide separate control and data planes:

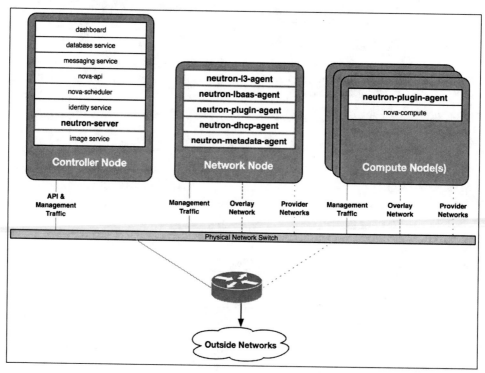

Figure 1.7

The preceding diagram reflects the use of a dedicated network node in a network configuration that utilizes the Neutron L3 agent. Software routers created with the Neutron API reside on the network node and handle routing between connected tenant networks and external provider networks. The `neutron-server` Neutron API service remains on the controller node.

Summary

OpenStack Networking offers the ability to create and manage different technologies found in a data center in a virtualized and programmable manner. If the built-in features and reference implementations are not enough, the pluggable architecture of OpenStack Networking allows for additional functionality to be provided by third-party commercial and open-source vendors. The security requirements of the organization building the cloud as well as the use cases of the cloud will ultimately dictate the physical layout and separation of services across the infrastructure nodes.

Throughout this book, you will learn how to build a functional OpenStack cloud utilizing advanced Neutron networking features available as of the Kilo release. In the next chapter, we will begin a package-based installation of OpenStack on the Ubuntu 14.04 LTS operating system. Topics covered include the installation, configuration, and verification of the database; messaging; and OpenStack identity, image, compute, and dashboard services. The installation and configuration of base OpenStack Networking services, including the Neutron API, can be found in *Chapter 3, Installing Neutron*.

2
Installing OpenStack

Installing, configuring, and maintaining OpenStack clouds can be an arduous task when performed by hand. Many third-party vendors offer downloadable cloud software based on OpenStack that provide deployment and management strategies using Chef, Puppet, Fuel, Ansible, and other tools.

This chapter will step you through a package-based installation of the following OpenStack components on the Ubuntu 14.04 LTS operating system:

- OpenStack Identity (Keystone)
- OpenStack Image Service (Glance)
- OpenStack Compute (Nova)
- OpenStack Block Storage (Cinder)
- OpenStack Dashboard (Horizon)

 The installation process documented within this chapter is based on the *OpenStack Installation Guide for Ubuntu 14.04* found at http://docs.openstack.org/. If you wish to install OpenStack on a different operating system, the guides available at that site provide instructions to do so.

If you'd rather download a third-party cloud distribution based on OpenStack, try one of the following distributions:

- **Rackspace Private Cloud** at http://www.rackspace.com/cloud/private/
- **Red Hat RDO** at http://openstack.redhat.com/
- **Mirantis OpenStack** at http://software.mirantis.com/

Once installed, many of the concepts and examples used throughout this book should still apply to the preceding distributions, but may require extra effort to implement.

System requirements

OpenStack components are intended to run on standard hardware that range from desktop machines to enterprise-grade servers. For optimal performance, the processors of the compute nodes must support hardware virtualization technologies, such as Intel's VT-x or AMD's AMD-v virtualization extensions.

This book assumes that OpenStack will be installed on physical hardware that meets the following minimum requirements:

Server	Hardware Requirements	Notes
Controller node (runs API, network, volume, scheduler, and image services)	• **Processor**: 64-bit x86 • **Memory**: 8 GB RAM • **Disk space**: 64 GB • **Network**: Three 1 Gbps **Network Interface Cards (NICs)**	While a single NIC can be used for all network traffic, that configuration is not addressed in this book
Compute nodes (run virtual instances)	• **Processor**: 64-bit x86 • **Memory**: 8 GB RAM • Disk Space: 64 GB • **Network**: Three 1 Gbps **Network Interface Cards (NICs)**	While a single NIC can be used for all network traffic, that configuration is not addressed in this book

While machines that fail to meet the minimum requirements may be capable of installation based on the documentation included here, these minimums have been defined to ensure a successful experience. Virtualization products, such as VirtualBox, may be used in lieu of physical hardware. However, they will require additional configuration to the environment and to OpenStack, which is outside the scope of this book.

Operating system requirements

OpenStack currently supports CentOS, Fedora, Red Hat Enterprise Linux, openSUSE, SUSE Linux Enterprise Server, and Ubuntu. Each new release of OpenStack tends to support the current releases of these operating systems, with little regard to backward compatibility. This book assumes that the Ubuntu 14.04 LTS server operating system has been installed on all hosts prior to the installation of OpenStack. You can find **Ubuntu 14.04 LTS Server** at http://www.ubuntu.com/download/server.

In order to support all the Neutron features discussed in this book, the minimum kernel version recommended is 3.16.0-38.

Initial network configuration

To understand how networking should initially be configured on each host, refer to the following diagram:

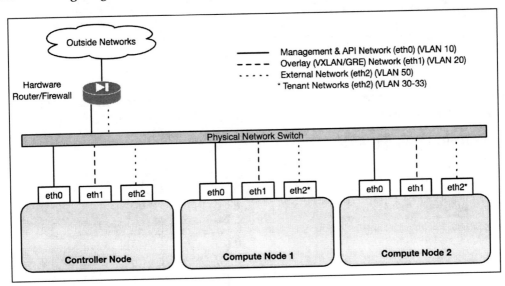

Figure 2.1

In the preceding diagram, three interfaces are cabled to each host. The **eth0** interface will serve as the management interface for OpenStack services and API access. The **eth1** interface will be used for overlay network traffic between hosts. On the controller node, **eth2** will be used for external network traffic to instances through Neutron routers. If VLAN tenant networks are used in lieu of overlay networks such as VXLAN and GRE, then **eth2** will be configured on the compute nodes to support those networks.

At a minimum, the management interface should be configured with an IP address that has outbound access to the Internet. Internet access is required to download OpenStack packages from the Ubuntu package repository. Inbound access to the management address of the servers from a trusted network via SSH (TCP port 22) is recommended.

Example networks

Throughout the book, there will be examples on configuring and using various OpenStack services. The following table provides the VLANs and associated networks used for those services:

VLAN name	VLAN ID	Network
MGMT_NET	10	10.254.254.0/24
OVERLAY_NET	20	172.18.0.0/24
GATEWAY_NET	50	10.50.0.0/24
TENANT_NET30	30	10.30.0.0/24
TENANT_NET31	31	10.31.0.0/24
TENANT_NET32	32	10.32.0.0/24
TENANT_NET33	33	10.33.0.0/24

The following tables provide IP addresses and VLAN IDs recommended for each host interface, should you choose to follow along with the examples:

controller01.learningneutron.com

Interface	IP address	Switchport	VLAN ID
eth0	10.254.254.100	Access port	VLAN 10 (Untagged)
eth1	172.18.0.100	Access port	VLAN 20 (Untagged)
eth2	None	Trunk port	VLAN 30-33,50 (Tagged)

compute01.learningneutron.com

Interface	IP address	Switchport	VLAN ID
eth0	10.254.254.101	Access port	VLAN 10 (Untagged)
eth1	172.18.0.101	Access port	VLAN 20 (Untagged)
eth2	None	Trunk port	VLAN 30-33,50 (Tagged)

compute02.learningneutron.com

Interface	IP address	Switchport	VLAN ID
eth0	10.254.254.102	Access port	VLAN 10 (Untagged)
eth1	172.18.0.102	Access port	VLAN 20 (Untagged)
eth2	None	Trunk port	VLAN 30-33,50 (Tagged)

In the event of connectivity loss, out-of-band management access to the servers via DRAC, iLo, or some other IPMI mechanism is highly recommended.

Interface configuration

Ubuntu uses a configuration file found at /etc/network/interfaces that describes how network interfaces should be configured.

Using a text editor, update the network interface file on each host as follows:

For controller01:

```
auto eth0
iface eth0 inet static
    address 10.254.254.100
    netmask 255.255.255.0
    gateway 10.254.254.1
    dns-nameserver 8.8.8.8

auto eth1
```

```
iface eth1 inet static
    address 172.18.0.100
    netmask 255.255.255.0

auto eth2
iface eth2 inet manual
```

For compute01:

```
auto eth0
iface eth0 inet static
    address 10.254.254.101
    netmask 255.255.255.0
    gateway 10.254.254.1
    dns-nameserver 8.8.8.8

auto eth1
iface eth1 inet static
    address 172.18.0.101
    netmask 255.255.255.0

auto eth2
iface eth2 inet manual
```

For compute02:

```
auto eth0
iface eth0 inet static
    address 10.254.254.102
    netmask 255.255.255.0
    gateway 10.254.254.1
    dns-nameserver 8.8.8.8

auto eth1
iface eth1 inet static
    address 172.18.0.102
    netmask 255.255.255.0

auto eth2
iface eth2 inet manual
```

Downloading the example code

You can download the example code files for all Packt books you have purchased from your account at http://www.packtpub.com. If you purchased this book elsewhere, you can visit http://www.packtpub.com/support and register to have the files e-mailed directly to you.

The `eth2` interface will be used in a network bridge described in further detail in *Chapter 4, Building a Virtual Switching Infrastructure*. To activate the changes, cycle the interfaces using the `ifdown` and `ifup` commands on each node:

```
# ifdown --all; ifup --all
```

> For more information on configuring network interfaces, refer to the Ubuntu man page found at `http://manpages.ubuntu.com/manpages/trusty/man5/interfaces.5.html`.

Initial steps

Before we can install OpenStack, some work must be done to prepare the system for a successful installation.

Updating the system

Before packages can be downloaded, run the following `apt-get` command to update package lists on all hosts:

```
# apt-get update
```

Permissions

OpenStack services can be installed either as root or as a user with `sudo` permissions. The latter may require that the user be added to the `sudoers` file on each host. For tips on configuring `sudoers`, visit `https://help.ubuntu.com/community/RootSudo`.

> For this installation, all commands should be run as root, unless specified otherwise.

Configuring the OpenStack repository

Installation of OpenStack on Ubuntu 14.04 LTS uses packages from the Ubuntu Cloud Archive repository when installing versions of OpenStack that are newer than what the operating system shipped with. To enable the Cloud Archive repository, download and install the `ubuntu-cloud-keyring` package on all hosts:

```
# apt-get install ubuntu-cloud-keyring
```

Once installed, the Kilo repository should be added to apt sources on all hosts:

```
# cat > /etc/apt/sources.list.d/cloudarchive-kilo.list <<EOF
deb http://ubuntu-cloud.archive.canonical.com/ubuntu trusty-updates/kilo
main

EOF
```

 The deb statement should be on one line, but is line-wrapped in this example.

Installing OpenStack utilities

The `crudini` utility is used throughout this book to make the configuration of various services easier and consistent. This utility overwrites or adds individual configuration settings without overwriting the entire file. The following command installs `crudini` and other required tools:

```
# apt-get install crudini curl
```

Setting the hostnames

Before installing OpenStack, be sure that each node in the environment has been configured with its proper hostname. Use the `hostnamectl` command on each host to set the hostname accordingly:

- For controller01, use:

  ```
  hostnamectl set-hostname controller01.learningneutron.com
  ```

- For compute01, use:

  ```
  hostnamectl set-hostname compute01.learningneutron.com
  ```

- For compute02, use:

  ```
  hostnamectl set-hostname compute02.learningneutron.com
  ```

To simplify communication between hosts, it is recommended that you use DNS or a local name resolver to resolve host names. Using a text editor, update the `/etc/hosts` file on each node to include the management IP address and hostname of all nodes:

```
10.254.254.100 controller01.learningneutron.com controller01
10.254.254.101 compute01.learningneutron.com compute01
10.254.254.102 compute02.learningneutron.com compute02
```

Installing and configuring Network Time Protocol

A time synchronization program, such as NTP, is a requirement, as OpenStack services depend on consistent and synchronized time between hosts. For Nova Compute, having synchronized time helps avoid problems when scheduling VM launches on compute nodes. Other services can experience similar issues when the time is not synchronized.

To install NTP, issue the following commands on all nodes in the environment:

```
# apt-get install ntp
```

Upgrading the system

Before installing OpenStack, it is imperative that the kernel and other system packages on each node be upgraded to the latest version provided by Ubuntu for the 14.04 LTS release. Issue the following `apt-get` commands on each node, followed by a reboot to allow the changes to take effect:

```
# apt-get update
# apt-get dist-upgrade
# reboot
```

Installing OpenStack

The steps in this section document the installation of OpenStack services, including Keystone, Glance, Nova Compute, and Horizon on a single controller and two compute nodes. Neutron, the OpenStack Networking service, will be installed in the next chapter.

Installing and configuring the MySQL database server

On the controller node, use `apt-get` to install the MySQL database service and related Python packages:

```
# apt-get install mariadb-server python-mysqldb
```

If prompted, set the password to `openstack`.

Insecure passwords are used throughout the book to simplify the configuration and demonstration of concepts and are not recommended for production environments. Visit http://www.strongpasswordgenerator.org to generate strong passwords for your environment.

Once installed, set the IP address that MySQL will bind to by editing the /etc/mysql/conf.d/mysqld_openstack.cnf configuration file and adding the bind-address definition. Doing so will allow connectivity to MySQL from other hosts in the environment. The value for bind-address should be the management IP of the controller node:

```
[mysqld]
...
bind-address = 10.254.254.100
```

In addition to adding the bind-address definition, add the options shown here to the [mysqld] section:

```
[mysqld]
...
default-storage-engine = innodb
innodb_file_per_table
collation-server = utf8_general_ci
init-connect = "SET NAMES utf8"
character-set-server = utf8
```

Save and close the file. Then, start the mysql service:

```
# service mysql restart
```

The MySQL secure installation utility is used to build the default MySQL database and set a password for the MySQL root user. The following command will begin the MySQL installation and configuration process:

```
# mysql_secure_installation
```

During the MySQL installation process, you will be prompted to enter a password and change various settings. For this installation, the chosen root password is openstack. A more secure password suitable for your environment is highly recommended.

Answer [Y]es to the remaining questions to exit the configuration process. At this point, the MySQL server has been successfully installed on the controller node.

Installing and configuring the messaging server

Advanced Message Queue Protocol (AMQP) is the messaging technology chosen for use with an OpenStack-based cloud. Components such as Nova, Cinder, and Neutron communicate internally and among one another using a message bus. Here are the instructions to install RabbitMQ, an AMQP broker.

On the controller node, install the messaging server:

```
# apt-get install rabbitmq-server
```

Add a user named `openstack` to RabbitMQ with the password as `rabbit`, as shown in the following command:

```
# rabbitmqctl add_user openstack rabbit
```

Set RabbitMQ permissions to allow configuration, read, and write access for the `openstack` user:

```
# rabbitmqctl set_permissions openstack ".*" ".*" ".*"
```

At this point, the installation and configuration of RabbitMQ is complete.

Installing and configuring the identity service

Keystone is the identity service for OpenStack, and is used to authenticate and authorize users and services in the OpenStack cloud. Keystone should only be installed on the controller node and will be covered in the following sections.

Installing Keystone

In the Kilo release of OpenStack, the Keystone project uses a WSGI server instead of Eventlet. An Apache HTTP server using `mod_wsgi` will serve Keystone requests on port `5000` and `35357` rather than the Keystone service itself. Execute the following command to disable the `keystone` service from starting on the controller node once it is installed to avoid issues:

```
# echo "manual" > /etc/init/keystone.override
```

Run the following command to install the Keystone packages on the controller node:

```
# apt-get install keystone python-openstackclient apache2 libapache2-mod-
wsgi memcached python-memcache
```

Update the [database] section in the /etc/keystone/keystone.conf file to configure Keystone to use MySQL as its database. In this installation, the username and password will be keystone. You will need to overwrite the existing connection string with the following value:

```
[database]
...
connection = mysql://keystone:keystone@controller01/keystone
```

Update the [memcache] section in the /etc/keystone/keystone.conf file to configure Keystone to use the local memcache service:

```
[memcache]
...
servers = localhost:11211
```

Configuring the database

Keystone comes equipped with a SQLite database by default. Remove the database with the following command:

```
# rm -f /var/lib/keystone/keystone.db
```

Using the mysql client, create the Keystone database and associated user. When prompted for the root password, use openstack:

```
# mysql -u root -p
```

Enter the following SQL statements in the MariaDB [(none)] > prompt:

```
CREATE DATABASE keystone;
GRANT ALL PRIVILEGES ON keystone.* TO 'keystone'@'localhost'
IDENTIFIED BY 'keystone';
GRANT ALL PRIVILEGES ON keystone.* TO 'keystone'@'%' IDENTIFIED BY
'keystone';
quit;
```

Configuring tokens and drivers

Before an administrative user has been configured in Keystone, an authorization token can be used as a shared secret between Keystone and other OpenStack services. When defined, the authorization token, admin_token, could be used to make changes to Keystone if an administrative user has not been configured or the password has been forgotten. Clients making calls to Keystone can pass the authorization token, which is then validated by Keystone before actions are taken.

Update the `[DEFAULT]` section in the `/etc/keystone/keystone.conf` file to set a simple admin token:

```
[DEFAULT]
...
admin_token = insecuretoken123
```

Keystone supports customizable token providers that can be defined within the `[token]` section of the configuration file. Keystone provides both UUID and PKI token providers. In this installation, the UUID token provider will be used. Update the `token` and `revoke` sections in the `/etc/keystone/keystone.conf` file accordingly:

```
[token]
...
provider = keystone.token.providers.uuid.Provider
driver = keystone.token.persistence.backends.memcache.Token
[revoke]
...
driver = keystone.contrib.revoke.backends.sql.Revoke
```

Populate the Keystone database using the `keystone-manage` utility:

```
# su -s /bin/sh -c "keystone-manage db_sync" keystone
```

Configuring the Apache HTTP server

Keystone now uses an HTTP server to process the Keystone API requests rather than a dedicated service. As a result, Apache must be configured accordingly.

Add the `ServerName` option to the Apache configuration file that references the short name of the controller node:

```
# sed -i '1s/^/ServerName controller01\n&/' /etc/apache2/apache2.conf
```

Next, create a file named `/etc/apache2/sites-available/wsgi-keystone.conf` that includes virtual host definitions for the WSGI server:

```
# cat >> /etc/apache2/sites-available/wsgi-keystone.conf <<EOF
Listen 5000
Listen 35357

<VirtualHost *:5000>
    WSGIDaemonProcess keystone-public processes=5 threads=1
user=keystone display-name=%{GROUP}
    WSGIProcessGroup keystone-public
    WSGIScriptAlias / /var/www/cgi-bin/keystone/main
    WSGIApplicationGroup %{GLOBAL}
```

```
    WSGIPassAuthorization On
    <IfVersion >= 2.4>
      ErrorLogFormat "%{cu}t %M"
    </IfVersion>
    LogLevel info
    ErrorLog /var/log/apache2/keystone-error.log
    CustomLog /var/log/apache2/keystone-access.log combined
</VirtualHost>

<VirtualHost *:35357>
    WSGIDaemonProcess keystone-admin processes=5 threads=1
user=keystone display-name=%{GROUP}
    WSGIProcessGroup keystone-admin
    WSGIScriptAlias / /var/www/cgi-bin/keystone/admin
    WSGIApplicationGroup %{GLOBAL}
    WSGIPassAuthorization On
    <IfVersion >= 2.4>
      ErrorLogFormat "%{cu}t %M"
    </IfVersion>
    LogLevel info
    ErrorLog /var/log/apache2/keystone-error.log
    CustomLog /var/log/apache2/keystone-access.log combined
</VirtualHost>
EOF
```

Once complete, enable the virtual hosts for the Identity service with the following command:

```
# ln -s /etc/apache2/sites-available/wsgi-keystone.conf /etc/apache2/
sites-enabled
```

Download WSGI components

Create a directory structure for the WSGI components:

```
# mkdir -p /var/www/cgi-bin/keystone
```

Then, copy the WSGI components from the upstream Kilo repository to the new directory using `curl`:

```
# curl http://git.openstack.org/cgit/openstack/keystone/plain/httpd/
keystone.py?h=stable/kilo | tee /var/www/cgi-bin/keystone/main /var/www/
cgi-bin/keystone/admin
```

 The `curl` statement should be on one line, but is line-wrapped in this example.

Adjust the ownership and permissions of the files just created:

```
# chown -R keystone:keystone /var/www/cgi-bin/keystone
# chmod 755 /var/www/cgi-bin/keystone/*
```

Finally, restart the Apache web service for the changes to take effect:

```
# service apache2 restart
```

Define services and API endpoints in Keystone

Each OpenStack service that is installed should be registered with Keystone so that its location on the network can be tracked. There are two commands involved in registering a service:

- `openstack service create`: This describes the service that is being created
- `openstack endpoint create`: This associates API endpoints with the service

Typically, a username and password is used to authenticate against Keystone. As users have not yet been created, it is necessary that you use the authorization token created earlier. The token can be passed using the `--os-token` option of the Keystone command or by setting the OS_TOKEN environment variable. We will use both the OS_TOKEN and OS_URL environment variables to provide the authorization token and to specify where the Keystone service is running.

Use the `export` command to export the variables and their values to your environment. OS_TOKEN should be set to the admin token value determined earlier:

```
# export OS_TOKEN=insecuretoken123
# export OS_URL=http://controller01:35357/v2.0
```

Keystone itself is among the services that must be registered. You can create a service entry for Keystone with the following command:

```
# openstack service create --name keystone --description "OpenStack Identity" identity
```

The resulting output is as follows:

```
+--------------+----------------------------------+
| Field        | Value                            |
+--------------+----------------------------------+
| description  | OpenStack Identity               |
| enabled      | True                             |
| id           | 0f261702a746429c90a60c8292785e6f |
| name         | keystone                         |
| type         | identity                         |
+--------------+----------------------------------+
```

Figure 2.2

Next, specify an API endpoint for the Identity service. When specifying an endpoint, you must provide URLs for the public API, internal API, and the admin API. The three URLs can potentially be on three different IP networks depending on your network setup and can have different hostnames. The short name of the controller will be used to populate the URLs. Each host can reference the other based on the hostname via DNS or the local /etc/hosts entries created earlier:

```
# openstack endpoint create \
  --publicurl http://controller01:5000/v2.0 \
  --internalurl http://controller01:5000/v2.0 \
  --adminurl http://controller01:35357/v2.0 \
  --region RegionOne \
  identity
```

The resulting output is as follows:

```
+--------------+----------------------------------+
| Field        | Value                            |
+--------------+----------------------------------+
| adminurl     | http://controller01:35357/v2.0   |
| enabled      | True                             |
| id           | 2bcce9da8309497e974082f21d7168fb |
| internalurl  | http://controller01:5000/v2.0    |
| publicurl    | http://controller01:5000/v2.0    |
| region       | RegionOne                        |
| service_id   | 0f261702a746429c90a60c8292785e6f |
| service_name | keystone                         |
| service_type | identity                         |
+--------------+----------------------------------+
```

Figure 2.3

IDs of various resources are unique and will vary between environments.

Defining users, tenants, and roles in Keystone

Once the installation of Keystone is complete, it is necessary to set up domains, users, projects (tenants), roles, and endpoints that will be used by various OpenStack services.

 In this installation, the `default` domain will be used.

In Keystone, a project or tenant represents a logical group of users to which resources are assigned. The terms "project" and "tenant" are used interchangeably throughout various OpenStack services. Resources are assigned to projects and not directly to users. Create an `admin` project for the administrative user, a `demo` project for regular users, and a `service` project for other OpenStack services to use:

```
# openstack project create --description "Admin Project" admin
# openstack project create --description "Service Project" service
# openstack project create --description "Demo Project" demo
```

Next, create an administrative user called `admin`. Specify a secure password for the `admin` user:

```
# openstack user create admin --password=secrete
```

Once the `admin` user has been created, create a role for administrative tasks called `admin`:

```
# openstack role create admin
```

Any roles that are created should map to roles specified in the `policy.json` files of the corresponding OpenStack services. The default policy files use the `admin` role to allow access to services.

 For more information on user management in Keystone, refer to `http://docs.openstack.org/admin-guide-cloud/content/keystone-user-management.html`.

Associate the `admin` role to the `admin` user in the `admin` project:

```
# openstack role add --project admin --user admin admin
```

Create a regular user called `demo`. Specify a secure password for the `demo` user:

```
# openstack user create demo --password=demo
```

Create the user role:

```
# openstack role create user
```

Finally, add the user role to the demo project and user:

```
# openstack role add --project demo --user demo user
```

Verifying the Keystone installation

To verify that Keystone was installed and configured properly, use the unset command to unset the OS_TOKEN and OS_URL environment variables. These variables are only needed to bootstrap the administrative user and to register the Keystone service:

```
# unset OS_TOKEN OS_URL
```

Once the environment variables are unset, it should be possible to use username-based authentication. Request an authentication token using the admin user and the password specified earlier:

```
# openstack --os-auth-url http://controller01:35357 --os-project-name
admin --os-username admin --os-password secrete token issue
```

Keystone should respond with a token that is paired with the specified user ID. This verifies that the user account is established in Keystone with the expected credentials:

```
+------------+----------------------------------+
| Field      | Value                            |
+------------+----------------------------------+
| expires    | 2015-10-12T15:06:47.304126Z      |
| id         | a4fbe4b90d7b4ef893278e4c15df8efd |
| project_id | 65ff4cf1a04846f1ab2bc1ff0efb1090 |
| user_id    | ee254b5fd5e44e61884a1286223253c9 |
+------------+----------------------------------+
```

Figure 2.4

As the admin user, request a list of projects to verify that the admin user can execute admin-only CLI commands and that the Identity service contains all of the projects created earlier in this chapter:

```
# openstack --os-auth-url http://controller01:35357 \
  --os-project-name admin --os-username admin \
  --os-password secrete project list
```

The command will result in the following output:

Figure 2.5

You should receive a list of projects containing the admin, demo, and service projects created earlier in the chapter.

Setting environment variables

To avoid having to provide credentials every time you run an OpenStack command, create a file containing environment variables that can be loaded at any time. The following commands will create a file named adminrc containing environment variables for the admin user:

```
# cat >> ~/adminrc <<EOF
export OS_PROJECT_DOMAIN_ID=default
export OS_USER_DOMAIN_ID=default
export OS_PROJECT_NAME=admin
export OS_TENANT_NAME=admin
export OS_USERNAME=admin
export OS_PASSWORD=secrete
export OS_AUTH_URL=http://controller01:35357/v3
EOF
```

The following commands will create a file named demorc containing environment variables for the demo user:

```
# cat >> ~/demorc <<EOF
export OS_PROJECT_DOMAIN_ID=default
export OS_USER_DOMAIN_ID=default
export OS_PROJECT_NAME=demo
export OS_TENANT_NAME=demo
export OS_USERNAME=demo
export OS_PASSWORD=demo
export OS_AUTH_URL=http://controller01:5000/v3
EOF
```

Use the `source` command to load the environment variables from the file. To test Keystone, issue the following commands:

```
# source ~/adminrc
# openstack user list
```

As the `admin` user, Keystone should return the user list as requested:

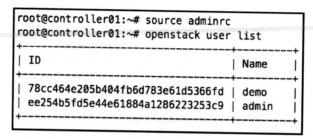

```
root@controller01:~# source adminrc
root@controller01:~# openstack user list
+------------------------------------+-------+
| ID                                 | Name  |
+------------------------------------+-------+
| 78cc464e205b404fb6d783e61d5366fd   | demo  |
| ee254b5fd5e44e61884a1286223253c9   | admin |
+------------------------------------+-------+
```

Figure 2.6

As the `demo` user, access is denied:

```
root@controller01:~# source demorc
root@controller01:~# openstack user list
ERROR: openstack You are not authorized to perform the requested action: admin_required (HTTP 403)
```

Figure 2.7

Depending on the command, non-admin users may not have appropriate access.

Installing and configuring the image service

Glance is the image service for OpenStack. It is responsible for storing images and snapshots of instances, and for providing images to compute nodes when instances are created.

To install Glance, run the following command from the controller node:

```
# apt-get install glance python-glanceclient
```

Configuring the database

Glance comes equipped with a SQLite database by default. Remove the database with the following command:

```
# rm -f /var/lib/glance/glance.sqlite
```

Using the `mysql` client, create the Keystone database and associated user. When prompted for the root password, use `openstack`:

```
# mysql -u root -p
```

Enter the following SQL statements in the `MariaDB [(none)] >` prompt:

```
CREATE DATABASE glance;
GRANT ALL PRIVILEGES ON glance.* TO 'glance'@'localhost' IDENTIFIED BY
'glance';
GRANT ALL PRIVILEGES ON glance.* TO 'glance'@'%' IDENTIFIED BY
'glance';
quit;
```

Update the `[database]` connection string in the `glance-api` configuration file found at `/etc/glance/glance-api.conf` to use the previously defined MySQL database:

```
[database]
...
connection = mysql://glance:glance@controller01/glance
```

Repeat the process for the `glance-registry` configuration file found at `/etc/glance/glance-registry.conf`:

```
[database]
...
connection = mysql://glance:glance@controller01/glance
```

Add the `glance` user to Keystone and create the appropriate role:

```
# openstack user create --password glance glance
# openstack role add --project service --user glance admin
```

Configuring authentication settings

Both the `glance-api` and `glance-registry` service configuration files must be updated with the appropriate authentication settings for the services to operate.

Update the `[keystone_authtoken]` settings in the `glance-api` configuration file found at `/etc/glance/glance-api.conf`:

```
[keystone_authtoken]
...
auth_uri = http://controller01:5000/v2.0
auth_url = http://controller01:35357
auth_plugin = password
user_domain_id = default
project_domain_id = default
```

```
project_name = service
username = glance
password = glance
```

Repeat the process for the `glance-registry` configuration file found at `/etc/glance/glance-registry.conf`:

```
[keystone_authtoken]
...
auth_uri = http://controller01:5000/v2.0
auth_url = http://controller01:35357
auth_plugin = password
user_domain_id = default
project_domain_id = default
project_name = service
username = glance
password = glance
```

Configuring additional settings

Update the `glance-api` configuration file found at `/etc/glance/glance-api.conf` with the following additional settings:

```
[paste_deploy]
...
flavor = keystone

[glance_store]
...
default_store = file
filesystem_store_datadir = /var/lib/glance/images

[DEFAULT]
...
notification_driver = noop
```

Update the `glance-registry` configuration file found at `/etc/glance/glance-registry.conf` with the following additional settings:

```
[paste_deploy]
...
flavor = keystone

[DEFAULT]
...
notification_driver = noop
```

Populate the Glance database using the `glance-manage` utility:

```
# su -s /bin/sh -c "glance-manage db_sync" glance
```

Restart the Glance services with the following commands:

```
# service glance-registry restart
# service glance-api restart
```

Defining the Glance service and API endpoints in Keystone

Like other OpenStack services, Glance should be added to the Keystone database using the `openstack service create` and `endpoint create` commands:

```
# openstack service create --name glance \
  --description "OpenStack Image service" image
```

The resulting output can be seen as follows:

```
+-------------+----------------------------------+
| Field       | Value                            |
+-------------+----------------------------------+
| description | OpenStack Image service          |
| enabled     | True                             |
| id          | 6530def6d6de4176a9712a2a9471cab9 |
| name        | glance                           |
| type        | image                            |
+-------------+----------------------------------+
```

Figure 2.8

Create the Glance API endpoints with the following command:

```
# openstack endpoint create \
  --publicurl http://controller01:9292 \
  --internalurl http://controller01:9292 \
  --adminurl http://controller01:9292 \
  --region RegionOne \
  image
```

The resulting output is as follows:

```
+---------------+------------------------------------------+
| Field         | Value                                    |
+---------------+------------------------------------------+
| adminurl      | http://controller01:9292                 |
| enabled       | True                                     |
| id            | f7ca29f54d2b431f96df20864b1a0369         |
| internalurl   | http://controller01:9292                 |
| publicurl     | http://controller01:9292                 |
| region        | RegionOne                                |
| service_id    | 6530def6d6de4176a9712a2a9471cab9         |
| service_name  | glance                                   |
| service_type  | image                                    |
+---------------+------------------------------------------+
```

Figure 2.9

Verifying the Glance image service installation

Update each environment script created earlier in the chapter to define an environment variable that instructs the OpenStack client to use v2 of the Glance API:

```
# echo "export OS_IMAGE_API_VERSION=2" | tee -a ~/adminrc ~/demorc
```

Source the `adminrc` script to set or update the environment variables:

```
# source ~/adminrc
```

To verify that Glance was installed and configured properly, download a test image from the Internet and verify that it can be uploaded to the image server:

```
# mkdir /tmp/images
# wget -P /tmp/images http://download.cirros-cloud.net/0.3.4/cirros-
0.3.4-x86_64-disk.img
```

Upload the image to Glance using the following command:

```
# glance image-create --name "cirros-0.3.4-x86_64" \
  --file /tmp/images/cirros-0.3.4-x86_64-disk.img \
  --disk-format qcow2 --container-format bare \
  --visibility public --progress
```

Verify that the image exists in Glance using the `openstack image list` or `glance image-list` command:

```
root@controller01:~# openstack image list
+--------------------------------------+-----------------------+
| ID                                   | Name                  |
+--------------------------------------+-----------------------+
| 3dd4f4e5-f82d-435e-8d25-0f9f6193dc61 | cirros-0.3.4-x86_64   |
+--------------------------------------+-----------------------+
```

Figure 2.10

Installing additional images

The CirrOS image is limited in functionality and is recommended only for testing network connectivity and operational Compute functionality. Multiple vendors provide cloud-ready images for use with OpenStack:

- **Ubuntu Cloud Images** at http://cloud-images.ubuntu.com/
- **Red Hat-Based Cloud Images** at https://www.rdoproject.org/resources/image-resources/

To install the Ubuntu 14.04 LTS image, download the file to /tmp/images and upload it to Glance:

```
# wget -P /tmp/images https://cloud-images.ubuntu.com/trusty/current/
trusty-server-cloudimg-amd64-disk1.img
```

Use the Glance `image-create` command to upload the new image:

```
# glance image-create --name "Ubuntu 14.04 LTS Cloud Image" \
  --file /tmp/images/trusty-server-cloudimg-amd64-disk1.img \
  --disk-format qcow2 --container-format bare \
  --visibility public --progress
```

Another look at the image list shows that the new Ubuntu image is available for use:

```
root@controller01:~# openstack image list
+--------------------------------------+------------------------------+
| ID                                   | Name                         |
+--------------------------------------+------------------------------+
| 5ecfac0c-98eb-4c81-8448-02249ee89aae | Ubuntu 14.04 LTS Cloud Image |
| 3dd4f4e5-f82d-435e-8d25-0f9f6193dc61 | cirros-0.3.4-x86_64          |
+--------------------------------------+------------------------------+
```

Figure 2.11

Installing and configuring the Compute service

OpenStack Compute is a collection of services that enable cloud operators and tenants to launch virtual machine instances. Most services run on the controller node. The only exception is the `nova-compute` service, which runs on the compute nodes and is responsible for launching the virtual machine instances on those nodes.

Installing and configuring controller node components

Execute the following command on the controller node to install the various Nova Compute services used by the controller:

```
# apt-get install nova-api nova-cert nova-conductor \
  nova-consoleauth nova-novncproxy nova-scheduler python-novaclient
```

Configuring the database

Nova comes equipped with a SQLite database by default. Remove the database with the following command:

```
# rm -f /var/lib/nova/nova.sqlite
```

Using the `mysql` client, create the Nova database and associated user. When prompted for the root password, use `openstack`:

```
# mysql -u root -p
```

Enter the following SQL statements in the `MariaDB [(none)] >` prompt:

```
CREATE DATABASE nova;
GRANT ALL PRIVILEGES ON nova.* TO 'nova'@'localhost' IDENTIFIED BY
'nova';
GRANT ALL PRIVILEGES ON nova.* TO 'nova'@'%' IDENTIFIED BY 'nova';
quit;
```

Update the `[database]` section of the Nova configuration file found at `/etc/nova/nova.conf` to set the connection string to use the previously configured MySQL database:

```
[database]
...
connection = mysql://nova:nova@controller01/nova
```

 The `[database]` and other sections referenced here may not exist in a new installation and can be safely created.

Update the [DEFAULT] and [oslo_messaging_rabbit] sections of the Nova configuration file to configure Nova to use the RabbitMQ message broker:

```
[DEFAULT]
...
rpc_backend = rabbit

[oslo_messaging_rabbit]
...
rabbit_host = controller01
rabbit_userid = openstack
rabbit_password = rabbit
```

VNC Proxy is an OpenStack component that allows users to access their instances through VNC clients. VNC stands for **virtual network computing** and is a graphical desktop-sharing system that uses the Remote Frame Buffer protocol to control another computer over a network. The controller must be able to communicate with compute nodes for VNC services to work properly through the Horizon dashboard or other VNC clients.

Update the [DEFAULT] section of the Nova configuration file to configure the appropriate VNC settings for the controller node:

```
[DEFAULT]
...
my_ip = 10.254.254.100
vncserver_listen = 10.254.254.100
vncserver_proxyclient_address = 10.254.254.100
```

Configuring authentication settings

Create a user called nova in Keystone. The Nova service will use this user for authentication. After this, associate the user with the service project and give the user the admin role:

```
# openstack user create --password nova nova

# openstack role add --project service --user nova admin
```

Update the Nova configuration file at `/etc/nova/nova.conf` with the following Keystone-related attributes:

```
[DEFAULT]
...
auth_strategy = keystone

[keystone_authtoken]
...
auth_uri = http://controller01:5000
auth_url = http://controller01:35357
auth_plugin = password
project_domain_id = default
user_domain_id = default
project_name = service
username = nova
password = nova
```

You must then register Nova with the Identity service so that other OpenStack services can locate it. Register the service and specify the endpoint:

```
# openstack service create --name nova --description "OpenStack Compute"
compute
```

The resulting output should resemble the output shown here:

```
+-------------+----------------------------------+
| Field       | Value                            |
+-------------+----------------------------------+
| description | OpenStack Compute                |
| enabled     | True                             |
| id          | 81b347f70d9c4c18a331221fcf6561d7 |
| name        | nova                             |
| type        | compute                          |
+-------------+----------------------------------+
```

Figure 2.12

Create the Nova endpoint with the following command:

```
# openstack endpoint create \
  --publicurl http://controller01:8774/v2/%\(tenant_id\)s \
  --internalurl http://controller01:8774/v2/%\(tenant_id\)s \
  --adminurl http://controller01:8774/v2/%\(tenant_id\)s \
  --region RegionOne \
  compute
```

The output should resemble the one shown here:

```
+-----------------+------------------------------------------------+
| Field           | Value                                          |
+-----------------+------------------------------------------------+
| adminurl        | http://controller01:8774/v2/%(tenant_id)s      |
| enabled         | True                                           |
| id              | 1f50d1770e224b0195c7b38b2513fabc               |
| internalurl     | http://controller01:8774/v2/%(tenant_id)s      |
| publicurl       | http://controller01:8774/v2/%(tenant_id)s      |
| region          | RegionOne                                      |
| service_id      | 81b347f70d9c4c18a331221fcf6561d7               |
| service_name    | nova                                           |
| service_type    | compute                                        |
+-----------------+------------------------------------------------+
```

Figure 2.13

Additional controller tasks

Update the Nova configuration file at /etc/nova/nova.conf to specify the
controller node as the Glance host:

```
[glance]
. . .
host = controller01
```

Update the Nova configuration file to set the lock file path for Nova services:

```
[oslo_concurrency]
. . .
lock_path = /var/lib/nova/tmp
```

Populate the Nova database using the nova-manage utility:

```
# su -s /bin/sh -c "nova-manage db sync" nova
```

Restart the controller-based Nova services for the changes to take effect:

```
# service nova-api restart
```

```
# service nova-cert restart
```

```
# service nova-consoleauth restart
```

```
# service nova-scheduler restart
```

```
# service nova-conductor restart
```

```
# service nova-novncproxy restart
```

Installing and configuring compute node components

Once the controller-based Nova services have been configured on the controller node, at least one other host must be configured as a compute node. The compute node receives requests from the controller node to host virtual machine instances. Separating the services by running dedicated compute nodes means that Nova compute services can be scaled horizontally by adding additional compute nodes, once all available resources have been utilized.

On the compute nodes, install the `nova-compute` package and related packages. These packages provide virtualization support services to the compute node:

```
# apt-get install nova-compute sysfsutils
```

Update the Nova configuration file at `/etc/nova/nova.conf` on the compute nodes with the following Keystone-related attributes:

```
[DEFAULT]
...
auth_strategy = keystone

[keystone_authtoken]
...
auth_uri = http://controller01:5000
auth_url = http://controller01:35357
auth_plugin = password
project_domain_id = default
user_domain_id = default
project_name = service
username = nova
password = nova
```

Next, update the `[DEFAULT]` and `[oslo_messaging_rabbit]` sections of the Nova configuration file to configure Nova to use the RabbitMQ message broker:

```
[DEFAULT]
...
rpc_backend = rabbit

[oslo_messaging_rabbit]
...
rabbit_host = controller01
rabbit_userid = openstack
rabbit_password = rabbit
```

Then, update the Nova configuration file to provide remote console access to instances through a proxy on the controller node. The remote console is accessible through the Horizon dashboard. The IP configured as my_ip should be the respective management IP of each compute node:

Compute01:

```
[DEFAULT]
. . .
my_ip = 10.254.254.101
vncserver_proxyclient_address = 10.254.254.101
vnc_enabled = True
vncserver_listen = 0.0.0.0
novncproxy_base_url = http://controller01:6080/vnc_auto.html
```

Compute02:

```
[DEFAULT]
. . .
my_ip = 10.254.254.102
vncserver_proxyclient_address = 10.254.254.102
vnc_enabled = True
vncserver_listen = 0.0.0.0
novncproxy_base_url   http://controller01:6080/vnc_auto.html
```

Additional compute tasks

Update the Nova configuration file at /etc/nova/nova.conf to specify the controller node as the Glance host:

```
[glance]
. . .
host = controller01
```

Update the Nova configuration file to set the lock file path for Nova services:

```
[oslo_concurrency]
. . .
lock_path = /var/lib/nova/tmp
```

Restart the nova-compute service on all compute nodes:

```
# service nova-compute restart
```

Verifying communication between services

To check the status of Nova services throughout the environment, use the Nova `service-list` command on the controller node as follows:

```
# nova service-list
```

The command should return statuses on all Nova services that have checked in:

```
root@controller01:~# nova service-list
+----+------------------+-------------------------------+----------+---------+-------+----------------------------+-----------------+
| Id | Binary           | Host                          | Zone     | Status  | State | Updated_at                 | Disabled Reason |
+----+------------------+-------------------------------+----------+---------+-------+----------------------------+-----------------+
| 1  | nova-cert        | controller01.learningneutron.com | internal | enabled | up    | 2015-10-12T14:10:17.000000 | -               |
| 2  | nova-consoleauth | controller01.learningneutron.com | internal | enabled | up    | 2015-10-12T14:10:20.000000 | -               |
| 3  | nova-scheduler   | controller01.learningneutron.com | internal | enabled | up    | 2015-10-12T14:10:22.000000 | -               |
| 4  | nova-conductor   | controller01.learningneutron.com | internal | enabled | up    | 2015-10-12T14:10:17.000000 | -               |
| 6  | nova-compute     | compute01.learningneutron.com | nova     | enabled | up    | 2015-10-12T14:10:19.000000 | -               |
| 7  | nova-compute     | compute02.learningneutron.com | nova     | enabled | up    | 2015-10-12T14:10:20.000000 | -               |
+----+------------------+-------------------------------+----------+---------+-------+----------------------------+-----------------+
```

Figure 2.14

In the preceding output, the state of the services on both the controller and compute nodes are reflected under the `Status` column. The `nova service-list` command can be run on any node in the environment, but will require proper authentication credentials. If there are inconsistencies in the output among multiple nodes, it's worth ensuring that **Network Time Protocol (NTP)** is synchronized properly on all nodes.

Installing the OpenStack dashboard

The OpenStack dashboard, also known as Horizon, provides a web-based user interface to OpenStack services, including Compute, Networking, Storage, and Identity, among others.

To install Horizon, install the following package on the controller node:

```
# apt-get install openstack-dashboard
```

Identifying the Keystone server

Edit the `/etc/openstack-dashboard/local_settings.py` file to set the hostname of the Identity server. In this installation, the Keystone services are running on the controller node. Change the `OPENSTACK_HOST` value from its default to the following:

```
OPENSTACK_HOST = controller01
```

Configuring a default role

The `OPENSTACK_KEYSTONE_DEFAULT_ROLE` setting in the `/etc/openstack-dashboard/local_settings.py` file must also be modified before the dashboard can be used. Change the `OPENSTACK_KEYSTONE_DEFAULT_ROLE` value from its default to the following:

```
OPENSTACK_KEYSTONE_DEFAULT_ROLE = "user"
```

Save and close the file.

Reload Apache

Once the preceding changes have been made, reload the Apache web server configuration using the following command:

```
# service apache2 reload
```

Uninstalling the default Ubuntu theme (optional)

By default, installations of the OpenStack dashboard on Ubuntu include a theme that has been customized by Canonical. To remove the theme, execute the following command:

```
# apt-get remove openstack-dashboard-ubuntu-theme
```

The examples in this book assume that the custom theme has been uninstalled.

Testing connectivity to the dashboard

From a machine that has access to the management network of the controller node, open `http://controller01/horizon/` in a web browser.

The API network is reachable from my workstation, and the /etc/hosts file on my client workstation has been updated to include the same hostname-to-IP mappings configured earlier in this chapter. The following screenshot demonstrates a successful connection to the dashboard. The username and password were created in the *Defining users, tenants, and roles in Keystone* section earlier in this chapter. In this installation, the username is admin and the password is secrete:

Figure 2.15

Once you have successfully logged in, the dashboard defaults to the **Admin** tab. From here, information about the environment is provided in a graphical format. Looking at the following screenshot, the **System Information** panel provides the user with information about the environment, including **Services** and **Compute Services**. The services listed in the following screenshot are services that were installed earlier in this chapter:

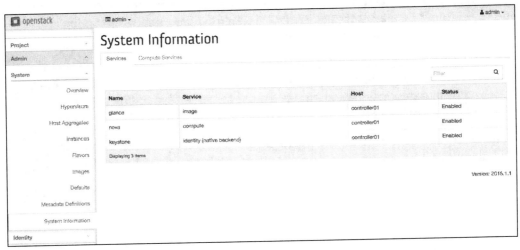

Figure 2.16

To view the status of Nova Compute services, click on the **Compute Services** tab. This will return output similar to that of `nova service-list` in the CLI:

System Information

Services   Compute Services

Name	Host	Zone	Status	State	Last Updated
nova-cert	controller01.learningneutron.com	internal	Enabled	Up	0 minutes
nova-consoleauth	controller01.learningneutron.com	internal	Enabled	Up	0 minutes
nova-scheduler	controller01.learningneutron.com	internal	Enabled	Up	0 minutes
nova-conductor	controller01.learningneutron.com	internal	Enabled	Up	0 minutes
nova-compute	compute01.learningneutron.com	nova	Enabled	Up	0 minutes

Displaying 5 items

Version: 2015.1.1

Figure 2.17

Summary

At this point in the installation, the OpenStack Identity, Image, Dashboard, and Compute services have been successfully deployed across the nodes of the cloud. The environment is not ready to host instances just yet, as OpenStack Networking services have not been installed or configured. If issues arise during the installation and test procedures documented throughout this chapter, be sure to check the log messages found in `/var/log/nova/`, `/var/log/glance/`, `/var/log/apache2/`, and `/var/log/keystone/` for assistance in troubleshooting.

It is important to note that the frequent OpenStack release cycle means that older releases may no longer be available for download 12–18 months after their initial release. For updated installation guides for the latest version of OpenStack, visit `http://docs.openstack.org`.

In the next chapter, we will begin the installation of Neutron networking services and discover additional information about the internal architecture of OpenStack Networking.

3
Installing Neutron

OpenStack Networking, also known as **Neutron**, provides a network **Infrastructure as a Server (IaaS)** platform to users of the cloud. In the last chapter, we installed some of the base services of OpenStack, including Keystone, Glance, and Nova. In this chapter, I will guide you through the installation of Neutron networking services on top of the OpenStack environment installed in the previous chapter.

Components to be installed include:

- Neutron API server
- Modular Layer 2 (ML2) plugin
- DHCP agent
- Metadata agent

By the end of this chapter, you will have a basic understanding of the function and operation of various Neutron plugins and agents, as well as a foundation on top of which a virtual switching infrastructure can be built.

Basic networking elements in Neutron

Neutron constructs the virtual network using elements that are familiar to all system and network administrators, including networks, subnets, ports, routers, load balancers, and more.

Using version 2.0 of the core Neutron API, users can build a network foundation composed of the following entities:

- **Network**: A network is an isolated layer 2 broadcast domain. Typically reserved for the tenants that created them, networks could be shared among tenants if configured accordingly. The network is the core entity of the Neutron API. Subnets and ports must always be associated with a network.

- **Subnet**: A subnet is an IPv4 or IPv6 address block from which IP addresses can be assigned to virtual machine instances. Each subnet must have a CIDR and must be associated with a network. Multiple subnets can be associated with a single network and can be noncontiguous. A DHCP allocation range can be set for a subnet that limits the addresses provided to instances.

- **Port**: A port in Neutron represents a virtual switch port on a logical virtual switch. Virtual machine interfaces are mapped to Neutron ports, and the ports define both the MAC address and the IP address to be assigned to the interfaces plugged into them. Neutron port definitions are stored in the Neutron database, which is then used by the respective plugin agent to build and connect the virtual switching infrastructure.

Cloud operators and users alike can configure network topologies by creating and configuring networks and subnets, and then instruct services such as Nova to attach virtual devices to ports on these networks. Users can create multiple networks, subnets, and ports, but are limited to thresholds defined by per-tenant quotas set by the cloud administrator.

Extending functionality with plugins

Neutron introduces support for third-party plugins and drivers that extend network functionality and implementation of the Neutron API. Plugins and drivers can be created that use a variety of software- and hardware-based technologies to implement the network built by operators and users.

There are two major plugin types within the Neutron architecture:

- Core plugin
- Service plugin

A **core plugin** implements the core Neutron API and is responsible for adapting the logical network described by networks, ports, and subnets into something that can be implemented by the L2 agent and IP address management system running on the host.

A **service plugin** provides additional network services such as routing, load balancing, firewalling, and more.

In this book, the Modular Layer 2 core plugin is discussed.

The following service plugins will be covered in later chapters:

- Router
- Load balancer
- Firewall
- Virtual private network

 The Neutron API provides a consistent experience to the user despite the chosen networking plugin. For more information on interacting with the Neutron API, visit `http://developer.openstack.org/api-ref-networking-v2.html`.

Modular Layer 2 plugin

Prior to the inclusion of the **Modular Layer 2 (ML2)** plugin in the Havana release of OpenStack, Neutron was limited to using a single core plugin at a time. The ML2 plugin replaces two monolithic plugins in its reference implementation: the LinuxBridge plugin and the Open vSwitch plugin. Their respective agents, however, continue to be utilized and can be configured to work with the ML2 plugin.

Drivers

The ML2 plugin introduced the concept of type drivers and mechanism drivers to separate the types of networks being *implemented* and the mechanisms for *implementing* networks of those types.

Type drivers

An ML2 **type driver** maintains type-specific network state, validates provider network attributes, and describes network segments using provider attributes. Provider attributes include network interface labels, segmentation IDs, and network types. Supported network types include `local`, `flat`, `vlan`, `gre`, and `vxlan`.

Mechanism drivers

An ML2 **mechanism driver** is responsible for taking information established by the type driver and ensuring that it is properly implemented. Multiple mechanism drivers can be configured to operate simultaneously, and can be described using three types of models:

- **Agent-based:** This includes LinuxBridge, Open vSwitch, and others
- **Controller-based:** This includes OpenDaylight, VMWare NSX, and others
- **Top-of-Rack:** This includes Cisco Nexus, Arista, Mellanox, and others

Mechanism drivers to be discussed in this book include:

- LinuxBridge
- Open vSwitch
- L2 Population

The LinuxBridge and Open vSwitch ML2 mechanism drivers are used to configure their respective switching technologies within nodes that host instances and network services. The LinuxBridge driver supports `local`, `flat`, `vlan`, and `vxlan` network types, while the Open vSwitch driver supports all of those as well as the `gre` network type.

The L2 population driver is used to limit the amount of broadcast traffic that is forwarded across the overlay network fabric. Traditional switching behavior dictates that unknown unicast, multicast, and broadcast traffic is flooded out all switch ports until the location is learned. This behavior can have a negative impact on the overlay network fabric, especially as the number of hosts in the cloud scales out. As an authority on what instances and other network resources exist in the cloud, Neutron can prepopulate forwarding databases on all hosts to avoid a costly learning operation. When ARP proxy is used, Neutron prepopulates the ARP table on all hosts in a similar manner to avoid ARP traffic from being broadcast across the overlay fabric.

ML2 architecture

The following diagram demonstrates at a high level how the Neutron API service interacts with the various plugins and agents responsible for constructing the virtual and physical network:

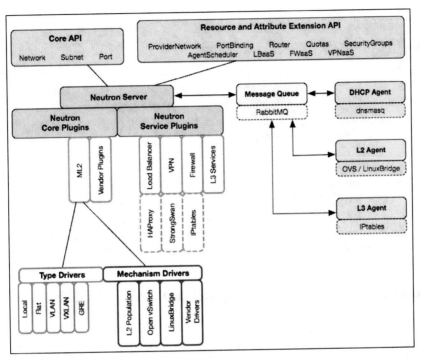

Figure 3.1

The preceding diagram demonstrates the interaction between the Neutron API, Neutron plugins and drivers, and services such as the L2 and L3 agents. For more information on the Neutron ML2 plugin architecture, refer to the *OpenStack Neutron Modular Layer 2 Plugin Deep Dive* video from the 2013 OpenStack Summit in Hong Kong available at https://www.youtube.com/watch?v=whmcQ-vHams.

Third-party support

Third-party vendors such as PLUMGrid and OpenContrail have implemented support for their respective SDN technologies by developing their own monolithic or ML2 plugins that implement the Neutron API and extended network services. Others, including Cisco, Arista, Brocade, Radware, F5, VMWare, and more, have created plugins that allow Neutron to interface with OpenFlow controllers, load balancers, switches, and other network hardware. For a look at some of the commands related to these plugins, refer to *Appendix A, Additional Neutron Commands*.

The configuration and use of these plugins is outside the scope of this book. For more information on the available plugins for Neutron, visit http://docs.openstack.org/admin-guide-cloud/content/section_plugin-arch.html.

Network namespaces

OpenStack was designed with multitenancy in mind and provides users with the ability to create and manage their own compute and network resources. Neutron supports each tenant having multiple private networks, routers, firewalls, load balancers, and other networking resources. It is able to isolate many of those objects through the use of network namespaces.

A **network namespace** is defined as a logical copy of the network stack with its own routes, firewall rules, and network interface devices. When using the open source reference plugins and drivers, every network, router, and load balancer that is created by a user is represented by a network namespace. When network namespaces are enabled, Neutron is able to provide isolated DHCP and routing services to each network. These services allow users to create overlapping networks with other users in other projects and even other networks in the same project.

The following naming convention for network namespaces should be observed:

- **DHCP namespace**: qdhcp-<network UUID>
- **Router namespace**: qrouter-<router UUID>
- **Load Balancer namespace**: qlbaas-<load balancer UUID>

A qdhcp namespace contains a DHCP service that provides IP addresses to instances using the DHCP protocol. In a reference implementation, dnsmasq is the process that services DHCP requests. The qdhcp namespace has an interface plugged into the virtual switch and is able to communicate with instances and other devices in the same network or subnet. A qdhcp namespace is created for every network where the associated subnet(s) have DHCP enabled.

A qrouter namespace represents a virtual router and is responsible for routing traffic to and from instances in the subnets it is connected to. Like the qdhcp namespace, the qrouter namespace is connected to one or more virtual switches depending on the configuration.

A `qlbaas` namespace represents a virtual load balancer and may run a service such as HAProxy that load balances traffic to instances. The `qlbaas` namespace is connected to a virtual switch and can communicate with instances and other devices in the same network or subnet.

 The leading q in the name of the network namespaces stands for Quantum, the original name for the OpenStack Networking service.

Network namespaces will only be seen on nodes running the Neutron DHCP, L3, and LBaaS agents. These services are typically configured only on controllers or dedicated network nodes. The `ip netns list` command can be used to list available namespaces, and commands can be executed within the namespace using the following syntax:

```
ip netns exec NAMESPACE_NAME <command>
```

Commands that can be executed in the namespace include `ip`, `route`, `iptables`, and more. The output of these commands corresponds to data specific to the namespace they are executed in.

For more information on network namespaces, see the man page for `ip netns` at `http://man7.org/linux/man-pages/man8/ip-netns.8.html`.

Installing and configuring Neutron services

In this installation, the various services that make up OpenStack Networking will be installed on the controller node rather than a dedicated networking node. The compute nodes will run L2 agents that interface with the controller node and provide virtual switch connections to instances.

 Remember that the configuration settings recommended here and online at `docs.openstack.org` may not be appropriate for production systems.

To install the Neutron API server, the DHCP and metadata agents, and the ML2 plugin on the controller, issue the following command:

```
# apt-get install neutron-server neutron-dhcp-agent \
neutron-metadata-agent neutron-plugin-ml2 neutron-common \
python-neutronclient
```

On the compute nodes, only the ML2 plugin is required:

```
# apt-get install neutron-plugin-ml2
```

Creating the Neutron database

Using the `mysql` client, create the Neutron database and associated user. When prompted for the root password, use `openstack`:

```
# mysql -u root -p
```

Enter the following SQL statements in the `MariaDB [(none)] >` prompt:

```
CREATE DATABASE neutron;
GRANT ALL PRIVILEGES ON neutron.* TO 'neutron'@'localhost' IDENTIFIED
BY 'neutron';
GRANT ALL PRIVILEGES ON neutron.* TO 'neutron'@'%' IDENTIFIED BY
'neutron';
quit;
```

Update the `[database]` section of the Neutron configuration file at `/etc/neutron/neutron.conf` on all nodes to use the proper MySQL database connection string based on the preceding values rather than the default value:

```
[database]
...
connection = mysql://neutron:neutron@controller01/neutron
```

Configuring the Neutron user, role, and endpoint in Keystone

Neutron requires that you create a user, role, and endpoint in Keystone in order to function properly. When executed from the controller node, the following commands will create a user called `neutron` in Keystone, associate the `admin` role with the `neutron` user, and add the `neutron` user to the `service` project:

```
# openstack user create neutron --password neutron
# openstack role add --project service --user neutron admin
```

Create a service in Keystone that describes the OpenStack Networking service by executing the following command on the controller node:

```
# openstack service create --name neutron \
  --description "OpenStack Networking" network
```

The `service create` command will result in the following output:

```
+-------------+----------------------------------+
| Field       | Value                            |
+-------------+----------------------------------+
| description | OpenStack Networking             |
| enabled     | True                             |
| id          | bc9ab04a39a9488491685195a845f285 |
| name        | neutron                          |
| type        | network                          |
+-------------+----------------------------------+
```

Figure 3.2

To create the endpoint, use the following `openstack endpoint create` command:

```
# openstack endpoint create \
    --publicurl http://controller01:9696 \
    --adminurl http://controller01:9696 \
    --internalurl http://controller01:9696 \
    --region RegionOne \
    network
```

The resulting endpoint is as follows:

```
+--------------+----------------------------------+
| Field        | Value                            |
+--------------+----------------------------------+
| adminurl     | http://controller01:9696         |
| enabled      | True                             |
| id           | 4ffdd681b17d444a9cda174e35b78bcc |
| internalurl  | http://controller01:9696         |
| publicurl    | http://controller01:9696         |
| region       | RegionOne                        |
| service_id   | bc9ab04a39a9488491685195a845f285 |
| service_name | neutron                          |
| service_type | network                          |
+--------------+----------------------------------+
```

Figure 3.3

Enabling packet forwarding

Before the nodes can properly forward or route traffic for virtual machine instances, there are three kernel parameters that must be configured on all nodes:

- `net.ipv4.ip_forward`
- `net.ipv4.conf.all.rp_filter`
- `net.ipv4.conf.default.rp_filter`

The `net.ipv4.ip_forward` kernel parameter allows the nodes to forward traffic from the instances to the network. The default value is 0 and should be set to 1 to enable IP forwarding. Use the following command on all nodes to implement this change:

```
# sysctl -w "net.ipv4.ip_forward=1"
```

The `net.ipv4.conf.default.rp_filter` and `net.ipv4.conf.all.rp_filter` kernel parameters are related to **reverse path filtering**, a mechanism intended to prevent certain types of denial of service attacks. When enabled, the Linux kernel will examine every packet to ensure that the source address of the packet is routable back through the interface in which it came. Without this validation, a router can be used to forward malicious packets from a sender who has spoofed the source address to prevent the target machine from responding properly.

In OpenStack, anti-spoofing rules are implemented by Neutron on each compute node within iptables. Therefore, the preferred configuration for these two `rp_filter` values is to disable them by setting them to 0. Use the following `sysctl` commands on all nodes to implement this change:

```
# sysctl -w "net.ipv4.conf.default.rp_filter=0"
# sysctl -w "net.ipv4.conf.all.rp_filter=0"
```

Using `sysctl -w` makes the changes take effect immediately. However, the changes are not persistent across reboots. To make the changes persistent, edit the `/etc/sysctl.conf` file on all hosts and add the following lines:

```
net.ipv4.ip_forward = 1
net.ipv4.conf.default.rp_filter = 0
net.ipv4.conf.all.rp_filter = 0
```

Load the changes into memory on all nodes with the following `sysctl` command:

```
# sysctl -p
```

Configuring Neutron to use Keystone

The Neutron configuration file found at `/etc/neutron/neutron.conf` has dozens of settings that can be modified to meet the needs of the OpenStack cloud administrator. A handful of these settings must be changed from their defaults as part of this installation.

To specify Keystone as the authentication method for Neutron, update the [DEFAULT] section of the Neutron configuration file on all hosts with the following setting:

```
[DEFAULT]
...
auth_strategy = keystone
```

Neutron must also be configured with the appropriate Keystone authentication settings. The username and password for the neutron user in Keystone were set earlier in this chapter. Update the [keystone_authtoken] section of the Neutron configuration file on all hosts with the following settings:

```
[keystone_authtoken]
...
auth_uri = http://controller01:5000
auth_url = http://controller01:35357
auth_plugin = password
project_domain_id = default
user_domain_id = default
project_name = service
username = neutron
password = neutron
```

Configuring Neutron to use a messaging service

Neutron communicates with various OpenStack services on the AMQP messaging bus. Update the [DEFAULT] and [oslo_messaging_rabbit] sections of the Neutron configuration file on all hosts to specify RabbitMQ as the messaging broker:

```
[DEFAULT]
...
rpc_backend = rabbit
```

The RabbitMQ authentication settings should match what was previously configured for the other OpenStack services:

```
[oslo_messaging_rabbit]
...
rabbit_host = controller01
rabbit_userid = openstack
rabbit_password = rabbit
```

Configuring Nova to utilize Neutron networking

Before Neutron can be utilized as the network manager for Nova Compute services, the appropriate configuration options must be set in the Nova configuration file located at /etc/nova/nova.conf on all hosts.

Start by updating the following sections with information on the Neutron API class and URL:

```
[DEFAULT]
...
network_api_class = nova.network.neutronv2.api.API

[neutron]
...
url = http://controller01:9696
```

Then, update the [neutron] section with the proper Neutron credentials:

```
[neutron]
...
auth_strategy = keystone
admin_tenant_name = service
admin_username = neutron
admin_password = neutron
admin_auth_url = http://controller01:35357/v2.0
```

Nova uses the firewall_driver configuration option to determine how to implement firewalling. As the option is meant for use with the nova-network networking service, it should be set to nova.virt.firewall.NoopFirewallDriver to instruct Nova *not* to implement firewalling when Neutron is in use:

```
[DEFAULT]
...
firewall_driver = nova.virt.firewall.NoopFirewallDriver
```

The security_group_api configuration option specifies which API Nova should use when working with security groups. For installations using Neutron instead of nova-network, this option should be set to neutron as follows:

```
[DEFAULT]
...
security_group_api = neutron
```

Nova requires additional configuration once a mechanism driver has been determined. The LinuxBridge and Open vSwitch mechanism drivers and their respective agents and Nova configuration changes will be discussed in further detail in *Chapter 4, Building a Virtual Switching Infrastructure*.

Configuring Neutron to notify Nova

Neutron must be configured to notify Nova of network topology changes. Update the [DEFAULT] and [nova] sections of the Neutron configuration file on the controller node located at /etc/neutron/neutron.conf with the following settings:

```
[DEFAULT]
...
notify_nova_on_port_status_changes = True
notify_nova_on_port_data_changes = True
nova_url = http://controller01:8774/v2

[nova]
...
auth_url = http://controller01:35357
auth_plugin = password
project_domain_id = default
user_domain_id = default
region_name = RegionOne
project_name = service
username = nova
password = nova
```

Configuring Neutron services

The neutron-server service exposes the Neutron API to users and passes all calls to the configured Neutron plugins for processing.

By default, Neutron is configured to listen for API calls on all configured addresses as seen by the default bind_hosts option in the Neutron configuration file:

```
bind_host = 0.0.0.0
```

As an additional security measure, it is possible to expose the API only on the management or API network. On the controller node, update the bind_host value in the [DEFAULT] section of the Neutron configuration located at /etc/neutron/neutron.conf with the management address of the controller node:

```
[DEFAULT]
...
bind_host = 10.254.254.100
```

Other configuration options that may require tweaking include:

- core_plugin
- service_plugins
- dhcp_lease_duration

Some of these settings apply to all nodes, while others apply only to the network or controller node. The `core_plugin` configuration option instructs Neutron to use the specified networking plugin. Beginning with the Icehouse release, the ML2 plugin supersedes both the LinuxBridge and Open vSwitch monolithic plugins.

On all nodes, update the `core_plugin` value in the `[DEFAULT]` section of the Neutron configuration file located at `/etc/neutron/neutron.conf` and specify the ML2 plugin:

```
[DEFAULT]
...
core_plugin = ml2
```

The `service_plugins` configuration option is used to define plugins that are loaded by Neutron for additional functionality. Examples of plugins include `router`, `firewall`, `lbaas`, `vpnaas`, and `metering`. This option should only be configured on the controller node or any other node running the `neutron-server` service. Specific plugins will be defined in later chapters.

> Due to a bug in Horizon, the `router` plugin must be defined before users can create and manage networks within the dashboard. On the controller node, update the `service_plugins` configuration option accordingly:
>
> ```
> [DEFAULT]
> service_plugins = router
> ```

The `dhcp_lease_duration` configuration option specifies the duration of an IP address lease by an instance. The default value is 86400 seconds, or 24 hours. If the value is set too low, the network may be flooded with broadcast traffic due to short leases and frequent renewal attempts. The DHCP client on the instance itself is responsible for renewing the lease, and this operation varies between operating systems. It is not uncommon for instances to attempt to renew their lease well before exceeding the lease duration. However, the value set for `dhcp_lease_duration` does not dictate how long an IP address stays associated with an instance. Once an IP address has been allocated to an instance by Neutron, it remains associated with the instance until the instance or the port is deleted, even if the instance is shut off. Instances typically rely on DHCP to obtain their address, though, which is why this configuration option is important.

Starting neutron-server

Before the `neutron-server` service can be started, the Neutron database must be updated based on options configured earlier in this chapter. Use the `neutron-db-manage` command on the controller node to update the database accordingly:

```
# su -s /bin/sh -c "neutron-db-manage \
--config-file /etc/neutron/neutron.conf \
--config-file /etc/neutron/plugins/ml2/ml2_conf.ini \
upgrade head" neutron
```

Restart the Nova compute services on the controller node:

```
# service nova-api restart
# service nova-scheduler restart
# service nova-conductor restart
```

Restart the Nova compute service on the compute nodes:

```
# service nova-compute restart
```

Finally, restart the `neutron-server` service on the controller node:

```
# service neutron-server restart
```

Configuring the Neutron DHCP agent

Neutron utilizes `dnsmasq`, a free, lightweight DNS forwarder and DHCP server, which is used to provide DHCP services to networks. The `neutron-dhcp-agent` service is responsible for spawning and configuring `dnsmasq` and metadata processes for each network that leverages DHCP.

The DHCP driver is specified in the `dhcp_agent.ini` configuration file found in the `/etc/neutron` directory. The agent can be configured to use other DHCP drivers, but `dnsmasq` support is built in and requires no additional setup. The default `dhcp_driver` value is `neutron.agent.linux.dhcp.Dnsmasq` and can be left unmodified.

Other notable configuration options found in the dhcp_agent.ini configuration file include:

- interface_driver
- use_namespaces
- enable_isolated_metadata
- enable_metadata_network
- dhcp_domain
- dhcp_delete_namespaces

The interface_driver configuration option should be configured appropriately based on the network mechanism driver chosen for your environment:

- **LinuxBridge**: neutron.agent.linux.interface.BridgeInterfaceDriver
- **Open vSwitch**: neutron.agent.linux.interface.OVSInterfaceDriver

Both LinuxBridge and Open vSwitch will be discussed in further detail in *Chapter 4, Building a Virtual Switching Infrastructure*. For now, update the interface_driver value in the [DEFAULT] section of the DHCP agent configuration file located at /etc/neutron/dhcp_agent.ini on the controller node to specify the OVS driver:

```
[DEFAULT]
...
interface_driver = neutron.agent.linux.interface.OVSInterfaceDriver
```

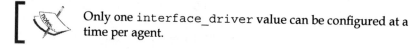

> Only one interface_driver value can be configured at a time per agent.

The use_namespaces configuration option instructs Neutron to disable or enable the use of network namespaces for DHCP. When True, every network scheduled to a DHCP agent will have a namespace by the name qdhcp-<Network UUID>, where <Network UUID> is a unique UUID associated with every network. By default, use_namespaces is set to True. When set to False, overlapping networks between tenants are not allowed. Not all distributions and kernels support network namespaces, which may limit how tenant networks are built out. The operating system and kernel recommended in *Chapter 2, Installing OpenStack*, does support network namespaces. For this installation, leave the value set to True.

The enable_isolated_metadata configuration option is useful in cases where a physical network device, such as a firewall or router, serves as the default gateway for instances, but Neutron is still required to provide metadata services to instances. When the L3 agent is used, an instance reaches the metadata service through the Neutron router that serves as its default gateway. An isolated network is assumed to be one in which a Neutron router is not serving as the gateway, but Neutron handles DHCP requests for the instances. Often, this is the case when instances are leveraging flat or VLAN networks and the L3 agent is not used. The default value for enable_ isolated_metadata is False. When set to True, Neutron can provide instances with a static route to the metadata service via DHCP in certain cases. More information on the use of metadata and this configuration can be found in *Chapter 5, Creating Networks with Neutron*. On the controller node, update the enable_isolated_ metadata option in the DHCP agent configuration file located at /etc/neutron/ dhcp_agent.ini to True:

```
[DEFAULT]
...
enable_isolated_metadata = True
```

The enable_metadata_network configuration option is useful in cases where the L3 agent may be used, but the metadata agent is not on the same host as the router. By setting enable_metadata_network to True, Neutron networks whose subnet CIDR is included in 169.254.0.0/16 will be regarded as metadata networks. When connected to a Neutron router, a metadata proxy is spawned on the node hosting the router, granting metadata access to all the networks connected to the router.

The dhcp_domain configuration option specifies the DNS search domain that is provided to instances via DHCP when they obtain a lease. The default value is openstacklocal. This can be changed to whatever fits your organization. For the purpose of this installation, change the value from openstacklocal to learningneutron.com. On the controller node, update the dhcp_domain option in the DHCP agent configuration file located at /etc/neutron/dhcp_agent.ini to learningneutron.com:

```
[DEFAULT]
...
dhcp_domain = learningneutron.com
```

The dhcp_delete_namespaces configuration option, when set to true, allows Neutron to automatically delete DHCP namespaces from the host when a DHCP server is disabled on a network. It is set to false by default and should be set to true for most modern operating systems, including Ubuntu 14.04 LTS. Update the dhcp_delete_namespaces option in the DHCP agent configuration file from false to true:

```
[DEFAULT]
...
dhcp_delete_namespaces = true
```

Configuration options not mentioned here have sufficient default values and should not be changed unless your environment requires it.

Restarting the Neutron DHCP agent

Use the following command to restart the neutron-dhcp-agent service on the controller node:

```
# service neutron-dhcp-agent restart
```

Confirm the status of the neutron-dhcp-agent as follows:

```
root@controller01:~# service neutron-dhcp-agent status
neutron-dhcp-agent start/running, process 12233
```

Figure 3.4

The agent should be in a running status. Using the neutron agent-list command, verify that the service has checked in:

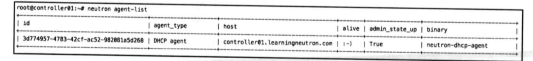

```
root@controller01:~# neutron agent-list
+--------------------------------------+------------+-------------------------------+-------+----------------+--------------------+
| id                                   | agent_type | host                          | alive | admin_state_up | binary             |
+--------------------------------------+------------+-------------------------------+-------+----------------+--------------------+
| 3d774957-4783-42cf-ac52-982081a5d268 | DHCP agent | controller01.learningneutron.com | :-)   | True           | neutron-dhcp-agent |
+--------------------------------------+------------+-------------------------------+-------+----------------+--------------------+
```

Figure 3.5

A smiley face under the alive column means the agent is properly communicating with the Neutron service.

> The metadata agent may have checked in prior to its configuration due to base settings in the configuration file. The base configuration will be replaced in the following section.

Configuring the Neutron metadata agent

OpenStack provides metadata services that enable users to retrieve information about their instances that can be used to configure or manage the running instance. **Metadata** includes information such as the hostname, fixed and floating IPs, public keys, and more. In addition to metadata, users can access **user data**, such as scripts, that are provided during the launching of an instance and are executed during the boot process.

Instances typically access the metadata service over HTTP at `http://169.254.169.254` during the boot process. This mechanism is implemented by `cloud-init`, a utility found on most cloud-ready images and available at `https://launchpad.net/cloud-init`.

The following diagram provides a high-level overview of the retrieval of metadata from an instance when the controller node hosts Neutron networking services:

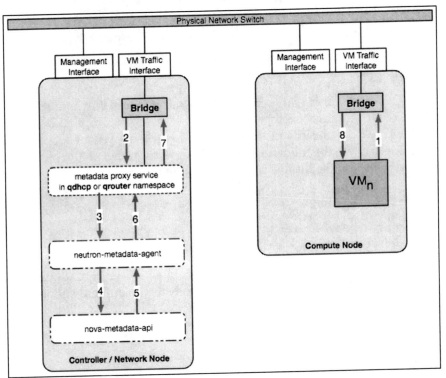

Figure 3.6

In the preceding diagram, the following actions take place when an instance makes a request to the metadata service:

1. An instance sends a request for metadata to 169.254.269.254 via HTTP at boot.

2. The metadata request hits either the router or DHCP namespace depending on the route in the instance.

3. The metadata proxy service in the namespace sends the request to the Neutron metadata agent service via a Unix socket.

4. The Neutron metadata agent service forwards the request to the Nova metadata API service.

5. The Nova metadata API service responds to the request and forwards the response back to the Neutron metadata agent service.

6. The Neutron metadata agent service sends the response back to the metadata proxy service in the namespace.

7. The metadata proxy service forwards the HTTP response to the instance.

8. The instance receives the metadata and/or the user data and continues the boot process.

For proper operation of metadata services, both Neutron and Nova must be configured to communicate together with a shared secret. Neutron uses this secret to sign the Instance-ID header of the metadata request to prevent spoofing. On the controller node, update the following metadata options in the [neutron] section of the Nova configuration file located at /etc/nova/nova.conf:

```
[neutron]
. . .

metadata_proxy_shared_secret = metadatasecret123
service_metadata_proxy = true
```

Next, update the [DEFAULT] section of the metadata agent configuration file located at /etc/neutron/metadata_agent.ini with the Neutron authentication details and the metadata proxy shared secret:

```
[DEFAULT]
. . .
auth_url = http://controller01:5000/v2.0
auth_region = regionOne
admin_tenant_name = service
admin_user = neutron
admin_password = neutron
nova_metadata_ip = controller01
metadata_proxy_shared_secret = metadatasecret123
```

Configuration options not mentioned here have sufficient default values and should not be changed unless your environment requires it.

Restarting the Neutron metadata agent

Use the following command to restart the `neutron-metadata-agent` and `nova-api` services on the controller node for the changes to take effect:

```
# service nova-api restart
# service neutron-metadata-agent restart
```

Confirm the status of `neutron-metadata-agent` as follows:

```
root@controller01:~# service neutron-metadata-agent status
neutron-metadata-agent start/running, process 28239
```

Figure 3.7

The agent should be in a running status. Using the neutron `agent-list` command, verify that the service has checked in:

```
root@controller01:~# neutron agent-list
+--------------------------------------+----------------+-----------------------------+-------+----------------+------------------------+
| id                                   | agent_type     | host                        | alive | admin_state_up | binary                 |
+--------------------------------------+----------------+-----------------------------+-------+----------------+------------------------+
| 154aea15-2b39-417f-a697-56352fd8ada6 | Metadata agent | controller01.learningneutron.com | :-)   | True           | neutron-metadata-agent |
| 3d774957-4783-42cf-ac52-982081a5d268 | DHCP agent     | controller01.learningneutron.com | :-)   | True           | neutron-dhcp-agent     |
+--------------------------------------+----------------+-----------------------------+-------+----------------+------------------------+
```

Figure 3.8

A smiley face under the `alive` column means the agent is properly communicating with the Neutron service. If the services do not appear or have xxx under the `alive` column, check the Neutron logs found at `/var/log/neutron` for assistance in troubleshooting. More information on the use of metadata can be found in *Chapter 5, Creating Networks with Neutron*, and later chapters.

Configuring the Neutron L3 agent

OpenStack Networking includes an extension that provides users with the ability to dynamically provision and configure virtual routers using the API. These routers interconnect L2 networks and provide floating IP functionality that make instances on private networks externally accessible. The Neutron L3 agent uses the Linux IP stack and iptables to perform both L3 forwarding and network address translation, or NAT. In order to support multiple routers with potentially overlapping IP networks, the Neutron L3 agent defaults to using network namespaces to provide isolated forwarding contexts. More information on creating and managing routers in Neutron begins with *Chapter 7, Creating Standalone Routers with Neutron*.

Configuring the Neutron LBaaS agent

OpenStack Networking includes an extension that provides users the ability to dynamically provision and configure virtual load balancers using the API. Neutron includes a reference implementation for LBaaS that utilizes the HAProxy software load balancer. Network namespaces are used to provide isolated load balancing contexts per virtual IP, or VIP, in version 1.0 of the LBaaS API. More information on creating and managing virtual load balancers in Neutron can be found in *Chapter 10, Load Balancing Traffic to Instances*.

Using the Neutron command-line interface

Neutron provides a command-line client to interface with its API. Neutron commands can be run directly from the Linux command line, or the Neutron shell can be invoked by issuing the neutron command:

```
root@controller01:~# neutron
(neutron)
```

Figure 3.9

The neutron shell provides commands that can be used to create, read, update, and delete the networking configuration within the OpenStack cloud. By typing a question mark or help within the Neutron shell, a list of commands can be found. Additionally, running neutron help from the Linux command line provides a brief description of each command's function.

Many of the commands listed will be covered in subsequent chapters of this book. Commands outside the scope of basic Neutron functionality, such as those relying on third-party plugins, can be found in *Appendix A, Additional Neutron Commands*.

Summary

Neutron has seen major internal architectural improvements over the last few releases. These improvements have made developing and implementing network features easier for developers and operators, respectively. Neutron maintains the logical network architecture in its database, and network plugins and agents on each node are responsible for configuring virtual and physical network devices accordingly. With the introduction of the ML2 plugin, developers can spend less time implementing the core Neutron API functionality and more time developing value-added features.

Now that OpenStack Networking services have been installed across all nodes in the environment, configuration of a layer 2 networking plugin is all that remains before instances can be created.

In the next chapter, you will be guided through the configuration of the ML2 plugin and both the LinuxBridge and Open vSwitch network agents. We will also explore the differences between LinuxBridge and Open vSwitch in terms of how they function and provide connectivity to instances.

Building a Virtual Switching Infrastructure

One of the core functions of OpenStack Networking is to provide connectivity to and from instances by programmatically configuring the network infrastructure of the cloud.

In the last chapter, we installed various Neutron services and the ML2 plugin across all nodes in the cloud. In this chapter, you will be introduced to networking concepts and architectures that Neutron relies on to provide connectivity to instances as well as multiple mechanism drivers that extend the functionality of the ML2 network plugin: the LinuxBridge, Open vSwitch, and L2 population drivers. You will be guided through the installation and configuration of the drivers and their respective agents, and we will lay a foundation for the creation of networks and instances in the chapters to come.

Virtual network devices

OpenStack is responsible for configuring and managing many different types of virtual and physical network devices and technologies across the cloud infrastructure.

Virtual network interfaces

OpenStack uses the libvirt KVM/QEMU driver to provide platform virtualization in default Nova configurations. When an instance is booted for the first time, Neutron assigns a virtual port to each network interface of the instance. KVM creates a virtual network interface called a **tap interface** on the compute node hosting the instance. The tap interface corresponds directly to a network interface within the guest instance. Through the use of a bridge, the host can expose the guest instance to a physical network.

> In OpenStack, the name of a tap interface associated with an instance corresponds to the Neutron port UUID, or unique identifier, which the instance is plugged into.

Virtual network switches

Neutron supports many types of virtual and physical switches and includes built-in support for Linux bridges and Open vSwitch virtual switches.

> The terms **bridge** and **switch** are often used interchangeably in the context of Neutron and may be used in the same way throughout this book.

A **Linux bridge** is a virtual switch on a host that connects multiple network interfaces. When using Neutron, a bridge usually connects a physical interface to one or more virtual or tap interfaces. A physical interface includes Ethernet interfaces, such as eth1, or bonded interfaces, such as bond0. A virtual interface includes VLAN interfaces, such as eth1.100, as well as tap interfaces created by KVM. You can connect multiple physical or virtual network interfaces to a Linux bridge.

The following diagram provides a high-level view of a Linux bridge leveraged by Neutron:

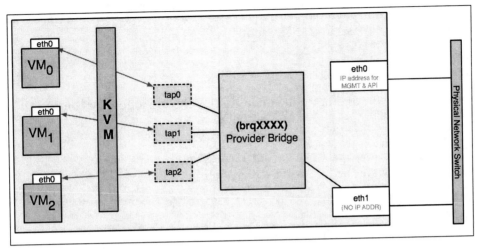

Figure 4.1

In *Figure 4.1*, the Linux bridge, **brqXXXX**, is connected to a single physical interface, **eth1**, and three virtual interfaces, **tap0**, **tap1**, and **tap2**. The three tap interfaces correspond to a network interface within the respective guest instance. Traffic from **eth0** in a virtual machine instance can be observed on the respective tap interface on the host as well as on the bridge interface and the physical interface connected to the bridge.

Open vSwitch operates as a software-based switch that uses virtual network bridges and flow rules to forward packets between hosts. Most Neutron setups that leverage Open vSwitch utilize at least three virtual switches or bridges, including a provider, integration, and tunnel bridge. These virtual switches are cross connected with one another, similar to how a physical switch may be connected to another physical switch with a cross connect cable.

When wrong combinations of interfaces exist in a bridge, bridging loops may occur and cause issues with the network. Be sure not to manually modify the bridges managed by OpenStack to avoid these issues.

More information on how Linux bridges and Open vSwitch bridges connect instances to the network will be covered later in this chapter.

Configuring the bridge interface

In this installation, the `eth2` physical network interface will be utilized for bridging purposes. On the controller and compute nodes, configure the `eth2` interface within the `/etc/network/interfaces` file, as follows:

```
auto eth2
iface eth2 inet manual
```

Close and save the file and bring the interface up with the following command:

 # ip link set dev eth2 up

Confirm that the interface is in an UP state using the `ip link show dev eth2` command, as shown in the following screenshot:

```
root@controller01:~# ip link set eth2 up
root@controller01:~# ip link show dev eth2
4: eth2: <BROADCAST,MULTICAST,UP,LOWER_UP> mtu 1500 qdisc pfifo_fast state UP mode DEFAULT group default qlen 1000
    link/ether 8c:ae:4c:fe:9a:d0 brd ff:ff:ff:ff:ff:ff
```

Figure 4.2

If the interface is up, it is ready for use in a Linux or Open vSwitch bridge.

> As the interface will be used in a bridge, an IP address cannot be applied directly to it. If there is an IP address applied to `eth2`, it will become inaccessible once the interface is placed in a bridge. Instead, consider applying the IP address to the bridge if you must have connectivity to this interface.

Overlay networks

Neutron supports overlay networking technologies that allow virtual networks to scale across the cloud with little to no change in the underlying physical infrastructure. To accomplish this, Neutron leverages L2-in-L3 overlay networking technologies, such as GRE and VXLAN. When configured accordingly, Neutron builds point-to-point tunnels between all network and compute nodes in the cloud using the management or another dedicated interface. These point-to-point tunnels create what is called a **mesh network**, where every host is connected to every other host. A cloud consisting of one controller running network services and three compute nodes will have a fully meshed overlay network that resembles *Figure 4.3*:

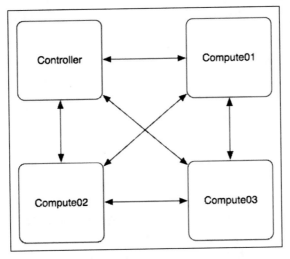

Figure 4.3

Using the ML2 plugin, GRE- and VXLAN-based networks can be created by users at scale without any changes to the underlying switching infrastructure. When GRE- or VXLAN-based networks are created, a unique ID is specified that is used to encapsulate the traffic. Every packet between instances on different hosts is encapsulated on one host and sent to the other through a point-to-point GRE or VXLAN tunnel. When the packet reaches the destination host, the tunnel-related headers are stripped, and the packet is forwarded through the connected bridge to the instance.

The following diagram shows a packet encapsulated by a host:

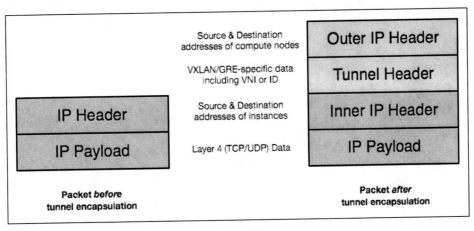

Figure 4.4

In *Figure 4.4*, the outer IP header source and destination addresses identify the endpoints of the tunnel. Tunnel endpoints include compute nodes and any node running the L3 and DHCP services, such as a network node. The inner IP header source and destination addresses identify the original sender and recipient of the payload.

Because GRE and VXLAN network traffic is encapsulated between hosts, many physical network devices cannot participate in these networks. As a result, GRE and VXLAN networks are effectively isolated from other networks in the cloud without the use of a Neutron router. More information on creating Neutron routers can be found in *Chapter 7, Creating Standalone Routers with Neutron*.

Connectivity issues when using overlay networks

One thing to be aware of when using overlay networking technologies is that the additional headers added to the packets may cause the packet to exceed the maximum transmission unit, or MTU. The MTU is the largest size of packet or frame that can be sent over a network. Encapsulating a packet with VXLAN headers may cause the packet size to exceed the default maximum, which is 1500 bytes. Connection issues caused by exceeding the MTU manifest themselves in strange ways; they can be seen in partial failures in connecting to instances over SSH or in a failure to transfer large payloads between instances, among others. Consider lowering the MTU of interfaces within virtual machine instances from 1500 bytes to 1450 bytes to account for the overhead of VXLAN encapsulation so as to avoid connectivity issues.

The DHCP agent and dnsmasq can be configured to push a lower MTU to instances within the DHCP lease offer. To configure a lower MTU, complete the following steps:

1. On the controller node, modify the DHCP configuration file at /etc/neutron/dhcp_agent.ini and specify a custom dnsmasq configuration file, as follows:

    ```
    [DEFAULT]
    dnsmasq_config_file = /etc/neutron/dnsmasq-neutron.conf
    ```

2. Next, create the custom dnsmasq configuration file at /etc/neutron/dnsmasq-neutron.conf and add the following contents:

    ```
    dhcp-option-force=26,1450
    ```

3. Save and close the file. Restart the Neutron DHCP agent with the following command:

```
# service neutron-dhcp-agent restart
```

When the instances are later created, the MTU can be observed within the instance using the `ip link show <interface>` command.

Network types supported by Neutron

With the ML2 plugin, Neutron supports a range of traditional and overlay networking types provided by type drivers, including:

- Local
- Flat
- VLAN
- VXLAN
- GRE

A **local network** is one that is isolated from other networks and nodes. Instances connected to a local network may communicate with other instances in the same network on the same compute node but may be unable to communicate with instances in the same network that reside on another host. Because of this designed limitation, local networks are recommended for testing purposes only.

In a **flat network**, no VLAN tagging or other network segregation takes place. In some configurations, instances can reside in the same network as the host machines.

VLAN networks are networks that utilize 802.1q tagging to segregate network traffic. Instances in the same VLAN are considered part of the same network and are in the same layer 2 broadcast domain. InterVLAN routing, or routing between VLANs, is only possible through the use of a router.

A **VXLAN network** uses a unique segmentation ID, called VNI, to differentiate traffic from other VXLAN networks. Traffic from one instance to another is encapsulated by the host using the VNI and sent over an existing layer 3 network using UDP, where it is decapsulated and forwarded to the instance. The use of VXLAN to encapsulate packets over an existing network is meant to solve limitations of VLANs and physical switching infrastructures. More information on how VXLAN encapsulation works is described in RFC 7348, available at `https://tools.ietf.org/html/rfc7348`.

A **GRE network** is similar to a VXLAN network in that traffic from one instance to another is encapsulated and sent over an existing layer 3 network. A unique segmentation ID is used to differentiate traffic from other GRE networks. Rather than using UDP as the transport mechanism, GRE traffic uses IP protocol 47. More information on how GRE encapsulation works is described in RFC 2784, available at `https://tools.ietf.org/html/rfc2784`.

 As of the Kilo release of OpenStack, the LinuxBridge driver does not implement GRE networks.

Choosing a plugin and driver

Neutron networking plugins, drivers, and agents are responsible for implementing features that provide network connectivity to and from instances. The ML2 plugin can leverage multiple layer 2 technologies simultaneously through the use of mechanism drivers. The two drivers discussed in this book, LinuxBridge and Open vSwitch, implement network connectivity in different ways.

Using the LinuxBridge driver

When configured to utilize the ML2 plugin and LinuxBridge driver, Neutron relies on the `bridge`, `8021q`, and `vxlan` kernel modules to properly connect instances and other network resources to the virtual switch and forward the traffic. The LinuxBridge driver is popular for its dependability and ease of troubleshooting but lacks support for some advanced Neutron features, such as distributed virtual routers.

In a LinuxBridge-based network implementation, there are five types of interfaces managed by Neutron, which are:

- Tap interfaces
- Physical interfaces
- VLAN interfaces
- VXLAN interfaces
- Linux bridges

A **tap interface** is created and used by a hypervisor, such as QEMU/KVM, to connect the guest operating system in a virtual machine instance to the host. These virtual interfaces on the host correspond to a network interface inside the guest instance. An Ethernet frame sent to the tap device on the host is received by the guest operating system, and the frames received from a guest operating system are injected into the host network stack.

A physical interface represents an interface on the host that is plugged into physical network hardware. Physical interfaces are often labeled eth0, eth1, em0, em1, and so on, and vary depending on the host operating system.

Linux supports 802.1q VLAN tagging through the use of virtual VLAN interfaces. A VLAN interface can be created using iproute2 commands or the traditional vlan utility and 8021q kernel module. A VLAN interface is often labeled ethX.<vlan> and is associated with its respective physical interface, ethX.

A VXLAN interface is a virtual interface that is used to encapsulate and forward traffic based on the parameters configured during the creation of an interface, such as a **VXLAN Network Identifier (VNI)** and **VXLAN Tunnel End Point (VTEP)**. The function of a VTEP is to encapsulate the virtual machine instance traffic within an IP header across an IP network. Traffic is segregated from other VXLAN traffic using an ID provided by the VNI. The instances themselves are unaware of the outer network topology providing connectivity between VTEPs.

A Linux bridge is a virtual interface that connects multiple network interfaces. In Neutron, a bridge usually includes a physical interface and one or more virtual or tap interfaces. Linux bridges are a form of virtual switches.

Using the Open vSwitch driver

Within OpenStack Networking, Open vSwitch operates as a software-based switch that uses virtual network bridges and flow rules to forward packets between hosts. Although it is capable of supporting many technologies and protocols, only a subset of Open vSwitch features are leveraged by Neutron.

There are three main components of Open vSwitch to be aware of:

- **The kernel module**: The Open vSwitch kernel module is the equivalent of ASICs on a hardware switch. It is the data plane of the switch where all packet processing takes place.
- **The vSwitch daemon**: The Open vSwitch daemon, ovs-vswitchd, is a Linux process that runs in user space on every physical host and dictates how the kernel module will be programmed.

- **The database server**: Open vSwitch uses a local database on every physical host called **Open vSwitch Database Server (OVSDB)**, which maintains the configuration of virtual switches.

When configured to utilize the Open vSwitch mechanism driver, Neutron relies on the `bridge` and `openvswitch` kernel modules along with user-space utilities, such as `ovs-vsctl` and `ovs-ofctl`, to properly manage the Open vSwitch database and connect instances and other network resources to virtual switches.

In an Open vSwitch-based network implementation, there are five distinct types of virtual networking devices:

- Tap devices
- Linux bridges
- Virtual Ethernet cables
- OVS bridges
- OVS patch ports

Tap devices and Linux bridges were described briefly in the previous section, and their use in an Open vSwitch-based network remains the same. **Virtual Ethernet**, or **veth**, cables are virtual interfaces that mimic network patch cables. An Ethernet frame sent to one end of a veth cable is received by the other end, much like a real network patch cable. Neutron also makes use of veth cables to make connections between various network resources, including namespaces and bridges.

An OVS bridge behaves like a physical switch, only one that is virtualized. Neutron connects the interfaces used by DHCP or router namespaces and instance tap interfaces to OVS bridge ports. The ports themselves can be configured much like a physical switch port. Open vSwitch maintains information about connected devices, including MAC addresses and interface statistics.

Open vSwitch has a built-in port type that mimics the behavior of a Linux veth cable, but it is optimized for use with OVS bridges. When connecting two Open vSwitch bridges, a port on each switch is reserved as a **patch port**. Patch ports are configured with a peer name that corresponds to the patch port on the other switch. Graphically, it looks something similar to this:

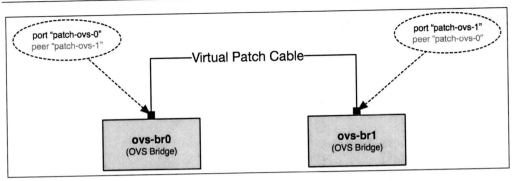

Figure 4.5

In *Figure 4.5,* two OVS bridges are cross connected via a patch port on each switch.

Open vSwitch patch ports are used to connect Open vSwitch bridges to each other, while Linux veth interfaces are used to connect Open vSwitch bridges to Linux bridges or Linux bridges to other Linux bridges.

Using the L2 population driver

The L2 population driver was introduced in the Havana release alongside the ML2 plugin. It enables broadcast, multicast, and unicast traffic to scale out on large overlay networks.

The L2 population driver works to prepopulate bridge-forwarding tables on all hosts to eliminate normal switch learning behaviors as broadcasts through an overlay network are costly operations due to encapsulation. As Neutron is seen as the source of truth for the logical layout of networks and instances created by tenants, it can easily prepopulate forwarding tables consisting of MAC addresses and destination hosts with this information. The L2 population driver also implements an ARP proxy on each host, eliminating the need to broadcast ARP requests across the overlay network. Each node is able to intercept an ARP request from an instance or router and proxy the response to the requestor.

 When using overlay networks, it is highly recommended to configure the L2 population mechanism driver along with the LinuxBridge or Open vSwitch driver.

Visualizing traffic flow when using LinuxBridge

While an Ethernet frame travels from the virtual machine instance to a remote physical network, it passes through three or four of the following devices depending on the network type:

- **The tap interface**: `tapN`
- **The Linux bridge**: `brqXXXX`
- **The VXLAN interface**: `vxlan-Z` (where `z` is the VNI)
- **The VLAN interface**: `ethX.Y` (where `x` is the interface and `Y` is the VLAN ID)
- **The physical interface**: `ethX` (where `x` is the interface)

To help conceptualize how Neutron uses Linux bridges, a few examples of LinuxBridge architectures are provided in the following sections.

VLAN

Imagine a basic OpenStack cloud that consists of a single network on VLAN 100 for use with instances. The network architecture within the compute node resembles the following:

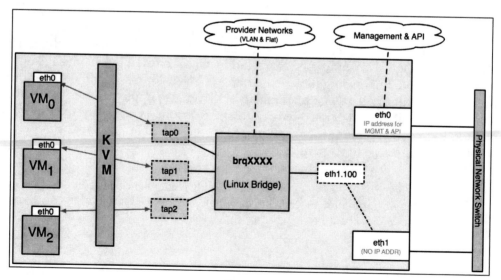

Figure 4.6

In *Figure 4.6*, three virtual machine instances are connected to a Linux bridge named brqXXXX via their respective tap interfaces. When an instance was launched in the network mapped to VLAN 100, a virtual interface named eth1.100 was automatically created and connected to a network bridge by Neutron. The eth1.100 interface is bound to the physical interface, eth1. As the traffic from instances traverses the Linux bridge and out towards the physical interface, the eth1.100 interface tags this traffic as VLAN 100 and drops it on eth1. The ingress traffic towards the instances through eth1 is inversely untagged by eth1.100 and sent to the appropriate instance through the bridge.

Using the brctl show command, the preceding diagram can be realized in the Linux CLI as the following:

```
# brctl show

bridge name        bridge id          STP enabled        interfaces
brqXXXX            <based on NIC>         no              eth1.100
                                                          tap0
                                                          tap1
                                                          tap2
```

Figure 4.7

The bridge ID in the output is dynamically generated based on the parent NIC of the virtual VLAN interface. In this bridge, the parent interface is eth1.

The bridge name, beginning with the brq prefix, is generated based on the UUID of the corresponding Neutron network that it is associated with. Each network uses its own bridge.

If more than one VLAN is needed, another Linux bridge will be created that contains a separate virtual VLAN interface. The new virtual interface, eth1.101, is connected to a new bridge, brqYYYY, as seen in *Figure 4.8*:

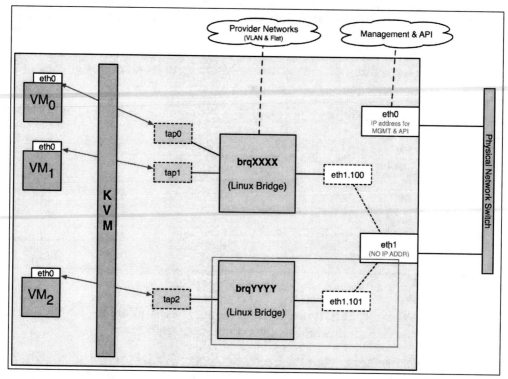

Figure 4.8

On the compute node, the preceding diagram can be realized as the following:

```
# brctl show

bridge name        bridge id          STP enabled      interfaces
brqXXXX            <based on NIC>          no           eth1.100
                                                        tap0
                                                        tap1

bridge name        bridge id          STP enabled      interfaces
brqYYYY            <based on NIC>          no           eth1.101
                                                        tap2
```

Figure 4.9

Flat

A flat network in Neutron is meant to describe a network in which VLAN tagging does not take place. Unlike VLAN tagged networks, flat networks require the physical interface of the host associated with the network to be connected directly to the bridge. This means that only a single flat network can exist per bridge and physical interface.

Figure 4.10 demonstrates a physical interface connecting to the bridge in a flat network scenario:

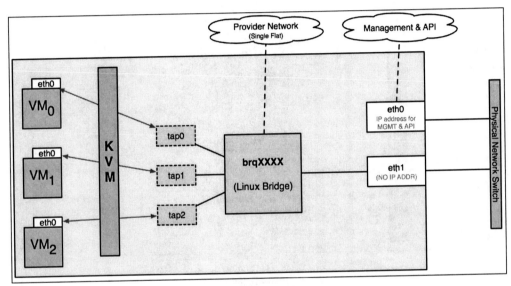

Figure 4.10

In *Figure 4.10*, `eth1` is connected to the bridge named `brqXXXX` along with three tap interfaces that correspond to guest instances. The Linux kernel does not perform any VLAN tagging on the host.

On the compute node, the preceding diagram can be realized as the following:

```
# brctl show

bridge name      bridge id          STP enabled       interfaces
brqXXXX          <based on NIC>         no             eth1
                                                       tap0
                                                       tap1
                                                       tap2
```

Figure 4.11

When multiple flat networks are created, a separate physical interface must be associated with each flat network. *Figure 4.12* demonstrates the use of a second physical interface used for flat networks:

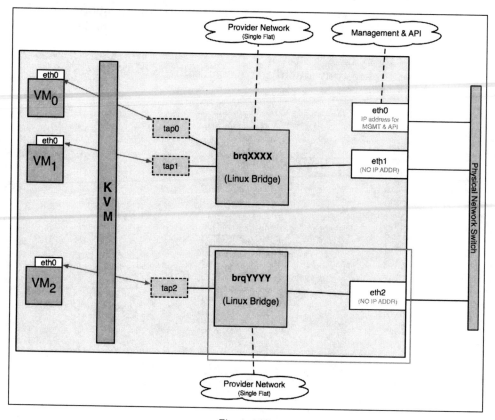

Figure 4.12

On the compute node, the use of two physical interfaces for separate flat networks can be realized as the following:

```
# brctl show

bridge name       bridge id          STP enabled       interfaces
brqXXXX           <based on NIC>         no             eth1
                                                        tap0
                                                        tap1

bridge name       bridge id          STP enabled       interfaces
brqYYYY           <based on NIC>         no             eth2
                                                        tap2
```

Figure 4.13

With two flat networks, the host does not perform any VLAN tagging on the traffic traversing these bridges. The instances connected to the two bridges require a router to communicate with one another.

VXLAN

When VXLAN networks are created, the LinuxBridge agent creates a corresponding VXLAN interface using the `iproute2` user-space utilities and connects it to a network bridge in lieu of a tagged or physical interface. The VXLAN interface is programmed with information such as the VNI and local VTEP address.

When the L2 population driver is configured, Neutron prepopulates the forwarding database with static entries consisting of the MAC addresses of instances and their respective host VTEP addresses. As a packet from an instance traverses the bridge, the host determines how to forward the packet by looking in the forwarding database. If an entry is found, Neutron will forward the packet out the corresponding local interface and encapsulate the traffic accordingly. To view the bridge table on each host, use the `bridge fdb show` command.

Local

When creating a local network in Neutron, it is not possible to specify a VLAN ID or even a physical interface. The LinuxBridge plugin agent will create a bridge and connect only the tap interface of the instance to the bridge. Instances in the same local network will be connected to the same bridge and are free to communicate among one another. Because the host does not have a physical or virtual VLAN interface connected to the bridge, traffic between instances is limited to the host on which the instances reside.

Figure 4.14 demonstrates the lack of physical or virtual VLAN interfaces connected to the bridge:

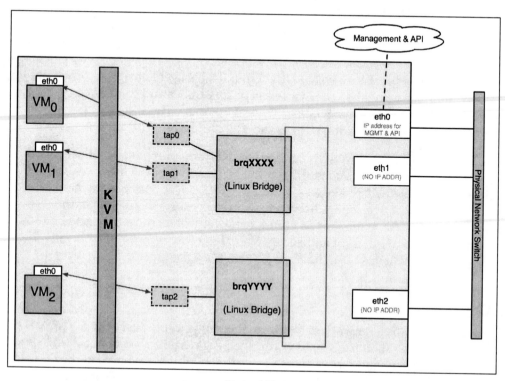

Figure 4.14

In *Figure 4.14*, two local networks exist that utilize their respective bridges: brqXXXX and brqYYYY. Instances connected to the same bridge can communicate with one another but with nothing else outside of the bridge. There is no mechanism to permit traffic between instances on different bridges or hosts when using local networks.

Visualizing the traffic flow when using Open vSwitch

When using the Open vSwitch driver, for an Ethernet frame to travel from the virtual machine instance out through the physical server interface, it will potentially pass through nine devices inside the host:

- **The tap interface**: tapXXXX
- **The Linux bridge**: qbrXXXX
- **The veth pair**: qvbXXXX, qvoXXXX
- **The OVS integration bridge**: br-int
- **OVS patch ports**: int-br-ethX and phy-br-ethX
- **The OVS provider bridge**: br-ethX
- **The physical interface**: ethX
- **The OVS tunnel bridge**: br-tun

The Open vSwitch bridge br-int is known as the **integration bridge**. The integration bridge is the central virtual switch that most virtual devices are connected to, including instances, DHCP servers, routers, and more. When Neutron security groups are enabled, however, instances are *not* directly connected to the integration bridge. Instead, instances are connected to individual Linux bridges that are cross connected to the integration bridge using a veth cable.

> The reliance on Linux bridges in an Open vSwitch-based network implementation stems from the current inability to place iptables rules on tap interfaces connected to Open vSwitch bridge ports, a core function of Neutron security groups. To work around this limitation, tap interfaces are placed into Linux bridges, which in turn are connected to the integration bridge. More information on security group rules and how they are applied to interfaces can be found in *Chapter 6, Managing Security Groups*.

The `br-ethX` Open vSwitch bridge is known as a **provider bridge**. The provider bridge provides connectivity to the physical network via a connected physical interface. The provider bridge is also connected to the integration bridge by a virtual patch cable provided by the `int-br-ethX` and `phy-br-ethX` patch ports.

A visual representation of the architecture described can be seen in *Figure 4.15*:

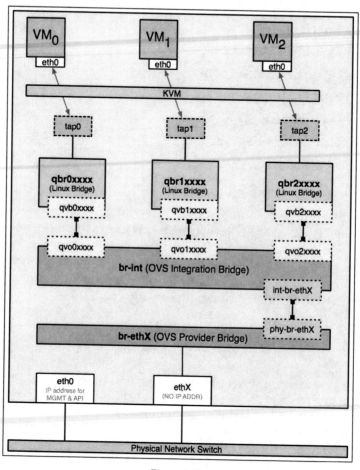

Figure 4.15

In *Figure 4.15*, instances are connected to an individual Linux bridge via their respective tap interface. Linux bridges are connected to the OVS integration bridge using a veth cable. OpenFlow rules on the integration bridge dictate how traffic is forwarded through the virtual switch. The integration bridge is connected to the provider bridge using an OVS patch cable. Lastly, the provider bridge is connected to the physical network interface, which allows traffic to enter and exit the host onto the physical network infrastructure.

When using the Open vSwitch driver, every network and compute node in the environment has its own integration, provider, and tunnel bridge. The virtual switches across nodes are effectively cross connected to one another through the physical network. More than one provider bridge can be configured on a host, but it often requires the use of a dedicated physical interface per provider bridge.

Identifying ports on the virtual switch

Using the `ovs-ofctl show <bridge>` command, we can see a logical representation of the specified virtual switch. The following screenshot demonstrates the use of this command to show the switch ports of the integration bridge on `compute01`:

```
root@compute01:~# ovs-ofctl show br-int
OFPT_FEATURES_REPLY (xid=0x2): dpid:0000de416cbe2b46
n_tables:254, n_buffers:256
capabilities: FLOW_STATS TABLE_STATS PORT_STATS QUEUE_STATS ARP_MATCH_IP
actions: OUTPUT SET_VLAN_VID SET_VLAN_PCP STRIP_VLAN SET_DL_SRC SET_DL_DST SET_NW_SRC SET_NW_DST SET_NW_TOS SET_TP_SRC SET_TP_DST ENQUEUE
 6(int-br-eth2): addr:2e:97:d1:79:57:44
     config:     0
     state:      0
     speed: 0 Mbps now, 0 Mbps max
 7(patch-tun): addr:56:a3:b0:ab:99:eb
     config:     0
     state:      0
     speed: 0 Mbps now, 0 Mbps max
 8(qvo017db302-dc): addr:36:75:da:ef:7a:f6
     config:     0
     state:      0
     current:    10GB-FD COPPER
     speed: 10000 Mbps now, 0 Mbps max
 9(qvo7140bc00-75): addr:96:dd:15:3b:14:21
     config:     0
     state:      0
     current:    10GB-FD COPPER
     speed: 10000 Mbps now, 0 Mbps max
 LOCAL(br-int): addr:de:41:6c:be:2b:46
     config:     PORT_DOWN
     state:      LINK_DOWN
     speed: 0 Mbps now, 0 Mbps max
OFPT_GET_CONFIG_REPLY (xid=0x4): frags=normal miss_send_len=0
```

Figure 4.16

The following are the components demonstrated in the preceding screenshot:

- Port number 6 is named `int-br-eth2`, and it is one end of a Linux veth cable. The other end connects to the provider bridge, `br-eth2` (not pictured).

- Port number 7 is named `patch-tun`, and it is one end of an OVS patch cable. The other end connects to the tunnel bridge, `br-tun` (not pictured).

- Port number 8 is named `qvo017db302-dc`, and it corresponds to a Neutron port UUID starting with `017db302-dc`.

- Port number 9 is named `qvo7140bc00-75`, and it corresponds to a Neutron port UUID starting with `7140bc00-75`.

- The `LOCAL` port is named `br-int`, and it is used for the management of traffic to and from the virtual switch.

The following screenshot demonstrates the switch configuration in a graphical manner:

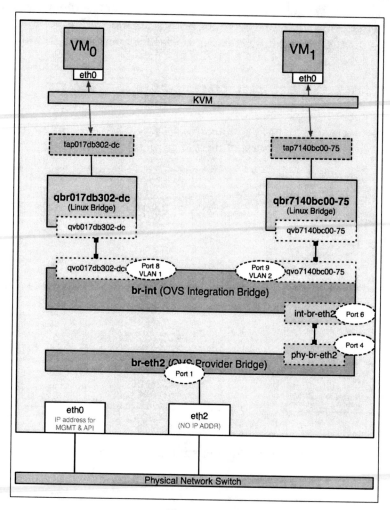

Figure 4.17

Identifying the VLANs associated with ports

Every port on the integration bridge connected to an instance or other network resource is placed in a VLAN, which is local to this virtual switch. The Open vSwitch database on each host is independent of all other hosts, and the VLAN database is not related to the physical network infrastructure. Instances in the same Neutron network on a particular host are placed in the same VLAN on the local integration bridge.

Using the `ovs-vsctl show` command, you can identify the internal VLAN tag of all ports on all virtual switches on the host. The following screenshot demonstrates this command in action on `compute01`:

```
root@compute01:~# ovs-vsctl show
77379f94-35f8-4efc-8039-3d82f7bbb365
    Bridge "br-eth2"
        Port "phy-br-eth2"
            Interface "phy-br-eth2"
                type: patch
                options: {peer="int-br-eth2"}
        Port "eth2"
            Interface "eth2"
        Port "br-eth2"
            Interface "br-eth2"
                type: internal
    Bridge br-tun
        fail_mode: secure
        Port "vxlan-0afefec8"
            Interface "vxlan-0afefec8"
                type: vxlan
                options: {df_default="true", in_key=flow, local_ip="10.254.254.201", out_key=flow, remote_ip="10.254.254.200"}
        Port patch-int
            Interface patch-int
                type: patch
                options: {peer=patch-tun}
        Port "vxlan-0afefeca"
            Interface "vxlan-0afefeca"
                type: vxlan
                options: {df_default="true", in_key=flow, local_ip="10.254.254.201", out_key=flow, remote_ip="10.254.254.202"}
        Port br-tun
            Interface br-tun
                type: internal
    Bridge br-int
        fail_mode: secure
        Port "qvo7140bc00-75"
            tag: 2
            Interface "qvo7140bc00-75"
        Port patch-tun
            Interface patch-tun
                type: patch
                options: {peer=patch-int}
        Port "int-br-eth2"
            Interface "int-br-eth2"
                type: patch
                options: {peer="phy-br-eth2"}
        Port int-br-ex
            Interface int-br-ex
                type: patch
                options: {peer=phy-br-ex}
        Port "qvo017db302-dc"
            tag: 1
            Interface "qvo017db302-dc"
        Port br-int
            Interface br-int
                type: internal
    ovs_version: "2.3.2"
```

Figure 4.18

Inside the integration bridge reside two ports named `qvo7140bc00-75` and `qvo017db302-dc`, and each is assigned its own VLAN tag. These ports correspond to two instances in two different Neutron networks, as evidenced by the difference in their VLAN IDs.

The VLAN IDs are arbitrarily assigned by the local Open vSwitch process and may change upon the restart of the `openvswitch-switch` service or after a reboot.

Programming flow rules

Unlike the LinuxBridge driver architecture, the Open vSwitch driver does not use VLAN interfaces on the host to tag traffic. Instead, the Open vSwitch agent programs flow rules on the virtual switches that dictate how the traffic traversing the switch should be manipulated before forwarding. When the traffic traverses a virtual switch, flow rules on the switch can transform, add, or strip the VLAN tags before forwarding the traffic. In addition, flow rules can be added to this drop traffic if it matches certain characteristics. Open vSwitch is capable of performing other types of actions on traffic, but these actions are outside the scope of this book.

Using the `ovs-ofctl dump-flows <bridge>` command, we can observe the flows currently programmed on the specified bridge. The Open vSwitch plugin agent is responsible for converting information about the network in the Neutron database to Open vSwitch flows and constantly maintains the flows as changes are made to the network.

Flow rules for VLANs

In the following example, the VLANs, 30 and 33, represent two networks in the data center. Both VLANs are trunked down to the controller and compute nodes, and Neutron networks that utilize these VLAN IDs are configured. Traffic that enters the `eth2` physical interface is processed by the flow rules on the `br-eth2` bridge that it is connected to:

```
root@compute01:~# ovs-ofctl dump-flows br-eth2
NXST_FLOW reply (xid=0x4):
 cookie=0x0, duration=1869.589s, table=0, n_packets=2870, n_bytes=401611, idle_age=0, priority=1 actions=NORMAL
 cookie=0x0, duration=1406.766s, table=0, n_packets=124, n_bytes=11606, idle_age=1377, priority=4,in_port=4,dl_vlan=1 actions=mod_vlan_vid:30,NORMAL
 cookie=0x0, duration=288.560s, table=0, n_packets=124, n_bytes=11606, idle_age=261, priority=4,in_port=4,dl_vlan=2 actions=mod_vlan_vid:33,NORMAL
 cookie=0x0, duration=1869.120s, table=0, n_packets=19, n_bytes=1594, idle_age=288, priority=2,in_port=4 actions=drop
```

Figure 4.19

Flow rules are processed in the order of priority, from highest to lowest. By default, `ovs-ofctl` returns flow entries in the same order that the virtual switch sends them in; however, they may be out of order. Using `--rsort`, it is possible to return the results in the order of priority, from highest to lowest:

```
root@compute01:~# ovs-ofctl dump-flows br-eth2 --rsort
 cookie=0x0, duration=2075.648s, table=0, n_packets=124, n_bytes=11606, priority=4,in_port=4,dl_vlan=1 actions=mod_vlan_vid:30,NORMAL
 cookie=0x0, duration=957.442s, table=0, n_packets=124, n_bytes=11606, priority=4,in_port=4,dl_vlan=2 actions=mod_vlan_vid:33,NORMAL
 cookie=0x0, duration=2538.002s, table=0, n_packets=19, n_bytes=1594, priority=2,in_port=4 actions=drop
 cookie=0x0, duration=2538.471s, table=0, n_packets=3814, n_bytes=534793, priority=1 actions=NORMAL
```

Figure 4.20

The first three rules specify a particular inbound port:

```
in_port=4
```

According to the diagram in *Figure 4.17*, traffic entering the `br-eth2` bridge from the `eth2` physical interface does so through port 1, not port 4; so, the first three rules do not apply. Traffic is forwarded to the integration bridge via the fourth rule, where no particular port is specified:

```
root@compute01:~# ovs-ofctl dump-flows br-eth2 --rsort
 cookie=0x0, duration=2075.648s, table=0, n_packets=124, n_bytes=11606, priority=4,in_port=4,dl_vlan=1 actions=mod_vlan_vid:30,NORMAL
 cookie=0x0, duration=957.442s, table=0, n_packets=124, n_bytes=11606, priority=4,in_port=4,dl_vlan=2 actions=mod_vlan_vid:33,NORMAL
 cookie=0x0, duration=2538.002s, table=0, n_packets=19, n_bytes=1594, priority=2,in_port=4 actions=drop
 cookie=0x0, duration=2538.471s, table=0, n_packets=3814, n_bytes=534793, priority=1 actions=NORMAL
```

Figure 4.21

Flows with a NORMAL action instruct Open vSwitch to act as a learning switch, which means that traffic will be forwarded out of all ports until the switch learns and updates its forwarding database, also known as the FDB table. Traffic is forwarded out the port connected to the integration bridge.

The FDB table is the equivalent of a CAM or MAC address table. This learning behavior is similar to that of a hardware switch that floods traffic out of all ports until it learns the proper path.

As traffic exits port 4 of the `br-eth2` provider bridge and enters port 6 of the `br-int` integration bridge, it is evaluated by the flow rules on `br-int`, as follows:

```
root@compute01:~# ovs-ofctl dump-flows br-int --rsort
 cookie=0x0, duration=2679.292s, table=0, n_packets=75, n_bytes=8133, priority=3,in_port=6,dl_vlan=30 actions=mod_vlan_vid:1,NORMAL
 cookie=0x0, duration=1561.085s, table=0, n_packets=75, n_bytes=8129, priority=3,in_port=6,dl_vlan=33 actions=mod_vlan_vid:2,NORMAL
 cookie=0x0, duration=3141.760s, table=0, n_packets=2835, n_bytes=533927, priority=2,in_port=6 actions=drop
 cookie=0x0, duration=3142.406s, table=0, n_packets=267, n_bytes=24806, priority=1 actions=NORMAL
 cookie=0x0, duration=3142.350s, table=23, n_packets=0, n_bytes=0, priority=0 actions=drop
```

Figure 4.22

The first rule performs the action of modifying the VLAN ID of a packet from its original VLAN to a VLAN that is local to the integration bridge on the compute node when the original VLAN ID is 30:

```
root@compute01:~# ovs-ofctl dump-flows br-int --rsort
 cookie=0x0, duration=2679.292s, table=0, n_packets=75, n_bytes=8133, priority=3,in_port=6,dl_vlan=30 actions=mod_vlan_vid:1,NORMAL
 cookie=0x0, duration=1561.085s, table=0, n_packets=75, n_bytes=8129, priority=3,in_port=6,dl_vlan=33 actions=mod_vlan_vid:2,NORMAL
 cookie=0x0, duration=3141.760s, table=0, n_packets=2835, n_bytes=533927, priority=2,in_port=6 actions=drop
 cookie=0x0, duration=3142.406s, table=0, n_packets=267, n_bytes=24806, priority=1 actions=NORMAL
 cookie=0x0, duration=3142.350s, table=23, n_packets=0, n_bytes=0, priority=0 actions=drop
```

Figure 4.23

When the traffic tagged as VLAN 30 is sent to an instance and forwarded through the provider bridge to the integration bridge, the VLAN tag is modified from 30 to local VLAN 1. It is then forwarded to a port on br-int that is connected to the instance that matches the destination MAC address.

The third rule performs a similar action when the original VLAN is 33 by replacing it with local VLAN 2. If the third rule is matched, it means that no other rules of a higher priority matching port 6 were found and traffic will be dropped:

```
root@compute01:~# ovs-ofctl dump-flows br-int --rsort
 cookie=0x0, duration=2679.292s, table=0, n_packets=75, n_bytes=8133, priority=3,in_port=6,dl_vlan=30 actions=mod_vlan_vid:1,NORMAL
 cookie=0x0, duration=1561.085s, table=0, n_packets=75, n_bytes=8129, priority=3,in_port=6,dl_vlan=33 actions=mod_vlan_vid:2,NORMAL
 cookie=0x0, duration=3141.760s, table=0, n_packets=2835, n_bytes=533927, priority=2,in_port=6 actions=drop
 cookie=0x0, duration=3142.406s, table=0, n_packets=267, n_bytes=24806, priority=1 actions=NORMAL
 cookie=0x0, duration=3142.350s, table=23, n_packets=0, n_bytes=0, priority=0 actions=drop
```

Figure 4.24

The return traffic from the instances through the br-int integration bridge is forwarded to the provider bridge by the third rule:

```
root@compute01:~# ovs-ofctl dump-flows br-int --rsort
 cookie=0x0, duration=2679.292s, table=0, n_packets=75, n_bytes=8133, priority=3,in_port=6,dl_vlan=30 actions=mod_vlan_vid:1,NORMAL
 cookie=0x0, duration=1561.085s, table=0, n_packets=75, n_bytes=8129, priority=3,in_port=6,dl_vlan=33 actions=mod_vlan_vid:2,NORMAL
 cookie=0x0, duration=3141.760s, table=0, n_packets=2835, n_bytes=533927, priority=2,in_port=6 actions=drop
 cookie=0x0, duration=3142.406s, table=0, n_packets=267, n_bytes=24806, priority=1 actions=NORMAL
 cookie=0x0, duration=3142.350s, table=23, n_packets=0, n_bytes=0, priority=0 actions=drop
```

Figure 4.25

Once the traffic hits the br-eth2 provider bridge, it is processed by the flow rules, as follows:

```
root@compute01:~# ovs-ofctl dump-flows br-eth2 --rsort
 cookie=0x0, duration=2075.648s, table=0, n_packets=124, n_bytes=11606, priority=4,in_port=4,dl_vlan=1 actions=mod_vlan_vid:30,NORMAL
 cookie=0x0, duration=957.442s, table=0, n_packets=124, n_bytes=11606, priority=4,in_port=4,dl_vlan=2 actions=mod_vlan_vid:33,NORMAL
 cookie=0x0, duration=2538.002s, table=0, n_packets=19, n_bytes=1594, priority=2,in_port=4 actions=drop
 cookie=0x0, duration=2538.471s, table=0, n_packets=3814, n_bytes=534793, priority=1 actions=NORMAL
```

Figure 4.26

These rules should look familiar as they are the same flow rules on the provider bridge shown earlier. This time, however, traffic from the integration bridge connected to port 4 is processed by the first three rules.

The first flow rule on the provider bridge checks the VLAN ID in the Ethernet header, and if it is 1, modifies it to 30 before forwarding the traffic to the physical interface. The second rule modifies the VLAN tag of the packet from 2 to 33 before it exits the bridge. All other traffic from the integration bridge on port 4 not tagged as VLAN 1 or 2 will be dropped.

Flow rules for a particular network do not exist on a bridge if there are no instances or resources in this network scheduled to this node. The Neutron Open vSwitch agent on each node is responsible for creating the appropriate flow rules for virtual switches on this node.

Flow rules for flat networks

Flat networks in Neutron are untagged networks, meaning there is no 802.1q VLAN tag associated with the network when it is created. Internally, however, Open vSwitch treats flat networks similarly to VLANs when programming the virtual switches. Flat networks are assigned a local VLAN ID in the Open vSwitch database, similar to a VLAN network, and instances in the same flat network connected to the same integration bridge are placed in the same local VLAN. However, there is a difference between VLAN and flat networks, which can be observed in the flow rules that are created on the integration and provider bridges. Instead of mapping the local VLAN ID to a physical VLAN ID and vice versa, as traffic traverses the bridges, the local VLAN ID is added to or stripped from the Ethernet header by flow rules.

In another example, a flat network that has no VLAN tag is added in Neutron:

```
Created a new network:
+--------------------------+--------------------------------------+
| Field                    | Value                                |
+--------------------------+--------------------------------------+
| admin_state_up           | True                                 |
| id                       | 5060cb15-6178-4704-ade7-a7c04044c002 |
| mtu                      | 0                                    |
| name                     | MyFlatNetwork                        |
| provider:network_type    | flat                                 |
| provider:physical_network| physnet2                             |
| provider:segmentation_id |                                      |
| router:external          | False                                |
| shared                   | False                                |
| status                   | ACTIVE                               |
| subnets                  |                                      |
| tenant_id                | da6c995d9f834090bd7a00d13d40b817     |
+--------------------------+--------------------------------------+
```

Figure 4.27

On the physical switch, this network may be configured as the native VLAN (untagged) on the switch port connected to `eth2` of `compute01`. An instance spun up on the `MyFlatNetwork` network results in the following virtual switch configuration:

```
Bridge br-int
    fail_mode: secure
    Port "qvo7140bc00-75"
        tag: 2
        Interface "qvo7140bc00-75"
    Port patch-tun
        Interface patch-tun
            type: patch
            options: {peer=patch-int}
    Port "qvo1a05aa90-23"
        tag: 3
        Interface "qvo1a05aa90-23"
    Port "int-br-eth2"
        Interface "int-br-eth2"
            type: patch
            options: {peer="phy-br-eth2"}
    Port int-br-ex
        Interface int-br-ex
            type: patch
            options: {peer=phy-br-ex}
    Port "qvo017db302-dc"
        tag: 1
        Interface "qvo017db302-dc"
    Port br-int
        Interface br-int
            type: internal
ovs_version: "2.3.2"
```

Figure 4.28

Note that the port associated with the instance is assigned a VLAN ID of 3 even though it is a flat network. On the integration bridge, there exists a flow rule that modifies the VLAN header of an incoming Ethernet frame when it has no real VLAN ID set:

```
root@compute01:~# ovs-ofctl dump-flows br-int --rsort
 cookie=0x0, duration=4279.351s, table=0, n_packets=75, n_bytes=8133, priority=3,in_port=6,dl_vlan=30 actions=mod_vlan_vid:1,NORMAL
 cookie=0x0, duration=3161.144s, table=0, n_packets=75, n_bytes=8129, priority=3,in_port=6,dl_vlan=33 actions=mod_vlan_vid:2,NORMAL
 cookie=0x0, duration=211.055s, table=0, n_packets=279, n_bytes=44647, priority=3,in_port=6,vlan_tci=0x0000 actions=mod_vlan_vid:3,NORMAL
 cookie=0x0, duration=4741.819s, table=0, n_packets=4099, n_bytes=770671, priority=2,in_port=6 actions=drop
 cookie=0x0, duration=4742.465s, table=0, n_packets=401, n_bytes=37248, priority=1 actions=NORMAL
 cookie=0x0, duration=4742.410s, table=23, n_packets=0, n_bytes=0, priority=0 actions=drop
```

Figure 4.29

TCI stands for **Tag Control Information**; it is a 2-byte field of the 802.1q header. For packets with an 802.1q header, this field contains VLAN information, including the VLAN ID. For packets without an 802.1q header, also known as the untagged packets, `vlan_tci` is set to 0 (0x0000).

The result is that the incoming traffic is tagged as VLAN 3 and forwarded to the instances connected to the integration bridge that reside in VLAN 3.

As the return traffic from the instance is processed by the flow rules on the provider bridge, the local VLAN ID is stripped and the traffic becomes untagged:

```
root@compute01:~# ovs-ofctl dump-flows br-eth2 --rsort
 cookie=0x0, duration=793.193s, table=0, n_packets=129, n_bytes=12036, priority=4,in_port=4,dl_vlan=3 actions=strip_vlan,NORMAL
 cookie=0x0, duration=4861.486s, table=0, n_packets=124, n_bytes=11606, priority=4,in_port=4,dl_vlan=1 actions=mod_vlan_vid:30,NORMAL
 cookie=0x0, duration=3743.280s, table=0, n_packets=124, n_bytes=11606, priority=4,in_port=4,dl_vlan=2 actions=mod_vlan_vid:33,NORMAL
 cookie=0x0, duration=5323.840s, table=0, n_packets=24, n_bytes=2000, priority=2,in_port=4 actions=drop
 cookie=0x0, duration=5324.309s, table=0, n_packets=7967, n_bytes=1118958, priority=1 actions=NORMAL
```

Figure 4.30

The untagged traffic is then forwarded out of the eth2 physical interface and processed by the physical switch.

Flow rules for local networks

Local networks in an Open vSwitch implementation behave in a similar way to that of a LinuxBridge implementation. Instances in local networks are connected to the integration bridge and can communicate with other instances in the same network and local VLAN. There are no flow rules created for local networks. Traffic between instances in the same network remains local to the virtual switch, and by definition, local to the compute node on which they reside. This means that DHCP and metadata services will be unavailable to any instances that are not on the same host as these services.

Configuring the ML2 networking plugin

Before you can consume the Neutron API and build networking resources, a networking plugin must be defined and configured. The remainder of this chapter is dedicated to providing instructions on installing and configuring the ML2 plugin and LinuxBridge or Open vSwitch drivers and respective network agents.

Prior to the ML2 plugin and a common database schema, the LinuxBridge and Open vSwitch plugins could not easily interoperate with one another. When using the ML2 plugin, it is possible to use both the LinuxBridge and Open vSwitch drivers simultaneously within an environment but on different hosts. Some agents, such as the L3 and DHCP agents, require a network driver to be defined as part of their configuration. These changes will be highlighted as part of the configuration outlined in this chapter.

Configuring the LinuxBridge and Open vSwitch drivers for simultaneous operation is outside the scope of this book. For simplicity, I recommend deploying the LinuxBridge driver if advanced routing features, such as distributed virtual routers, are not required. The configuration and architecture of distributed virtual routers are outlined in *Chapter 9, Distributed Virtual Routers*.

ML2 plugin configuration options

The ML2 plugin was installed in the previous chapter, and its configuration file located at `/etc/neutron/plugins/ml2/ml2_conf.ini` must be configured before Neutron networking services can be used.

The `ml2_conf.ini` file is broken into configuration blocks and contains the following commonly used options:

```
[ml2]
type drivers
mechanism drivers
tenant_network_types

[ml2_type_flat]
flat_networks

[ml2_type_vlan]
network_vlan_ranges

[ml2_type_gre]
tunnel_id_ranges

[ml2_type_vxlan]
vni_ranges

[securitygroup]
firewall_driver
enable_security_group
enable_ipset
```

Other blocks are required for the LinuxBridge and Open vSwitch agents, and their configuration will be discussed later in this chapter.

> Configuration options must remain in the appropriate block; otherwise, Neutron services may not start or operate properly.

Type drivers

Type drivers describe the type of networks that can be created and implemented by mechanism drivers. Type drivers included with the ML2 plugin include `local`, `flat`, `vlan`, `gre`, and `vxlan`. Not all mechanism drivers can implement all types of networks, however. The Open vSwitch driver can support all five, but the LinuxBridge driver lacks support for GRE networks.

Update the ML2 configuration file on all hosts and add the following type drivers:

```
[ml2]
...
type_drivers = local,flat,vlan,gre,vxlan
```

 If you are using the LinuxBridge mechanism driver, it is not necessary to specify the `gre` type driver.

Mechanism drivers

Mechanism drivers are responsible for implementing the networks described by the type driver. Mechanism drivers included with the ML2 plugin are `linuxbridge`, `openvswitch`, and `l2population`.

Update the ML2 configuration file on all hosts and add the following mechanism drivers.

For LinuxBridge, you can use the following code:

```
[ml2]
...
mechanism_drivers = linuxbridge,l2population
```

For Open vSwitch, you can use the following code:

```
[ml2]
...
mechanism_drivers = openvswitch,l2population
```

Both the LinuxBridge and Open vSwitch agents require specific configuration options, which will be discussed later in this chapter.

Tenant network types

The `tenant_network_types` configuration option describes the type of networks that a tenant can create. When using the Open vSwitch driver, the supported tenant network types are `flat`, `vlan`, `local`, `gre`, `vxlan`, and `none`. The LinuxBridge driver supports the same type drivers, with the exception of `gre`.

The configuration option takes values in an ordered list, such as `vxlan,vlan`. In this example, when a tenant creates a network, Neutron will automatically provision a VXLAN network. When all available VXLAN VNI's are allocated, Neutron allocates a network of the next type in the list. In this case, a VLAN network would be allocated. When all available networks are allocated, tenants can no longer create networks.

 Administrators can override the behavior of `tenant_network_types` by specifying provider attributes using the `--provider:network_type` flag in the network creation process.

Update the ML2 configuration file on all hosts and add the following tenant network types to the `[ml2]` section:

```
[ml2]
...
tenant_network_types = vlan,vxlan
```

If at any time you wish to change the value of `tenant_network_types`, edit the plugin configuration file accordingly on all nodes and restart the `neutron-server` service.

Flat networks

The `flat_networks` configuration option defines interfaces that support the use of untagged networks, commonly referred to as a native VLAN. This option requires that a provider label be specified. A **provider label** is an arbitrary label or name that is mapped to a physical interface or bridge. These mappings will be discussed in further detail in the LinuxBridge- and Open vSwitch-specific sections later in this chapter.

In the following example, the `physnet1` interface is configured to support a flat network:

```
flat_networks = physnet1
```

Multiple interfaces can be defined using a comma-separated list, as follows:

```
flat_networks = physnet1,physnet2
```

 Due to the lack of an identifier to segregate untagged traffic on the same interface, an interface can only support a single flat network.

In this environment, the `flat_networks` option can remain unconfigured.

Network VLAN ranges

The `network_vlan_ranges` configuration option defines a range of VLAN IDs that tenant networks will be associated with upon their creation when Neutron allocates a VLAN network. When the number of the available VLAN IDs reaches zero, tenants will no longer be able to create VLAN networks.

In the following example, VLANs 30 through 33 are available for tenant network allocation:

```
network_vlan_ranges = physnet2:30:33
```

Noncontiguous VLANs can be allocated using a comma-separated list, as follows:

```
network_vlan_ranges = physnet2:30:33,physnet2:51:55
```

In this installation, the `physnet2` provider label is used with VLANs 30 through 33 available for tenant allocation.

Update the ML2 configuration file on all hosts and add the following network VLAN ranges configuration to the `[ml2_type_vlan]` section:

```
[ml2_type_vlan]
...
network_vlan_ranges = physnet2:30:33
```

If at any time this configuration option is updated, you must restart the `neutron-server` service for the changes to take effect.

Tunnel ID ranges

When GRE networks are created, each network is assigned a unique segmentation ID that is used to encapsulate traffic. As traffic traverses the Open vSwitch tunnel bridge, the segmentation ID is used to populate a field in the encapsulation header of the packet. For GRE packets, the KEY header field is used.

The `tunnel_id_ranges` configuration option is a comma-separated list of ID ranges that are available for tenant network allocation when `tunnel_type` is set to `gre`.

In the following example, segmentation IDs 1 through `1000` are reserved for allocation to tenant networks upon creation:

```
tunnel_id_ranges = 1:1000
```

The `tunnel_id_ranges` option supports noncontiguous IDs using a comma-separated list as follows:

```
tunnel_id_ranges = 1:1000,2000:2500
```

VNI ranges

When VXLAN networks are created, each network is assigned a unique segmentation ID, which is used to encapsulate traffic. As traffic traverses the Open vSwitch tunnel bridge, the segmentation ID is used to populate a field in the encapsulation header of the packet. For VXLAN encapsulation, the `VXLAN ID` header field is used. When the LinuxBridge driver is used, the segmentation ID is used when creating the respective VXLAN interface on each host.

The `vni_ranges` configuration option is a comma-separated list of ID ranges that are available for tenant network allocation when `tunnel_type` is set to `vxlan`.

In the following example, segmentation IDs 1 through `1000` are reserved for allocation to tenant networks upon creation:

```
vni_ranges = 1:1000
```

The `vni_ranges` option supports noncontiguous IDs using a comma-separated list, as follows:

```
vni_ranges = 1:1000,2000:2500
```

Update the ML2 configuration file on all hosts and add the following VNI range to the `[ml2_type_vxlan]` section:

```
[ml2_type_vxlan]
...
vni_ranges = 1:1000
```

If at any time this configuration option is updated, you must restart the `neutron-server` service for the changes to take effect.

Firewall driver

The `firewall_driver` configuration option instructs Neutron to use a particular firewall driver for security group functionality. There may be different firewall drivers configured based on the mechanism driver in use.

Update the ML2 configuration file on all hosts and define the appropriate `firewall_driver` configuration option in the `[securitygroup]` section.

For LinuxBridge, use the following code:

```
[securitygroup]
...
firewall_driver = neutron.agent.linux.iptables_firewall.
IptablesFirewallDriver
```

For Open vSwitch, run the following code:

```
[securitygroup]
...
firewall_driver = neutron.agent.linux.iptables_firewall.
OVSHybridIptablesFirewallDriver
```

If you do not want to use a firewall and want to disable the application of the security group rules, set `firewall_driver` to `neutron.agent.firewall.NoopFirewallDriver`.

Enable security group

The `enable_security_group` configuration option instructs Neutron to enable or disable the security group API. The option is set to `true` by default.

If at any time this configuration option is updated, you must restart the `neutron-server` service for the changes to take effect.

Enable ipset

The `enable_ipset` configuration option instructs Neutron to enable or disable the ipset extension for iptables that allows for the creation of firewall rules that match entire sets of addresses at once. The use of ipsets makes lookups very efficient compared to the traditional linear lookups. The option is set to `true` by default.

Configuring the LinuxBridge driver and agent

The LinuxBridge mechanism driver is included with the ML2 plugin and was installed in *Chapter 3, Installing Neutron*. The following sections will walk you through the configuration of Neutron and Nova to utilize the LinuxBridge driver and agent.

> While the LinuxBridge and Open vSwitch agents and drivers can coexist in the same environment, they should not be installed and configured simultaneously on the same host.

Installing the LinuxBridge agent

To install the LinuxBridge agent, issue the following command on all nodes:

```
# apt-get install neutron-plugin-linuxbridge-agent
```

If prompted to overwrite the neutron.conf file, type N at the [default=N] prompt.

Configuring Nova to use LinuxBridge

In order to properly connect instances to the network, Nova Compute must be aware that LinuxBridge is the networking plugin. The linuxnet_interface_driver configuration option in /etc/nova/nova.conf instructs Nova Compute on how to properly connect instances to the network.

Update the linuxnet_interface_driver configuration option in the Nova configuration file at /etc/nova/nova.conf on all hosts to use the LinuxBridge interface driver with the following code:

```
[DEFAULT]
...
linuxnet_interface_driver = nova.network.linux_net.
LinuxBridgeInterfaceDriver
```

Configuring the DHCP agent to use LinuxBridge

For Neutron to properly connect DHCP namespace interfaces to the appropriate network bridge, the DHCP agent must be configured to use the LinuxBridge interface driver.

Update the `interface_driver` configuration option in the Neutron DHCP agent configuration file at `/etc/neutron/dhcp_agent.ini` on the controller node to use the LinuxBridge interface driver:

```
[DEFAULT]
...
interface_driver = neutron.agent.linux.interface.BridgeInterfaceDriver
```

Additional DHCP agent configuration options can be found in the previous chapter.

ML2 configuration options for LinuxBridge

Prior to ML2, the LinuxBridge plugin used its own configuration file and options. The `[linux_bridge]` and `[vxlan]` option blocks are moved to the ML2 configuration file, and the most common options can be seen in the following code:

```
[linux_bridge]
...
physical_interface_mappings


[vxlan]
...
enable_vxlan
12_population
local_ip
```

Physical interface mappings

The `physical_interface_mappings` configuration option describes the mapping of an artificial interface name or label to a physical interface in the server. When networks are created, they are associated with an interface label, such as `physnet2`. The `physnet2` label is then mapped to a physical interface, such as `eth2`, by the `physical_interface_mappings` option. This mapping can be observed as follows:

```
physical_interface_mappings = physnet2:eth2
```

The chosen label must be consistent between all nodes in the environment. However, the physical interface mapped to the label may be different. A difference in mappings is often observed when one node maps `physnet2` to a 1-Gbit interface and another maps `physnet2` to a 10-Gbit interface.

More than one interface mapping is allowed, and they can be added to the list using a comma as the separator:

```
physical_interface_mappings = physnet1:eth1,physnet2:eth2
```

In this installation, the `eth2` interface will be utilized as the physical network interface, which means that any VLAN provided for use by tenants must traverse `eth2`. The physical switch port connected to `eth2` must support 802.1q VLAN tagging if VLAN networks are to be created by tenants.

Configure the LinuxBridge plugin to use `physnet2` as the physical interface label and `eth2` as the physical network interface by updating the ML2 configuration file accordingly on all hosts, as follows:

```
[linux_bridge]
...
physical_interface_mappings = physnet2:eth2
```

Enable VXLAN

To enable support for VXLAN, the `enable_vxlan` configuration option must be set to `true`. Update the `enable_vxlan` configuration option in the `[vxlan]` section of the ML2 configuration file accordingly on all hosts with the following code:

```
[vxlan]
...
enable_vxlan = true
```

L2 population

To enable support for the L2 population driver, the `l2_population` configuration option must be set to `true`. Update the `l2_population` configuration option in the `[vxlan]` section of the ML2 configuration file accordingly on all hosts using the following code:

```
[vxlan]
...
l2_population = true
```

Local IP

The local_ip configuration option specifies the local IP address on the node that will be used to build the VXLAN overlay between hosts when enable_vxlan is set to true. Refer to *Chapter 1, Preparing the Network for OpenStack,* for ideas on how the overlay network should be architected. In this installation, all guest traffic through overlay networks will traverse a dedicated VLAN over the eth1 interface configured in *Chapter 2, Installing OpenStack.*

The following table provides the interfaces and addresses to be configured on each host:

Hostname	Interface	IP address
Controller01	eth1	172.18.0.100
Compute01	eth1	172.18.0.101
Compute02	eth1	172.18.0.102

Update the local_ip configuration option in the [vxlan] section of the ML2 configuration file accordingly on all hosts.

On the controller node, use the following address:

```
[vxlan]
...
local_ip = 172.18.0.100
```

On compute01, use the following address:

```
[vxlan]
...
local_ip = 172.18.0.101
```

On compute02, use the following address:

```
[vxlan]
...
local_ip = 172.18.0.102
```

Restarting services

If the OpenStack configuration files have been modified to use LinuxBridge as the networking plugin, certain services must be restarted for the changes to take effect.

The following service should be restarted on all hosts in the environment:

```
# service neutron-plugin-linuxbridge-agent restart
```

Also, the following services should be restarted on the controller node:

```
# service nova-api restart
# service neutron-server restart
# service neutron-dhcp-agent restart
```

Then, the following service should be restarted on the compute nodes:

```
# service nova-compute restart
```

Verifying LinuxBridge agents

To verify that the LinuxBridge network agents on all nodes have properly checked in, issue the `neutron agent-list` command on the controller node:

```
# neutron agent-list
+--------------------------------------+--------------------+----------------------------------+-------+----------------+----------------------------+
| id                                   | agent_type         | host                             | alive | admin_state_up | binary                     |
+--------------------------------------+--------------------+----------------------------------+-------+----------------+----------------------------+
| 154aea15-2b39-417f-a697-56352fd8ada6 | Metadata agent     | controller01.learningneutron.com | :-)   | True           | neutron-metadata-agent     |
| 284eefed-21a9-43f2-b865-3c7a9f09ca69 | Linux bridge agent | compute01.learningneutron.com    | :-)   | True           | neutron-linuxbridge-agent  |
| 3d774957-4783-42cf-ac52-982081a5d268 | DHCP agent         | controller01.learningneutron.com | :-)   | True           | neutron-dhcp-agent         |
| f22df576-1286-4df7-828c-cf623fefb058 | Linux bridge agent | controller01.learningneutron.com | :-)   | True           | neutron-linuxbridge-agent  |
+--------------------------------------+--------------------+----------------------------------+-------+----------------+----------------------------+
```

Figure 4.31

The LinuxBridge agents on the controller and compute nodes should be visible in the output with a smiley face under the `alive` column. If a node is not present or the status is XXX, troubleshoot agent connectivity issues by observing the log messages found in `/var/log/neutron/neutron-plugin-linuxbridge-agent.log` on the respective host.

Configuring the Open vSwitch driver and agent

The Open vSwitch mechanism driver is included with the ML2 plugin and was installed in *Chapter 3, Installing Neutron*. The following sections will walk you through the configuration of Neutron and Nova to utilize the Open vSwitch driver and agent.

 While the LinuxBridge and Open vSwitch agents and drivers can coexist in the same environment, they should not be installed and configured simultaneously on the same host.

Installing the Open vSwitch agent

To install the Open vSwitch agent, issue the following command on all nodes:

```
# apt-get install neutron-plugin-openvswitch-agent
```

Dependencies, such as the Open vSwitch components openvswitch-common and openvswitch-switch, will be installed. If prompted to overwrite the neutron.conf file, type N at the [default=N] prompt.

Configuring Nova to use Open vSwitch

For Nova to properly connect instances to the network when using the Open vSwitch driver, the linuxnet_interface_driver configuration option in /etc/nova/nova. conf must be modified.

Update the linuxnet_interface_driver configuration option in the Nova configuration file at /etc/nova/nova.conf on all hosts to use the OVS interface driver:

```
[DEFAULT]
...
linuxnet_interface_driver = nova.network.linux_net.
LinuxOVSInterfaceDriver
```

Configuring the DHCP agent to use Open vSwitch

To properly connect the DHCP namespace tap interfaces to the integration bridge, the DHCP agent must be configured to use the Open vSwitch interface driver.

Update the `interface_driver` configuration option in the Neutron DHCP agent configuration file at `/etc/neutron/dhcp_agent.ini` on the controller node to use the OVS interface driver using the following code:

```
[DEFAULT]
...
interface_driver = neutron.agent.linux.interface.OVSInterfaceDriver
```

ML2 configuration options for Open vSwitch

Prior to ML2, the Open vSwitch plugin used its own configuration file and options. The [ovs] and [agent] option blocks are moved to the ML2 configuration file, and the most common options can be seen in the following code:

```
[ovs]
bridge_mappings
enable_tunneling
tunnel_type
integration_bridge
tunnel_bridge
local_ip

[agent]
tunnel_types
```

Bridge mappings

The `bridge_mappings` configuration option describes the mapping of an artificial interface name or label to a network bridge configured on the server. Unlike the LinuxBridge plugin that configures multiple bridges containing individual VLAN or VXLAN interfaces, the Open vSwitch plugin uses a single bridge interface containing a single physical interface and flow rules to add, modify, or remove VLAN headers if necessary.

When networks are created, they are associated with an interface label, such as physnet1. The physnet1 label is then mapped to a bridge, such as br-eth1, which contains the eth1 physical interface. The mapping of the label to the bridge interface is handled by the bridge_mappings option. This mapping can be observed as follows:

```
bridge_mappings = physnet1:br-eth1
```

The label itself must be consistent between all nodes in the environment. However, the bridge interface mapped to the label as well as the interface in the bridge itself, may be different. A difference in mappings is often observed when one node maps physnet1 to a bridge interface capable of 1 gigabit and another maps physnet1 to a bridge interface capable of 10 gigabits.

More than one interface mapping is allowed and can be added to the list using a comma as a separator, as seen in the following example:

```
bridge_mappings = physnet1:br-eth1,physnet2:br-eth2
```

In this installation, physnet2 will be used as the interface label and be mapped to the br-eth2 bridge. Update the ML2 configuration file at /etc/neutron/plugins/ml2/ml2_conf.ini accordingly on all hosts by executing the following code:

```
[OVS]
...
bridge_mappings = physnet2:br-eth2
```

Configuring the bridges

To configure a bridge with Open vSwitch, use the Open vSwitch utility ovs-vsctl. Create the br-eth2 bridge on all the hosts, as follows:

```
# ovs-vsctl add-br br-eth2
```

Use the ovs-vsctl add-port command to add the eth2 physical interface to the bridge, as follows:

```
# ovs-vsctl add-port br-eth2 eth2
```

 Note that the physical switch port connected to eth2 must support 802.1q VLAN tagging if VLANs of any type are to be created. On many switches, the switch port can be configured as a trunk port.

Enable tunneling

To enable support for GRE and VXLAN, the `enable_tunneling` configuration option must be set to `true`. Open vSwitch versions newer than Version 1.10 should support both technologies. To determine the version of Open vSwitch you have installed, run `ovs-vsctl -V`, as follows:

```
root@controller01:~# ovs-vsctl -V
ovs-vsctl (Open vSwitch) 2.3.1
Compiled Jan 14 2015 12:34:24
DB Schema 7.6.2
```

Figure 4.32

For better performance and reliability, Open vSwitch 2.3 or higher is recommended. For more information on how to download and install the latest Open vSwitch release, visit www.openvswitch.org.

To enable GRE and VXLAN tunneling support, update the `enable_tunneling` configuration option in the `[OVS]` section of the ML2 configuration file on all hosts:

```
[OVS]
...
enable_tunneling = true
```

Tunnel type

The `tunnel_type` configuration option specifies the type of tunnel to use when utilizing tunnels. The two available options are `gre` and/or `vxlan`.

To enable only GRE tunnels, set `tunnel_type` to `gre` in the `[OVS]` section of the ML2 configuration file:

```
[OVS]
...
tunnel_type = gre
```

To enable only the VXLAN tunnels, set `tunnel_type` to `vxlan` in the `[OVS]` section of the ML2 configuration file:

```
[OVS]
...
tunnel_type = vxlan
```

To enable both GRE and VXLAN tunnels, specify both tunnel types separated by a comma:

```
[OVS]
...
tunnel_type = vxlan,gre
```

Integration bridge

The `integration_bridge` configuration option specifies the name of the integration bridge used on each node. There is a single integration bridge per node that acts as the virtual switch where all virtual machine VIFs, otherwise known as **virtual network interfaces**, are connected. The default name of the integration bridge is `br-int` and should not be modified.

 Starting with the Icehouse release of OpenStack, the Open vSwitch agent automatically creates the integration bridge the first time the agent service is started. You do not need to add an interface to the integration bridge as Neutron is responsible for connecting network devices to this virtual switch.

Tunnel bridge

The tunnel bridge is a virtual switch, which is similar to the integration and provider bridges, and is used to connect the GRE and VXLAN tunnel endpoints. Flow rules exist on this bridge that are responsible for properly encapsulating and decapsulating tenant traffic as it traverses the bridge.

The `tunnel_bridge` configuration option specifies the name of the tunnel bridge. The default value is `br-tun` and should not be modified. It is not necessary to create this bridge manually as Neutron does it automatically.

Local IP

The `local_ip` configuration option specifies the local IP address on the node that will be used to build the GRE or VXLAN overlay network between hosts when `enable_tunneling` is set to `true`. Refer to *Chapter 1, Preparing the Network for OpenStack,* for ideas on how the overlay network should be architected. In this installation, all guest traffic through overlay networks will traverse a dedicated VLAN over the `eth1` interface configured in *Chapter 2, Installing OpenStack.*

The following table provides the interfaces and addresses to be configured on each host:

Hostname	Interface	IP address
Controller01	eth1	172.18.0.100
Compute01	eth1	172.18.0.101
Compute02	eth1	172.18.0.102

Update the `local_ip` configuration option in the `[OVS]` section of the ML2 configuration file accordingly on all hosts.

On the `controller` node:

```
[OVS]
...
local_ip = 172.18.0.100
```

On `compute01`:

```
[OVS]
...
local_ip = 172.18.0.101
```

On `compute02`:

```
[OVS]
...
local_ip = 172.18.0.102
```

Tunnel types

The `tunnel_types` configuration option specifies the types of tunnels supported by the agent. The two available options are `gre` and/or `vxlan`. If left unconfigured, the default value is `gre` when `enable_tunneling` is set to `true`. If you are using only `vxlan`, set this option to `vxlan`.

Update the `tunnel_types` configuration option in the `[agent]` section of the ML2 configuration file accordingly on all hosts:

```
[agent]
tunnel_types = vxlan,gre
```

Restarting services to enable the Open vSwitch plugin

Now that the appropriate OpenStack configuration files have been modified to use Open vSwitch as the networking driver, certain services must be started or restarted for the changes to take effect.

The Open vSwitch network agent should be restarted on all nodes; the following code needs to be executed:

```
# service neutron-plugin-openvswitch-agent restart
```

The following services should be restarted on the controller node:

```
# service nova-api restart
```

```
# service neutron-server restart
```

```
# service neutron-dhcp-agent restart
```

The following service should be restarted on the compute nodes:

```
# service nova-compute restart
```

Verifying Open vSwitch agents

To verify that the Open vSwitch network agents on all nodes have properly checked in, issue the `neutron agent-list` command on the controller node:

```
# neutron agent-list
+--------------------------------------+--------------------+--------------+-------+----------------+---------------------------+
| id                                   | agent_type         | host         | alive | admin_state_up | binary                    |
+--------------------------------------+--------------------+--------------+-------+----------------+---------------------------+
| 4882a39b-f636-475f-9075-f37abd2e74d2 | Open vSwitch agent | compute02    | :-)   | True           | neutron-openvswitch-agent |
| 6a7d5e2f-f9bc-4623-9614-17b1db06c068 | L3 agent           | controller01 | :-)   | True           | neutron-l3-agent          |
| a82d6b3e-9bc1-4dbc-87ec-bd7d809024db | Open vSwitch agent | controller01 | :-)   | True           | neutron-openvswitch-agent |
| ab7d9388-9db0-43f1-9055-bba1df231410 | Metadata agent     | controller01 | :-)   | True           | neutron-metadata-agent    |
| b429cccd-2e6b-411f-9b1b-46a828395806 | Open vSwitch agent | compute01    | :-)   | True           | neutron-openvswitch-agent |
| b5e7dbc2-acc9-450b-8401-2517f76a308e | DHCP agent         | controller01 | :-)   | True           | neutron-dhcp-agent        |
+--------------------------------------+--------------------+--------------+-------+----------------+---------------------------+
```

Figure 4.33

The Open vSwitch agents on the controller and compute nodes should be visible in the output with a smiley face under the `alive` column. If a node is not present or the status is xxx, troubleshoot agent connectivity issues by observing the log messages found in `/var/log/neutron/openvswitch-agent.log` on the respective host.

Summary

Both the LinuxBridge and Open vSwitch drivers and agents for Neutron provide unique solutions to the same problem of connecting virtual machine instances to the network. The use of Open vSwitch relies on flow rules to determine how traffic in and out of the environment should be processed and requires both user-space utilities and kernel modules to perform such actions. On the other hand, the use of Linux bridges requires the 8021q and bridge kernel modules and relies on the use of VLAN and VXLAN interfaces on the host to bridge instances to the physical network. For most environments, I recommend using the ML2 plugin and LinuxBridge driver and agent unless integration with OpenFlow controllers or the use of a third-party solution or plugin is required.

In the next chapter, you will be guided through the process of creating different types of networks to provide connectivity to instances. The process of creating networks is the same for both LinuxBridge- and Open vSwitch-based environments, but the underlying network implementation will vary based on the driver and agent in use.

5
Creating Networks with Neutron

In the previous chapter, we laid down a virtual switching infrastructure that will support OpenStack Neutron networking features moving forward. In this chapter, we will build network resources on this foundation. I will guide you through the following tasks:

- Creating networks and subnets
- Attaching instances to networks
- Demonstrating DHCP and metadata services

Networks, subnets, and ports—the core resources of the Neutron API—were introduced in *Chapter 3, Installing Neutron*. The relationship between these core resources and instances, DHCP, and metadata services can be observed in the following sections.

Network management

OpenStack can be managed in a variety of ways, including through the GUI, API, and CLI. Neutron provides users with the ability to execute commands from a shell that interfaces with the Neutron API. To enter the Neutron shell, type neutron in a shell on the controller node:

```
root@controller01:~# neutron
(neutron)
```

Figure 5.1

Alternatively, Neutron commands can be executed straight from the Linux command line using the Neutron client. The client provides a number of commands that assist with the creation, modification, and deletion of networks, subnets, and ports.

The primary commands associated with network management are:

- `net-create`
- `net-delete`
- `net-list`
- `net-external-list`
- `net-update`
- `subnet-create`
- `subnet-delete`
- `subnet-list`
- `subnet-show`
- `subnet-update`
- `port-create`
- `port-delete`
- `port-list`
- `port-show`
- `port-update`

Whether you choose a LinuxBridge- or Open vSwitch-based virtual networking infrastructure, the process to create, modify, and delete networks and subnets is the same. Behind the scenes, however, the process of connecting instances and other resources to the network differs greatly between them.

Provider and tenant networks

There are two categories of networks that can provide connectivity to instances and other network resources, including virtual routers:

- Provider networks
- Tenant networks

Every network created in Neutron, whether created by an administrator or tenant, has **provider attributes** that describe it. Attributes that describe a network include the network's type (such as `flat`, `vlan`, `gre`, `vxlan`, or `local`), the physical network interface that the traffic will traverse, and the segmentation ID of the network. The difference between a provider and tenant network is in who or what sets these attributes and how they are managed within OpenStack.

Provider networks can *only* be created and managed by an OpenStack administrator as they require knowledge and configuration of the physical network infrastructure. When a provider network is created, the administrator must manually specify the provider attributes for the network in question. The administrator is expected to have some understanding of the physical network infrastructure and may be required to configure switch ports for proper operation. Provider networks allow for either virtual machine instances or virtual routers created by tenants to be connected to them. When a provider network is configured to act as an external network for Neutron routers, the provider network is known as an **external provider network**. Provider networks are often configured as flat or VLAN networks and utilize an external routing device to properly route traffic in and out of the cloud.

Tenant networks, unlike provider networks, are created by users and are isolated from other networks in the cloud by default. The inability to configure the physical infrastructure means that tenants will likely connect their networks to Neutron routers when external connectivity is required. Tenants are unable to specify provider attributes manually and restricted to creating networks whose attributes are predefined by the administrator in Neutron configuration files. More information on the configuration and use of Neutron routers begins with *Chapter 7, Creating Standalone Routers with Neutron*.

Managing networks in the CLI

To create networks using the Neutron client, use the Neutron `net-create` command:

```
usage:    net-create [--tenant-id TENANT_ID]
          [--admin-state-down] [--shared] [--router:external]
          [--provider:network_type <network_type>]
          [--provider:physical_network <physical_network_name>]
          [--provider:segmentation_id <segmentation_id>]
          NAME
```

There are three provider attributes that can be defined for a network, which are:

- `provider:network_type`
- `provider:physical_network`
- `provider:segmentation_id`

Other attributes that can be set for provider networks include:

- `router:external`
- `shared`

Options that can be set for both provider and tenant networks include:

- `admin-state-down`
- `tenant-id`

The `network_type` provider attribute defines the type of network being created. Available options include `flat`, `vlan`, `local`, `gre`, and `vxlan`. For a network type to be functional, the corresponding type driver must be enabled in the ML2 configuration file and supported by the enabled mechanism driver. As an external provider network, an overlay network type, such as GRE or VXLAN, is uncommon. However, an OpenStack administrator can create GRE or VXLAN networks on behalf of tenants by specifying a tenant ID and the appropriate provider attributes.

The `physical_network` provider attribute defines the physical interface that will be used to forward traffic through the host. The value specified here corresponds to the `bridge_mappings` or `physical_interface_mappings` option set in the LinuxBridge or Open vSwitch blocks of the ML2 plugin configuration file.

The `segmentation_id` provider attribute specifies the unique ID for the network. If you are creating a VLAN network, the value used for `segmentation_id` should be the 802.1q VLAN ID trunked to the host. If you are creating a GRE or VXLAN network, the `segmentation_id` value should be an arbitrary but unique integer that is not used by any other network of the same type. This ID is used to provide network isolation via the GRE `key` or VXLAN `vni` header fields for GRE and VXLAN networks, respectively. When the `segmentation_id` attribute is not specified, one is automatically allocated from the tenant range specified in the plugin configuration file. Users have no visibility or option to specify an ID when creating networks. When all available IDs in the range available to tenants are exhausted, users will no longer be able to create networks of this type.

The `router:external` attribute is a Boolean value that, when set to `true`, allows a network to be utilized as a gateway network for Neutron routers. For more information on Neutron routers, refer to *Chapter 7, Creating Standalone Routers with Neutron*.

The `shared` switch is a Boolean value that, when set to `true`, allows a network to be utilized among all tenants. This attribute is available *only* for networks created by administrators and is not available for networks created by users.

The `admin-state-down` switch is a Boolean value that, when set to `true`, means that the network is not available upon creation.

Finally, the `tenant-id` option allows for the administrator to create networks on behalf of tenants.

Creating a flat network in the CLI

If you recall from *Chapter 4, Building a Virtual Switching Infrastructure*, a flat network is a network in which no 802.1q VLAN tagging takes place.

The syntax to create a flat provider network as an administrator can be seen here:

```
usage:     net-create [--tenant-id TENANT_ID]
           [--admin-state-down] [--shared] [--router:external]
           --provider:network_type flat
           --provider:physical_network <provider label>
           NAME
```

 Attributes in the [] brackets are considered optional and are not required to create the network.

The following is an example of using the Neutron `net-create` command to create a flat network by the name of `MyFlatNetwork`. The network will utilize an interface or bridge represented by the `physnet2` label and will be shared among all tenants:

```
root@controller01:~# neutron net-create MyFlatNetwork --provider:network_type=flat \
> --provider:physical_network=physnet2 --shared
Created a new network:
+----------------------------+--------------------------------------+
| Field                      | Value                                |
+----------------------------+--------------------------------------+
| admin_state_up             | True                                 |
| id                         | 3282acdf-85d1-47ea-b734-f5625cfca027 |
| mtu                        | 0                                    |
| name                       | MyFlatNetwork                        |
| provider:network_type      | flat                                 |
| provider:physical_network  | physnet2                             |
| provider:segmentation_id   |                                      |
| router:external            | False                                |
| shared                     | True                                 |
| status                     | ACTIVE                               |
| subnets                    |                                      |
| tenant_id                  | 65ff4cf1a04846f1ab2bc1ff0efb1090     |
+----------------------------+--------------------------------------+
```

Figure 5.2

In the preceding output, the tenant ID corresponds to the `admin` tenant where the `net-create` command was executed. As the network is shared, all tenants can create instances and network resources that utilize the `MyFlatNetwork` network.

Attempting to create an additional flat network using the same bridge or interface will result in an error, as seen in the following screenshot:

```
root@controller01:~# neutron net-create MyFlatNetwork2 --provider:network_type=flat \
> --provider:physical_network=physnet2 --shared
Unable to create the flat network. Physical network physnet2 is in use.
```

Figure 5.3

Creating a VLAN network in the CLI

A VLAN network is one in which Neutron tags traffic based on the 802.1q segmentation ID. The syntax used to create a VLAN network as an administrator can be seen here:

```
usage:     net-create [--tenant-id TENANT_ID]
           [--admin-state-down] [--shared] [--router:external]
           --provider:network_type vlan
           --provider:physical_network <provider label>
           [--provider:segmentation_id <vlan id>]
           NAME
```

 Attributes in the [] brackets are considered optional and are not required to create the network.

The following is an example of using the Neutron net-create command to create a VLAN network by the name of MyVLANNetwork. The network will utilize the same bridge or interface represented by physnet2, and the traffic will be tagged as VLAN 200. By specifying the --shared flag, the network can be shared by all tenants. The resulting output is as follows:

```
root@controller01:~# neutron net-create --provider:network_type=vlan --provider:physical_network=physnet2 \
> --provider:segmentation_id=200 --shared MyVLANNetwork
Created a new network:
+---------------------------+--------------------------------------+
| Field                     | Value                                |
+---------------------------+--------------------------------------+
| admin_state_up            | True                                 |
| id                        | 3a342db3-f918-4760-972a-cb700d5b6d2c |
| mtu                       | 0                                    |
| name                      | MyVLANNetwork                        |
| provider:network_type     | vlan                                 |
| provider:physical_network | physnet2                             |
| provider:segmentation_id  | 200                                  |
| router:external           | False                                |
| shared                    | True                                 |
| status                    | ACTIVE                               |
| subnets                   |                                      |
| tenant_id                 | 65ff4cf1a04846f1ab2bc1ff0efb1090     |
+---------------------------+--------------------------------------+
```

Figure 5.4

To create an additional VLAN network that utilizes the same bridge or interface, simply specify a different segmentation ID. In the following example, VLAN 201 is used for the new network, MyVLANNetwork2. The resulting output is as follows:

```
root@controller01:~# neutron net-create --provider:network_type=vlan --provider:physical_network=physnet2 \
> --provider:segmentation_id=201 --shared MyVLANNetwork2
Created a new network:
+---------------------------+--------------------------------------+
| Field                     | Value                                |
+---------------------------+--------------------------------------+
| admin_state_up            | True                                 |
| id                        | c6933c77-9adc-4d29-8da0-f186329b8e0e |
| mtu                       | 0                                    |
| name                      | MyVLANNetwork2                       |
| provider:network_type     | vlan                                 |
| provider:physical_network | physnet2                             |
| provider:segmentation_id  | 201                                  |
| router:external           | False                                |
| shared                    | True                                 |
| status                    | ACTIVE                               |
| subnets                   |                                      |
| tenant_id                 | 65ff4cf1a04846f1ab2bc1ff0efb1090     |
+---------------------------+--------------------------------------+
```

Figure 5.5

Remember that any VLAN network that is created requires that the underlying switching infrastructure be configured to support the specified VLAN. At a minimum, this may require the switch port be configured as a trunk port.

Creating a local network in the CLI

When an instance sends traffic on a local network, the traffic remains isolated to the instance and other interfaces connected to the same bridge or segment. Services such as DHCP and metadata might not be available to instances on local networks, especially if they are located on a different node.

To create a local network, use the following syntax:

```
usage:    net-create [--tenant-id TENANT_ID] [--admin-state-down]
          [--shared] [--router:external]
          --provider:network_type local
          NAME
```

When using the LinuxBridge driver, a bridge is created for the local network, but no physical or virtual VLAN interface is added. Traffic is kept local to the bridge and connected instances. When using the Open vSwitch driver, instances are attached to the integration bridge and can only communicate with other instances in the same local VLAN.

Listing networks in the CLI

To list the existing networks in Neutron, use the `net-list` command, as shown in the following screenshot:

```
root@controller01:~# neutron net-list
+--------------------------------------+----------------+---------+
| id                                   | name           | subnets |
+--------------------------------------+----------------+---------+
| 3282acdf-85d1-47ea-b734-f5625cfca027 | MyFlatNetwork  |         |
| 3a342db3-f918-4760-972a-cb700d5b6d2c | MyVLANNetwork  |         |
| c6933c77-9adc-4d29-8da0-f186329b8e0e | MyVLANNetwork2 |         |
+--------------------------------------+----------------+---------+
```

Figure 5.6

The list output provides the network ID, network name, and any associated subnets. The OpenStack administrator can see all networks, while tenants can see shared networks and the networks that they created.

Showing network properties in the CLI

To show the properties of a network, use the Neutron `net-show` command, as follows:

usage: **net-show NETWORK**

The output of the command can be observed in the following screenshot:

```
root@controller01:~# neutron net-show MyVLANNetwork
+---------------------------+--------------------------------------+
| Field                     | Value                                |
+---------------------------+--------------------------------------+
| admin_state_up            | True                                 |
| id                        | 3a342db3-f918-4760-972a-cb700d5b6d2c |
| mtu                       | 0                                    |
| name                      | MyVLANNetwork                        |
| provider:network_type     | vlan                                 |
| provider:physical_network | physnet2                             |
| provider:segmentation_id  | 200                                  |
| router:external           | False                                |
| shared                    | True                                 |
| status                    | ACTIVE                               |
| subnets                   |                                      |
| tenant_id                 | 65ff4cf1a04846f1ab2bc1ff0efb1090     |
+---------------------------+--------------------------------------+
```

Figure 5.7

Information about the specified network, including the network type, provider bridge label, segmentation ID, and more, can be observed in the `net-show` output when executed by an administrator. Network provider attributes are hidden from ordinary, non-admin users.

Updating networks in the CLI

At times, it may be necessary to update the attributes of a network after it has been created. To update a network, use the Neutron `net-update` command, as follows:

```
usage:    net-update NETWORK
          [--router:external] [--shared] [--admin-state-up] [--name]
```

Provider attributes are among those that cannot be changed once a network has been created. The following attributes, however, can be modified:

* `name`
* `router:external`
* `shared`
* `admin-state-up`

The `router:external` attribute is a Boolean value that, when set to `true`, allows the network to be utilized as a gateway network for Neutron routers. For more information on Neutron routers, refer to *Chapter 7, Creating Standalone Routers with Neutron*.

The `shared` switch is a Boolean value that, when set to `true`, allows the network to be utilized among all tenants.

The `admin-state-up` switch is a Boolean value. When this is set to `false`, DHCP and metadata services are no longer available on the network. The network interfaces within the DHCP namespace are destroyed, and any instance that attempts to obtain or renew a lease will fail. When set to `true`, DHCP and metadata services are restored.

Deleting networks in the CLI

To delete a network, use the Neutron `net-delete` command and specify the UUID or name of the network:

```
usage:    net-delete NETWORK
```

To delete a network named "MyVLANNetwork", you can enter the following Neutron command:

```
net-delete MyVLANNetwork
```

Alternatively, you can use the network's UUID, as follows:

```
net-delete 3a342db3-f918-4760-972a-cb700d5b6d2c
```

Neutron will successfully delete the network as long as there are no instances or other network resources, including floating IPs or load balancer VIPs, utilizing it.

Creating networks in the dashboard

Networks can be created in the dashboard either by an administrator or a user. Both have their own methods, which are described in the following sections.

Creating a network via the Admin tab as an administrator

In order to create a network in the dashboard as a cloud administrator, perform the following steps:

1. Navigate to **Admin | System | Networks**:

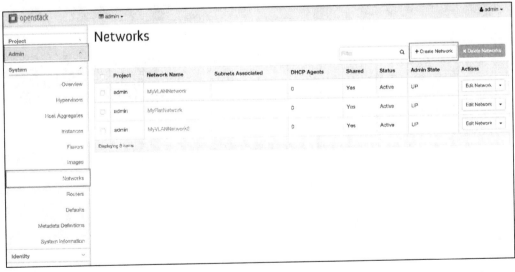

Figure 5.8

2. Click on **Create Network** in the upper right-hand corner of the screen. A window will appear and allow you to specify network properties:

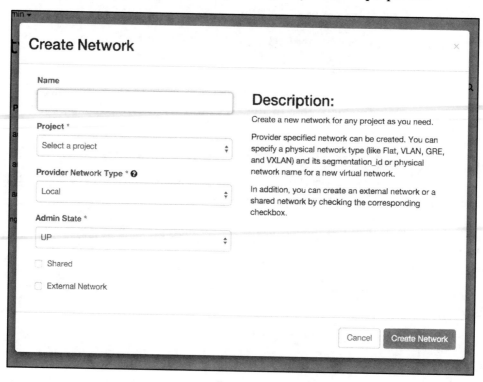

Figure 5.9

The available options include associating the network with a project, setting the network type, setting the admin state as on or off, enabling sharing, and enabling the network to be used as an external network for Neutron routers. Click on the **Create Network** button to create the network.

Creating a network via the Project tab as a user

As an ordinary user, networks are created under the **Project** tab in the dashboard. To create a network as a user, log in as the user and perform the following steps:

1. Navigate to **Project** | **Network** | **Networks**:

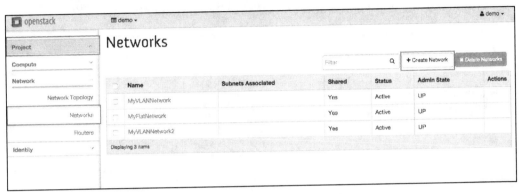

Figure 5.10

From here, note that there are no actions available next to the networks currently defined. Even though the networks are shared, they are not editable by users and can only be edited by an administrator.

2. Click on **Create Network** in the upper right-hand corner of the screen. A window will appear and allow you to specify network properties:

Create Network

| Network | Subnet * | Subnet Details |

Network Name

MyUserNetwork

Create a new network. In addition, a subnet associated with the network can be created in the next panel.

Admin State * ❷

UP

Cancel   « Back   Next »

Figure 5.11

From the **Network** tab, you can define the **Network Name** and **Admin Status** (on or off) values. Marking a network as **Shared** or **External**, as seen in the admin panel earlier, is only available to the networks created by an administrator.

Users creating networks within the dashboard are not required to create a subnet at the time that the network is created. By unselecting the **Create Subnet** checkbox in the **Subnet** tab, the network creation process can be completed:

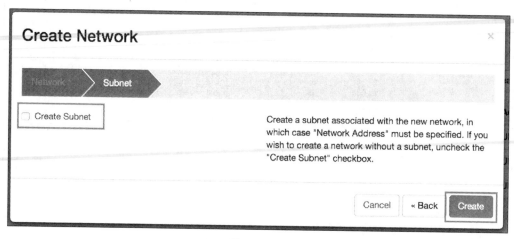

Figure 5.12

The process to create subnets within the dashboard will be explained later in this chapter.

Subnets in Neutron

Once a network is created, the next step is to create a subnet within the network. A subnet in Neutron is a layer 3 object and can be an IPv4 or IPv6 network defined using the **classless inter-domain routing (CIDR)** notation. CIDR is a method of allocating IP addresses and routing IP packets, and it is based on **variable-length subnet masking (VLSM)**. VLSM allows a network to be divided into various sized subnets, providing the opportunity to size a network more appropriately for local needs.

More information on CIDR and VLSM can be found on Wikipedia at
`http://en.wikipedia.org/wiki/Classless_Inter-Domain_Routing`.

A few examples of IPv4 subnets described using the CIDR notation are as follows:

- `192.168.100.50/24` represents the IP address, `192.168.100.50`; its associated routing prefix, `192.168.100.0`; and the subnet mask, `255.255.255.0` (which is 24 "1" bits)

- `172.16.1.200/23` represents the IP address, `172.16.0.200`; its associated routing prefix, `172.16.0.0`; and the subnet mask, `255.255.254.0` (which is 23 "1" bits)

- `10.0.10.4/22` represents the IP address, `10.0.10.4`; its associated routing prefix, `10.0.8.0`; and the subnet mask, `255.255.252.0` (which is 22 "1" bits)

The CIDR notation can be used to quickly identify the total number of IP addresses in a subnet. For example, the subnet mask, `255.255.255.0`, in the CIDR notation is `/24`. To determine the number of host IP addresses available in `/24`, subtract 24 from 32 (which is the total number of bits in an IPv4 address.) Take the remainder, which is 8, and use it as x in the following formula:

```
2^x = number of addresses in a subnet
```

Using the preceding formula, it can be determined that there are 256 IP addresses in a `/24`, as $2^8 = 256$. An advantage to working with powers of two is that every incremental increase of the exponent doubles the number of available host addresses. A `/23` subnet can be written as 2^9, resulting in 512 addresses, and a `/22` subnet can be written as 2^{10}, resulting in 1,024 addresses. On the other hand, every incremental decrease of the exponent halves the number of available addresses. Using the formula, a `/25` subnet can be written as 2^7, resulting in 128 addresses; a `/26` can be written as 2^6, resulting in 64 host addresses; and so on.

Not every address in the subnet might be useable, however, as the first and last addresses are usually reserved as the network and broadcast addresses, respectively. As a result, Neutron will *not* assign the first or last address of a subnet to network resources, including instances. Use the following formula to determine the total number of useable addresses in a subnet when sizing your network. The x variable represents the number of host bits available in the subnet mask:

```
2^x-2 = number of useable addresses in a subnet
```

Keep in mind that when creating a subnet, it is important to plan ahead as the subnet mask, or CIDR, is currently *not* an updateable attribute. When instances and other resources consume all of the available IP addresses in a subnet, devices can no longer be added to the network. To resolve this, a new subnet will need to be created and added to the existing network or an entirely new network, and a subnet will need to be created. Depending on your network infrastructure, this might not be an easy change to implement.

IPv6 is an advanced topic that will not be covered in this book. For more information on IPv6, please refer to the Wikipedia article on the subject at https://en.wikipedia.org/wiki/IPv6.

An informational slideshow on IPv6 concepts has also been made available by the Asia-Pacific Network Information Centre and is available at https://training.apnic.net/docs/eIP602_IPv6-AaS.pdf.

Creating subnets in the CLI

To create a subnet using the Neutron client, use the following subnet-create command:

```
usage:  subnet-create [--tenant-id TENANT_ID] [--name NAME]
        [--gateway GATEWAY_IP] [--no-gateway]
        [--allocation-pool start=IP_ADDR,end=IP_ADDR]
        [--host-route destination=CIDR,nexthop=IP_ADDR]
        [--dns-nameserver DNS_NAMESERVER]
        [--disable-dhcp] [--enable-dhcp]
        [--ip-version {4,6}]
        [--ipv6-ra-mode {dhcpv6-stateful,dhcpv6-stateless,slaac}]
        [--ipv6-address-mode {dhcpv6-stateful,dhcpv6-stateless,slaac}]
        NETWORK CIDR
```

Attributes identified in [] brackets are optional and not required for subnet creation.

The tenant-id attribute specifies the ID of the tenant that the subnet should be associated with. This should be the same tenant associated with the parent network.

The name attribute specifies the name of the subnet. While you can create multiple subnets with the same name, it is recommended that subnet names remain unique for easy identification.

The `gateway` attribute defines the gateway address for the subnet. When the subnet is attached to the instance side of a Neutron router, the router's interface will be configured with the address specified here. The address is then used as the default gateway for instances in the subnet. If the subnet is attached to the external side of a Neutron router, the address is used as the default gateway for the router itself. To see this behavior in action, refer to *Chapter 7, Creating Standalone Routers with Neutron*. If a gateway is not specified, Neutron defaults to the first available address in the CIDR range.

The `no-gateway` attribute instructs Neutron to *not* automatically reserve an IP for use as the gateway for the subnet. It also triggers the injection of a metadata route via DHCP when `enable_isolated_metadata` is set to `true` in the DHCP configuration file.

The `allocation-pool` attribute defines the range of IP addresses within the subnet that can be assigned to instances or as floating IPs. IP addresses cannot be excluded from a single range. However, multiple allocation pools can be defined excluding addresses. For example, to exclude 192.168.1.50-55 from 192.168.1.0/24, the following syntax would be needed:

```
# neutron subnet-create MyFlatNetwork 192.168.1.0/24 \
--allocation-pool start=192.168.1.2,end=192.168.1.49 \
--allocation-pool start=192.168.1.56,end=192.168.1.254
```

Depending on the type of network in use, it is possible for devices outside of OpenStack to coexist with instances in the same subnet. The allocation pool(s) should be defined so that addresses allocated to instances do not overlap with devices outside of the OpenStack cloud.

The `host-route` attribute defines one or more static routes to be injected via DHCP. Multiple routes listed as `destination`, and `nexthop` pairs can be separated by a space. The default maximum number of routes per subnet is 20 and can be modified in the `/etc/neutron/neutron.conf` file. The maximum number of routes per router is 30 and can also be modified in the Neutron configuration file.

The `dns-nameserver` attribute sets the nameservers for the subnet. The default maximum number of nameservers is five per subnet and can be modified in the `/etc/neutron/neutron.conf` file.

Using `--dns-nameservers` rather than `--dns-nameserver` allows you to specify more than one nameserver address using a space-separated list.

The disable-dhcp switch disables DHCP services for the subnet.

The enable-dhcp switch enables DHCP services for the subnet. DHCP is enabled by default.

 DHCP is not required for network operation. Disabling DHCP simply means that the network interface within an instance will not be configured automatically. Instances are still allocated IP addresses within the allocation pool range, whether DHCP is disabled or enabled.

The ip-version attribute defines the version of the Internet protocol in use by the subnet. Possible options include 4 for IPv4 and 6 for IPv6. IPv4 is the default when the version is not specified.

The ipv6-ra-mode attribute defines the router advertisement mode for the subnet when IPv6 is used. Possible options include dhcpv6-stateful, dhcpv6-stateless, and slaac.

The ipv6-address-mode attribute defines the address mode for the subnet when IPv6 is used. Possible options include dhcpv6-stateful, dhcpv6-stateless, and slaac.

 Not all combinations of the ipv6-ra-mode and ipv6-address-mode parameters are valid. To review both valid and invalid use cases, refer to the API guide at http://specs.openstack.org/openstack/neutron-specs/specs/juno/ipv6-radvd-ra.html#rest-api-impact.

The NETWORK argument defines the network the subnet should be associated with. Multiple subnets can be associated with a single network as long as the subnet does not overlap with another in the same network. The NETWORK argument can be the UUID or the name of a network.

The CIDR argument defines the CIDR notation of the subnet being created.

 The NETWORK and CIDR arguments are positional arguments and should be placed in this order when using the subnet-create command to avoid issues with the command.

Creating a subnet in the CLI

To demonstrate this command in action, create a subnet within the `MyFlatNetwork` network with the following characteristics:

- **Internet Protocol**: `IPv4`
- **Subnet**: `192.168.100.0/24`
- **Subnet mask**: `255.255.255.0`
- **External gateway**: `192.168.100.1`
- **DNS servers**: `8.8.8.8, 8.8.4.4`

To create the subnet and associate it with `MyFlatNetwork`, refer to the following screenshot:

```
root@controller01:~# neutron subnet-create MyFlatNetwork 192.168.100.0/24 --name MyFlatSubnet \
> --ip-version=4 --dns-nameservers 8.8.8.8 8.8.4.4
Created a new subnet:
+--------------------+------------------------------------------------------+
| Field              | Value                                                |
+--------------------+------------------------------------------------------+
| allocation_pools   | {"start": "192.168.100.2", "end": "192.168.100.254"} |
| cidr               | 192.168.100.0/24                                     |
| dns_nameservers    | 8.8.4.4                                              |
|                    | 8.8.8.8                                              |
| enable_dhcp        | True                                                 |
| gateway_ip         | 192.168.100.1                                        |
| host_routes        |                                                      |
| id                 | f48901fd-0b56-4483-af09-dc995936ae76                 |
| ip_version         | 4                                                    |
| ipv6_address_mode  |                                                      |
| ipv6_ra_mode       |                                                      |
| name               | MyFlatSubnet                                         |
| network_id         | 3282acdf-85d1-47ea-b734-f5625cfca027                 |
| subnetpool_id      |                                                      |
| tenant_id          | 65ff4cf1a04846f1ab2bc1ff0efb1090                     |
+--------------------+------------------------------------------------------+
```

Figure 5.13

Listing subnets in the CLI

To list existing subnets in Neutron, use the `subnet-list` command, as shown in the following screenshot:

```
root@controller01:~# neutron subnet-list
+--------------------------------------+--------------+------------------+------------------------------------------------------+
| id                                   | name         | cidr             | allocation_pools                                     |
+--------------------------------------+--------------+------------------+------------------------------------------------------+
| f48901fd-0b56-4483-af09-dc995936ae76 | MyFlatSubnet | 192.168.100.0/24 | {"start": "192.168.100.2", "end": "192.168.100.254"} |
+--------------------------------------+--------------+------------------+------------------------------------------------------+
```

Figure 5.14

The command output provides the ID, name, CIDR notation, and IP address allocation pools of all subnets when executed as an administrator. As a user, the command returns subnets within the project or subnets associated with shared networks.

Showing subnet properties in the CLI

To show the properties of a subnet, use the Neutron subnet-show command:

```
usage:      subnet-show SUBNET
```

The output of the command can be observed in the following screenshot:

```
root@controller01:~# neutron subnet-show MyFlatSubnet
+---------------------+--------------------------------------------------------+
| Field               | Value                                                  |
+---------------------+--------------------------------------------------------+
| allocation_pools    | {"start": "192.168.100.2", "end": "192.168.100.254"}   |
| cidr                | 192.168.100.0/24                                       |
| dns_nameservers     | 8.8.4.4                                                |
|                     | 8.8.8.8                                                |
| enable_dhcp         | True                                                   |
| gateway_ip          | 192.168.100.1                                          |
| host_routes         |                                                        |
| id                  | f48901fd-0b56-4483-af09-dc995936ae76                   |
| ip_version          | 4                                                      |
| ipv6_address_mode   |                                                        |
| ipv6_ra_mode        |                                                        |
| name                | MyFlatSubnet                                           |
| network_id          | 3282acdf-85d1-47ea-b734-f5625cfca027                   |
| subnetpool_id       |                                                        |
| tenant_id           | 65ff4cf1a04846f1ab2bc1ff0efb1090                       |
+---------------------+--------------------------------------------------------+
```

Figure 5.15

Updating a subnet in the CLI

To update a subnet in the CLI, use the Neutron subnet-update command:

```
usage:      subnet-update [--name NAME] [--gateway GATEWAY_IP]
            [--no-gateway] [--allocation-pool start=IP_ADDR,end=IP_ADDR]
            [--host-route destination=CIDR,nexthop=IP_ADDR]
            [--dns-nameserver DNS_NAMESERVER]
            [--disable-dhcp] [--enable-dhcp]
            SUBNET
```

Not all attributes of a subnet can be updated after it has been created. The following attributes can be updated:

- `name`
- `dns_nameservers`
- `enable_dhcp/disable-dhcp`
- `gateway_ip`
- `allocation_pools`
- `host_routes`

The `dns_nameserver` attribute defines the domain name server for the subnet. To overwrite the existing value with a single name server, use `--dns-nameserver`. To overwrite the existing value(s) with multiple name servers, use `--dns-nameservers`, as shown in the following command:

```
(neutron) subnet-update SUBNET --dns-nameservers <dns 1> <dns 2>
```

To enable DHCP in a subnet, use `--enable-dhcp`. To disable DHCP in a subnet, use `--disable-dhcp`.

 Instances that rely on DHCP to procure or renew a lease might lose network connectivity if DHCP is disabled.

The `gateway_ip` attribute defines the default gateway for the subnet. To overwrite an existing gateway address, use the Neutron `subnet-update` command with `--gateway-ip`, as shown in the following command:

```
(neutron) subnet-update SUBNET --gateway_ip=<gateway addr>
```

To completely remove a gateway address from the subnet, use the `action=clear` directive, as follows:

```
(neutron) subnet-update SUBNET --gateway_ip action=clear
```

 The `action=clear` directive can be used to clear the values of some attributes but may not be available on all objects.

The host_routes attribute defines one or more routes to be injected into a virtual machine instance's routing table via DHCP. To update a subnet to provide a route via DHCP, use the Neutron subnet-update command with the --host-route option, as demonstrated in the following command:

```
# neutron subnet-update SUBNET \
--host-route destination=10.0.0.0/24,nexthop=192.168.100.254
```

To specify multiple routes, use multiple --host-route options, as demonstrated in the following command:

```
# neutron subnet-update SUBNET \
--host-route destination=10.0.0.0/24,nexthop=192.168.100.254 \
--host-route destination=172.16.0.0/24,nexthop=192.168.100.254
```

> Using subnet-update to update the name servers, routes, and gateway IP of a subnet will result in an overwriting of the existing values. To avoid possible downtime or other network connectivity issues, care should be taken to ensure that the environment is not affected by the changes made to subnet attributes.

Creating subnets in the dashboard

Subnets can be created in the dashboard either by an administrator or user. The process of creating subnets as either type of user is described in the upcoming sections.

Creating subnets via the Admin tab as an administrator

To create a subnet as the cloud administrator, perform the following steps:

1. Navigate to **Admin | System | Networks** and click on the name of the network that you wish to add a subnet to:

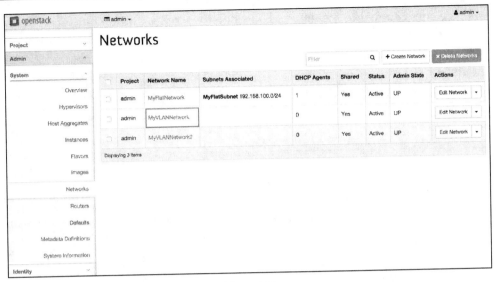

Figure 5.16

2. Clicking on **MyVLANNetwork** provides a list of details of the network, including the associated subnets and ports:

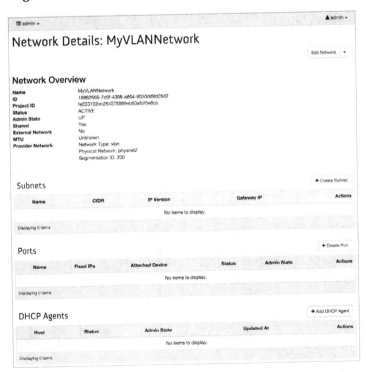

Figure 5.17

3. To add a subnet to the network, click on the **Create Subnet** button on the right-hand side:

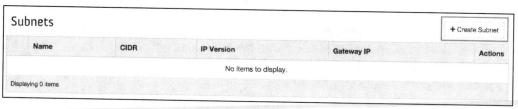

Figure 5.18

4. A window will appear that allows you to define the properties of the subnet:

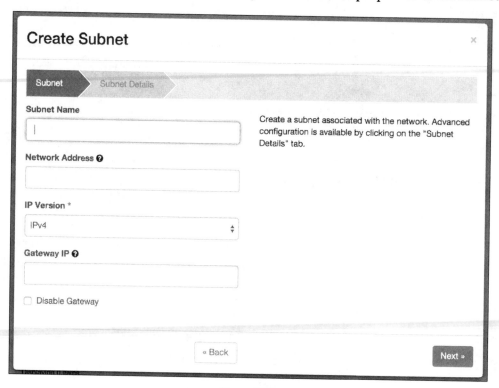

Figure 5.19

5. Each option pictured here corresponds to an option available with the Neutron `subnet-create` command in the CLI. Clicking on **Next** reveals additional configuration options:

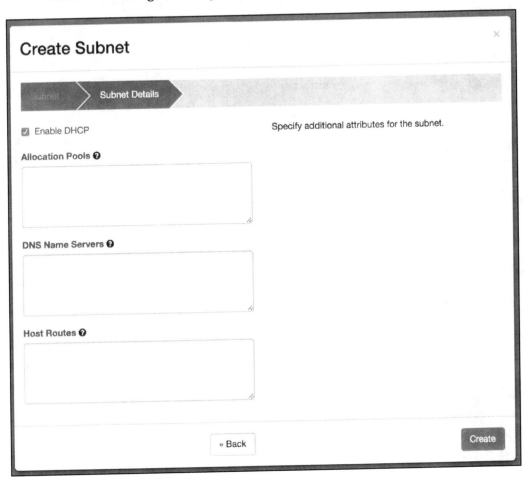

Figure 5.20

6. To complete the creation of the subnet, click on the blue **Create** button.

Creating subnets via the Project tab as a user

In the dashboard, users can create subnets at the time of network creation or add subnets to an existing network. To create a network and subnet as a user, perform the following steps:

1. Navigate to **Project | Network | Networks** and click on the **Create Network** button:

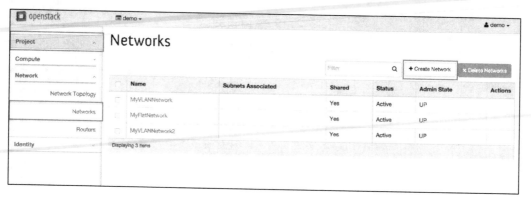

Figure 5.21

2. Clicking on **Create Network** will open a window where you can specify the network and subnet details:

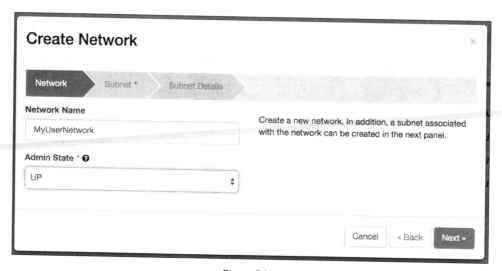

Figure 5.22

3. Clicking on the **Subnet** tab or **Next** button allows you to specify information on the subnet, including the network address, CIDR, and gateway information:

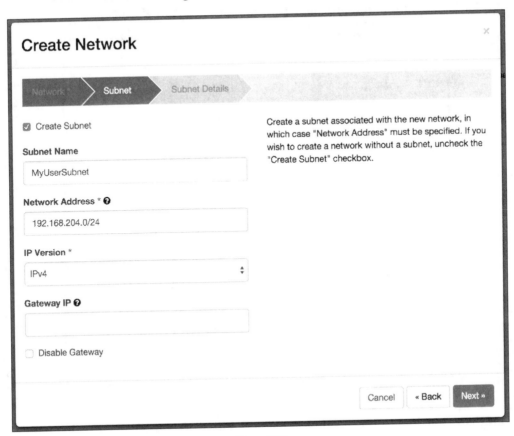

Figure 5.23

4. Finally, clicking on **Subnet Detail** or **Next** allows you to specify details such as IP allocation pools, DNS name servers, and static routes. Click on the blue **Create** button to complete the creation of the network and subnet:

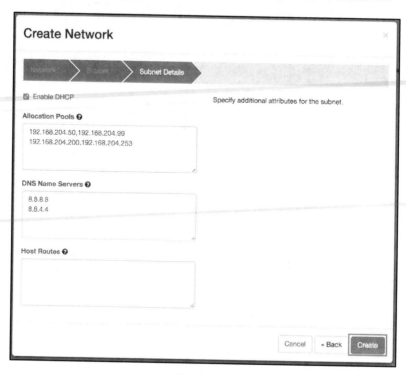

Figure 5.24

The ability to add additional subnets or delete a network entirely is provided within the menu located under the **Actions** column, as pictured in the following screenshot:

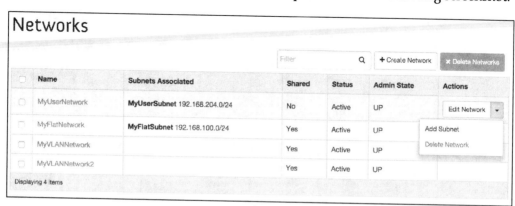

Figure 5.25

Neutron ports

A port in Neutron is a logical connection of a virtual network interface to a subnet. Ports can be associated with virtual machine instances, DHCP servers, routers, firewalls, load balancers, and more. Ports can even be created simply to reserve IP addresses from a subnet. Neutron stores port relationships in the Neutron database and uses this information to build switching connections at the physical or virtual switch layer through the networking plugin and agent.

To retrieve a list of all Neutron ports, use the Neutron `port-list` command, as shown in the following screenshot:

```
root@controller01:~# neutron port-list
+--------------------------------------+------+-------------------+--------------------------------------------------------------------------------------+
| id                                   | name | mac_address       | fixed_ips                                                                            |
+--------------------------------------+------+-------------------+--------------------------------------------------------------------------------------+
| 5ff7b16c-f028-4bb1-aff9-40a2ce293d39 |      | fa:16:3e:59:0c:68 | {"subnet_id": "f48901fd-0b56-4483-af09-dc995936ae76", "ip_address": "192.168.100.2"} |
| 971fda0d-eae8-45ce-b8b9-893b1c3dc17e |      | fa:16:3e:7c:2f:9b | {"subnet_id": "93c3c625-80c2-4282-98db-9ffd13fa9922", "ip_address": "192.168.204.50"}|
+--------------------------------------+------+-------------------+--------------------------------------------------------------------------------------+
```

Figure 5.26

Use the Neutron `port-show` command to see the details of a particular port:

```
root@controller01:/var/log/neutron# neutron port-show 5ff7b16c-f028-4bb1-aff9-40a2ce293d39
+------------------------+--------------------------------------------------------------------------------------+
| Field                  | Value                                                                                |
+------------------------+--------------------------------------------------------------------------------------+
| admin_state_up         | True                                                                                 |
| allowed_address_pairs  |                                                                                      |
| binding:host_id        | controller01.learningneutron.com                                                     |
| binding:profile        | {}                                                                                   |
| binding:vif_details    | {"port_filter": true}                                                                |
| binding:vif_type       | bridge                                                                               |
| binding:vnic_type      | normal                                                                               |
| device_id              | dhcpcdedd354-5b13-51e7-8b25-47e9fd5b6ad3-3282acdf-85d1-47ea-b734-f5625cfca027         |
| device_owner           | network:dhcp                                                                         |
| extra_dhcp_opts        |                                                                                      |
| fixed_ips              | {"subnet_id": "f48901fd-0b56-4483-af09-dc995936ae76", "ip_address": "192.168.100.2"} |
| id                     | 5ff7b16c-f028-4bb1-aff9-40a2ce293d39                                                 |
| mac_address            | fa:16:3e:59:0c:68                                                                    |
| name                   |                                                                                      |
| network_id             | 3282acdf-85d1-47ea-b734-f5625cfca027                                                 |
| security_groups        |                                                                                      |
| status                 | ACTIVE                                                                               |
| tenant_id              | 65ff4cf1a04846f1ab2bc1ff0efb1090                                                     |
+------------------------+--------------------------------------------------------------------------------------+
```

Figure 5.27

The port pictured in *Figure 5.27* is owned by an interface used within a DHCP namespace. The `network_id` field reveals the network to be `3282acdf-85d1-47ea-b734-f5625cfca027`, otherwise known as the `MyFlatNetwork` network, which was created earlier in this chapter.

Use the `ip netns exec` command to execute `ip addr` within the DHCP namespace to list its interfaces and their details:

```
root@controller01:~# ip netns exec qdhcp-3282acdf-85d1-47ea-b734-f5625cfca027 ip addr
1: lo: <LOOPBACK,UP,LOWER_UP> mtu 65536 qdisc noqueue state UNKNOWN group default
    link/loopback 00:00:00:00:00:00 brd 00:00:00:00:00:00
    inet 127.0.0.1/8 scope host lo
       valid_lft forever preferred_lft forever
    inet6 ::1/128 scope host
       valid_lft forever preferred_lft forever
2: ns-5ff7b16c-f0: <BROADCAST,MULTICAST,UP,LOWER_UP> mtu 1500 qdisc pfifo_fast state UP group default qlen 1000
    link/ether fa:16:3e:59:0c:68 brd ff:ff:ff:ff:ff:ff
    inet 192.168.100.2/24 brd 192.168.100.255 scope global ns-5ff7b16c-f0
       valid_lft forever preferred_lft forever
    inet 169.254.169.254/16 brd 169.254.255.255 scope global ns-5ff7b16c-f0
       valid_lft forever preferred_lft forever
    inet6 fe80::f816:3eff:fe59:c68/64 scope link
       valid_lft forever preferred_lft forever
```

Figure 5.28

In the DHCP namespace, the interface's MAC address corresponds to the port's `mac_address` field, while the name of the interface corresponds to the first 10 characters of the Neutron port UUID:

```
root@controller01:~# neutron port-show 5ff7b16c-f028-4bb1-aff9-40a2ce293d39 -F id -F mac_address
+--------------+---------------------------------------+
| Field        | Value                                 |
+--------------+---------------------------------------+
| id           | 5ff7b16c-f028-4bb1-aff9-40a2ce293d39  |
| mac_address  | fa:16:3e:59:0c:68                     |
+--------------+---------------------------------------+
```

Figure 5.29

Creating a port

By creating a Neutron port manually, users have the ability to specify a particular fixed IP address, MAC address, security group, and more.

To create a port, use the Neutron `port-create` command, as follows:

```
usage:      neutron port-create [--tenant-id TENANT_ID] [--name NAME]
            [--fixed-ip subnet_id=SUBNET,ip_address=IP_ADDR]
            [--device-id DEVICE_ID]
            [--device-owner DEVICE_OWNER] [--admin-state-down]
            [--mac-address MAC_ADDRESS]
            [--security-group SECURITY_GROUP | --no-security-groups]
            [--extra-dhcp-opt EXTRA_DHCP_OPTS]
            NETWORK
```

Once created, the port can then be associated with a virtual machine instance or other virtual network device or can simply be used to reserve an IP address in a subnet.

Attaching instances to networks

Using the Nova command-line client, instances can be attached to networks in a couple of ways. When first booted, instances can be attached to one or more networks using the nova boot command. Running instances can be attached to additional networks using the nova interface-attach command. Both methods are explained in the upcoming sections.

Attaching instances to networks using nova boot

The following nova boot options provide a single network interface to an instance.

Users can specify a network identified by the network's UUID, as follows:

```
--nic net-id=<UUID of Neutron network>
```

In the preceding example, Nova interfaces with the Neutron API to create a port using the network ID provided by the user, and Neutron returns details of the port back to Nova for use by the instance.

As an alternative, users can specify a port identified by the port's UUID, as follows:

```
--nic port-id=<UUID of Neutron network>
```

In the preceding example, Neutron associates the instance with an existing port and sets the port's device_id attribute accordingly.

By passing the --nic switch multiple times, it is possible to provide multiple virtual interfaces to an instance that is attached to specified networks or ports. The interfaces within the instance may be enumerated as eth0, eth1, eth2, and so on, depending on the operating system.

The following nova boot command demonstrates the procedure of connecting an instance to multiple networks when first booting an instance:

```
# nova boot --flavor FLAVOR --image IMAGE \
    --nic net-id=NETWORK1_UUID \
    --nic net-id=NETWORK2_UUID \
    --nic net-id=NETWORK3_UUID \
    INSTANCE
```

For many cloud-ready images, a single interface within the instance is brought online automatically. Modification of the network interface file(s) within an instance may be required to activate and configure additional network interfaces once the instance is active.

Nova attaches instances to the virtual switch on the compute node with a **virtual interface**, or **VIF**. Each VIF has a corresponding Neutron port in the database. In the preceding example, the instance was connected to three different Neutron networks. When using the Open vSwitch driver, each VIF plugs into the integration bridge on the respective compute node hosting the instance. The virtual switch port is configured with a local VLAN ID that corresponds to the network associated with the Neutron port and VIF.

 When security groups are used, the OVS hybrid firewall driver utilizes Linux bridges for iptables support. The VIF may first plug into a Linux bridge (qbr) that connects to the integration bridge with a veth pair (qvo,qva). More information on this can be found in *Chapter 6, Managing Security Groups*.

When using the LinuxBridge driver, each VIF connects to a Linux bridge that corresponds to the associated network. Every network has a corresponding bridge that is used to segregate traffic.

Attaching multiple network interfaces to an instance is referred to as **multihoming**. When an instance is multihomed, neither Neutron nor the instance itself is aware of which network takes precedence over another. When attached networks and subnets have their own respective gateway addresses set, an instance's routing table can be populated with multiple default routes. This scenario can wreak havoc on the connectivity and routing behavior of an instance.

 Paravirtualized devices, including network and storage devices that use virtio drivers, are PCI devices. Virtual machine instances under KVM are currently limited to 32 total PCI devices. Some PCI devices are critical for operation, including the host bridge, the ISA/USB bridge, the graphics card, and the memory balloon device, leaving up to 28 PCI slots available for use. Every paravirtualized network or block device uses one slot. This means that users may have issues attempting to connect upwards of 20-25 networks to an instance depending on the characteristics of the instance.

Attaching network interfaces

There are times when it may be necessary to add an additional network interface to a running instance and have it connect to a network. Use cases may include the need to access other instances on an isolated backend network or communicate with physical devices on a flat or VLAN network. Using the `nova interface-attach` command, you can specify an existing port or create a new port based on specific network or IP requirements.

The `nova interface-attach` command syntax is as follows:

```
usage:    nova interface-attach [--port-id <port_id>]
          [--net-id <net-id>] [--fixed-ip <fixed_ip>]
          INSTANCE
```

The `--port-id` option allows users to attach an existing Neutron port to an instance. The port must be one that is not currently associated with any other instance or resource.

The `--net-id` option allows users to attach a new interface to an instance from the specified network. A new port that has a unique MAC address and an IP from the specified network is created in Neutron. It is possible to attach an instance to the same network multiple times using multiple `nova interface-attach` commands.

The `--fixed-ip` option can be used in conjunction with the `--net-id` options and allows users to specify a particular IP address for use rather than the next available address in the subnet.

 While additional network interfaces may be added to running instances using hot-plug technology, the interfaces themselves may need to be configured within the operating system before they can be used.

If no options are specified, Nova will attempt to attach an interface from an existing network. If more than one network exists, the following error will be observed:

```
root@controller01:~# nova interface-attach MyFlatInstance
ERROR (BadRequest): Multiple possible networks found, use a Network ID to be more specific. (HTTP 400)
```

Figure 5.30

Detaching network interfaces

To detach an interface from an instance, use the `nova interface-detach` command, as follows:

```
usage:    nova interface-detach INSTANCE <port_id>
```

Interfaces detached from instances are removed completely from the Neutron port database.

Exploring how instances get their addresses

When a network is created and DHCP is enabled on a subnet within the network, the network is scheduled to one or more DHCP agents in the environment. A `dnsmasq` process is spawned in a network namespace that corresponds to the network. If a `dnsmasq` process already exists for the network and a new subnet is added, the existing process is updated to support the additional subnet.

When DHCP is not enabled on a subnet, a `dnsmasq` process is not spawned. An IP address is still associated with the Neutron port that corresponds to the interface within the instance, however. Without DHCP services, it is up to the user to manually configure the IP address on the interface within the guest operating system through a console session.

Most instances rely on DHCP to obtain their associated IP addresses. DHCP goes through the following stages:

- A DHCP client sends a `DHCPDISCOVER` broadcast packet that requests IP information from a DHCP server.
- A DHCP server responds to the request with a `DHCPOFFER` packet. The packet contains the MAC address of the instance that makes the request, IP address, subnet mask, lease duration, and IP address of the DHCP server. A Neutron network can be scheduled to multiple DHCP agents simultaneously, and each DHCP server may respond with a `DHCPOFFER` packet. However, the client will only accept the first one.
- In response to the offer, the DHCP client sends a `DHCPREQUEST` packet back to the DHCP server, requesting the offered address.
- In response to the request, the DHCP server issues a `DHCPACK` or acknowledgement packet to the instance. At this point, the IP configuration is complete. The DHCP server sends other DHCP options, such as name servers, routes, and so on, to the instance.

Network namespaces associated with DHCP servers begin with qdhcp in their names, followed by the network UUID. DHCP namespaces will only reside on hosts running the neutron-dhcp-agent service. Even then, the network must be scheduled to the DHCP agent for the namespace to be created on this host. In this example, the DHCP agent runs on the controller node.

To view a list of namespaces on the controller node, type ip netns in the host prompt, as follows:

```
root@controller01:~# ip netns
qdhcp-34265955-56be-4486-853d-2f0ed5cebb44
qdhcp-3282acdf-85d1-47ea-b734-f5625cfca027
```

Figure 5.31

The two namespaces correspond to the two networks that DHCP is enabled for:

```
root@controller01:~# neutron net-list
+--------------------------------------+----------------+-------------------------------------------------------------------+
| id                                   | name           | subnets                                                           |
+--------------------------------------+----------------+-------------------------------------------------------------------+
| 34265955-56be-4486-853d-2f0ed5cebb44 | MyUserNetwork  | 93c3c625-80c2-4282-98db-9ffd13fa9922 192.168.204.0/24             |
| 3282acdf-85d1-47ea-b734-f5625cfca027 | MyFlatNetwork  | f48901fd-0b56-4483-af09-dc995936ae76 192.168.100.0/24            |
| 3a342db3-f918-4760-972a-cb700d5b6d2c | MyVLANNetwork  |                                                                   |
| c6933c77-9adc-4d29-8da0-f186329b8e0e | MyVLANNetwork2 |                                                                   |
+--------------------------------------+----------------+-------------------------------------------------------------------+
```

Figure 5.32

Within the qdhcp namespace, there exists an interface that is used to connect the namespace to the network, as shown in the following figure:

```
root@controller01:~# ip netns exec qdhcp-34265955-56be-4486-853d-2f0ed5cebb44 ip a
1: lo: <LOOPBACK,UP,LOWER_UP> mtu 65536 qdisc noqueue state UNKNOWN group default
    link/loopback 00:00:00:00:00:00 brd 00:00:00:00:00:00
    inet 127.0.0.1/8 scope host lo
       valid_lft forever preferred_lft forever
    inet6 ::1/128 scope host
       valid_lft forever preferred_lft forever
2: ns-971fda0d-ea: <BROADCAST,MULTICAST,UP,LOWER_UP> mtu 1500 qdisc pfifo_fast state UP group default qlen 1000
    link/ether fa:16:3e:7c:2f:9b brd ff:ff:ff:ff:ff:ff
    inet 192.168.204.50/24 brd 192.168.204.255 scope global ns-971fda0d-ea
       valid_lft forever preferred_lft forever
    inet 169.254.169.254/16 brd 169.254.255.255 scope global ns-971fda0d-ea
       valid_lft forever preferred_lft forever
    inet6 fe80::f816:3eff:fe7c:2f9b/64 scope link
       valid_lft forever preferred_lft forever
```

Figure 5.33

The IP address assigned to the interface within the namespace, 192.168.204.50/24, is automatically assigned by Neutron and procured from the subnet's allocation pool.

The `ns-971fda0d-ea` interface within the namespace is one end of a veth cable. When using the LinuxBridge driver, the other end of the cable is connected to a bridge that corresponds to the network and is represented by the `tap971fda0d-ea` interface, as shown in the following figure:

```
root@controller01:~# brctl show
bridge name        bridge id              STP enabled    interfaces
brq3282acdf-85     8000.52fc6c3ccdf1          no         eth2
                                                         tap5ff7b16c-f0

brq34265955-56     8000.621a2ddf2cfc          no         tap971fda0d-ea
                                                         vxlan-48
```

Figure 5.34

In the preceding screenshot, the bridge labeled "`brq34265955-56`" corresponds to the `MyUserNetwork` network, which is a VXLAN network. The `tap971fda0d-ea` interface is the other end of the veth cable connected to the DHCP namespace.

Watching the DHCP lease cycle

To observe an instance requesting a DHCP lease, start a packet capture within the corresponding DHCP network namespace using the following command:

```
# ip netns exec <namespace> tcpdump -i any -ne port 67 or port 68
```

As an instance starts up, it will send broadcast packets that will be answered by the DHCP server within the namespace:

```
root@controller01:~# ip netns exec qdhcp-34265955-56be-4486-853d-2f0ed5cebb44 tcpdump -i any -ne port 67 or port 68
tcpdump: verbose output suppressed, use -v or -vv for full protocol decode
listening on any, link-type LINUX_SLL (Linux cooked), capture size 65535 bytes
16:06:07.051982   B fa:16:3e:25:ab:a3 length 334: 0.0.0.68 > 255.255.255.67: BOOTP/DHCP, Request from fa:16:3e:25:ab:a3, length 290
16:06:07.052515 Out fa:16:3e:7c:2f:9b length 377: 192.168.204.50.67 > 192.168.204.51.68: BOOTP/DHCP, Reply, length 333
16:06:07.054195   B fa:16:3e:25:ab:a3 length 346: 0.0.0.68 > 255.255.255.255.67: BOOTP/DHCP, Request from fa:16:3e:25:ab:a3, length 302
16:06:07.058622 Out fa:16:3e:7c:2f:9b length 398: 192.168.204.50.67 > 192.168.204.51.68: BOOTP/DHCP, Reply, length 354
```

Figure 5.35

A similar output can be observed by performing the capture on the tap interface of the instance on the compute node:

```
root@compute01:~# tcpdump -i tap60fcacdb-92 -ne port 67 or port 68
tcpdump: WARNING: tap60fcacdb-92: no IPv4 address assigned
tcpdump: verbose output suppressed, use -v or -vv for full protocol decode
listening on tap60fcacdb-92, link-type EN10MB (Ethernet), capture size 65535 bytes
16:12:59.709076 fa:16:3e:25:ab:a3 > ff:ff:ff:ff:ff:ff length 340: 0.0.0.68 > 255.255.255.255.67: BOOTP/DHCP, Request from fa:16:3e:25:ab:a3, length 298
16:12:59.710360 fa:16:3e:7c:2f:9b > fa:16:3e:25:ab:a3 length 375: 192.168.204.50.67 > 192.168.204.51.68: BOOTP/DHCP, Reply, length 333
16:12:59.710973 fa:16:3e:25:ab:a3 > ff:ff:ff:ff:ff:ff length 352: 0.0.0.68 > 255.255.255.255.67: BOOTP/DHCP, Request from fa:16:3e:25:ab:a3, length 310
16:12:59.716567 fa:16:3e:7c:2f:9b > fa:16:3e:25:ab:a3 length 396: 192.168.204.50.67 > 192.168.204.51.68: BOOTP/DHCP, Reply, length 354
```

Figure 5.36

Using the `dhcpdump` utility, we can observe a more verbose output of the DHCP lease cycle:

```
root@controller01:~# ip netns exec qdhcp-34265955-56be-4486-853d-
2f0ed5cebb44 dhcpdump -i ns-971fda0d-ea
```

The `DHCPDISCOVER` packet is shown in the following figure:

```
  TIME: 2015-10-12 16:20:27.197
    IP: 0.0.0.0 (fa:16:3e:3a:db:a9) > 255.255.255.255 (ff:ff:ff:ff:ff:ff)
    OP: 1 (BOOTPREQUEST)
 HTYPE: 1 (Ethernet)
  HLEN: 6
  HOPS: 0
   XID: e82e9424
  SECS: 0
 FLAGS: 0
CIADDR: 0.0.0.0
YIADDR: 0.0.0.0
SIADDR: 0.0.0.0
GIADDR: 0.0.0.0
CHADDR: fa:16:3e:3a:db:a9:00:00:00:00:00:00:00:00:00:00
 SNAME: .
 FNAME: .
OPTION:  53 (  1) DHCP message type            1 (DHCPDISCOVER)
OPTION:  61 (  7) Client-identifier            01:fa:16:3e:3a:db:a9
OPTION:  57 (  2) Maximum DHCP message size 576
OPTION:  55 (  9) Parameter Request List       1 (Subnet mask)
                              3 (Routers)
                              6 (DNS server)
                             12 (Host name)
                             15 (Domainname)
                             26 (Interface MTU)
                             28 (Broadcast address)
                             42 (NTP servers)
                            121 (Classless Static Route)

OPTION:  60 ( 12) Vendor class identifier   udhcp 1.20.1
OPTION:  12 (  6) Host name                 cirros
```

Figure 5.37

The DHCPOFFER packet is as follows:

```
   TIME: 2015-10-12 16:20:27.197
     IP: 192.168.204.50 (fa:16:3e:7c:2f:9b) > 192.168.204.52 (fa:16:3e:3a:db:a9)
     OP: 2 (BOOTPREPLY)
  HTYPE: 1 (Ethernet)
   HLEN: 6
   HOPS: 0
    XID: e82e9424
   SECS: 0
  FLAGS: 0
 CIADDR: 0.0.0.0
 YIADDR: 192.168.204.52
 SIADDR: 192.168.204.50
 GIADDR: 0.0.0.0
 CHADDR: fa:16:3e:3a:db:a9:00:00:00:00:00:00:00:00:00:00
  SNAME: .
  FNAME: .
 OPTION:  53 (  1) DHCP message type         2 (DHCPOFFER)
 OPTION:  54 (  4) Server identifier         192.168.204.50
 OPTION:  51 (  4) IP address leasetime      86400 (24h)
 OPTION:  58 (  4) T1                        43200 (12h)
 OPTION:  59 (  4) T2                        75600 (21h)
 OPTION:   1 (  4) Subnet mask               255.255.255.0
 OPTION:  28 (  4) Broadcast address         192.168.204.255
 OPTION:  15 ( 19) Domainname                learningneutron.com
 OPTION:   3 (  4) Routers                   192.168.204.1
 OPTION: 121 ( 14) Classless Static Route    20a9fea9fec0a8cc  .......
                   3200c0a8cc01           2.....
 OPTION:   6 (  8) DNS server                8.8.4.4,8.8.8.8
```

Figure 5.38

Here's what the DHCPREQUEST packet looks like:

```
   TIME: 2015-10-12 16:20:27.197
     IP: 0.0.0.0 (fa:16:3e:3a:db:a9) > 255.255.255.255 (ff:ff:ff:ff:ff:ff)
     OP: 1 (BOOTPREQUEST)
  HTYPE: 1 (Ethernet)
   HLEN: 6
   HOPS: 0
    XID: e82e9424
   SECS: 0
  FLAGS: 0
 CIADDR: 0.0.0.0
 YIADDR: 0.0.0.0
 SIADDR: 0.0.0.0
 GIADDR: 0.0.0.0
 CHADDR: fa:16:3e:3a:db:a9:00:00:00:00:00:00:00:00:00:00
  SNAME: .
  FNAME: .
 OPTION:  53 (  1) DHCP message type            3 (DHCPREQUEST)
 OPTION:  61 (  7) Client-identifier     01:fa:16:3e:3a:db:a9
 OPTION:  50 (  4) Request IP address        192.168.204.52
 OPTION:  54 (  4) Server identifier         192.168.204.50
 OPTION:  57 (  2) Maximum DHCP message size 576
 OPTION:  55 (  9) Parameter Request List       1 (Subnet mask)
                                  3 (Routers)
                                  6 (DNS server)
                                 12 (Host name)
                                 15 (Domainname)
                                 26 (Interface MTU)
                                 28 (Broadcast address)
                                 42 (NTP servers)
                                121 (Classless Static Route)

 OPTION:  60 ( 12) Vendor class identifier    udhcp 1.20.1
 OPTION:  12 (  6) Host name                  cirros
```

Figure 5.39

Finally, here's the DHCPACK packet:

```
   TIME: 2015-10-12 16:20:27.197
     IP: 192.168.204.50 (fa:16:3e:7c:2f:9b) > 192.168.204.52 (fa:16:3e:3a:db:a9)
     OP: 2 (BOOTPREPLY)
  HTYPE: 1 (Ethernet)
   HLEN: 6
   HOPS: 0
    XID: e82e9424
   SECS: 0
  FLAGS: 0
 CIADDR: 0.0.0.0
 YIADDR: 192.168.204.52
 SIADDR: 192.168.204.50
 GIADDR: 0.0.0.0
 CHADDR: fa:16:3e:3a:db:a9:00:00:00:00:00:00:00:00:00:00
  SNAME: .
  FNAME: .
 OPTION:  53 (  1) DHCP message type          5 (DHCPACK)
 OPTION:  54 (  4) Server identifier          192.168.204.50
 OPTION:  51 (  4) IP address leasetime       86400 (24h)
 OPTION:  58 (  4) T1                         43200 (12h)
 OPTION:  59 (  4) T2                         75600 (21h)
 OPTION:   1 (  4) Subnet mask                255.255.255.0
 OPTION:  28 (  4) Broadcast address          192.168.204.255
 OPTION:  15 ( 19) Domainname                 learningneutron.com
 OPTION:  12 ( 19) Host name                  host-192-168-204-52
 OPTION:   3 (  4) Routers                    192.168.204.1
 OPTION: 121 ( 14) Classless Static Route     20a9fea9fec0a8cc  .......
                   3200c0a8cc01          2.....
 OPTION:   6 (  8) DNS server                 8.8.4.4,8.8.8.8
```

Figure 5.40

 The dhcpdump utility can be installed on any host with the following command:

```
# apt-get install dhcpdump
```

Troubleshooting DHCP

If an instance is unable to procure its address from DHCP, it may be helpful to run a packet capture from various points in the network to see where the request or reply is failing.

Using `tcpdump` or `dhcpdump`, one can capture a DHCP request and response packets on the UDP ports, `67` and `68`, from the following locations:

- Within the DHCP namespace
- On the physical interface of the network and/or compute nodes
- On the tap interface of the instance
- Within the guest operating system

Further investigation may be required once the node responsible for dropping traffic is identified.

Exploring how instances retrieve their metadata

In *Chapter 3, Installing Neutron*, we briefly covered the process instances accessing metadata over the network, through either a proxy in the router namespace or the DHCP namespace. The latter is described in the following section.

The DHCP namespace

Instances can access metadata at `http://169.254.169.254`, followed by a URI that corresponds to the version of metadata, usually `/latest`. When an instance is connected to a network that does not utilize a Neutron router as the gateway, the instance must learn how to reach the metadata service. This can be accomplished in a few different ways, including:

- Setting a route manually on the instance
- Allowing DHCP to provide a route

When `enable_isolated_metadata` is set to `true` in the DHCP configuration file at `/etc/neutron/dhcp_agent.ini`, each DHCP namespace provides a proxy to the metadata service running on the controller node. The proxy service listens directly on port `80`, as shown in the following figure:

```
root@controller01:~# ip netns exec qdhcp-34265955-56be-4486-853d-2f0ed5cebb44 netstat -ntlp
Active Internet connections (only servers)
Proto Recv-Q Send-Q Local Address          Foreign Address         State       PID/Program name
tcp        0      0 0.0.0.0:80             0.0.0.0:*               LISTEN      24848/python
tcp        0      0 192.168.204.50:53      0.0.0.0:*               LISTEN      24768/dnsmasq
tcp        0      0 169.254.169.254:53     0.0.0.0:*               LISTEN      24768/dnsmasq
tcp6       0      0 fe80::f816:3eff:fe7c:53 :::*                   LISTEN      24768/dnsmasq
```

Figure 5.41

Using the `ps` command within the namespace, you can note that the process associated with this listener is the Neutron metadata proxy:

```
root@controller01:~# ip netns exec qdhcp-34265955-56be-4486-853d-2f0ed5cebb44 ps 24848
  PID TTY      STAT   TIME COMMAND
24848 ?        S      0:00 /usr/bin/python /usr/bin/neutron-ns-metadata-proxy --pid_file=/var/lib/neutr
```

Figure 5.42

Adding a manual route to 169.254.169.254

Before an instance can reach the metadata service in the DHCP namespace at `169.254.169.254`, a route must be configured to use the DHCP namespace interface as the next hop rather than the default gateway of the instance.

Observe the IP addresses within the following DHCP namespace:

```
root@controller01:~# ip netns exec qdhcp-34265955-56be-4486-853d-2f0ed5cebb44 ip a
1: lo: <LOOPBACK,UP,LOWER_UP> mtu 65536 qdisc noqueue state UNKNOWN group default
    link/loopback 00:00:00:00:00:00 brd 00:00:00:00:00:00
    inet 127.0.0.1/8 scope host lo
       valid_lft forever preferred_lft forever
    inet6 ::1/128 scope host
       valid_lft forever preferred_lft forever
2: ns-971fda0d-ea: <BROADCAST,MULTICAST,UP,LOWER_UP> mtu 1500 qdisc pfifo_fast state UP group default qlen 1000
    link/ether fa:16:3e:7c:2f:9b brd ff:ff:ff:ff:ff:ff
    inet 192.168.204.50/24 brd 192.168.204.255 scope global ns-971fda0d-ea
       valid_lft forever preferred_lft forever
    inet 169.254.169.254/16 brd 169.254.255.255 scope global ns-971fda0d-ea
       valid_lft forever preferred_lft forever
    inet6 fe80::f816:3eff:fe7c:2f9b/64 scope link
       valid_lft forever preferred_lft forever
```

Figure 5.43

The `169.254.169.254/16` address is automatically configured as a secondary address on the interface inside the namespace. To reach `169.254.169.254` from an instance in the `192.168.204.0/24` network, the following `ip route` command can be used within the guest instance that sets `192.168.204.50` as the next hop:

```
# ip route add 169.254.169.254/32 via 192.168.204.50
```

While this method works, the process of adding a route to each instance does not scale well, especially when multiple DHCP agents exist in the environment. A single network can be scheduled to multiple agents that, in turn, have their own respective namespaces and IP addresses in the same subnet. Users need prior knowledge of the IP to use it in their route statement, and the address is subject to change. Allowing DHCP to inject the route automatically is the recommended method, which will be discussed in the next section.

Using DHCP to inject the route

When `enable_isolated_metadata` is set to `true` and the gateway for a subnet is either *not* set or *not* a Neutron router, the DHCP service is capable of injecting a route to the metadata service via the `classless-static-route` DHCP option, which is otherwise known as option 121.

Once an instance connected to a subnet with the mentioned characteristics is created, observe the following routes passed to the instance via DHCP:

```
$ ip r
169.254.169.254 via 192.168.204.50 dev eth0
192.168.204.0/24 dev eth0  src 192.168.204.52
```

Figure 5.44

The next hop address for the metadata route is the IP address of the DHCP server that responds to the initial DHCP request from the client. If there were multiple DHCP agents in the environment and the same network was scheduled to all of them, it is possible that the next hop address would vary between instances as any of the DHCP servers could respond to the request.

Summary

This chapter laid a foundation for creating networks and subnets that can be utilized by instances and other virtual and physical network devices. Both the Horizon dashboard and the Neutron command-line client can be used to manage networks, subnets, and ports, though the latter is recommended for most administrative tasks.

For more information on network, subnet, and port attributes as well as for guidance on how to use the Neutron API, refer to the OpenStack Wikipedia page at `https://wiki.openstack.org/wiki/Neutron/APIv2-specification`.

For additional details on deployment scenarios based on provider networks, refer to *OpenStack Networking Guide* available at `http://docs.openstack.org/networking-guide/`.

In the next chapter, you will learn how to leverage the Neutron security group functionality to provide network-level security to instances. The configuration of virtual firewalls can be found in *Chapter 11, Firewall as a Service*.

Managing Security Groups

Neutron includes two methods of providing network-level security to instances: security groups and virtual firewalls. The security group functionality relies on iptables rules to filter traffic on the compute node hosting the instance. Virtual firewalls are provided by the advanced Neutron service known as **Firewall as a Service**, or **FWaaS**, which relies on iptables to filter traffic at the perimeter of the network in a Neutron router.

In this chapter, we will focus on security groups and cover some fundamental security features of Neutron, including:

- A brief introduction to iptables
- Creating and managing security groups
- Demonstrating how security groups leverage iptables
- Disabling port security

Security groups in OpenStack

A **security group** is a collection of network access rules, known as **security group rules**, which limits the types of traffic an instance can send or receive. In the reference architecture, security group rules are converted to iptables rules that are applied on the compute nodes hosting the instances. Each tenant is provided with a default security group that can be modified by users within the tenant. Neutron provides an API to create, modify, apply, and delete security group rules.

There are multiple ways to apply security groups to instances. For example, one or more instances, usually of similar functionality or role, can be placed in a security group. Security group rules can reference IPv4 and IPv6 hosts and networks as well as security groups themselves. Referencing a particular security group in a rule, rather than a particular host or network, frees the user from having to specify individual addresses. Neutron constructs the filtering rules applied on the host automatically based on the information in the database.

Rules within a security group are applied at a port level on the compute node, as demonstrated in the following diagram:

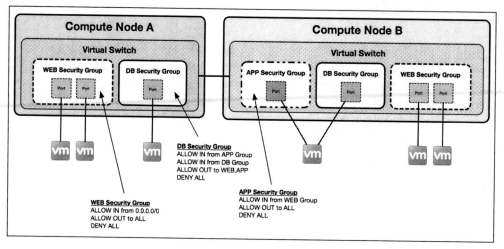

Figure 6.1

In the preceding diagram, ports within the virtual switch belong to one of three security groups: WEB, DB, or APP. When a change is made to a security group, such as adding or removing rules, corresponding iptables rule changes are made automatically on the compute nodes.

Some users may use security groups to describe certain types of rules that should be applied to a particular instance port. For example, a security group can be used to categorize multiple hosts or subnets that are allowed access to a port. Multiple security groups can be applied to a port, and all rules defined in these groups are applied to the port. As all traffic is implicitly denied and security group rules define only the allowed traffic through a port, there is no chance of a rule in one security group applied to a port counteracting a rule in another security group applied to the same port.

The following example demonstrates the use of security groups to categorize traffic that is allowed access through a port:

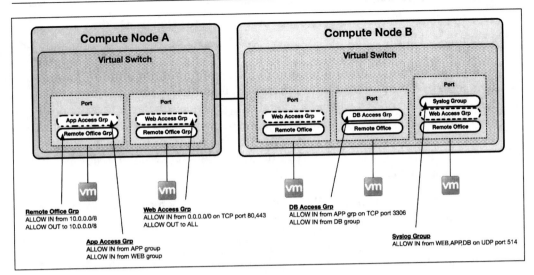

Figure 6.2

When a port is created in Neutron, it is associated with a default security group unless a specific security group is specified. The default security group drops all ingress traffic and allows all egress traffic from instances. Rules can be added to or removed from the default security group to change its behavior. In addition, standard rules are applied to every instance that prohibits IP, DHCP, and MAC address spoofing. This behavior can be changed and will be discussed later in this chapter.

Once a security group is applied to a Neutron port, the corresponding security group rules are translated by Neutron into iptables rules that are then applied to the respective compute node hosting the instances.

An introduction to iptables

In the reference architecture, the security group functionality relies on iptables to perform traffic filtering. Iptables is a firewall built into Linux that allows a system administrator to define tables containing chains of rules that determine how network packets should be treated. Packets are processed by sequentially traversing rules in chains within the following tables:

- **Raw**: This is a default table that filters packets before any other table. It is mainly used to configure exemptions from connection tracking and is not used by security groups or FWaaS.
- **Filter**: This is a default table to filter packets.

- **NAT**: This is a default table used for network address translation.
- **Mangle**: This is a default table used for specialized packet alteration and is not used by security groups or FWaaS.

A rule in a chain can cause a jump to another chain, which in turn can jump to another chain and so on. This behavior can be repeated to whatever level of nesting is desired. If the traffic does not match the rules of a subchain, the system recalls the point at which the jump occurred and returns to this point for further processing. When iptables is enabled, every network packet arriving at or leaving an interface traverses at least one chain.

There are five default chains, and the origin of the packet determines which chain will be initially traversed. The five default chains include:

- PREROUTING: Packets will enter this chain before a routing decision is made. This chain is not used for security group rules but for the floating IP functionality within a router namespace. The PREROUTING chain is used by the raw, mangle, and NAT tables.
- INPUT: This is used when a packet is to be locally delivered to the host machine. The INPUT chain is used by the mangle and filter tables.
- FORWARD: All packets that are routed and not used for local delivery will traverse this chain. The FORWARD chain is used by the mangle and filter tables.
- OUTPUT: Packets sent from the host machine itself will traverse this chain. The OUTPUT chain is used by the raw, mangle, NAT, and filter tables.
- POSTROUTING: Packets will enter this chain when a routing decision has been made. This chain is not used for security group rules but for the floating IP functionality within a router namespace. The POSTROUTING chain is used by the mangle and NAT tables.

Each rule in a chain contains criteria that packets can be matched against. The rule may also contain a target, such as another chain or a verdict such as DROP or ACCEPT. As a packet traverses a chain, each rule is examined. If a rule does not match the packet, the packet is passed to the next rule. If a rule does match the packet, the rule takes the action indicated by the target or verdict.

Possible verdicts include:

- ACCEPT: The packet is accepted and sent to the application for processing
- DROP: The packet is dropped silently
- REJECT: The packet is dropped and an error message is sent to the sender
- LOG: the packet details are logged

- DNAT: This rewrites the destination IP of the packet
- SNAT: This rewrites the source IP of the packet
- RETURN: This returns the processing to the calling chain

The ACCEPT, DROP, and REJECT verdicts are often used by the filter table. Common rule criteria include:

- -p <protocol>: This matches protocols such as TCP, UDP, ICMP, and more
- -s <ip_addr>: This matches the source IP address
- -d <ip_addr>: This matches the destination IP address
- --sport: This matches the source port
- --dport: This matches the destination port
- -i <interface>: This matches the interface from which the packet entered
- -o <interface>: This matches the interface from which the packet exits

The difference in the application of iptables rules between security groups and FWaaS can be seen in further detail later in this chapter and in *Chapter 11, Firewall as a Service*.

For more information on iptables, visit the following resources:

- `http://bencane.com/2012/09/iptables-linux-firewall-rules-for-a-basic-web-server/`
- `https://help.ubuntu.com/community/IptablesHowTo`
- `http://rlworkman.net/howtos/iptables/iptables-tutorial.html`

Using ipset

In past OpenStack releases, for every security group referenced in a rule that was created, an exponential number of iptables rules were created that corresponded to each source and destination pair of addresses and ports. This behavior resulted in poor L2 agent performance as well as race conditions, where virtual machine instances were connected to the virtual bridge but unable to successfully connect to the network.

Beginning with the Juno release, the **ipset** extension to iptables is utilized in an attempt to reduce the number of iptables rules required by creating groups of addresses and ports that are stored efficiently for a fast lookup.

Without ipset, iptables rules that allow connections on port 80 to a set of web instances may resemble the following:

```
iptables -A INPUT -p tcp -d 1.1.1.1 --dport 80 -j ACCEPT
iptables -A INPUT -p tcp -d 2.2.2.2 --dport 80 -j ACCEPT
iptables -A INPUT -p tcp -d 3.3.3.3 --dport 80 -j ACCEPT
iptables -A INPUT -p tcp -d 4.4.4.4 --dport 80 -j ACCEPT
```

The preceding match syntax, -d x.x.x.x, means the "match packets whose destination address is x.x.x.x". To allow all four addresses, four separate iptables rules with four separate match specifications must be defined.

Alternatively, a combination of ipset and iptables commands can used to achieve the same result:

```
ipset -N webset iphash
ipset -A webset 1.1.1.1
ipset -A webset 2.2.2.2
ipset -A webset 3.3.3.3
ipset -A webset 4.4.4.4
iptables -A INPUT -p tcp -m set --match-set webset dst --dport 80 -j
ACCEPT
```

The ipset command creates a new set, webset, with four addresses. The iptables command references the set with --m set --match-set webset dst, which means "match packets whose destination matches an entry within the set named webset".

Using an ipset, only one rule is required to accomplish what took four rules before. The savings are small in this example, but as instances are added to security groups and security group rules are configured, the reduction in rules has a noticeable impact on performance and reliability.

Working with security groups

Security groups can be managed in either the Neutron CLI or the Horizon dashboard. Both methods offer a fairly comprehensive experience and are discussed in the following sections.

Managing security groups in the CLI

From within the Neutron command-line client, a number of commands can be used to manage security groups, including:

- security-group-create

- `security-group-delete`
- `security-group-list`
- `security-group-rule-create`
- `security-group-rule-delete`
- `security-group-rule-list`
- `security-group-rule-show`
- `security-group-show`
- `security-group-update`

Creating security groups in the CLI

To create a security group within the CLI, use the Neutron `security-group-create` command as follows:

Usage: `security-group-create [--tenant-id TENANT_ID]`

`[--description DESCRIPTION] NAME`

 By default, security groups in Neutron are prepopulated with two egress rules that allow all outbound traffic over IPv4 and IPv6. Ingress traffic from hosts outside of the associated group is not permitted by default.

Deleting security groups in the CLI

To delete a security group within the CLI, use the Neutron `security-group-delete` command as follows:

Usage: `security-group-delete SECURITY_GROUP`

The keyword, `SECURITY_GROUP`, can be the ID or name of the security group to delete.

 A security group must be removed from all ports before it can be deleted.

Listing security groups in the CLI

To obtain a listing of security groups within the CLI, use the Neutron `security-group-list` command as follows:

`Usage:     security-group-list`

The output returned includes the ID, name, and description of all security groups within the tenant where the command was run. If run as an administrator, all security groups across all tenants will be listed.

Showing the details of a security group in the CLI

To display the details of a security group, use the Neutron `security-group-show` command as follows:

`Usage:     security-group-show SECURITY_GROUP`

The keyword, `SECURITY_GROUP`, can be the ID or name of the security group to show. The output returned includes the description, ID, name, associated tenant ID, and the individual rules within the security group.

Updating security groups in the CLI

To update the attributes of a security group, use the Neutron `security-group-update` command as follows:

`Usage:     security-group-update [--description DESCRIPTION]`
`           [--name NAME]`

 It is not possible to change the name of the default security groups provided by Neutron.

Creating security group rules in the CLI

To create a security group rule, use the Neutron `security-group-rule-create` command as follows:

```
usage:     security-group-rule-create
           [--tenant-id TENANT_ID] [--direction {ingress,egress}]
           [--ethertype ETHERTYPE] [--protocol PROTOCOL]
           [--port-range-min PORT_RANGE_MIN]
           [--port-range-max PORT_RANGE_MAX]
```

```
[--remote-ip-prefix REMOTE_IP_PREFIX]
[--remote-group-id REMOTE_GROUP]
SECURITY_GROUP
```

The `--direction` flag is optional and allows you to specify the direction of traffic that should be affected. Specifying `ingress` means the rule applies to incoming traffic, while specifying `egress` means the rule applies to outgoing traffic from the instance. The default value is `ingress`.

The `--ethertype` flag is optional and allows you to specify whether the rule applies to the IPv4 or IPv6 traffic. The default value is `IPv4`.

The `--protocol` flag is optional and allows you to specify the type of traffic the rule applies to. Possible options include ICMP, TCP, UDP, or an IP protocol number.

The `--port-range-min` flag is optional and allows you to specify the starting port of a range of ports. If this option is specified, a protocol must also be defined.

The `--port-range-max` flag is optional and allows you to specify the ending port of a range of ports. If this option is specified, a protocol must also be defined.

The `--remote-ip-prefix` flag is optional and allows you to specify the source address or network the rule applies to. The address or network should be defined in the CIDR format.

The `--remote-group-id` flag is optional and allows you to specify the ID of a security group the rule should apply to rather than individual IP addresses or networks. For example, when creating a rule to allow inbound SQL traffic to database servers, you can specify the ID of a security group that application servers are a member of without having to specify their individual IP addresses.

The `SECURITY_GROUP` keyword is used to specify the ID of the security group that the rule should be placed in.

Deleting security group rules in the CLI

To delete a security group rule, use the Neutron `security-group-rule-delete` command as follows:

```
Usage:   security-group-rule-delete SECURITY_GROUP_RULE_ID
```

While it is possible to delete the rules within the default security group, it is not possible to delete the group itself.

Listing security group rules in the CLI

To list the security group rules within a security group, use the Neutron `security-group-rule-list` command as follows:

```
Usage:    security-group-rule-list
```

The output returned includes details of individual security group rules, such as their ID, associated security group, direction, protocol, remote IP prefix, and remote group name.

Showing the details of a security group rule in the CLI

To display the details of a particular security group rule, use the Neutron `security-group-rule-show` command as follows:

```
Usage:    security-group-rule-show SECURITY_GROUP_RULE_ID
```

The output returned includes the ID, direction, ethertype, port range, protocol, remote group IP, remote IP prefix, tenant ID, and associated security group ID of the specified security group rule.

Applying security groups to instances and ports in the CLI

Applying security groups to instances within the CLI is typically done at instance creation using `nova boot`, as follows:

```
nova boot --flavor <FLAVOR_ID> --image <IMAGE_ID> \
--nic net-id=<NETWORK_ID> --security-group <SECURITY_GROUP_ID> \
INSTANCE_NAME
```

Security groups can also be applied to running instances using either the Neutron `port-update` command or the Nova `add-secgroup` command. The following example demonstrates the use of `port-update` to apply security groups to a port:

```
neutron port-update <PORT_ID> --security-group <SECURITY_GROUP_ID>
```

 Using `port-update` to assign security groups to a port will overwrite the existing security group associations.

Multiple security groups can be associated with a Neutron port simultaneously. To apply multiple security groups to a port, use the `--security-group` flag before each security group, as follows:

```
neutron port-update <PORT_ID> \
--security-group <SECURITY_GROUP_ID1> \
--security-group <SECURITY_GROUP_ID2> \
--security-group <SECURITY_GROUP_ID3>
```

The following example demonstrates the use of the Nova `add-secgroup` command to apply a security group to all ports connected to an instance:

```
nova add-secgroup <INSTANCE_ID> <SECURITY_GROUP_ID>
```

Removing security groups from instances and ports in the CLI

To remove an individual security group rule, execute the Nova `remove-secgroup` command as shown in the following example:

```
nova remove-secgroup <INSTANCE_ID> <SECURITY_GROUP_ID>
```

To remove all security groups from a port, use the Neutron `port-update` command with the `--no-security-groups` flag, as shown in the following example:

```
neutron port-update <neutron_port_id> --no-security-groups
```

 It is not possible to remove single security groups from a port using the `port-update` command. All security groups should be removed from the port and then the select groups should be added back.

Implementing security group rules

In the following example, an instance named WEB1 will be created that acts as a web server running Apache on ports 80 and 443. To demonstrate how security group rules are implemented on a compute node, take note of the following WEB_SERVERS security group created with the Neutron security-group-create command:

```
root@controller01:~# neutron security-group-list
+--------------------------------------+-------------+------------------------------+
| id                                   | name        | description                  |
+--------------------------------------+-------------+------------------------------+
| 4decc566-7bd7-40bb-bd73-731a7a83f334 | default     | Default security group       |
| 60ca9b2c-dc87-40c7-a5ff-5e5037b08c56 | default     | Default security group       |
| b009d622-4a05-4ff1-a870-a3e9f22ff7b6 | WEB_SERVERS | Security group for web servers |
| c0c27f3d-cab1-4b2e-ad63-0339b3510d2f | default     | Default security group       |
+--------------------------------------+-------------+------------------------------+
```

Figure 6.3

The following screenshot shows two security group rules being added to the WEB_SERVERS security group using the security-group-rule-create command. The rules allow inbound connections on ports 80 and 443 from any remote host:

```
root@controller01:~# neutron security-group-rule-create --protocol tcp --port-range-min 80 \
> --port-range-max 80 --remote-ip-prefix 0.0.0.0/0 WEB_SERVERS
Created a new security_group_rule:
+-------------------+--------------------------------------+
| Field             | Value                                |
+-------------------+--------------------------------------+
| direction         | ingress                              |
| ethertype         | IPv4                                 |
| id                | 74e11bbb-19df-40cc-a84d-6c2a4fb7a10c |
| port_range_max    | 80                                   |
| port_range_min    | 80                                   |
| protocol          | tcp                                  |
| remote_group_id   |                                      |
| remote_ip_prefix  | 0.0.0.0/0                            |
| security_group_id | b009d622-4a05-4ff1-a870-a3e9f22ff7b6 |
| tenant_id         | 65ff4cf1a04846f1ab2bc1ff0efb1090     |
+-------------------+--------------------------------------+

root@controller01:~# neutron security-group-rule-create --protocol tcp --port-range-min 443 \
> --port-range-max 443 --remote-ip-prefix 0.0.0.0/0 WEB_SERVERS
Created a new security_group_rule:
+-------------------+--------------------------------------+
| Field             | Value                                |
+-------------------+--------------------------------------+
| direction         | ingress                              |
| ethertype         | IPv4                                 |
| id                | 0a7c00ef-5f65-4729-bdc5-34ff976f0927 |
| port_range_max    | 443                                  |
| port_range_min    | 443                                  |
| protocol          | tcp                                  |
| remote_group_id   |                                      |
| remote_ip_prefix  | 0.0.0.0/0                            |
| security_group_id | b009d622-4a05-4ff1-a870-a3e9f22ff7b6 |
| tenant_id         | 65ff4cf1a04846f1ab2bc1ff0efb1090     |
+-------------------+--------------------------------------+
```

Figure 6.4

Using the Neutron `port-update` command, the WEB_SERVERS security group can be applied to the Neutron port of the WEB1 instance, as shown in the following screenshot:

```
root@controller01:~# nova list
+--------------------------------------+------+--------+------------+-------------+-------------------+
| ID                                   | Name | Status | Task State | Power State | Networks          |
+--------------------------------------+------+--------+------------+-------------+-------------------+
| d92fea06-d71e-4009-bf87-d3dfcfc03333 | WEB1 | ACTIVE | -          | Running     | WEB_NET=10.30.0.3 |
+--------------------------------------+------+--------+------------+-------------+-------------------+

root@controller01:~# neutron port-list --device-id=d92fea06-d71e-4009-bf87-d3dfcfc03333 -c id
+--------------------------------------+
| id                                   |
+--------------------------------------+
| 6d7340c8-b1af-4cf0-b393-916a32acb18b |
+--------------------------------------+

root@controller01:~# neutron port-update 6d7340c8-b1af-4cf0-b393-916a32acb18b --security-group WEB_SERVERS
Updated port: 6d7340c8-b1af-4cf0-b393-916a32acb18b

root@controller01:~# neutron port-show 6d7340c8-b1af-4cf0-b393-916a32acb18b
+-----------------------+-----------------------------------------------------------------------------------+
| Field                 | Value                                                                             |
+-----------------------+-----------------------------------------------------------------------------------+
| admin_state_up        | True                                                                              |
| allowed_address_pairs |                                                                                   |
| binding:host_id       | compute02.learningneutron.com                                                     |
| binding:profile       | {}                                                                                |
| binding:vif_details   | {"port_filter": true}                                                             |
| binding:vif_type      | bridge                                                                            |
| binding:vnic_type     | normal                                                                            |
| device_id             | d92fea06-d71e-4009-bf87-d3dfcfc03333                                              |
| device_owner          | compute:None                                                                      |
| extra_dhcp_opts       |                                                                                   |
| fixed_ips             | {"subnet_id": "d5cbbcb6-f039-4364-b1db-0392cd232dd9", "ip_address": "10.30.0.3"}  |
| id                    | 6d7340c8-b1af-4cf0-b393-916a32acb18b                                              |
| mac_address           | fa:16:3e:a4:c3:f9                                                                 |
| name                  |                                                                                   |
| network_id            | ebea7ab6-93f3-45db-b44a-bf284bac54ac                                              |
| security_groups       | b009d622-4a05-4ff1-a870-a3e9f22ff7b6                                              |
| status                | ACTIVE                                                                            |
| tenant_id             | 65ff4cf1a04846f1ab2bc1ff0efb1090                                                  |
+-----------------------+-----------------------------------------------------------------------------------+
```

Figure 6.5

Once a security group is applied to the corresponding Neutron port of an instance, a series of iptables rules and chains are implemented on the compute node hosting the instance.

Stepping through the chains

The implementation of security group rules using iptables is similar in both LinuxBridge- and Open vSwitch-based environments. On `compute02`, which is a compute node running the LinuxBridge agent and hosting the instance, the iptables rules can be observed using the `iptables-save` command. For readability, only the `filter` table is shown in the following screenshot and some comments have been removed or truncated to fit the page:

```
# Generated by iptables-save v1.4.21 on Tue Oct 27 17:35:56 2015
*filter
:INPUT ACCEPT [44:3963]
:FORWARD ACCEPT [0:0]
:OUTPUT ACCEPT [33:4099]
:neutron-filter-top - [0:0]
:neutron-linuxbri-FORWARD - [0:0]
:neutron-linuxbri-INPUT - [0:0]
:neutron-linuxbri-OUTPUT - [0:0]
:neutron-linuxbri-i6d7340c8-b - [0:0]
:neutron-linuxbri-local - [0:0]
:neutron-linuxbri-o6d7340c8-b - [0:0]
:neutron-linuxbri-s6d7340c8-b - [0:0]
:neutron-linuxbri-sg-chain - [0:0]
:neutron-linuxbri-sg-fallback - [0:0]
-A INPUT -j neutron-linuxbri-INPUT
-A FORWARD -j neutron-filter-top
-A FORWARD -j neutron-linuxbri-FORWARD
-A OUTPUT -j neutron-filter-top
-A OUTPUT -j neutron-linuxbri-OUTPUT
-A neutron-filter-top -j neutron-linuxbri-local
-A neutron-linuxbri-FORWARD -m physdev --physdev-out tap6d7340c8-b1 --physdev-is-bridged  -j neutron-linuxbri-sg-chain
-A neutron-linuxbri-FORWARD -m physdev --physdev-in tap6d7340c8-b1 --physdev-is-bridged  -j neutron-linuxbri-sg-chain
-A neutron-linuxbri-INPUT -m physdev --physdev-in tap6d7340c8-b1 --physdev-is-bridged  -j neutron-linuxbri-o6d7340c8-b
-A neutron-linuxbri-i6d7340c8-b -m state --state INVALID -j DROP
-A neutron-linuxbri-i6d7340c8-b -m state --state RELATED,ESTABLISHED -j RETURN
-A neutron-linuxbri-i6d7340c8-b -s 10.30.0.2/32 -p udp -m udp --sport 67 --dport 68 -j RETURN
-A neutron-linuxbri-i6d7340c8-b -p tcp -m tcp --dport 443 -j RETURN
-A neutron-linuxbri-i6d7340c8-b -p tcp -m tcp --dport 80 -j RETURN
-A neutron-linuxbri-i6d7340c8-b -m comment --comment "Send unmatched traffic to the fallback chain." -j neutron-linuxbri-sg-fallback
-A neutron-linuxbri-o6d7340c8-b -p udp -m udp --sport 68 --dport 67 -m comment --comment "Allow DHCP client traffic." -j RETURN
-A neutron-linuxbri-o6d7340c8-b -j neutron-linuxbri-s6d7340c8-b
-A neutron-linuxbri-o6d7340c8-b -p udp -m udp --sport 67 --dport 68 -m comment --comment "Prevent DHCP Spoofing by VM." -j DROP
-A neutron-linuxbri-o6d7340c8-b -m state --state INVALID -j DROP
-A neutron-linuxbri-o6d7340c8-b -m state --state RELATED,ESTABLISHED -j RETURN
-A neutron-linuxbri-o6d7340c8-b -j RETURN
-A neutron-linuxbri-o6d7340c8-b -m comment --comment "Send unmatched traffic to the fallback chain." -j neutron-linuxbri-sg-fallback
-A neutron-linuxbri-s6d7340c8-b -s 10.30.0.3/32 -m mac --mac-source FA:16:3E:A4:C3:F9 -j RETURN
-A neutron-linuxbri-s6d7340c8-b -m comment --comment "Drop traffic without an IP/MAC allow rule." -j DROP
-A neutron-linuxbri-sg-chain -m physdev --physdev-out tap6d7340c8-b1 --physdev-is-bridged -j neutron-linuxbri-i6d7340c8-b
-A neutron-linuxbri-sg-chain -m physdev --physdev-in tap6d7340c8-b1 --physdev-is-bridged -j neutron-linuxbri-o6d7340c8-b
-A neutron-linuxbri-sg-chain -j ACCEPT
-A neutron-linuxbri-sg-fallback -m comment --comment "Default drop rule for unmatched traffic." -j DROP
COMMIT
# Completed on Tue Oct 27 17:35:56 2015
```

Figure 6.6

Network traffic to or from an instance will first traverse the FORWARD chain, as follows:

```
-A FORWARD -j neutron-filter-top
-A FORWARD -j neutron-linuxbri-FORWARD
```

The first rule causes iptables to jump to the `neutron-filter-top` chain for further processing:

```
-A neutron-filter-top -j neutron-linuxbri-local
```

From here, iptables jumps to the `neutron-linuxbri-local` chain for further processing. As there are no rules defined in this chain, iptables returns to the calling chain, `neutron-filter-top`. Once all rules are processed, iptables returns to the previous calling chain, `FORWARD`.

The next rule in the `FORWARD` chain that is processed is as follows:

```
-A FORWARD -j neutron-linuxbri-FORWARD
```

The mentioned rule causes iptables to jump to the `neutron-linuxbri-FORWARD` chain, as follows:

```
-A neutron-linuxbri-FORWARD -m physdev --physdev-out tap6d7340c8-b1 --physdev-is-bridged -j neutron-linuxbri-sg-chain
-A neutron-linuxbri-FORWARD -m physdev --physdev-in tap6d7340c8-b1 --physdev-is-bridged -j neutron-linuxbri-sg-chain
```

Figure 6.7

The `-m` flag, followed by `physdev`, is a directive to iptables to use an extended packet matching a module that supports the devices enslaved to a bridge device.

Remember that when the LinuxBridge agent is used, tap interfaces for instances are connected to network bridges that are prefaced with `brq-*`. When the OVS agent is used, the tap interfaces are connected to their own Linux bridge, prefaced with `qbr-*`.

The packet will match one of the two rules based on the direction that the packet is heading through the interface. In either case, iptables jumps to the `neutron-linuxbri-sg-chain` chain, as follows:

```
-A neutron-linuxbri-sg-chain -m physdev --physdev-out tap6d7340c8-b1 --physdev-is-bridged -j neutron-linuxbri-i6d7340c8-b
-A neutron-linuxbri-sg-chain -m physdev --physdev-in tap6d7340c8-b1 --physdev-is-bridged -j neutron-linuxbri-o6d7340c8-b
-A neutron-linuxbri-sg-chain -j ACCEPT
```

Figure 6.8

The direction of the packet will again dictate which rule is matched. Traffic entering the instance through the `tap6d7340c8-b1` interface will be processed by the `neutron-linuxbri-i6d7340c8-b` chain, as follows:

```
-A neutron-linuxbri-i6d7340c8-b -m state --state INVALID -j DROP
-A neutron-linuxbri-i6d7340c8-b -m state --state RELATED,ESTABLISHED -j RETURN
-A neutron-linuxbri-i6d7340c8-b -s 10.30.0.2/32 -p udp -m udp --sport 67 --dport 68 -j RETURN
-A neutron-linuxbri-i6d7340c8-b -p tcp -m tcp --dport 443 -j RETURN
-A neutron-linuxbri-i6d7340c8-b -p tcp -m tcp --dport 80 -j RETURN
-A neutron-linuxbri-i6d7340c8-b -j neutron-linuxbri-sg-fallback
```

Figure 6.9

The name of a security group chain corresponds to the first nine characters of the UUID of the Neutron port with which it is associated.

In the mentioned rule, iptables uses the `state` module to determine the state of the packet. Combined with connection tracking, iptables is able to track the connection and determine the states of the packet—whether it is INVALID, NEW, RELATED, or ESTABLISHED. The state of the packet results in an appropriate action being taken. The `-s` flag instructs iptables to match the source address of the packet against the address defined in the rule. The UDP rule allows for inbound DHCP response traffic from the DHCP server at `10.30.0.2/32`. Traffic not matched by any rule is dropped by the `neutron-linuxbri-sg-fallback` chain, as follows:

```
-A neutron-linuxbri-sg-fallback -j DROP
```

Traffic exiting the instance through the `tap6d7340c8-b1` interface is processed by the `neutron-linuxbri-o6d7340c8-b` chain, as follows:

```
-A neutron-linuxbri-o6d7340c8-b -p udp -m udp --sport 68 --dport 67 -j RETURN
-A neutron-linuxbri-o6d7340c8-b -j neutron-linuxbri-s6d7340c8-b
-A neutron-linuxbri-o6d7340c8-b -p udp -m udp --sport 67 --dport 68 -j DROP
-A neutron-linuxbri-o6d7340c8-b -m state --state INVALID -j DROP
-A neutron-linuxbri-o6d7340c8-b -m state --state RELATED,ESTABLISHED -j RETURN
-A neutron-linuxbri-o6d7340c8-b -j RETURN
-A neutron-linuxbri-o6d7340c8-b -j neutron-linuxbri-sg-fallback
```

Figure 6.10

The first UDP rule allows the instance to send the DHCPDISCOVER and DHCPREQUEST broadcast packets on UDP port `67`. All other traffic is then processed by the `neutron-linuxbri-s6d7340c8-b` chain, as follows:

```
-A neutron-linuxbri-s6d7340c8-b -s 10.30.0.3/32 -m mac --mac-source FA:16:3E:A4:C3:F9 -j RETURN
-A neutron-linuxbri-s6d7340c8-b -m comment --comment "Drop traffic without an IP/MAC allow rule." -j DROP
```

Figure 6.11

The preceding rule prevents an instance from performing IP and MAC address spoofing. Any traffic exiting the `tap6d7340c8-b1` interface must be sourced from `10.30.0.3/32` and the MAC address, `FA:16:3E:A4:C3:F9`. To permit traffic from additional IP or MAC addresses, use the Neutron `allowed-address-pairs` extension, as discussed in *Chapter 5, Creating Networks with Neutron*.

When traffic is returned to the calling chain, the next UDP rule prohibits the instance from acting as a rogue DHCP server, as shown in the following screenshot:

```
-A neutron-linuxbri-o6d7340c8-b -p udp -m udp --sport 67 --dport 68 -j DROP
```

Figure 6.12

Further processing includes verifying the state of the packet and performing the appropriate action. Traffic eventually returns to the `neutron-linuxbri-sg-chain` calling chain, where it is allowed through, as follows:

```
-A neutron-linuxbri-sg-chain -j ACCEPT
```

Working with security groups in the dashboard

Within the Horizon dashboard, security groups are managed within the **Access & Security** section under the **Compute** tab:

Figure 6.13

Creating a security group

To create a security group, perform the following steps.

Click on the **Create Security Group** button in the upper right-hand corner of the screen. A window will appear that will allow you to create a security group, which is similar to the following screenshot:

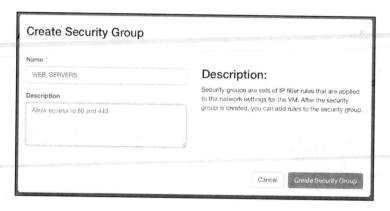

Figure 6.14

The **Name** field is required. When you are ready to proceed, click on the blue **Create Security Group** button to create the security group.

Managing security group rules

Once created, you will be returned to the **Access & Security** section, where you can add rules to the security group by clicking on the **Manage Rules** button of the corresponding group:

Figure 6.15

To delete a rule, click on the red **Delete Rule** button next to the corresponding security group rule. To add a rule, click on the **Add Rule** button in the upper right-hand corner:

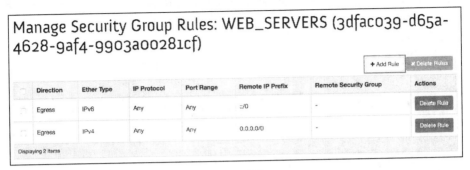

Figure 6.16

A window will appear that allows you to create rules. Within the rule list, you can choose from a predefined list of protocols or create a custom rule, as follows:

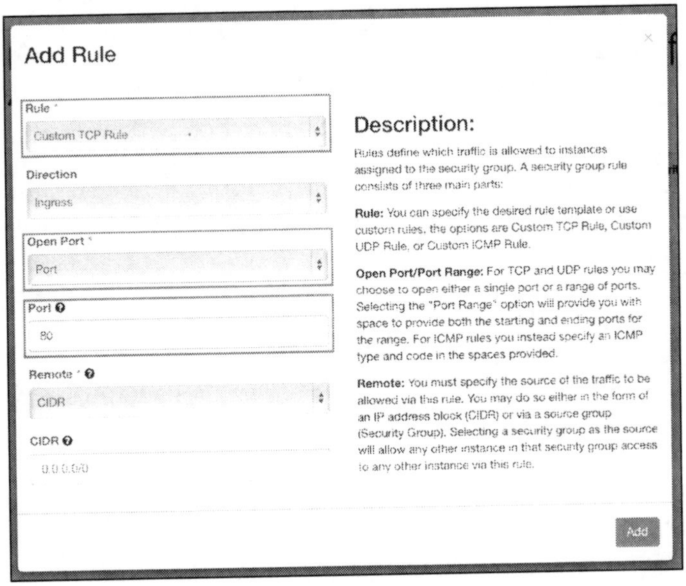

Figure 6.17

To complete the rule creation, click on the blue **Add** button.

Applying security groups to instances

To apply a security group to an instance, return to the **Instances** section of the **Compute** tab. Click on the arrow under the **Actions** menu next to the instance and select **Edit Security Groups**:

Figure 6.18

A window will appear that allows you to apply or remove security groups from an instance.

Hit the blue plus sign next to the group to apply it to an instance:

Figure 6.19

Once clicked, the group will move to the **Instance Security Groups** column. Click on the blue **Save** button to apply the changes:

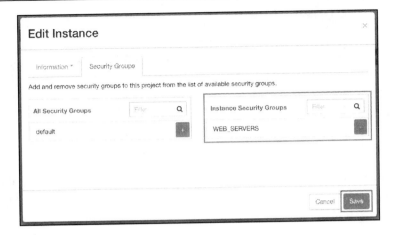

Figure 6.20

Disabling port security

By default, Neutron applies antispoofing rules to all ports to ensure that unexpected or undesired traffic cannot originate from or pass through a port. This includes rules that prohibit instances from running DHCP servers or acting as routers. To address the latter, the `allowed-address-pairs` extension can be used to allow additional subnets and MAC addresses through the port. However, additional functionality may be required that cannot be addressed by the `allowed-address-pairs` extension.

In Kilo, the `port security` extension was introduced for the ML2 plugin that allows all packet filtering to be disabled on a port. This is especially useful when deploying instances for NFV purposes. The `port security` extension requires additional configuration, which will be discussed in the following sections.

Configuring Neutron

To enable the `port security` extension, edit the ML2 configuration file on the controller node at `/etc/neutron/plugins/ml2/ml2_conf.ini`, and add the following to the `[ml2]` section:

```
[ml2]
...
extension_drivers = port_security
```

Restart the `neutron-server` service for changes to take effect:

```
# service neutron-server restart
```

Issues with enabling the port security extension

When the `port security` extension is enabled after networks are already created, users may find issues interacting with the Neutron and Nova API due to the following bug:

```
https://bugs.launchpad.net/neutron/+bug/1461519
```

To work around this bug, some changes may need to be made to the database to update existing tables and entries to support the port security functionality.

Using the `mysql` client, update the Neutron database using the following commands. When prompted for the root password, use `openstack`, as follows:

 # mysql -u root -p

Enter the following SQL statements at the `MariaDB [(none)] >` prompt:

```
use neutron;
INSERT INTO networksecuritybindings (network_id,
  port_security_enabled) SELECT id, True FROM networks
  WHERE id NOT IN (SELECT network_id FROM
  networksecuritybindings);
INSERT INTO portsecuritybindings (port_id,
  port_security_enabled) SELECT id, True FROM ports
  WHERE id NOT IN (SELECT port_id FROM
  portsecuritybindings);
exit;
```

Once these changes are made, it should no longer be necessary to run these commands in the future as long as the `port security` extension remains enabled.

Disabling port security for all ports on a network

Port security can be disabled on all ports connected to a particular network by setting the `port_security_enabled` attribute to `false` during network creation:

```
root@controller01:~# neutron net-create TENANT_NET2 --port-security-enabled=false
Created a new network:
+-----------------------------+---------------------------------------------+
| Field                       | Value                                       |
+-----------------------------+---------------------------------------------+
| admin_state_up              | True                                        |
| id                          | c1abc39c-498e-4cc9-ba75-c7ca53836e5d        |
| mtu                         | 0                                           |
| name                        | TENANT_NET2                                 |
| port_security_enabled       | False                                       |
| provider:network_type       | vxlan                                       |
| provider:physical_network   |                                             |
| provider:segmentation_id    | 37                                          |
| router:external             | False                                       |
| shared                      | False                                       |
| status                      | ACTIVE                                      |
| subnets                     |                                             |
| tenant_id                   | da6c995d9f834090bd7a00d13d40b817            |
+-----------------------------+---------------------------------------------+
```

Figure 6.21

When a port is created and attached to the network, its port_security_enabled attribute will be set to false automatically:

```
root@controller01:~# neutron port-create TENANT_NET2
Created a new port:
+-------------------------+-------------------------------------------+
| Field                   | Value                                     |
+-------------------------+-------------------------------------------+
| admin_state_up          | True                                      |
| allowed_address_pairs   |                                           |
| binding:host_id         |                                           |
| binding:profile         | {}                                        |
| binding:vif_details     | {}                                        |
| binding:vif_type        | unbound                                   |
| binding:vnic_type       | normal                                    |
| device_id               |                                           |
| device_owner            |                                           |
| fixed_ips               |                                           |
| id                      | 86b54fbd-16a5-40cf-b052-14fb4ec3a651      |
| mac_address             | fa:16:3e:c4:fd:ec                         |
| name                    |                                           |
| network_id              | c1abc39c-498e-4cc9-ba75-c7ca53836e5d      |
| port_security_enabled   | False                                     |
| security_groups         |                                           |
| status                  | DOWN                                      |
| tenant_id               | da6c995d9f834090bd7a00d13d40b817          |
+-------------------------+-------------------------------------------+
```

Figure 6.22

Due to limitations with the implementation of the port security extension, an instance cannot be booted with a port or network that does not have port security enabled. Instead, the port must be attached to a running instance. Once attached, only a handful of iptables rules are implemented on the respective compute node, as in the following screenshot:

```
root@compute02:~# iptables-save | grep 86b54fbd-16
-A neutron-openvswi-FORWARD -m physdev --physdev-out tap86b54fbd-16 --physdev-is-bridged -m comment --comment "Accept all packets when port security is disabled." -j ACCEPT
-A neutron-openvswi-FORWARD -m physdev --physdev-in tap86b54fbd-16 --physdev-is-bridged -m comment --comment "Accept all packets when port security is disabled." -j ACCEPT
-A neutron-openvswi-INPUT -m physdev --physdev-in tap86b54fbd-16 --physdev-is-bridged -m comment --comment "Accept all packets when port security is disabled." -j ACCEPT
```

Figure 6.23

The rules effectively allow *all* traffic to pass through a port. It is important to know that when port security is disabled on a port, the API will not allow the port to be associated with any security group. Disabling port security means that any filtering must be implemented within the guest operating system.

Disabling port security on an individual port

Port security can be disabled on an individual port by setting the port_security_ enabled attribute to false during the creation or update of a port. To do so requires that no security groups be associated with the port; otherwise, the attempt will result in an error.

The following screenshot demonstrates port security being disabled on an individual port despite port security being enabled on the network:

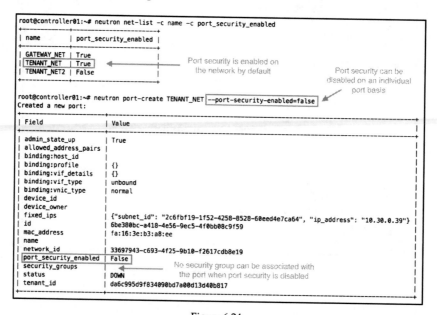

Figure 6.24

Summary

Security groups are fundamental to limiting access to Neutron ports and instances and allow users to create ingress and egress rules that allow traffic from specific addresses, ports, protocols, and even other security groups. It is important to keep in mind that security group rules can only be constructed to *allow* traffic as all traffic is denied by default in both directions—ingress and egress.

Using the reference plugin, Neutron converts security group rules to iptables rules that are applied on individual compute nodes and filter traffic as it passes through the virtual switches. No modifications are made to the instances themselves and firewalls within the instances can provide additional filtering if required.

In the next chapter, we will begin to look at Neutron routers, starting with the standalone variety. We will examine their involvement in routing traffic between tenant networks and cover the configuration and use of floating IPs to provide external connectivity to instances. The configuration of highly available and distributed virtual routers will be covered in later chapters.

7
Creating Standalone Routers with Neutron

Neutron enables users to build routers that provide connectivity between the networks created by users and external networks. In a reference implementation, the Neutron L3 agent provides IP routing and network address translation for virtual machine instances within a cloud by utilizing network namespaces to provide isolated routing instances. By creating networks and attaching them to routers, users can expose connected virtual machine instances and their applications to the Internet and other remote networks.

Prior to the Juno release of OpenStack, users were limited to building standalone routers that acted as single points of failure in the network stack. Since the advent of distributed virtual routers in Juno and beyond, standalone routers are now referred to as *legacy routers*.

In previous chapters, we discovered the difference between provider and tenant networks and demonstrated the process of booting an instance and connecting it to a network. In this chapter, we will work through the following:

- Installing and configuring the L3 agent
- Creating an external provider network
- Creating a standalone router in the CLI and Horizon dashboard
- Attaching a router to both external and tenant networks
- Booting instances
- Demonstrating instance and namespace connectivity using LinuxBridge
- Demonstrating SNAT and DNAT functionality provided by floating IPs

Routing traffic in a cloud

In a reference implementation, virtual routers created in Neutron exist as network namespaces that reside on nodes running the `neutron-l3-agent` service. A virtual router is often connected to a single external provider network and one or more tenant networks. Router interfaces connected to these networks can be identified as:

- qg – gateway interface
- qr – router interface

Neutron routers are responsible for providing inbound and outbound connectivity to and from tenant networks through the use of **network address translation** or **NAT**. The following diagram shows how a router namespace may be connected to multiple bridges in a LinuxBridge implementation:

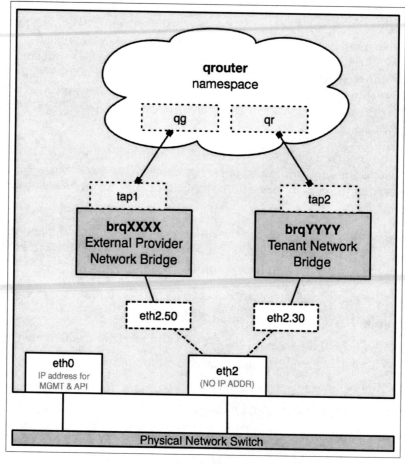

Figure 7.1

The preceding diagram demonstrates a Neutron router connected to multiple bridges in a LinuxBridge-based implementation. Traffic from tenant networks is routed in from qr interfaces and out the qg interface onto the external network. Routing tables within the namespace dictate how traffic is routed, and iptables rules dictate how traffic will be translated if necessary.

More information on creating and configuring standalone Neutron routers, along with examples on how they are connected to a network and provide connectivity to instances, can be found later in this chapter.

Installing and configuring the Neutron L3 agent

To install the Neutron L3 agent, run the following command on the controller node:

```
# apt-get install neutron-l3-agent
```

Neutron stores the L3 agent configuration in the /etc/neutron/l3_agent.ini file. The most common configuration options will be covered in the next section.

Defining an interface driver

The Neutron L3 agent must be configured to use an interface driver that corresponds to the chosen mechanism driver. In a reference implementation, that can be either the LinuxBridge or Open vSwitch drivers.

On the controller node, update the Neutron L3 agent configuration file at /etc/neutron/l3_agent.ini and specify one of the following interface drivers.

For LinuxBridge, use the following settings:

```
[DEFAULT]
...
interface_driver = neutron.agent.linux.interface.BridgeInterfaceDriver
```

For Open vSwitch, run the following settings:

```
[DEFAULT]
...
interface_driver = neutron.agent.linux.interface.OVSInterfaceDriver
```

Setting the external bridge

The `external_network_bridge` configuration option defines a single bridge on the host that can be used to connect external router interfaces to the network. When set, each L3 agent can be associated with no more than a single external network, and all routers are restricted to using the same external provider network. To allow the use of multiple external networks, both `external_network_bridge` and `gateway_external_network_id` must be left unset.

The default value of `external_network_bridge` is `br-ex`, which is a bridge expected to be configured manually and dedicated to a single external network. When this option is configured, Neutron places external (`qg`) router interfaces in the bridge but does not manage the creation of tagged or untagged interfaces or flows that would be used to connect to the physical infrastructure. Instead, the cloud administrator is expected to manually connect the respective interface to the bridge. Provider attributes of the external network created within Neutron, including the segmentation ID, network type, and provider bridge label, are ignored.

When left unset, Neutron treats external provider networks similarly to any other network, in that the user or administrator is not expected to make manual changes to the underlying network configuration. The respective agent is responsible for creating bridges, interfaces, and/or flow rules that allow routers to communicate with the physical infrastructure and external gateway devices.

On the controller node, set the `external_network_bridge` configuration option to an unset value in the L3 agent configuration file using the following settings:

```
[DEFAULT]
...
external_network_bridge =
```

Setting the external network

An external network connected to a router is one that not only provides external connectivity to the router and the instances behind it, but also serves as the network from which floating IPs are derived. In Havana, an L3 agent can be associated with only *one* external network at a time. In Icehouse and beyond, L3 agents are capable of supporting multiple external networks; to allow this, both `external_network_bridge` and `gateway_external_network_id` values must be left unset.

To be eligible to serve as an external network, a provider network must have its `router:external` attribute set to `true`. In Havana, if more than one provider network has the attribute set to `true`, the `gateway_external_network_id` configuration option must be used to associate a particular external network to the agent.

To define a specific external network, configure the `gateway_external_network_id` option, as in the following command:

```
gateway_external_network_id = <UUID of eligible provider network>
```

The default configuration contains an empty or unset value and is sufficient for most environments.

 Improvements to Neutron and L3 agent functionality in the last few releases have all but deprecated the use of `external_network_bridge` and `gateway_external_network_id` in most environments. Until the options are fully deprecated or defaulted to more useful values, it is important to understand how they should be configured to avoid issues in the environment.

Enabling router namespace deletion

By default, the Neutron L3 agent does not delete network namespaces when a router is deleted due to a bug found in older releases of the iproute2 utility. In modern operating systems, including the latest Ubuntu 14.04 LTS version discussed in this book, the `router_delete_namespaces` option can be set to `true`. Update the value from `false` to `true` in the L3 agent configuration file at `/etc/neutron/l3_agent.ini` according to the following example:

```
[DEFAULT]
...
router_delete_namespaces = true
```

Enabling the metadata proxy

When Neutron routers are used as the gateway for instances, requests for metadata are proxied by the router and forwarded to the Nova metadata service. This feature is enabled by default and can be disabled by setting the `enable_metadata_proxy` value to `false` in the `l3_agent.ini` configuration file and uncommenting the line. For this environment, leave the setting at its default `true` value.

Setting the agent mode

By default, the Neutron L3 agent works in legacy mode, which means that the L3 agent is deployed on a centralized node responsible for networking services. The default value for `agent_mode` is `legacy`, which will remain unchanged for the remainder of this chapter.

Restarting the Neutron L3 agent

After making changes to the configuration of the Neutron L3 agent, issue the following command on the controller node to restart the agent:

```
# service neutron-l3-agent restart
```

Verify that the agent is running through the following command:

```
# service neutron-l3-agent status
```

The service should return a similar output to that shown here:

```
root@controller01:~# service neutron-l3-agent status
neutron-l3-agent start/running, process 28332
```

If the service remains stopped, troubleshoot any errors that may be indicated in the /var/log/neutron/l3-agent.log log file.

Router management in the CLI

Neutron offers a number of commands that can be used to create and manage routers. The primary commands associated with router management include:

- `router-create`
- `router-delete`
- `router-gateway-clear`
- `router-gateway-set`
- `router-interface-add`
- `router-interface-delete`
- `router-list`
- `router-list-on-l3-agent`
- `router-port-list`
- `router-show`
- `router-update`

Creating routers in the CLI

Routers in Neutron are associated with projects or tenants and can only be managed by users within this tenant. Unlike networks, routers cannot be shared among tenants. However, shared networks can be attached to routers and potentially route traffic between different tenants. As an administrator, you can associate routers with tenants during the router creation process.

To create a standalone router in legacy mode, use the Neutron `router-create` command, as follows:

```
usage:    router-create [--tenant-id TENANT_ID] [--admin-state-down]
          NAME
```

The router will be created without any interfaces attached and will immediately be scheduled to an L3 agent. A corresponding network namespace should be visible on the node hosting the L3 agent.

Working with router interfaces in the CLI

Standalone Neutron routers have two types of interfaces: gateway and internal. The gateway interface of a Neutron router is analogous to the WAN interface of a physical router. It is an interface connected to an upstream device that provides connectivity to external resources. The internal interfaces of Neutron routers are analogous to the LAN interfaces of physical routers. Internal interfaces are connected to tenant networks and often serve as the gateway or next hop for instances in these networks.

Attaching internal interfaces to routers

To create an internal router interface and attach it to a subnet, use the Neutron `router-interface-add` command, as follows:

```
usage:    router-interface-add ROUTER INTERFACE
```

The `INTERFACE` keyword represents a subnet or port to be attached to the router. When an ID is specified without a hint to indicate whether it is a subnet or port ID, Neutron assumes that the ID is of a subnet. Neutron assigns the gateway IP of the subnet to the router when creating the `qr` interface and corresponding port. Instead of specifying a subnet, you can use `port=<portid>` to specify an existing port. A Neutron router can only have one interface in a subnet, but it can be attached to multiple subnets simultaneously. The L3 agent is responsible for connecting interfaces within the router namespace to the proper bridges on the host.

In Neutron, a network may contain multiple subnets. A router must be connected to all subnets in a network to properly route traffic for this network.

Attaching a gateway interface to a router

The external interface of a Neutron router is referred to as the gateway interface. A router is limited to a single gateway interface. To be eligible for use as an external network for router gateway interfaces, a provider network must have its `router:external` attribute set to `true`.

To attach a gateway interface to a router, use the Neutron `router-gateway-set` command, as shown here:

```
usage:    router-gateway-set [--disable-snat]
          ROUTER EXTERNAL-NETWORK
```

By default, Neutron routers perform **source network address translation**, or **SNAT**, on all traffic from instances that lack floating IPs. NAT and SNAT are covered in more detail later in this chapter. To disable this functionality, use the `--disable-snat` flag when using the `router-gateway-set` command.

Listing the interfaces attached to routers

To list the interfaces attached to routers, use the Neutron `router-port-list` command, as follows:

```
usage:    router-port-list ROUTER
```

The returned output includes the Neutron port ID, MAC address, IP address, and associated subnet of all attached interfaces.

Deleting internal interfaces

To delete an internal interface from a router, use the Neutron `router-interface-delete` command, as shown here:

```
usage:    router-interface-delete ROUTER INTERFACE
```

The INTERFACE keyword represents a subnet or port to be deleted from the router. When an ID is specified without a hint to indicate whether it is a subnet or port ID, Neutron assumes that the ID is of a subnet and defaults to deleting the interface associated with the subnet. If port=<portid> is specified as the interface, Neutron removes the router interface associated with the port and deletes the port. In either case, deleting an interface from a router results in the associated Neutron port being removed from the database.

Clearing the gateway interface

Gateway interfaces cannot be removed from a router using the router-interface-delete command. Instead, the router-gateway-clear command must be used.

To clear the gateway of a router, use the Neutron router-gateway-clear command, as follows:

```
usage:    router-gateway-clear ROUTER
```

Neutron includes checks that prohibit the clearing of a gateway interface in the event that floating IPs are associated with the router.

Listing routers in the CLI

To display a list of existing routers, use the Neutron router-list command, as shown here:

```
usage:    router-list [--tenant-id TENANT_ID]
```

The returned output includes the router ID, name, external gateway network, and SNAT state. Two additional attributes, distributed and ha, are used to identify the router as being highly available. For legacy routers, both attributes will be set to false.

Users only see routers that exist in their tenant or project. When router-list is executed by an administrator, Neutron returns a listing of all routers across all tenants, unless a tenant ID is specified.

Displaying router attributes in the CLI

To display the attributes of a router, use the following Neutron `router-show` command:

```
usage:    neutron router-show ROUTER
```

Among the items that the output returns are the admin state, external network, SNAT state, and tenant ID associated with the router. Two additional attributes, `distributed` and `ha`, are used to identify the router as being highly available. For legacy routers, both attributes will be set to `false`.

Updating router attributes in the CLI

To update the attributes of a router, use the Neutron `router-update` command, as shown here:

```
usage:    router-update ROUTER [--admin-state-up]

          [--name NAME]

          [--routes type=dict list=true destination=<network/
          cidr>,nexthop=<nexthop_addr>]
```

The `admin-state-up` attribute is a Boolean that, when set to `false`, does not allow Neutron to update interfaces within the router. This includes not adding floating IPs or additional internal interfaces to the router. Setting the value to `true` will allow queued changes to be applied.

The `routes` option allows you to add static routes to the routing table of a Neutron router. To add multiple routes, simply separate multiple destination and nexthop pairs with a space.

Deleting routers in the CLI

To delete a router, use the Neutron `router-delete` command, as follows:

```
usage:    router-delete ROUTER
```

Before a router can be deleted, all floating IPs and internal interfaces associated with the router must be unassociated or deleted.

Network address translation

Network address translation, or **NAT**, is a networking concept that was developed in the early 1990s in response to the rapid depletion of IP addresses throughout the world. Prior to NAT, every host connected to the Internet had a unique IP address.

Legacy routers support two types of NAT:

- One-to-one NAT
- Many-to-one NAT

One-to-one NAT is a method in which one IP address is directly mapped to another. Commonly referred to as static NAT, one-to-one NAT is often used to map a unique public address to a privately addressed host. Floating IPs utilize one-to-one NAT concepts.

Many-to-one NAT is a method in which multiple addresses are mapped to a single address. Many-to-one NAT employs the use of port address translation, or PAT. Neutron uses PAT to provide external access to instances behind the router when floating IPs are not assigned.

For more information on network address translation, please visit Wikipedia at `http://en.wikipedia.org/wiki/Network_address_translation`.

Floating IP addresses

Tenant networks, when attached to a Neutron router, often utilize the router as their default gateway. By default, when a router receives traffic from an instance and routes it upstream, the router performs a port address translation and modifies the source address of the packet to appear as its own external interface address. When the translation occurs, the ephemeral source port is mapped to the original client address in a table that is referred to when the response packet is received. This ensures that the packet can be routed upstream and returned to the router, where the packet is modified and returned to the instance that initiated the connection. Neutron refers to this type of behavior as **source NAT**.

When users require direct inbound access to instances, a floating IP address can be utilized. A **floating IP** address in OpenStack is a one-to-one static NAT that maps an external address from an external network to an internal address from a tenant network. This method of NAT allows instances to be accessible from remote networks, such as the Internet. Floating IP addresses are configured on the external interface of the router, which serves as a gateway for the instance and is then responsible for modifying both the source and destination address of packets, depending on their direction.

Floating IP management

Neutron offers a number of commands that can be used to create and manage floating IPs. The primary commands associated with floating IPs include:

- `floatingip-associate`
- `floatingip-create`
- `floatingip-delete`
- `floatingip-disassociate`
- `floatingip-list`
- `floatingip-show`

Creating floating IPs in the CLI

If you recall from previous chapters, IP addresses are not assigned directly to instances. Instead, an IP address is associated with a Neutron port, and this port is logically mapped to an instance or other network resource.

When a floating IP is created, it must be associated with a Neutron port. To create a floating IP from within the CLI, use the following Neutron `floatingip-create` command:

```
usage:    floatingip-create [--tenant-id TENANT_ID]
          [--port-id PORT_ID] [--fixed-ip-address FIXED_IP_ADDRESS]
          [--floating-ip-address FLOATING_IP_ADDRESS]
          FLOATING_NETWORK
```

Floating IP addresses can only be used within the tenant or project in which they were created. Using the `--tenant-id` option, an administrator is able to specify the tenant associated with the floating IP.

By specifying a port ID with the `--port-id` option, it is possible to immediately associate a floating IP with a Neutron port upon creation.

As a port can have multiple IP addresses associated with it, it may be necessary to define a specific fixed IP to associate the floating IP with. Use the `--fixed-ip-address` option to specify the fixed IP address that should be associated with the floating IP.

In previous releases of OpenStack, floating IPs were automatically assigned from the allocation pool of the external network. From Kilo onward, it is possible to create a floating IP using a specified address. Use the `--floating-ip-address` option to specify a particular address from the external network to be used as a floating IP.

Associating floating IPs with ports in the CLI

Once a floating IP has been created, it is available for use to any user within the tenant or project that created it. To associate a floating IP with an instance, it is first necessary to determine the Neutron port that is associated with the fixed IP of the instance.

The port ID associated with the fixed IP address of an instance can be determined in a couple of different ways. For example, the port ID of a device whose IP address is 10.30.0.2 can be determined in the following way:

```
# neutron port-list --fixed-ips ip_address=10.30.0.3
```

```
root@controller01:~# neutron port-list --fixed-ips ip_address=10.30.0.3
+--------------------------------------+------+-------------------+--------------------------------------------------------------------------------------+
| id                                   | name | mac_address       | fixed_ips                                                                            |
+--------------------------------------+------+-------------------+--------------------------------------------------------------------------------------+
| c1372dab-6362-48a6-892d-2c96f1cadf67 |      | fa:16:3e:15:63:2a | {"subnet_id": "7bfbc3b0-959c-4e60-bab0-7adb1100ca30", "ip_address": "10.30.0.3"} |
+--------------------------------------+------+-------------------+--------------------------------------------------------------------------------------+
```

Figure 7.2

Alternatively, if you know the ID of an instance, you can filter the output of neutron port-list to return the specific ports related to this instance.

For example, the ports of an instance whose ID is b00335cb-8c7e-4fc6-8115-a9d650801007 can be determined in the following way:

```
# neutron port-list --device_id=b00335cb-8c7e-4fc6-8115-a9d650801007
```

```
root@controller01:~# neutron port-list --device_id=b00335cb-8c7e-4fc6-8115-a9d650801007
+--------------------------------------+------+-------------------+--------------------------------------------------------------------------------------+
| id                                   | name | mac_address       | fixed_ips                                                                            |
+--------------------------------------+------+-------------------+--------------------------------------------------------------------------------------+
| c1372dab-6362-48a6-892d-2c96f1cadf67 |      | fa:16:3e:15:63:2a | {"subnet_id": "7bfbc3b0-959c-4e60-bab0-7adb1100ca30", "ip_address": "10.30.0.3"} |
+--------------------------------------+------+-------------------+--------------------------------------------------------------------------------------+
```

Figure 7.3

Once the port ID has been determined, use the following Neutron floatingip-associate command to associate the floating IP with the port:

```
usage:    floatingip-associate
          [--fixed-ip-address FIXED_IP_ADDRESS]
          FLOATINGIP_ID PORT
```

Using the preceding port ID and a floating IP whose ID is `da54d6a2-b8d4-4a08-91bf-c33fb2bb4ab5`, the `floatingip-associate` command can be used to associate the floating IP with the port, as shown in the following figure:

```
root@controller01:~# neutron floatingip-list
+--------------------------------------+-----------------+---------------------+---------+
| id                                   | fixed_ip_address | floating_ip_address | port_id |
+--------------------------------------+-----------------+---------------------+---------+
| da54d6a2-b8d4-4a08-91bf-c33fb2bb4ab5 |                 | 10.50.0.3           |         |
+--------------------------------------+-----------------+---------------------+---------+

root@controller01:~# neutron floatingip-associate da54d6a2-b8d4-4a08-91bf-c33fb2bb4ab5 c1372dab-6362-48a6-892d-2c96f1cadf67
                                                   Floating IP ID                       Port ID
```

Figure 7.4

Neutron uses the subnet ID of a specified port to determine the router in which to configure the floating IP address and respective NAT rules. The logic involved means that no more than one standalone router should be attached to a tenant network at any given time when floating IPs are used as unexpected results may occur otherwise.

Listing floating IPs in the CLI

To determine the association of floating IPs to Neutron ports and addresses, use the Neutron `floatingip-list` command, as shown here:

```
usage:     floatingip-list
```

The output returned includes the ID, fixed IP address, floating IP address, and port ID associated with the floating IP.

Displaying the floating IP attributes in the CLI

To display the attributes of a floating IP in the CLI, use the Neutron `floatingip-show` command, as follows:

```
usage:     floatingip-show FLOATINGIP
```

The output returned includes the floating IP address and associated external network, fixed IP address, port, tenant, and router IDs.

Disassociating floating IPs in the CLI

To disassociate a floating IP from a port, use the following Neutron `floatingip-disassociate` command:

```
usage:    floatingip-disassociate FLOATINGIP_ID
```

Disassociating a floating IP from a port makes the floating IP available for use to other users within the tenant or project.

Deleting floating IPs in the CLI

To delete a floating IP, use the Neutron `floatingip-delete` command, as follows:

```
usage:    floatingip-delete FLOATINGIP
```

Deleting a floating IP returns the IP address to the external network allocation pool, where it can be allocated to other network resources, including routers or floating IPs.

Demonstrating traffic flow from an instance to the Internet

To demonstrate the process of creating and connecting standalone Neutron routers to both tenant and external provider networks so as to provide network connectivity to instances, this section of the chapter is dedicated to a walkthrough that leverages the fundamental Neutron concepts that have been discussed in the book so far.

A VLAN provider network will be created and used as an external gateway network for the Neutron router, while a VLAN tenant network will be created and used by instances. A Neutron router will be created and used to route traffic from the instances in the tenant network to the Internet, and floating IPs will be created and used to provide direct connectivity to instances.

Setting the foundation

In this demonstration, a Cisco **Adaptive Security Appliance (ASA)** device serves as the physical network gateway device and is connected to the Internet. The inside interface of the Cisco ASA device has a configured IP address of 10.50.0.1/24 on VLAN 50 and will serve as the gateway for an external VLAN provider network created in the following section.

The following figure is the logical diagram of the network to be built as part of this demonstration:

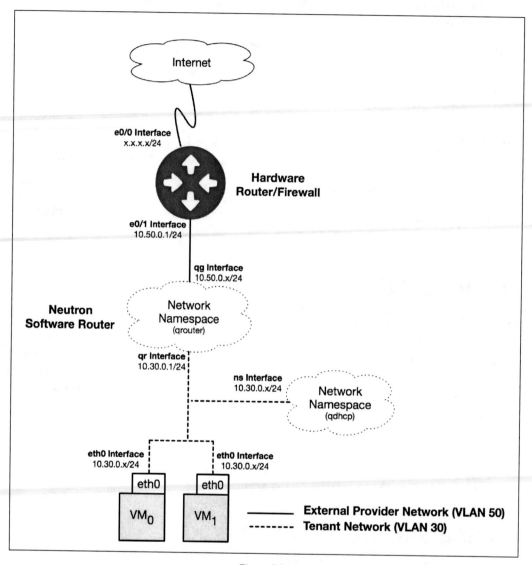

Figure 7.5

In the preceding figure, a Cisco ASA device serves as the external network device in front of the OpenStack Cloud.

Creating an external provider network

In order to provide instances with external connectivity, a Neutron router must be connected to a provider network that is eligible for use as an external network.

Using the Neutron `net-create` command, create a provider network with the following attributes:

- **Name**: GATEWAY_NET
- **Type**: VLAN
- **Segmentation ID**: 50
- **Physical network**: physnet2
- **External**: True
- **Shared**: True

The following screenshot displays the resulting output of the `net-create` command:

```
root@controller01:~# neutron net-create GATEWAY_NET --provider:network_type=vlan \
> --provider:segmentation_id=50 --provider:physical_network=physnet2 \
> --router:external --shared
Created a new network:
+---------------------------+--------------------------------------+
| Field                     | Value                                |
+---------------------------+--------------------------------------+
| admin_state_up            | True                                 |
| id                        | 55451e10-861e-49b8-9abc-a5996fe6adb3 |
| mtu                       | 0                                    |
| name                      | GATEWAY_NET                          |
| provider:network_type     | vlan                                 |
| provider:physical_network | physnet2                             |
| provider:segmentation_id  | 50                                   |
| router:external           | True                                 |
| shared                    | True                                 |
| status                    | ACTIVE                               |
| subnets                   |                                      |
| tenant_id                 | 65ff4cf1a04846f1ab2bc1ff0efb1090     |
+---------------------------+--------------------------------------+
```

Figure 7.6

Using the Neutron `subnet-create` command, create a subnet with the following attributes:

- **Name**: GATEWAY_SUBNET
- **Network**: 10.50.0.0
- **Subnet mask**: 255.255.255.0

- **Gateway**: 10.50.0.1
- **DHCP**: Disabled
- **Allocation pool**: 10.50.0.100 - 10.50.0.254

The following screenshot displays the resulting output of the subnet-create command:

```
root@controller01:~# neutron subnet-create GATEWAY_NET 10.50.0.0/24 --name GATEWAY_SUBNET \
> --disable-dhcp --allocation-pool start=10.50.0.100,end=10.50.0.254 --gateway 10.50.0.1
Created a new subnet:
+--------------------+-------------------------------------------------+
| Field              | Value                                           |
+--------------------+-------------------------------------------------+
| allocation_pools   | {"start": "10.50.0.100", "end": "10.50.0.254"}  |
| cidr               | 10.50.0.0/24                                    |
| dns_nameservers    |                                                 |
| enable_dhcp        | False                                           |
| gateway_ip         | 10.50.0.1                                       |
| host_routes        |                                                 |
| id                 | f2444660-69c6-4002-bc6c-62b5eb2bfc62            |
| ip_version         | 4                                               |
| ipv6_address_mode  |                                                 |
| ipv6_ra_mode       |                                                 |
| name               | GATEWAY_SUBNET                                  |
| network_id         | 55451e10-861e-49b8-9abc-a5996fe6adb3            |
| subnetpool_id      |                                                 |
| tenant_id          | 65ff4cf1a04846f1ab2bc1ff0efb1090                |
+--------------------+-------------------------------------------------+
```

Figure 7.7

Creating a Neutron router

Create a router using the Neutron router-create command with the following attribute:

- **Name**: MyRouter

The following screenshot displays the resulting output of the `router-create` command:

```
root@controller01:~# neutron router-create MyRouter
Created a new router:
+----------------------+-------------------------------------+
| Field                | Value                               |
+----------------------+-------------------------------------+
| admin_state_up       | True                                |
| distributed          | False                               |
| external_gateway_info |                                    |
| ha                   | False                               |
| id                   | bc2a45f6-db3b-4ca4-a5ee-340af36a8293 |
| name                 | MyRouter                            |
| routes               |                                     |
| status               | ACTIVE                              |
| tenant_id            | 65ff4cf1a04846f1ab2bc1ff0efb1090    |
+----------------------+-------------------------------------+
```

Figure 7.8

Attaching the router to the external network

When attaching a Neutron router to a provider network, the network must have its `router:external` attribute set to `true` to be eligible for use as an external network.

Using the following Neutron `router-gateway-set` command, attach the `MyRouter` router to the `GATEWAY_NET` network:

```
(neutron) router-gateway-set MyRouter GATEWAY_NET
Set gateway for router MyRouter
```

Using the Neutron `router-port-list` command, determine the external IP of the router, as follows:

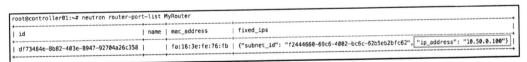

Figure 7.9

 The IP address assigned to the router is procured from the allocation pool of the external network's subnet. As of the Kilo release of OpenStack, there is no way to specify the external address of the router.

Identifying the L3 agent and namespace

Once the gateway interface has been added, the router will be scheduled to an eligible L3 agent. Using the Neutron `l3-agent-list-hosting-router` command, you can determine which L3 agent the router was scheduled to, as follows:

```
root@controller01:~# neutron l3-agent-list-hosting-router MyRouter
+--------------------------------------+-------------------------------+----------------+-------+
| id                                   | host                          | admin_state_up | alive |
+--------------------------------------+-------------------------------+----------------+-------+
| cd41db3f-4886-4446-8114-cccbde66cf95 | controller01.learningneutron.com | True         | :-)   |
+--------------------------------------+-------------------------------+----------------+-------+
```

Figure 7.10

The L3 agent is responsible for creating a network namespace that acts as the router. For easy identification, the name of the namespace incorporates the router's ID:

```
root@controller01:~# ip netns
qrouter-bc2a45f6-db3b-4ca4-a5ee-340af36a8293
```

Inside the namespace, you will find an interface with the prefix qg. The qg interface is the gateway or external interface of the router. Neutron automatically provides the qg interface with an IP address from the allocation pool of the external network's subnet:

```
root@controller01:~# ip netns exec qrouter-bc2a45f6-db3b-4ca4-a5ee-340af36a8293 ip a
1: lo: <LOOPBACK,UP,LOWER_UP> mtu 65536 qdisc noqueue state UNKNOWN group default
    link/loopback 00:00:00:00:00:00 brd 00:00:00:00:00:00
    inet 127.0.0.1/8 scope host lo
       valid_lft forever preferred_lft forever
    inet6 ::1/128 scope host
       valid_lft forever preferred_lft forever
2: qg-df73484e-8b: <BROADCAST,MULTICAST,UP,LOWER_UP> mtu 1500 qdisc pfifo_fast state UP group default qlen 1000
    link/ether fa:16:3e:fe:76:fb brd ff:ff:ff:ff:ff:ff
    inet 10.50.0.100/24 brd 10.50.0.255 scope global qg-df73484e-8b
       valid_lft forever preferred_lft forever
    inet6 fe80::f816:3eff:fefe:76fb/64 scope link
       valid_lft forever preferred_lft forever
```

Figure 7.11

When using the Open vSwitch driver, the interface is connected directly to the integration bridge. When using the LinuxBridge driver, as in this example, the qg interface is one end of a veth pair whose other end is connected to a bridge on the host. Using `ethtool`, we can determine the peer index of the corresponding interface on the host:

```
root@controller01:~# ip netns exec qrouter-bc2a45f6-db3b-4ca4-a5ee-340af36a8293 ethtool -S qg-df73484e-8b
NIC statistics:
    peer_ifindex: 23
```

Figure 7.12

Using `ip link show`, the corresponding interface (peer index 23) can be found by searching for the index on the controller:

```
root@controller01:~# ip link show | grep 23: -A1
23: tapdf73484e-8b: <BROADCAST,MULTICAST,UP,LOWER_UP> mtu 1500 qdisc pfifo_fast master brq55451e10-86 state UP mode DEFAULT group default qlen 1000
    link/ether 92:10:63:99:35:98 brd ff:ff:ff:ff:ff:ff
```

Figure 7.13

When using the LinuxBridge driver, the veth interface is connected to a bridge that corresponds to the *external* network:

```
root@controller01:~# brctl show
bridge name            bridge id              STP enabled        interfaces
brq55451e10-86         8000.8cae4cfe9ad0          no             eth2.50
                                                                 tapdf73484e-8b
       Network ID                                                       Port ID
```

Figure 7.14

 For easy identification, the bridge name includes the first 10 characters of the network ID. In addition, each end of the veth pair includes the first 10 characters of the port ID that is associated with the interface.

The namespace can communicate with other devices in the same subnet through the bridge. The other interface in the bridge, `eth2.50`, tags traffic as VLAN 50 as it exits the bridge out the physical interface `eth2`.

Observe the route table within the namespace. The default gateway address corresponds to the address defined in the subnet's `gateway_ip` attribute. In this case, it is `10.50.0.1`:

```
root@controller01:~# ip netns exec qrouter-bc2a45f6-db3b-4ca4-a5ee-340af36a8293 ip r
default via 10.50.0.1 dev qg-df73484e-8b
10.50.0.0/24 dev qg-df73484e-8b  proto kernel  scope link  src 10.50.0.100
```

Figure 7.15

Testing gateway connectivity

To test external connectivity from the Neutron router, ping the edge gateway device from within the router namespace:

```
root@controller01:~# ip netns exec qrouter-bc2a45f6-db3b-4ca4-a5ee-340af36a8293 ping 10.50.0.1 -c 5
PING 10.50.0.1 (10.50.0.1) 56(84) bytes of data.
64 bytes from 10.50.0.1: icmp_seq=1 ttl=255 time=1.11 ms
64 bytes from 10.50.0.1: icmp_seq=2 ttl=255 time=0.730 ms
64 bytes from 10.50.0.1: icmp_seq=3 ttl=255 time=0.830 ms
64 bytes from 10.50.0.1: icmp_seq=4 ttl=255 time=0.698 ms
64 bytes from 10.50.0.1: icmp_seq=5 ttl=255 time=0.737 ms

--- 10.50.0.1 ping statistics ---
5 packets transmitted, 5 received, 0% packet loss, time 3998ms
rtt min/avg/max/mdev = 0.698/0.822/1.116/0.154 ms
```

Figure 7.16

Successful ping attempts from the router namespace to the physical gateway device demonstrate a proper external VLAN configuration on both hardware- and software-based networking components.

Creating an internal network

Within the admin tenant, create an internal network for instances. In this demonstration, a network will be created with the following attribute:

- **Name**: TENANT_NET

The following screenshot demonstrates the resulting output of the net-create command:

```
root@controller01:~# neutron net-create TENANT_NET
Created a new network:
+-----------------------------+--------------------------------------+
| Field                       | Value                                |
+-----------------------------+--------------------------------------+
| admin_state_up              | True                                 |
| id                          | d305da03-960a-4ce4-aaec-4ee681fcff3d |
| mtu                         | 0                                    |
| name                        | TENANT_NET                           |
| provider:network_type       | vlan                                 |
| provider:physical_network   | physnet2                             |
| provider:segmentation_id    | 30                                   |
| router:external             | False                                |
| shared                      | False                                |
| status                      | ACTIVE                               |
| subnets                     |                                      |
| tenant_id                   | 65ff4cf1a04846f1ab2bc1ff0efb1090     |
+-----------------------------+--------------------------------------+
```

Figure 7.17

Note how Neutron automatically determines the network type, physical network, and segmentation ID for the network. As the `net-create` command was executed without specific provider attributes, Neutron relied on the configuration found in the plugin configuration file to determine the type of network to create.

The following configuration options in the ML2 configuration file were used to determine the network type, physical network, and segmentation ID:

```
tenant_network_types = vlan,vxlan
network_vlan_ranges = physnet2:30:33
```

Neutron consumes all available VLAN segmentation IDs as networks are created before moving on to VXLAN networks.

Using the Neutron `subnet-create` command, create a subnet with the following attributes:

- **Name**: TENANT_SUBNET
- **Network**: 10.30.0.0
- **Subnet mask**: 255.255.255.0
- **Gateway**: <auto>
- **DHCP range**: <auto>
- **DNS nameserver**: 8.8.8.8

The following screenshot demonstrates the resulting output of the `subnet-create` command:

```
root@controller01:~# neutron subnet-create TENANT_NET 10.30.0.0/24 --name TENANT_SUBNET --dns-nameserver 8.8.8.8
Created a new subnet:
+--------------------+----------------------------------------------+
| Field              | Value                                        |
+--------------------+----------------------------------------------+
| allocation_pools   | {"start": "10.30.0.2", "end": "10.30.0.254"} |
| cidr               | 10.30.0.0/24                                 |
| dns_nameservers    | 8.8.8.8                                      |
| enable_dhcp        | True                                         |
| gateway_ip         | 10.30.0.1                                    |
| host_routes        |                                              |
| id                 | bec74bb0-a8b9-448b-96e6-b4b8041dede5         |
| ip_version         | 4                                            |
| ipv6_address_mode  |                                              |
| ipv6_ra_mode       |                                              |
| name               | TENANT_SUBNET                                |
| network_id         | d305da03-960a-4ce4-aaec-4ee681fcff3d         |
| subnetpool_id      |                                              |
| tenant_id          | 65ff4cf1a04846f1ab2bc1ff0efb1090             |
+--------------------+----------------------------------------------+
```

Figure 7.18

Attaching the router to the internal network

Using the Neutron `router-interface-add` command, attach the `TENANT_SUBNET` subnet to `MyRouter`:

```
(neutron) router-interface-add MyRouter TENANT_SUBNET
Added interface 24b55e34-227f-4fe4-b341-35ff2f49a099 to router
MyRouter.
```

Using the Neutron `router-port-list` command, determine the internal IP of the router:

```
root@controller01:~# neutron router-port-list MyRouter
+--------------------------------------+------+-------------------+------------------------------------------------------------------------------------------------------------+
| id                                   | name | mac_address       | fixed_ips                                                                                                  |
+--------------------------------------+------+-------------------+------------------------------------------------------------------------------------------------------------+
| 24b55e34-227f-4fe4-b341-35ff2f49a099 |      | fa:16:3e:2d:89:41 | {"subnet_id": "bec74bb0-a8b9-448b-96e6-b4b8041dede5", "ip_address": "10.30.0.1"}                            |
| df73484e-8b82-403e-8947-92704a26c358 |      | fa:16:3e:fe:76:fb | {"subnet_id": "f2444660-69c6-4002-bc6c-62b5eb2bfc62", "ip_address": "10.50.0.100"}                          |
+--------------------------------------+------+-------------------+------------------------------------------------------------------------------------------------------------+
```

Figure 7.19

When a particular port ID is not specified while using the `router-interface-add` command, the IP address assigned to the internal router interface defaults to the address set in the `gateway_ip` attribute of the subnet.

Inside the router namespace, a new interface has been added with a prefix of `qr`. A `qr` interface is an internal interface of the router:

```
root@controller01:~# ip netns exec qrouter-bc2a45f6-db3b-4ca4-a5ee-340af36a8293 ip a
1: lo: <LOOPBACK,UP,LOWER_UP> mtu 65536 qdisc noqueue state UNKNOWN group default
    link/loopback 00:00:00:00:00:00 brd 00:00:00:00:00:00
    inet 127.0.0.1/8 scope host lo
       valid_lft forever preferred_lft forever
    inet6 ::1/128 scope host
       valid_lft forever preferred_lft forever
2: qg-df73484e-8b: <BROADCAST,MULTICAST,UP,LOWER_UP> mtu 1500 qdisc pfifo_fast state UP group default qlen 1000
    link/ether fa:16:3e:fe:76:fb brd ff:ff:ff:ff:ff:ff
    inet 10.50.0.100/24 brd 10.50.0.255 scope global qg-df73484e-8b
       valid_lft forever preferred_lft forever
    inet6 fe80::f816:3eff:fefe:76fb/64 scope link
       valid_lft forever preferred_lft forever
3: qr-24b55e34-22: <BROADCAST,MULTICAST,UP,LOWER_UP> mtu 1500 qdisc pfifo_fast state UP group default qlen 1000
    link/ether fa:16:3e:2d:89:41 brd ff:ff:ff:ff:ff:ff
    inet 10.30.0.1/24 brd 10.30.0.255 scope global qr-24b55e34-22
       valid_lft forever preferred_lft forever
    inet6 fe80::f816:3eff:fe2d:8941/64 scope link
       valid_lft forever preferred_lft forever
```

Figure 7.20

When using the Open vSwitch driver, the interface is connected directly to the integration bridge. When using the LinuxBridge driver, as in this example, every qr interface is at one end of a veth pair, whose other end is connected to a bridge on the host. When using the LinuxBridge driver, the interface is connected to a bridge that corresponds to a tenant network:

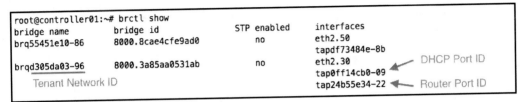

Figure 7.21

 For easy identification, the bridge name includes the first 10 characters of the network ID. In addition, each end of the veth pair includes the first 10 characters of the port ID associated with the interface.

The router namespace can communicate with other devices in the same subnet through the bridge. The eth2.30 interface in the bridge tags traffic as VLAN 30 as it exits the bridge out the eth2 parent interface.

Creating instances

Create two instances with the following characteristics:

- **Name**: MyInstance-1, MyInstance-2
- **Network**: TENANT_NET
- **Image**: CirrOS
- **Flavor**: m1.tiny

Use the glance image-list command to determine the ID of the CirrOS image downloaded in *Chapter 2, Installing OpenStack*:

```
root@controller01:~# glance image-list
+--------------------------------------+-------------------------------+
| ID                                   | Name                          |
+--------------------------------------+-------------------------------+
| 5ecfac0c-98eb-4c81-8448-02249ee89aae | Ubuntu 14.04 LTS Cloud Image  |
| 3dd4f4e5-f82d-435e-8d25-0f9f6193dc61 | cirros-0.3.4-x86_64           |
+--------------------------------------+-------------------------------+
```

Figure 7.22

Use the following `nova boot` command to boot two instances in the `TENANT_NET` network:

```
nova boot --flavor m1.tiny --image 3dd4f4e5-f82d-435e-8d25-0f9f6193dc61 \
--nic net-id=d305da03-960a-4ce4-aaec-4ee681fcff3d --min-count 2 \
--max-count 2 MyInstance
```

Figure 7.23

The `nova list` command can be used to return a list of instances and their IP addresses:

```
root@controller01:~# nova list
+--------------------------------------+-------------+--------+------------+-------------+------------------------+
| ID                                   | Name        | Status | Task State | Power State | Networks               |
+--------------------------------------+-------------+--------+------------+-------------+------------------------+
| 22710328-4432-4122-822f-a172d96f7ba5 | MyInstance-1 | ACTIVE | -          | Running     | TENANT_NET=10.30.0.3   |
| ec0a83a3-6670-4423-b342-2fb14e47b0c9 | MyInstance-2 | ACTIVE | -          | Running     | TENANT_NET=10.30.0.4   |
+--------------------------------------+-------------+--------+------------+-------------+------------------------+
```

Figure 7.24

On one or both of the compute nodes, depending on where the instances were scheduled, a Linux bridge is created that corresponds to the `TENANT_NET` network. Connected to the bridge, we can find a VLAN interface and one or more tap interfaces that correspond to the instances:

```
root@compute01:~# brctl show
bridge name         bridge id           STP enabled     interfaces
brqd305da03-96      8000.a0cec801f273      no            eth2.30
                                                         tap26b6f5af-c5   ◀─── MyInstance-2
                                                         tapd85d5718-e5   ◀─── MyInstance-1
```

Figure 7.25

Verifying instance connectivity

When a network and subnet are created with DHCP enabled, a network namespace is created by the `neutron-dhcp-agent` service, which serves as a DHCP server for the network. On the host running the `neutron-dhcp-agent` service, `ip netns` can be used to reveal the namespace:

```
root@controller01:~# ip netns
qdhcp-d305da03-960a-4ce4-aaec-4ee681fcff3d   ◀───   DHCP Namespace for
qrouter-bc2a45f6-db3b-4ca4-a5ee-340af36a8293              TENANT_NET
```

Figure 7.26

For easy identification, the name of a DHCP namespace corresponds to the ID of the network it is serving. Inside the namespace, an interface with the prefix ns is created and assigned an address from the allocation pool of the subnet:

```
root@controller01:~# ip netns exec qdhcp-d305da03-960a-4ce4-aaec-4ee681fcff3d ip a
1: lo: <LOOPBACK,UP,LOWER_UP> mtu 65536 qdisc noqueue state UNKNOWN group default
    link/loopback 00:00:00:00:00:00 brd 00:00:00:00:00:00
    inet 127.0.0.1/8 scope host lo
       valid_lft forever preferred_lft forever
    inet6 ::1/128 scope host
       valid_lft forever preferred_lft forever
2: ns-0ff14cb0-09: <BROADCAST,MULTICAST,UP,LOWER_UP> mtu 1500 qdisc pfifo_fast state UP group default qlen 1000
    link/ether fa:16:3e:1f:c1:c0 brd ff:ff:ff:ff:ff:ff
    inet 10.30.0.2/24 brd 10.30.0.255 scope global ns-0ff14cb0-09
       valid_lft forever preferred_lft forever
    inet 169.254.169.254/16 brd 169.254.255.255 scope global ns-0ff14cb0-09
       valid_lft forever preferred_lft forever
    inet6 fe80::f816:3eff:fe1f:c1c0/64 scope link
       valid_lft forever preferred_lft forever
```

Figure 7.27

When using the Open vSwitch driver, the ns interface is connected directly to the integration bridge. When using the LinuxBridge driver, as in this example, the ns interface is at one end of a veth pair, whose other end is connected to a bridge on the host. The namespace can communicate with other devices in the same subnet through the bridge. When using the LinuxBridge driver, the interface is connected to a bridge that corresponds to the network.

As the instances came online, they sent a DHCP request that was served by the dnsmasq process in the DHCP namespace. A populated ARP table within the namespace confirms that the instances are functioning in the VLAN on layer 2:

```
root@controller01:~# ip netns exec qdhcp-d305da03-960a-4ce4-aaec-4ee681fcff3d arp -an
? (10.30.0.3) at fa:16:3e:2e:0f:e9 [ether] on ns-0ff14cb0-09  ◄──── MyInstance-1
? (10.30.0.4) at fa:16:3e:53:6f:97 [ether] on ns-0ff14cb0-09  ◄──── MyInstance-2
```

Figure 7.28

 A populated ARP table can only be used to verify connectivity when the l2population driver is not in use. The l2population driver is used to prepopulate the ARP and forward tables to reduce the overhead on overlay networks. So, it may not provide an accurate picture of connectivity in these networks.

Before you can connect to the instances, security group rules must be updated to allow ICMP and SSH. *Chapter 6, Managing Security Groups*, focuses on the implementation and administration of security group rules in more detail. To test connectivity, add ICMP and SSH access to a security group applied to the instances. Use the following command to determine the security group for this particular instance:

```
# neutron port-list --device-id=<instance id> -c security_groups
```

The resulting output can be seen in the following screenshot:

```
root@controller01:~# neutron port-list --fixed-ips ip_address=10.30.0.3 -c security_groups
+-------------------------------------------------+
| security_groups                                 |
+-------------------------------------------------+
| [u'60ca9b2c-dc87-40c7-a5ff-5e5037b08c56']       |
+-------------------------------------------------+
```

Figure 7.29

Use the Neutron `security-group-rule-create` command to create rules within the respective security group, as follows:

```
root@controller01:~# neutron security-group-rule-create --protocol icmp 60ca9b2c-dc87-40c7-a5ff-5e5037b08c56
Created a new security_group_rule:
+-------------------+--------------------------------------+
| Field             | Value                                |
+-------------------+--------------------------------------+
| direction         | ingress                              |
| ethertype         | IPv4                                 |
| id                | 1c95dad2-6532-4049-ac66-7e04e730bd60 |
| port_range_max    |                                      |
| port_range_min    |                                      |
| protocol          | icmp                                 |
| remote_group_id   |                                      |
| remote_ip_prefix  |                                      |
| security_group_id | 60ca9b2c-dc87-40c7-a5ff-5e5037b08c56 |
| tenant_id         | 65ff4cf1a04846f1ab2bc1ff0efb1090     |
+-------------------+--------------------------------------+

root@controller01:~# neutron security-group-rule-create --protocol tcp --port-range-min 22 \
> --port-range-max 22 60ca9b2c-dc87-40c7-a5ff-5e5037b08c56
Created a new security_group_rule:
+-------------------+--------------------------------------+
| Field             | Value                                |
+-------------------+--------------------------------------+
| direction         | ingress                              |
| ethertype         | IPv4                                 |
| id                | 367aabaf-a13e-4adb-a5ce-bfeba7e8df40 |
| port_range_max    | 22                                   |
| port_range_min    | 22                                   |
| protocol          | tcp                                  |
| remote_group_id   |                                      |
| remote_ip_prefix  |                                      |
| security_group_id | 60ca9b2c-dc87-40c7-a5ff-5e5037b08c56 |
| tenant_id         | 65ff4cf1a04846f1ab2bc1ff0efb1090     |
+-------------------+--------------------------------------+
```

Figure 7.30

Using an SSH client, connect to an instance from either the router or DHCP namespace. The CirrOS image has a built-in user named `cirros` with the password `cubswin:)`:

```
root@controller01:~# ip netns exec qrouter-bc2a45f6-db3b-4ca4-a5ee-340af36a8293 ssh cirros@10.30.0.3
The authenticity of host '10.30.0.3 (10.30.0.3)' can't be established.
RSA key fingerprint is d3:af:d7:7a:09:0d:72:63:60:b0:5f:ee:e0:48:42:31.
Are you sure you want to continue connecting (yes/no)? yes
Warning: Permanently added '10.30.0.3' (RSA) to the list of known hosts.
cirros@10.30.0.3's password:
$ hostname
myinstance-1
$ ip r
default via 10.30.0.1 dev eth0
10.30.0.0/24 dev eth0   src 10.30.0.3
169.254.169.254 via 10.30.0.2 dev eth0
$ exit
Connection to 10.30.0.3 closed.
```

Figure 7.31

Observe the routing table of the instance. The default gateway of the instance is the Neutron router created earlier in this chapter. Pinging an external resource from an instance should be successful provided external connectivity from the Neutron router exists:

```
root@controller01:~# ip netns exec qrouter-bc2a45f6-db3b-4ca4-a5ee-340af36a8293 ssh cirros@10.30.0.3
cirros@10.30.0.3's password:
$ ping 8.8.8.8 -c 5
PING 8.8.8.8 (8.8.8.8): 56 data bytes
64 bytes from 8.8.8.8: seq=0 ttl=51 time=158.547 ms
64 bytes from 8.8.8.8: seq=1 ttl=51 time=176.579 ms
64 bytes from 8.8.8.8: seq=2 ttl=51 time=193.426 ms
64 bytes from 8.8.8.8: seq=3 ttl=51 time=86.279 ms
64 bytes from 8.8.8.8: seq=4 ttl=51 time=182.579 ms

--- 8.8.8.8 ping statistics ---
5 packets transmitted, 5 packets received, 0% packet loss
round-trip min/avg/max = 86.279/159.482/193.426 ms
```

Figure 7.32

Observing default NAT behavior

The default behavior of the Neutron router is to source NAT traffic from instances that lack floating IPs when traffic egresses the external or gateway interface of the router. From the `eth2.30` interface of the controller node, we can observe the ICMP traffic from the instances — sourcing from the real address, `10.30.0.3` — as it heads toward the router:

```
root@controller01:~# tcpdump -i eth2.30 -n icmp
tcpdump: WARNING: eth2.30: no IPv4 address assigned
tcpdump: verbose output suppressed, use -v or -vv for full protocol decode
listening on eth2.30, link-type EN10MB (Ethernet), capture size 65535 bytes
17:18:07.452319 IP 10.30.0.3 > 8.8.8.8: ICMP echo request, id 24577, seq 0, length 64
17:18:07.645486 IP 8.8.8.8 > 10.30.0.3: ICMP echo reply, id 24577, seq 0, length 64
```

Figure 7.33

From the `eth2.50` interface on the controller node, we can observe the ICMP traffic from the instances after it traverses the router sourcing as the router's address, `10.50.0.100`:

```
root@controller01:~# tcpdump -i eth2.50 -n icmp
tcpdump: WARNING: eth2.50: no IPv4 address assigned
tcpdump: verbose output suppressed, use -v or -vv for full protocol decode
listening on eth2.50, link-type EN10MB (Ethernet), capture size 65535 bytes
17:16:28.384680 IP 10.50.0.100 > 8.8.8.8: ICMP echo request, id 24321, seq 0, length 64
17:16:28.414260 IP 8.8.8.8 > 10.50.0.100: ICMP echo reply, id 24321, seq 0, length 64
```

Figure 7.34

A look at the iptables chains within the router namespace reveals the NAT rules responsible for this behavior:

```
root@controller01:~# ip netns exec qrouter-bc2a45f6-db3b-4ca4-a5ee-340af36a8293 iptables-save
...
# Generated by iptables-save v1.4.21 on Thu Oct 15 17:23:39 2015
*nat
:PREROUTING ACCEPT [14:1310]
:INPUT ACCEPT [3:486]
:OUTPUT ACCEPT [14:1094]
:POSTROUTING ACCEPT [0:0]
:neutron-l3-agent-OUTPUT - [0:0]
:neutron-l3-agent-POSTROUTING - [0:0]
:neutron-l3-agent-PREROUTING - [0:0]
:neutron-l3-agent-float-snat - [0:0]
:neutron-l3-agent-snat - [0:0]
:neutron-postrouting-bottom - [0:0]
-A PREROUTING -j neutron-l3-agent-PREROUTING
-A OUTPUT -j neutron-l3-agent-OUTPUT
-A POSTROUTING -j neutron-l3-agent-POSTROUTING
-A POSTROUTING -j neutron-postrouting-bottom
-A neutron-l3-agent-POSTROUTING ! -i qg-df73484e-8b ! -o qg-df73484e-8b -m conntrack ! --ctstate DNAT -j ACCEPT
-A neutron-l3-agent-PREROUTING -d 169.254.169.254/32 -i qr-+ -p tcp -m tcp --dport 80 -j REDIRECT --to-ports 9697
-A neutron-l3-agent-snat -j neutron-l3-agent-float-snat
-A neutron-l3-agent-snat -o qg-df73484e-8b -j SNAT --to-source 10.50.0.100
-A neutron-l3-agent-snat -m mark ! --mark 0x2 -m conntrack --ctstate DNAT -j SNAT --to-source 10.50.0.100
-A neutron-postrouting-bottom -m comment --comment "Perform source NAT on outgoing traffic." -j neutron-l3-agent-snat
COMMIT
# Completed on Thu Oct 15 17:23:39 2015
```

Figure 7.35

In this configuration, instances can communicate with outside resources through the router as long as the instances initiate the connection. Outside resources cannot initiate connections directly to instances via their fixed IP address.

Assigning floating IPs

To initiate connections to instances behind Neutron routers from outside networks, you must configure a floating IP address and associate it with the instance. With Neutron, a floating IP is associated with the Neutron port that corresponds to the interface of the instance accepting connections.

Using the Neutron `port-list` command, determine the port ID of each instance that has been recently booted. The `port-list` command allows results to be filtered by device or instance ID, as shown in the following screenshot:

```
root@controller01:~# for id in $(nova list | grep MyInstance | awk '{print $2}'); do neutron port-list --device_id=$id; done
+--------------------------------------+------+-------------------+----------------------------------------------------------------------------------------+
| id                                   | name | mac_address       | fixed_ips                                                                              |
+--------------------------------------+------+-------------------+----------------------------------------------------------------------------------------+
| d85d5718-e5d7-4ecd-b550-7cda9f09058c |      | fa:16:3e:2e:0f:e9 | {"subnet_id": "bec74bb0-a8b9-448b-96e6-b4b8041dede5", "ip_address": "10.30.0.3"} |
+--------------------------------------+------+-------------------+----------------------------------------------------------------------------------------+
| id                                   | name | mac_address       | fixed_ips                                                                              |
+--------------------------------------+------+-------------------+----------------------------------------------------------------------------------------+
| 26b6f5af-c533-45a6-aa90-3d2cd19f5951 |      | fa:16:3e:53:6f:97 | {"subnet_id": "bec74bb0-a8b9-448b-96e6-b4b8041dede5", "ip_address": "10.30.0.4"} |
+--------------------------------------+------+-------------------+----------------------------------------------------------------------------------------+
```

Figure 7.36

Using the Neutron `floatingip-create` command, create a single floating IP address and associate it with the port of the instance known as `MyInstance-1`:

```
root@controller01:~# neutron floatingip-create GATEWAY_NET --port-id=d85d5718-e5d7-4ecd-b550-7cda9f09058c
Created a new floatingip:
+---------------------+--------------------------------------+
| Field               | Value                                |
+---------------------+--------------------------------------+
| fixed_ip_address    | 10.30.0.3                            |
| floating_ip_address | 10.50.0.101                          |
| floating_network_id | 55451e10-861e-49b8-9abc-a5996fe6adb3 |
| id                  | 1e4ef721-6fd5-4e4c-9dca-43c44d28a277 |
| port_id             | d85d5718-e5d7-4ecd-b550-7cda9f09058c |
| router_id           | bc2a45f6-db3b-4ca4-a5ee-340af36a8293 |
| status              | DOWN                                 |
| tenant_id           | 65ff4cf1a04846f1ab2bc1ff0efb1090     |
+---------------------+--------------------------------------+
```

Figure 7.37

From within the guest OS, verify that the instance can still communicate with outside resources:

```
$ ping 8.8.8.8 -c1
PING 8.8.8.8 (8.8.8.8): 56 data bytes
64 bytes from 8.8.8.8: seq=0 ttl=51 time=32.523 ms

--- 8.8.8.8 ping statistics ---
1 packets transmitted, 1 packets received, 0% packet loss
round-trip min/avg/max = 32.523/32.523/32.523 ms
```

Figure 7.38

From the `eth2.50` interface on the controller node, we can observe the ICMP traffic from the instances after it traverses the router sourcing as the floating IP address, `10.50.0.101`:

```
root@controller01:~# tcpdump -i eth2.50 -n icmp
tcpdump: WARNING: eth2.50: no IPv4 address assigned
tcpdump: verbose output suppressed, use -v or -vv for full protocol decode
listening on eth2.50, link-type EN10MB (Ethernet), capture size 65535 bytes
17:36:34.176932 IP 10.50.0.101 > 8.8.8.8: ICMP echo request, id 26625, seq 0, length 64
17:36:34.206856 IP 8.8.8.8 > 10.50.0.101: ICMP echo reply, id 26625, seq 0, length 64
```

Figure 7.39

Within the router namespace, the floating IP is configured as a secondary address on the `qg` interface:

```
root@controller01:~# ip netns exec qrouter-bc2a45f6-db3b-4ca4-a5ee-340af36a8293 ip a
1: lo: <LOOPBACK,UP,LOWER_UP> mtu 65536 qdisc noqueue state UNKNOWN group default
    link/loopback 00:00:00:00:00:00 brd 00:00:00:00:00:00
    inet 127.0.0.1/8 scope host lo
       valid_lft forever preferred_lft forever
    inet6 ::1/128 scope host
       valid_lft forever preferred_lft forever
2: qg-df73484e-8b: <BROADCAST,MULTICAST,UP,LOWER_UP> mtu 1500 qdisc pfifo_fast state UP group default qlen 1000
    link/ether fa:16:3e:fe:76:fb brd ff:ff:ff:ff:ff:ff
    inet 10.50.0.100/24 brd 10.50.0.255 scope global qg-df73484e-8b
       valid_lft forever preferred_lft forever
    inet 10.50.0.101/32 brd 10.50.0.101 scope global qg-df73484e-8b     Floating IP as /32
       valid_lft forever preferred_lft forever                          secondary address
    inet6 fe80::f816:3eff:fefe:76fb/64 scope link
       valid_lft forever preferred_lft forever
3: qr-24b55e34-22: <BROADCAST,MULTICAST,UP,LOWER_UP> mtu 1500 qdisc pfifo_fast state UP group default qlen 1000
    link/ether fa:16:3e:2d:89:41 brd ff:ff:ff:ff:ff:ff
    inet 10.30.0.1/24 brd 10.30.0.255 scope global qr-24b55e34-22
       valid_lft forever preferred_lft forever
    inet6 fe80::f816:3eff:fe2d:8941/64 scope link
       valid_lft forever preferred_lft forever
```

Figure 7.40

When the floating IP is configured as a secondary network address on the `qg` interface, the router can respond to ARP requests to the floating IP from the upstream gateway device and other Neutron routers or devices in the same external network.

A look at the iptables chains within the router namespace shows that the rules have been added to perform the 1:1 NAT translation from the floating IP to the fixed IP of `MyInstance-1` and vice-versa:

```
Chain neutron-l3-agent-POSTROUTING (1 references)
target     prot opt source           destination
ACCEPT     all  --  anywhere         anywhere             ! ctstate DNAT

Chain neutron-l3-agent-PREROUTING (1 references)
target     prot opt source           destination
REDIRECT   tcp  --  anywhere         169.254.169.254      tcp dpt:http redir ports 9697
DNAT       all  --  anywhere         10.50.0.101          to:10.30.0.3

Chain neutron-l3-agent-float-snat (1 references)
target     prot opt source           destination
SNAT       all  --  10.30.0.3        anywhere             to:10.50.0.101
```

Figure 7.41

Provided our client workstation can route to the external provider network, traffic can be initiated directly to the instance via the floating IP:

```
workstation:~ james.denton$ ssh cirros@10.50.0.101
The authenticity of host '10.50.0.101 (10.50.0.101)' can't be established.
RSA key fingerprint is d3:af:d7:7a:09:0d:72:63:60:b0:5f:ee:e0:48:42:31.
Are you sure you want to continue connecting (yes/no)? yes
Warning: Permanently added '10.50.0.101' (RSA) to the list of known hosts.
cirros@10.50.0.101's password:
$ hostname
myinstance-1
$ ip r
default via 10.30.0.1 dev eth0
10.30.0.0/24 dev eth0  src 10.30.0.3
169.254.169.254 via 10.30.0.2 dev eth0
$ exit
Connection to 10.50.0.101 closed.
```

Figure 7.42

Reassigning floating IPs

Neutron provides the ability to quickly disassociate a floating IP from an instance or other network resource and associate it with another.

A listing of floating IPs shows the current association:

```
root@controller01:~# neutron floatingip-list
+--------------------------------------+-----------------+---------------------+--------------------------------------+
| id                                   | fixed_ip_address | floating_ip_address | port_id                              |
+--------------------------------------+-----------------+---------------------+--------------------------------------+
| 1e4ef721-6fd5-4e4c-9dca-43c44d28a277 | 10.30.0.3       | 10.50.0.101         | d85d5718-e5d7-4ecd-b550-7cda9f09058c |
+--------------------------------------+-----------------+---------------------+--------------------------------------+
```

Figure 7.43

Using the Neutron `floatingip-disassociate` and `floatingip-associate` commands, disassociate the floating IP from `MyInstance-1` and associate it with `MyInstance-2`. This disassociation can be seen in the following screenshot:

```
root@controller01:~# neutron floatingip-disassociate 1e4ef721-6fd5-4e4c-9dca-43c44d28a277
Disassociated floating IP 1e4ef721-6fd5-4e4c-9dca-43c44d28a277
```

Figure 7.44

A `floatingip-list` shows that the floating IP is no longer associated with a port:

```
root@controller01:~# neutron floatingip-list
+--------------------------------------+-----------------+---------------------+---------+
| id                                   | fixed_ip_address | floating_ip_address | port_id |
+--------------------------------------+-----------------+---------------------+---------+
| 1e4ef721-6fd5-4e4c-9dca-43c44d28a277 |                 | 10.50.0.101         |         |
+--------------------------------------+-----------------+---------------------+---------+
```

Figure 7.45

 The floating IP is still owned by the tenant who created it and cannot be assigned to another tenant without first being deleted.

Using the Neutron `floatingip-associate` command, associate the floating IP with the port of `MyInstance-2`, as shown in the following screenshot:

```
root@controller01:~# neutron floatingip-associate 1e4ef721-6fd5-4e4c-9dca-43c44d28a277 \
> $(neutron port-list | grep 10.30.0.4 | awk '{print $2}')
Associated floating IP 1e4ef721-6fd5-4e4c-9dca-43c44d28a277
```

Figure 7.46

Observe the iptables rules within the router namespace. The NAT relationship is modified, and the traffic from `MyInstance-2` will now appear as the floating IP:

```
Chain neutron-l3-agent-POSTROUTING (1 references)
target     prot opt source            destination
ACCEPT     all  --  anywhere          anywhere          ! ctstate DNAT

Chain neutron-l3-agent-PREROUTING (1 references)
target     prot opt source            destination
REDIRECT   tcp  --  anywhere          169.254.169.254   tcp dpt:http redir ports 9697
DNAT       all  --  anywhere          10.50.0.101       to:10.30.0.4    The destination IP has
                                                                        changed from .3 to .4
Chain neutron-l3-agent-float-snat (1 references)
target     prot opt source            destination                      The source IP has
SNAT       all  --  10.30.0.4         anywhere          to:10.50.0.101  changed from .3 to .4
```

Figure 7.47

As a result of the new association, attempting an SSH connection to the floating IP may result in the following message on the client machine:

```
workstation:~ james.denton$ ssh cirros@10.50.0.101
@@@@@@@@@@@@@@@@@@@@@@@@@@@@@@@@@@@@@@@@@@@@@@@@@@@@@@@@@@@
@    WARNING: REMOTE HOST IDENTIFICATION HAS CHANGED!     @
@@@@@@@@@@@@@@@@@@@@@@@@@@@@@@@@@@@@@@@@@@@@@@@@@@@@@@@@@@@
IT IS POSSIBLE THAT SOMEONE IS DOING SOMETHING NASTY!
Someone could be eavesdropping on you right now (man-in-the-middle attack)!
It is also possible that a host key has just been changed.
The fingerprint for the RSA key sent by the remote host is
a4:94:37:91:b4:cf:a7:f8:ed:50:ed:2d:dd:f6:89:6b.
Please contact your system administrator.
Add correct host key in /Users/jdenton/.ssh/known_hosts to get rid of this message.
Offending RSA key in /Users/jdenton/.ssh/known_hosts:11
RSA host key for 10.50.0.101 has changed and you have requested strict checking.
Host key verification failed.
```

Figure 7.48

The preceding message is a good indicator that traffic is being sent to a different host. Clearing the offending key and logging in to the instance reveals it to be `MyInstance-2`:

```
workstation:~ james.denton$ ssh cirros@10.50.0.101
The authenticity of host '10.50.0.101 (10.50.0.101)' can't be established.
RSA key fingerprint is a4:94:37:91:b4:cf:a7:f8:ed:50:ed:2d:dd:f6:89:6b.
Are you sure you want to continue connecting (yes/no)? yes
Warning: Permanently added '10.50.0.101' (RSA) to the list of known hosts.
cirros@10.50.0.101's password:
$ hostname
myinstance-2
$ ip a
1: lo: <LOOPBACK,UP,LOWER_UP> mtu 16436 qdisc noqueue
    link/loopback 00:00:00:00:00:00 brd 00:00:00:00:00:00
    inet 127.0.0.1/8 scope host lo
    inet6 ::1/128 scope host
       valid_lft forever preferred_lft forever
2: eth0: <BROADCAST,MULTICAST,UP,LOWER_UP> mtu 1500 qdisc pfifo_fast qlen 1000
    link/ether fa:16:3e:53:6f:97 brd ff:ff:ff:ff:ff:ff
    inet 10.30.0.4/24 brd 10.30.0.255 scope global eth0
    inet6 fe80::f816:3eff:fe53:6f97/64 scope link
       valid_lft forever preferred_lft forever
```

Figure 7.49

At this point, we have successfully deployed two instances behind a single virtual router and verified the connectivity to and from the instances using floating IPs. In the next section, we will explore how these same tasks can be accomplished within the Horizon dashboard.

Router management in the dashboard

From the Horizon dashboard, routers can be created and managed within the **Project** tab:

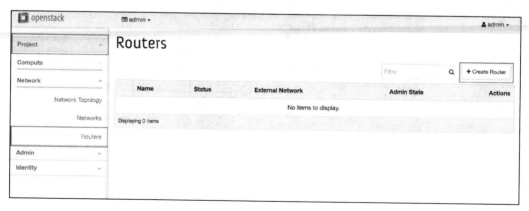

Figure 7.50

Creating a router in the dashboard

From the **Routers** page, click on **Create Router** in the upper right-hand corner to create a router. A window will open that resembles the following:

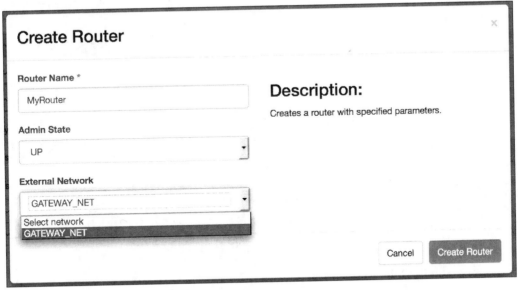

Figure 7.51

Enter the name of the router, its admin state, and the external network. Click on the blue **Create Router** button to complete the operation.

Attaching internal interfaces in the dashboard

To attach internal interfaces to routers in the dashboard, click on the router to reveal the **Router Details** page seen in the following figure:

Figure 7.52

Now, perform the following steps:

1. Click on the **Interfaces** tab to reveal details of the router's interfaces:

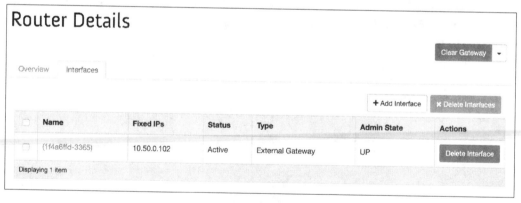

Figure 7.53

2. Clicking on the **Add Interface** button reveals a window that allows you to select the details of the interface to be added:

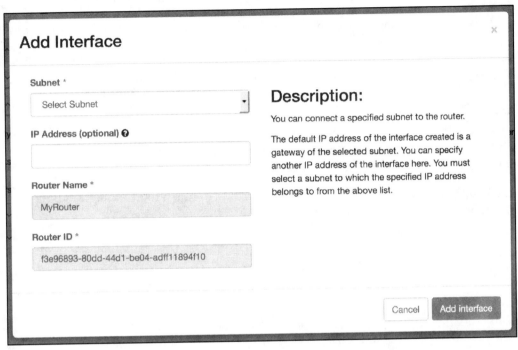

Figure 7.54

3. Select a tenant subnet that you wish to attach to the router from the **Subnet** menu, and click on the blue **Add Interface** button to attach the interface. The newly attached interface will be revealed on the **Interfaces** page:

Figure 7.55

It is normal for an interface's status to be **Down** immediately after adding the interface to the router. Neutron will not mark the interface as **Active** until the agents have completed their tasks. Refreshing the dashboard will update the status accordingly.

Viewing the network topology in the dashboard

From within the dashboard, users can view a logical topology of the network based on the network configuration managed by Neutron. For this, you need to do the following:

Click on **Network Topology** under the **Project** tab to find a logical diagram based on the networks, router, and instances created earlier:

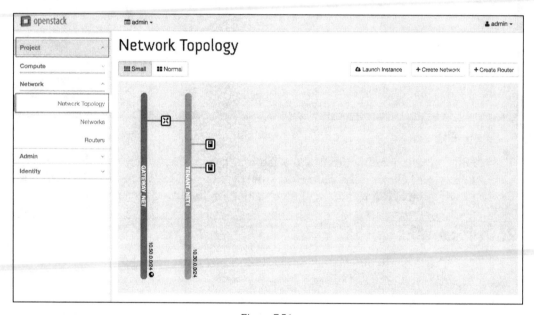

Figure 7.56

Letting the cursor hover over the router icon reveals a window displaying details about the router, such as the connected ports, IPs, and port status:

Figure 7.57

Associating floating IPs to instances in the dashboard

Floating IPs in the dashboard are managed on the **Instances** page under the **Project** tab. Click on the **More** button under the **Actions** tab next to the instance you wish to assign a floating IP to:

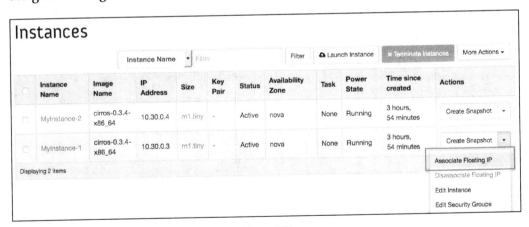

Figure 7.58

Clicking on **Associate Floating IP** reveals a window that allows you to manage floating IP allocations:

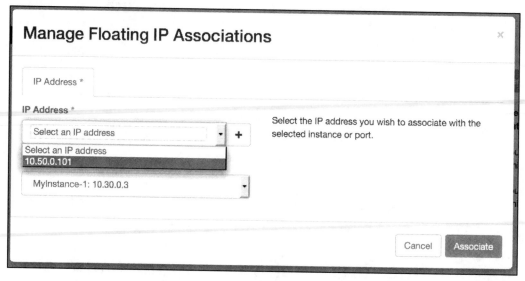

Figure 7.59

If there are no floating IP addresses available for allocation, click on the plus (+) sign to create one. A window will appear that allows new floating IPs to be created:

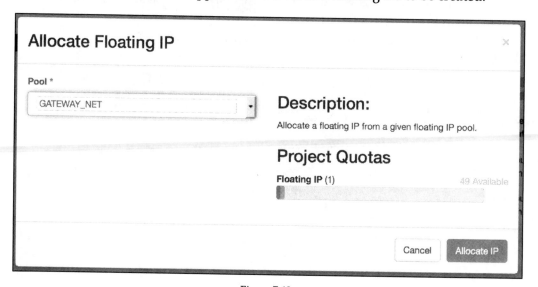

Figure 7.60

As floating IPs are procured from the allocation pool of external provider networks, only provider networks whose `router:external` attribute is set to `true` will appear in the list. Click on the blue **Allocate IP** button to allow Neutron to allocate the next available IP address:

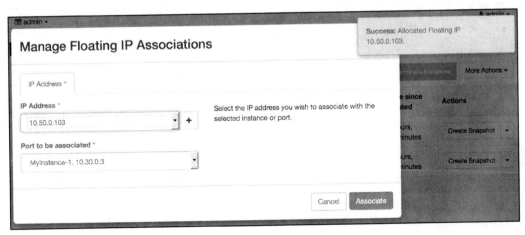

Figure 7.61

Once a floating IP is selected, click on the blue **Associate** button to associate the floating IP with the instance. The instance details page will be updated with the new association:

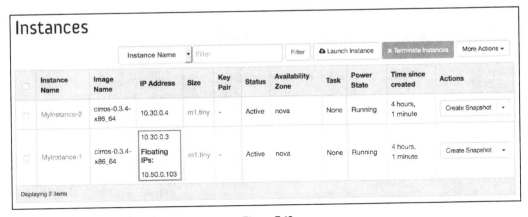

Figure 7.62

Disassociating floating IPs in the dashboard

To disassociate a floating IP from an instance in the dashboard, click on the **More** button under the **Actions** column that corresponds to the instance:

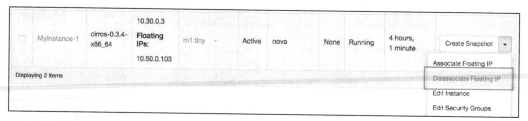

Figure 7.63

A message appears that warns you of the pending action:

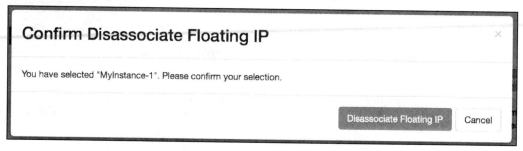

Figure 7.64

Click on the blue **Disassociate Floating IP** button to proceed with the action.

 While the floating IP is disassociated with the instance, it remains under the ownership of the tenant and is not returned to the allocation pool until it is deleted.

Summary

Neutron routers are a core component of networking in OpenStack and provide tenants with the flexibility to design a network best suiting their application. The use of floating IPs allows tenants to quickly and programmatically provide direct connectivity to applications while preserving limited IPv4 address space through the use of network address translation.

Standalone routers may be easy to implement, but they are a single point of failure in any network design. In the event of an L3 agent failure, all routers scheduled to the agent may become unavailable or unreliable. In the next chapter, we will discuss how Neutron implements highly available routers using Virtual Router Redundancy Protocol, or VRRP, to solve many of the shortcomings of standalone routers.

8
Router Redundancy
Using VRRP

In the Juno release of OpenStack, the Neutron community introduced two methods of attaining high availability in routing in a reference implementation. This chapter focuses on a method that uses **Virtual Routing Redundancy Protocol**, also known as **VRRP**, to implement redundancy between two or more Neutron routers. High availability using **distributed virtual routers**, otherwise known as **DVR**, will be discussed in *Chapter 9, Distributed Virtual Routers*.

In the previous chapter, we explored the concept of standalone routers and how they allow users to route traffic between tenant networks and external networks as well as provide network address translation for instances managed by the user. In this chapter, we will cover the following:

- High availability of routing using keepalived and VRRP
- Installing and configuring additional L3 agents
- Demonstrating the creation and management of a highly available router

Using keepalived and VRRP to provide redundancy

Keepalived is a software package for Linux that provides load balancing and high-availability to Linux-based software and infrastructures.

The **Virtual Router Redundancy Protocol**, or **VRRP**, is a first-hop redundancy protocol that aims to provide high availability of a network's default gateway by allowing two or more routers to provide backup for this address. If the active router fails, a backup router takes over the address within a brief period of time. VRRP is an open standard and is based on the proprietary protocol known as **Hot Standby Router Protocol (HSRP)** developed by Cisco.

Neutron uses keepalived, which utilizes VRRP, to provide failover between multiple sets of router namespaces.

VRRP groups

With VRRP, a group of routers can be configured to act as a single virtual router. Routers in the VRRP group elect a master to act as the gateway device, and hosts in the network only need to configure the virtual router to act as their default network gateway. When a failover occurs, another router in the group takes over the routing duties while the configuration of hosts in the network never changes.

In the following diagram, Router A, Router B, and Router C form a single virtual router. In standard configurations, the virtual router has its own IP address, and hosts in the network use the virtual router as their default gateway:

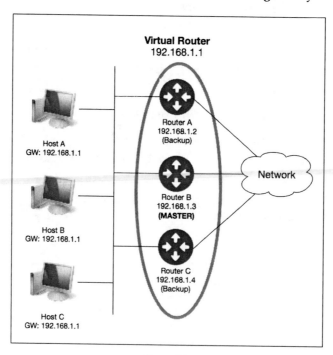

Figure 8.1

As the master router, Router B in the preceding figure is responsible for the virtual address, `192.168.1.1`, and routes traffic for hosts using this address as their gateway. The master router sends VRRP advertisements to the group that includes the priority and state of the master router using the multicast address `224.0.0.18`. The backup routers use a variety of timers and configuration options to determine when a master router has failed and change their state accordingly.

VRRP priority

Routers in the VRRP group elect a master router according to their priorities. The router with the highest priority is elected master, while the other routers in the group act as backups. When a master router fails to send its VRRP advertisements to the group, the backup routers in the VRRP group elect a new master to replace the failed master.

VRRP priorities range from `0` to `255`, with `255` being the highest priority. Neutron configures each router in a group with the same priority of 50. Because the priority is the same between routers, in the event of a failover, the election process falls back to the highest IP address.

VRRP's working mode

A router in a VRRP group works in one of two modes: preemptive and non-preemptive.

Preemptive

In the **preemptive** mode, when a master router fails, it becomes the master router again when it returns to the group if it has a higher priority than the newly elected master.

Non-preemptive

In the **non-preemptive** mode, when a router in a VRRP group becomes the master, it continues to operate as the master under normal working conditions. If a backup router is assigned a higher priority later, the active master router will continue to operate as master until it fails.

As of the Kilo release of OpenStack, Neutron configures each router to act in the non-preemptive mode, although this may change in the future. In the event of a failure of the HA network, the failed master router may not detect that it has failed and continue to operate as the master router even though another router has been elected master. The lack of connectivity between the routers means that all routers may not receive VRRP advertisements. When connectivity is reestablished, the routers may engage in an election to determine a single master router.

VRRP timers

Timers that are used within VRRP include an **advertisement interval timer** and a **preemption delay timer**.

Advertisement interval timer

The master router in a VRRP group periodically sends advertisements on an interval established by the **advertisement interval timer** to inform other routers in the group that it is operating properly. If a backup router does not receive advertisements in a period of three times the interval, the backup regards itself as the master and sends VRRP advertisements to start a new master election process. Neutron routers in a master state are configured to send advertisements every two seconds.

Preemption delay timer

After a backup router receives an advertisement with a priority lower than itself, it waits for a period of time established by the **preemption delay timer** before sending out VRRP advertisements to start a new master election. This delay helps the routers avoid frequent state changes among members of the VRRP group in cases of network flapping. Because preemption is not enabled within Neutron routers, this timer is not configured.

Networking of highly available routers

When a highly available router is created, Neutron creates a VRRP group composed of at least two router namespaces by default. The namespaces are spread across multiple hosts running the Neutron L3 agent, and each runs the keepalived service with its respective configuration. Traffic between the routers uses a dedicated network interface, which is discussed in the following section.

A dedicated HA network

The routers in the VRRP group communicate among one another over a dedicated HA network and interface prefixed with ha. The default HA network, 169.254.192.0/18, is created automatically by Neutron the first time an HA router is created and utilizes the default tenant network type. Only one network is created per tenant, and it is used by all HA routers created by this tenant. If all HA routers in a tenant are deleted, the HA network will remain and be reused for all other HA routers that get created by the tenant in the future.

Networks created by Neutron for VRRP communication between routers are not assigned to tenants. As a result, these networks are hidden from regular users in the CLI and GUI. The name of the network reflects the associated tenant and is used by the L3 agent for this purpose.

Limitations

VRRP utilizes a **virtual router identifier**, or **VRID**, within a subnet and exchanges VRRP protocol messages with other routers with the same VRID using multicast to determine the master router. The VRID is 8 bits in length, and the valid range is 1 to 255. As each tenant uses a single administrative network for VRRP communication between routers, tenants are limited to only 255 HA virtual routers.

The virtual IP

A virtual router has a virtual IP address that can act as the default gateway for hosts in the network. The master router owns the IP address until a failover event occurs, at which time a backup router becomes the new master and takes over the IP and associated routing duties.

Due to limitations with keepalived, Neutron HA routers do not completely follow the VRRP networking conventions described up to this point. Neutron assigns a single virtual IP to an HA router, and this virtual IP is only configured on the master router in the group at any given time. While the address fails over between routers during a failover event, it is not used as a gateway address for any network. As HA routers are created, a new virtual IP address is assigned to the respective group.

Neutron assigns virtual IP addresses from the 169.254.0.0/24 network by default. If an HA router's VRID is 5, then the assigned virtual IP would be 169.254.0.5. Using the VRID in the virtual IP assignment process assures that the address is consistent among HA router instances on different nodes without having to be stored in the database.

Instead of using virtual addresses for each connected subnet, Neutron uses the virtual_ipaddress_excluded configuration section found within the keepalived configuration file to specify routes, addresses, and their respective interfaces that should be configured when a router becomes master for the group. Likewise, the interface configuration is removed once the router becomes a backup router. The following screenshot demonstrates various interfaces and routes that will be modified:

```
vrrp_instance VR_1 {
    state BACKUP
    interface ha-a8675ca3-72
    virtual_router_id 1
    priority 50
    nopreempt
    advert_int 2
    track_interface {
        ha-a8675ca3-72
    }
    virtual_ipaddress {
        169.254.0.1/24 dev ha-a8675ca3-72
    }
    virtual_ipaddress_excluded {
        10.30.0.1/24 dev qr-c0a1d6e4-6d
        10.50.0.102/24 dev qg-d3b80979-74
        10.50.0.103/32 dev qg-d3b80979-74
        fe80::f816:3eff:fe6d:81d1/64 dev qg-d3b80979-74 scope link
        fe80::f816:3eff:fecc:9536/64 dev qr-c0a1d6e4-6d scope link
    }
    virtual_routes {
        0.0.0.0/0 via 10.50.0.1 dev qg-d3b80979-74
    }
}
```

Figure 8.2

The keepalived configuration file for an HA router will be discussed in further detail later in this chapter.

The keepalived service is limited to 20 configured virtual addresses, which could artificially limit the number of subnets attached to a Neutron router. The use of virtual_ipaddress_excluded is a known workaround of this limitation. The resulting behavior remains the same as that of a virtual address.

Determining the master router

In the following screenshot, an HA router without any connected gateway or tenant networks is scheduled across three L3 agents. One router acts as the master, while the other two are relegated to backup duties. The `ha` interfaces are used for communication between the routers:

```
root@controller01:~# ip netns exec qrouter-00b42869-7fbb-433b-93dd-e2359f58f204 ip a
<omit loopback>
2: ha-b1c7bb4c-6b: <BROADCAST,MULTICAST,UP,LOWER_UP> mtu 1500 qdisc pfifo_fast state UP group default qlen 1000
    link/ether fa:16:3e:e4:3a:67 brd ff:ff:ff:ff:ff:ff
    inet 169.254.192.1/18 brd 169.254.255.255 scope global ha-b1c7bb4c-6b
       valid_lft forever preferred_lft forever                           BACKUP
    inet6 fe80::f816:3eff:fee4:3a67/64 scope link
       valid_lft forever preferred_lft forever
```

```
root@compute01:~# ip netns exec qrouter-00b42869-7fbb-433b-93dd-e2359f58f204 ip a
<omit loopback>
2: ha-a8675ca3-72: <BROADCAST,MULTICAST,UP,LOWER_UP> mtu 1500 qdisc pfifo_fast state UP group default qlen 1000
    link/ether fa:16:3e:c5:98:20 brd ff:ff:ff:ff:ff:ff
    inet 169.254.192.3/18 brd 169.254.255.255 scope global ha-a8675ca3-72
       valid_lft forever preferred_lft forever                           BACKUP
    inet6 fe80::f816:3eff:fec5:9820/64 scope link
       valid_lft forever preferred_lft forever
```

```
root@compute02:~# ip netns exec qrouter-00b42869-7fbb-433b-93dd-e2359f58f204 ip a
<omit loopback>
2: ha-dbf90435-cf: <BROADCAST,MULTICAST,UP,LOWER_UP> mtu 1500 qdisc pfifo_fast state UP group default qlen 1000
    link/ether fa:16:3e:94:3a:9f brd ff:ff:ff:ff:ff:ff
    inet 169.254.192.2/18 brd 169.254.255.255 scope global ha-dbf90435-cf
       valid_lft forever preferred_lft forever
    inet 169.254.0.1/24 scope global ha-dbf90435-cf  ◄──── Virtual IP Address    MASTER
       valid_lft forever preferred_lft forever
    inet6 fe80::f816:3eff:fe94:3a9f/64 scope link
       valid_lft forever preferred_lft forever
```

Figure 8.3

At any given time, only the master router should have the virtual IP address configured on its `ha` interface.

> Other than examining namespaces, there is currently no way to tell which L3 agent is hosting the master router at any given time. This should be addressed with updates to the Neutron API and client in future releases.

Installing and configuring additional L3 agents

To configure HA routers, two or more L3 agents are required. To install the Neutron L3 agent, run the following command on the remaining compute nodes:

```
# apt-get install neutron-l3-agent
```

Defining an interface driver

Both the LinuxBridge and Open vSwitch mechanism drivers support HA routers, and the Neutron L3 agent must be configured to use the interface driver that corresponds to the chosen mechanism driver.

Update the Neutron L3 configuration file on the compute nodes at /etc/neutron/l3_agent.ini and specify one of the following interface drivers.

For LinuxBridge, use the following code:

```
[DEFAULT]
...
interface_driver = neutron.agent.linux.interface.BridgeInterfaceDriver
```

For Open vSwitch, use the following code:

```
[DEFAULT]
...
interface_driver = neutron.agent.linux.interface.OVSInterfaceDriver
```

Setting the external bridge

The external_network_bridge configuration option was discussed in detail in the previous chapter and should be configured identically across all L3 agents.

On all nodes, set the external_network_bridge configuration option to an unset value in the L3 agent configuration file, as follows:

```
[DEFAULT]
...
external_network_bridge =
```

Enabling router namespace deletion

By default, the Neutron L3 agent will not delete network namespaces when a router is deleted due to a bug found in older releases of the iproute2 utility. In modern operating systems, including the latest Ubuntu 14.04 LTS discussed in this book, the `router_delete_namespaces` option in the L3 agent configuration file can be set from `false` to `true` as follows:

```
[DEFAULT]
...
router_delete_namespaces = true
```

Setting the agent mode

The Neutron L3 agent considers HA routers as legacy routers, as many of the same mechanisms used for standalone routers are shared with HA routers. The default value for `agent_mode` is `legacy`, which will remain unchanged for the remainder of this chapter.

Restarting the Neutron L3 agent

After making changes to the configuration of the Neutron L3 agent, issue the following command on the compute nodes to restart the agent:

```
# service neutron-l3-agent restart
```

After a restart of the services, the additional agents should check in. Use the following Neutron `agent-list` command to return a listing of all L3 agents:

```
# neutron agent-list --agent_type="L3 Agent"
```

The API should return similar output to that shown in the following image:

```
root@controller01:~# neutron agent-list --agent_type="L3 Agent"
+--------------------------------------+----------+--------------------------------+-------+----------------+-----------------+
| id                                   | agent_type | host                         | alive | admin_state_up | binary          |
+--------------------------------------+----------+--------------------------------+-------+----------------+-----------------+
| 18abffc5-ea4d-43d1-9d10-5182dd9228de | L3 agent | compute01.learningneutron.com  | :-)   | True           | neutron-l3-agent |
| 69db2138-e4b4-4c3c-99ff-b8e13c377ff9 | L3 agent | compute02.learningneutron.com  | :-)   | True           | neutron-l3-agent |
| cd41db3f-4886-4446-8114-cccbde66cf95 | L3 agent | controller01.learningneutron.com | :-) | True           | neutron-l3-agent |
+--------------------------------------+----------+--------------------------------+-------+----------------+-----------------+
```

Figure 8.4

If an agent is not listed in the output as expected, troubleshoot any errors that may be indicated in the `/var/log/neutron/l3-agent.log` log file on the respective node.

Configuring Neutron

Neutron uses default settings to determine the type of routers that tenants are allowed to create as well as the number of routers that should be deployed across L3 agents.

The following default settings are specified within the Neutron configuration file at `/etc/neutron/neutron.conf` and only need to be modified on the host running the Neutron API service. In this environment, the `neutron-server` service runs on the controller node:

```
# =========== items for l3 extension =============
# Enable high availability for virtual routers.
# l3_ha = False
#
# Maximum number of l3 agents which a HA router will be
# scheduled on. If it is set to 0 the router will be scheduled on
# every agent.
# max_l3_agents_per_router = 3
#
# Minimum number of l3 agents which a HA router will be
# scheduled on. The default value is 2.
# min_l3_agents_per_router = 2
#
# CIDR of the administrative network if HA mode is enabled
# l3_ha_net_cidr = 169.254.192.0/18
# =========== end of items for l3 extension =======
```

To set HA routers as the default router type for tenants, set the `l3_ha` configuration option to `True` in `neutron.conf`. For this demonstration, the default value of `false` is sufficient.

When an HA router is created, multiple router namespaces are created and distributed among the L3 agents. At a minimum, two L3 agents are required.

To increase the number of L3 agents required for redundancy, increase the `min_l3_agents_per_router` value. For this demonstration, the default value is sufficient.

To set a maximum number of L3 agents used for a virtual router, set `max_l3_agents_per_router` accordingly. For this demonstration, the default value is sufficient.

Once the changes have been made, restart the `neutron-server` service on the controller node for the changes to take effect.

Working with highly available routers

With few exceptions, creating and managing an HA router is no different from its standalone counterpart. Neutron's router management commands were covered in the previous chapter, and the exceptions can be found in the following sections.

Creating highly available routers

As an administrator, HA routers can be created using the `--ha` flag with the Neutron `router-create` command, as follows:

```
usage:    router-create [--tenant-id TENANT_ID] [--admin-state-down]
          --ha {True,False}
          NAME
```

> As a regular user, the type of router that is created, whether it's a standalone, HA, or distributed virtual router, is determined by the `l3_ha` configuration option in the Neutron configuration file. Users do not have the ability to override the default router type and cannot specify the `--ha` option.

Deleting highly available routers

To delete an HA router, simply use the following Neutron `router-delete` command:

```
usage:    neutron router-delete ROUTER
```

> When all HA routers in a tenant are removed, the HA network used for communication between routers stays behind. This network will be reused upon the creation of HA routers at a later time.

Decomposing a highly available router

Using the concepts demonstrated in previous chapters, let's walk through the creation and decomposition of a highly available router. In the following example, I've started out with an external provider network and tenant network named GATEWAY_NET and TENANT_NET, respectively:

```
root@controller01:~# neutron net-list
+--------------------------------------+-------------+---------------------------------------------------------+
| id                                   | name        | subnets                                                 |
+--------------------------------------+-------------+---------------------------------------------------------+
| 55451e10-861e-49b8-9abc-a5996fe6adb3 | GATEWAY_NET | f2444660-69c6-4002-bc6c-62b5eb2bfc62 10.50.0.0/24       |
| d305da03-960a-4ce4-aaec-4ee681fcff3d | TENANT_NET  | bec74bb0-a8b9-448b-96e6-b4b8041dede5 10.30.0.0/24       |
+--------------------------------------+-------------+---------------------------------------------------------+
```

Figure 8.5

Using the router-create command with the --ha=true option, an HA router named MyRouter-HA will be created:

```
root@controller01:~# neutron router-create MyRouter-HA --ha=true
Created a new router:
+-----------------------+------------------------------------------+
| Field                 | Value                                    |
+-----------------------+------------------------------------------+
| admin_state_up        | True                                     |
| distributed           | False                                    |
| external_gateway_info |                                          |
| ha                    | True                                     |
| id                    | 00b42869-7fbb-433b-93dd-e2359f58f204     |
| name                  | MyRouter-HA                              |
| routes                |                                          |
| status                | ACTIVE                                   |
| tenant_id             | 65ff4cf1a04846f1ab2bc1ff0efb1090         |
+-----------------------+------------------------------------------+
```

Figure 8.6

Upon the creation of the HA router, a network namespace will be created on at least two hosts running the Neutron L3 agent. In this demonstration, the L3 agent is running on the controller and both compute nodes. Neutron has been configured to create a network namespace on up to three L3 agents.

In the following screenshot, a router namespace that corresponds to the `MyRouter-HA` router can be observed on each host:

```
root@controller01:~# ip netns
qrouter-00b42869-7fbb-433b-93dd-e2359f58f204
qdhcp-d305da03-960a-4ce4-aaec-4ee681fcff3d

root@compute01:~# ip netns
qrouter-00b42869-7fbb-433b-93dd-e2359f58f204

root@compute02:~# ip netns
qrouter-00b42869-7fbb-433b-93dd-e2359f58f204
```

Figure 8.7

Neutron automatically creates a network reserved for communication between the routers upon the creation of the first HA router within a tenant using the network defined by the `l3_ha_net_cidr` configuration option in the L3 agent configuration file:

```
root@controller01:~# neutron net-list
+--------------------------------------+----------------------------------------------+------------------------------------------------------------+
| id                                   | name                                         | subnets                                                    |
+--------------------------------------+----------------------------------------------+------------------------------------------------------------+
| 55451e10-861e-49b8-9abc-a5996fe6adb3 | GATEWAY_NET                                  | f2444660-69c6-4002-bc6c-62b5eb2bfc62 10.50.0.0/24          |
| d305da03-960a-4ce4-aaec-4ee681fcff3d | TENANT_NET                                   | bec74bb0-a8b9-448b-96e6-b4b8041dede5 10.30.0.0/24          |
| a99c3664-f771-4489-98c5-473d61aca55f | HA network tenant 65ff4cf1a04846f1ab2bc1ff0efb1090 | 24c8adce-1b87-4d28-b312-a33e19defdab 169.254.192.0/18 |
+--------------------------------------+----------------------------------------------+------------------------------------------------------------+
```

Figure 8.8

The HA network is not directly associated with the tenant and is not visible to anyone but an administrator, who can see all the networks:

```
root@controller01:~# neutron net-show a99c3664-f771-4489-98c5-473d61aca55f
+---------------------------+------------------------------------------------------+
| Field                     | Value                                                |
+---------------------------+------------------------------------------------------+
| admin_state_up            | True                                                 |
| id                        | a99c3664-f771-4489-98c5-473d61aca55f                 |
| mtu                       | 0                                                    |
| name                      | HA network tenant 65ff4cf1a04846f1ab2bc1ff0efb1090   |
| provider:network_type     | vlan                                                 |
| provider:physical_network | physnet2                                             |
| provider:segmentation_id  | 33                                                   |
| router:external           | False                                                |
| shared                    | False                                                |
| status                    | ACTIVE                                               |
| subnets                   | 24c8adce-1b87-4d28-b312-a33e19defdab                 |
| tenant_id                 |                                                      |
+---------------------------+------------------------------------------------------+
```

Figure 8.9

The name of the HA network includes the ID of the tenant who created the router, and the network is used by Neutron for all HA routers created by this tenant in the future.

 The HA network utilizes the default tenant network type and consumes a segmentation ID of this type.

Both a gateway and internal interface will be attached using the `router-gateway-set` and `router-interface-add` commands, respectively. Neutron's `router-port-list` command reveals the gateway, internal, and HA ports associated with the router:

```
root@controller01:~# neutron router-port-list MyRouter-HA
+--------------------------------------+-----------------------------------------------+-------------------+-------------------------------------------------------------------------------------------------+
| id                                   | name                                          | mac_address       | fixed_ips                                                                                       |
+--------------------------------------+-----------------------------------------------+-------------------+-------------------------------------------------------------------------------------------------+
| b1c7bb4c-6b9f-4373-89d0-7f307e7cab5f | HA port tenant 65ff4cf1a04846f1ab2bc1ff0efb1090 | fa:16:3e:e4:3a:67 | {"subnet_id": "24c8adce-1b87-4d28-b312-a33e19defdab", "ip_address": "169.254.192.1"} |
| dbf90435-cf8a-4e63-b0ae-c220f95d24aa | HA port tenant 65ff4cf1a04846f1ab2bc1ff0efb1090 | fa:16:3e:94:3a:9f | {"subnet_id": "24c8adce-1b87-4d28-b312-a33e19defdab", "ip_address": "169.254.192.2"} |
| a8675ca3-7200-436c-9c34-643a5a4e4c42 | HA port tenant 65ff4cf1a04846f1ab2bc1ff0efb1090 | fa:16:3e:c5:98:20 | {"subnet_id": "24c8adce-1b87-4d28-b312-a33e19defdab", "ip_address": "169.254.192.3"} |
| d3b80979-74a9-432e-8055-fc56ecd958ba | External Network Interface                    | fa:16:3e:6d:81:d1 | {"subnet_id": "f2444660-69c6-4002-bc6c-62b5eb2bfc62", "ip_address": "10.50.0.102"} |
| c0a1d6e4-6daa-4db5-b91a-7deac91e38ec | Internal Network Interface                    | fa:16:3e:cc:95:36 | {"subnet_id": "bec74bb0-a8b9-448b-96e6-b4b0041de6d5", "ip_address": "10.30.0.1"} |
+--------------------------------------+-----------------------------------------------+-------------------+-------------------------------------------------------------------------------------------------+
```

Figure 8.10

The three HA ports will be created automatically by Neutron and are used for communication between the router namespaces on the hosts. Inside the network namespaces, we can find the corresponding interfaces, as shown in the following figures:

```
root@controller01:~# ip netns exec qrouter-00b42869-7fbb-433b-93dd-e2359f58f204 ip a
<omit loopback>
2: ha-b1c7bb4c-6b: <BROADCAST,MULTICAST,UP,LOWER_UP> mtu 1500 qdisc pfifo_fast state UP group default qlen 1000
    link/ether fa:16:3e:e4:3a:67 brd ff:ff:ff:ff:ff:ff
    inet 169.254.192.1/18 brd 169.254.255.255 scope global ha-b1c7bb4c-6b
       valid_lft forever preferred_lft forever
    inet6 fe80::f816:3eff:fee4:3a67/64 scope link
       valid_lft forever preferred_lft forever
3: qg-d3b80979-74: <BROADCAST,MULTICAST,UP,LOWER_UP> mtu 1500 qdisc pfifo_fast state UP group default qlen 1000
    link/ether fa:16:3e:6d:81:d1 brd ff:ff:ff:ff:ff:ff
4: qr-c0a1d6e4-6d: <BROADCAST,MULTICAST,UP,LOWER_UP> mtu 1500 qdisc pfifo_fast state UP group default qlen 1000
    link/ether fa:16:3e:cc:95:36 brd ff:ff:ff:ff:ff:ff
```

Figure 8.11

```
root@compute01:~# ip netns exec qrouter-00b42869-7fbb-433b-93dd-e2359f58f204 ip a
<omit loopback>
2: ha-a8675ca3-72: <BROADCAST,MULTICAST,UP,LOWER_UP> mtu 1500 qdisc pfifo_fast state UP group default qlen 1000
    link/ether fa:16:3e:c5:98:20 brd ff:ff:ff:ff:ff:ff
    inet 169.254.192.3/18 brd 169.254.255.255 scope global ha-a8675ca3-72
       valid_lft forever preferred_lft forever
    inet6 fe80::f816:3eff:fec5:9820/64 scope link
       valid_lft forever preferred_lft forever
3: qg-d3b80979-74: <BROADCAST,MULTICAST,UP,LOWER_UP> mtu 1500 qdisc pfifo_fast state UP group default qlen 1000
    link/ether fa:16:3e:6d:81:d1 brd ff:ff:ff:ff:ff:ff
4: qr-c0a1d6e4-6d: <BROADCAST,MULTICAST,UP,LOWER_UP> mtu 1500 qdisc pfifo_fast state UP group default qlen 1000
    link/ether fa:16:3e:cc:95:36 brd ff:ff:ff:ff:ff:ff
```

Figure 8.12

```
root@compute02:~# ip netns exec qrouter-00b42869-7fbb-433b-93dd-e2359f58f204 ip a
<omit loopback>
2: ha-dbf90435-cf: <BROADCAST,MULTICAST,UP,LOWER_UP> mtu 1500 qdisc pfifo_fast state UP group default qlen 1000
    link/ether fa:16:3e:94:3a:9f brd ff:ff:ff:ff:ff:ff
    inet 169.254.192.2/18 brd 169.254.255.255 scope global ha-dbf90435-cf
       valid_lft forever preferred_lft forever                         VRRP
    inet 169.254.0.1/24 scope global ha-dbf90435-cf    ◄────────       Virtual IP
       valid_lft forever preferred_lft forever
    inet6 fe80::f816:3eff:fe94:3a9f/64 scope link
       valid_lft forever preferred_lft forever
3: qg-d3b80979-74: <BROADCAST,MULTICAST,UP,LOWER_UP> mtu 1500 qdisc pfifo_fast state UP group default qlen 1000
    link/ether fa:16:3e:6d:81:d1 brd ff:ff:ff:ff:ff:ff
    inet 10.50.0.102/24 scope global qg-d3b80979-74   ◄────────        Active qg
       valid_lft forever preferred_lft forever                         interface
    inet6 fe80::f816:3eff:fe6d:81d1/64 scope link
       valid_lft forever preferred_lft forever
4: qr-c0a1d6e4-6d: <BROADCAST,MULTICAST,UP,LOWER_UP> mtu 1500 qdisc pfifo_fast state UP group default qlen 1000
    link/ether fa:16:3e:cc:95:36 brd ff:ff:ff:ff:ff:ff
    inet 10.30.0.1/24 scope global qr-c0a1d6e4-6d     ◄────────        Active qr
       valid_lft forever preferred_lft forever                         interface
    inet6 fe80::f816:3eff:fecc:9536/64 scope link
       valid_lft forever preferred_lft forever
```

Figure 8.13

In the preceding figures, the router namespace on `compute02` was elected as the master router, as evidenced by the virtual IP, `169.254.0.1/24`, being configured on the `ha` interface within the namespace. In addition to the `ha` interface, the `qg` and `qr` interfaces are only fully configured on the master router. If more than one router owns the virtual IP or you see the `qg` and `qr` interfaces fully configured on more than one router, there may be communication issues between the routers on the HA network.

Based on Neutron's configuration of keepalived, the virtual IP is not used as a gateway address and is only used as a standardized address that can failover to other routers as part of the VRRP failover mechanisms. Neutron does not treat addresses on the qg or qr interfaces as virtual IPs. Along with the virtual IP, the qg and qr interfaces should only be configured and active on the master router at any given time.

Examining the keepalived configuration

Neutron configures keepalived in each namespace so that together the namespaces can act as a single virtual router. A `keepalived` service runs in each namespace and uses the following configuration file on the underlying host:

```
/var/lib/neutron/ha_confs/<router_id>/keepalived.conf
```

A look at the configuration file shows keepalived and VRRP configurations in use:

```
root@compute02:~# cat /var/lib/neutron/ha_confs/00b42869-7fbb-433b-93dd-e2359f58f204/keepalived.conf
vrrp_instance VR_1 {
    state BACKUP
    interface ha-dbf90435-cf
    virtual_router_id 1            ◄──────── Virtual Router ID (VRID)
    priority 50    ◄──────────  Router priority
    nopreempt      ◄──────────  Preempt mode
    advert_int 2   ◄──────────  Advertisement interval
    track_interface {
        ha-dbf90435-cf
    }
    virtual_ipaddress {
        169.254.0.1/24 dev ha-dbf90435-cf    ◄──────────  Virtual IP address
    }
    virtual_ipaddress_excluded {
        10.30.0.1/24 dev qr-c0a1d6e4-6d       ◄──────── Internal IP to be configured when master
        10.50.0.102/24 dev qg-d3b80979-74     ◄──────── External IP to be configured when master
        fe80::f816:3eff:fe6d:81d1/64 dev qg-d3b80979-74 scope link
        fe80::f816:3eff:fecc:9536/64 dev qr-c0a1d6e4-6d scope link
    }
    virtual_routes {
        0.0.0.0/0 via 10.50.0.1 dev qg-d3b80979-74    ◄──────── Route be configured when master
    }
```

Figure 8.14

Executing a failover

Under normal circumstances, a node is not likely to fail and router failover is unlikely to occur. A failure scenario can be recreated and failover tested by manually rebooting the node hosting the active router or by putting its physical interfaces in a down state.

Failover actions are logged in the following location within the router namespaces:

```
/var/lib/neutron/ha_confs/<router_id>/neutron-keepalived-state-change.
log
```

An example of a router going from a backup state to master state once failure is detected can be observed in the following screenshot:

```
root@compute01:~# tail -f /var/lib/neutron/ha_confs/00b42869-7fbb-433b-93dd-e2359f58f204/neutron-keepalived-state-change.log
2015-10-17 10:48:14.363 neutron.agent.l3.keepalived_state_change [-] Wrote router 00b42869-7fbb-433b-93dd-e2359f58f204 state backup write_state_change
2015-10-17 10:48:14.425 neutron.agent.l3.keepalived_state_change [-] Notified agent router 00b42869-7fbb-433b-93dd-e2359f58f204, state backup notify_agent
2015-10-17 11:09:37.073 neutron.agent.l3.keepalived_state_change [-] Wrote router 00b42869-7fbb-433b-93dd-e2359f58f204 state master write_state_change
2015-10-17 11:09:38.411 neutron.agent.l3.keepalived_state_change [-] Notified agent router 00b42869-7fbb-433b-93dd-e2359f58f204, state master notify_agent
```

Figure 8.15

Once the former master router detects that a new master is elected, it moves to a backup state:

```
root@compute02:~# tail -f /var/lib/neutron/ha_confs/00b42869-7fbb-433b-93dd-e2359f58f204/neutron-keepalived-state-change.log
2015-10-17 10:04:51.845 neutron.agent.l3.keepalived_state_change [-] Wrote router 00b42869-7fbb-433b-93dd-e2359f58f204 state master write_state_change
2015-10-17 10:04:52.403 neutron.agent.l3.keepalived_state_change [-] Notified agent router 00b42869-7fbb-433b-93dd-e2359f58f204, state master notify_agent
2015-10-17 11:12:31.897 neutron.agent.l3.keepalived_state_change [-] Wrote router 00b42869-7fbb-433b-93dd-e2359f58f204 state backup write_state_change
2015-10-17 11:12:31.972 neutron.agent.l3.keepalived_state_change [-] Notified agent router 00b42869-7fbb-433b-93dd-e2359f58f204, state backup notify_agent
```

Figure 8.16

Issues with failovers

In the current Kilo release of OpenStack, there are outstanding bugs in relation to router failover and L2 population that affect both LinuxBridge- and Open vSwitch-based environments. When the l2population and vxlan drivers are used, Neutron programs the forwarding table with manual entries on each host to indicate which VXLAN tunnel to use when communicating with particular addresses.

Normally, when a router fails over to another node, the newly elected master sends a gratuitous ARP to indicate its new location, and MAC address tables or bridge forwarding tables are updated accordingly. Because Neutron is responsible for updating these tables dynamically based on the information in the database, the lack of notification to the Neutron agent when a router fails over means that stale information may remain in the FDB table when a failover occurs. Instances attempting to communicate with their respective gateway may utilize the wrong VXLAN tunnel, among other issues.

A fix for this issue has been implemented for Open vSwitch in the latest Kilo release. However, the respective LinuxBridge fix remains incomplete. More information on this issue can be seen in the following Neutron bug report:

```
https://bugs.launchpad.net/neutron/+bug/1365476
```

Summary

Highly available routers can be created and managed using the same router command set that was discussed in the previous chapter. The L3 agents are responsible for configuring the routers in a VRRP group, and the routers are left to elect the master router and implement their respective keepalived configuration.

While HA routers provide a level of redundancy over their standalone counterparts, they are not without their drawbacks. A single node hosting a master router is still a bottleneck for traffic traversing this router. In addition, if the network used for dedicated VRRP traffic between routers experiences a loss of connectivity, the routers can become split-brained, causing two or more routers to become master routers and potentially causing ARP and MAC flapping issues in the network. Connection tracking between routers has not been implemented as of the Kilo release, which means that connections to and from instances may be severed during a failover event. In addition to the previously mentioned limitations, there are also outstanding bugs in relation to router failover and L2 population that affect both LinuxBridge- and Open vSwitch-based Juno and Kilo environments and should be addressed in a future release of OpenStack.

In the next chapter, we will look at distributed virtual routers: a method of distributing routers across compute nodes that are responsible for routing traffic for their respective instances.

9
Distributed Virtual Routers

Prior to the introduction of Neutron in the Folsom release of OpenStack, all network management was built into the Nova API and was known as nova-network. Nova-network remains an alternative to Neutron, although the networking models and functionality provided by it are limited when compared to the advanced features offered by Neutron. Despite its advanced feature set, up until the Juno release, Neutron was unable to replicate one of the most common networking scenarios available with nova-network: FlatDHCP with multi-host.

The multi-host functionality of nova-network offers high availability of networking by limiting the single points of failure to individual compute nodes rather than single network nodes or L2/L3 agents. High availability using distributed virtual routers borrows many concepts from the nova-network multi-host model while retaining support for many of the networking features provided by Neutron.

Distributing routers across the cloud

Much like nova-network does with its multi-host functionality, Neutron can distribute a virtual router across compute nodes in an effort to isolate the failure domain to a particular compute node rather than a traditional network node. By eliminating a centralized layer 3 agent, the routing that was performed on a single node is now handled by the compute nodes themselves.

Legacy routing using a centralized network node resembles the following diagram:

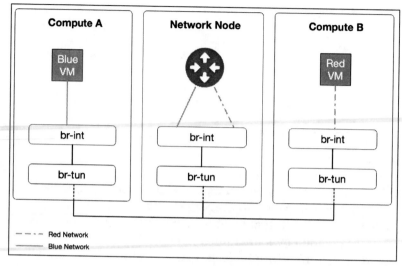

Figure 9.1

In the legacy model, traffic from the blue virtual machine to the red virtual machine on a different network would traverse a centralized network node hosting the router. If the node hosting the router were to fail, traffic between the instances and external networks, or the instances themselves, would be dropped.

In this chapter, I will discuss the following:

- Installing and configuring additional L3 agents
- Demonstrating the creation and management of a distributed virtual router
- Routing between networks behind the same router
- Outbound connectivity using SNAT
- Inbound and outbound connectivity using floating IPs

Installing and configuring Neutron components

To configure distributed virtual routers, there are a few required components that must be installed and configured:

- The ML2 plugin
- The L2population mechanism driver
- The Open vSwitch mechanism driver

- The layer 3 agent installed on all network and compute nodes
- The external bridge configured on all network and compute nodes

Installing additional L3 agents

To install the Neutron L3 agent, run the following command on the remaining compute nodes if it has not yet been installed:

```
# apt-get install neutron-l3-agent
```

Defining an interface driver

Open vSwitch and the Open vSwitch mechanism driver are required to enable and utilize distributed virtual routers.

Update the Neutron L3 configuration file on the compute nodes and specify the following interface driver:

```
[DEFAULT]
...
interface_driver = neutron.agent.linux.interface.OVSInterfaceDriver
```

Enabling distributed mode

The ML2 plugin is required to operate distributed virtual routers and must be configured accordingly.

Update the ML2 configuration file at /etc/neutron/plugins/ml2/ml2_conf.ini on all nodes to enable the OVS agent to support distributed virtual routing and L2 population:

```
[agent]
...
enable_distributed_routing = True
l2_population = True
```

Setting the external bridge

On all nodes, set the external_network_bridge configuration option to an unset value in the L3 agent configuration file:

```
[DEFAULT]
...
external_network_bridge =
```

Enabling router namespace deletion

By default, the Neutron L3 agent does not delete network namespaces when a router is deleted due to a bug found in older releases of the iproute2 utility. In modern operating systems, including the latest Ubuntu 14.04 LTS discussed in this book, the `router_delete_namespaces` option in the L3 agent configuration file can be set from `false` to `true` on all nodes:

```
[DEFAULT]
...
router_delete_namespaces = true
```

Setting the agent mode

When using distributed virtual routers, a node can operate in one of two modes: `dvr` or `dvr_snat`. A node configured in `dvr_snat` mode handles north-south SNAT traffic, while a node in `dvr` mode handles the north-south DNAT (for example, floating IP) and east-west traffic between instances.

In this book, the controller node serves as a network node in addition to handling API services and will handle SNAT traffic. On the controller node, configure the L3 agent to operate in `dvr_snat` mode by modifying the `agent_mode` option in the L3 agent configuration file:

```
[DEFAULT]
...
agent_mode = dvr_snat
```

On the compute nodes, configure the L3 agent to operate in `dvr` mode:

```
[DEFAULT]
...
agent_mode = dvr
```

Configuring Neutron

Neutron uses default settings to determine the type of routers that tenants are allowed to create as well as the number of routers that should be deployed across L3 agents.

The following default settings are specified within the `neutron.conf` configuration file and only need to be modified on the host running the Neutron API service. In this environment, the `neutron-server` service runs on the controller node:

```
# ==Start Global Config Option for Distributed L3 Router==
# Setting the "router_distributed" flag to "True" will default
```

```
# to the creation of distributed tenant routers. The admin can
# override this flag by specifying the type of the router on the
# create request (admin-only attribute). Default value is "False"
# to support legacy mode (centralized) routers.
#
# router_distributed = False
#
# ==End Global Config Option for Distributed L3 Router==
```

To set distributed routers as the default router type for tenants, set the `router_distributed` configuration option to `True` in `neutron.conf`. For this demonstration, the default value of `false` is sufficient.

Once the changes have been made, restart the `neutron-server` service on controller01 for the changes to take effect.

Restarting the Neutron L3 and Open vSwitch agent

After making changes to the configuration of the Neutron L3 and L2 agents, issue the following command on all nodes to restart the respective agents:

```
# service neutron-l3-agent restart
# service neutron-plugin-openvswitch-agent restart
```

After a restart of the services, the additional agents should check in. Use the following Neutron `agent-list` command to return a listing of all L3 agents:

```
# neutron agent-list --agent_type="L3 Agent"
```

The service should return a similar output to that shown in the following screenshot:

```
root@controller01:~# neutron agent-list --agent_type="L3 Agent"
+--------------------------------------+------------+-------------+-------+----------------+------------------+
| id                                   | agent_type | host        | alive | admin_state_up | binary           |
+--------------------------------------+------------+-------------+-------+----------------+------------------+
| fbb712cc-4a7f-4d13-a87c-af2bd3a8aa52 | L3 agent   | compute01   | :-)   | True           | neutron-l3-agent |
| 883e73b4-02f0-4d4b-bdb5-6b2dc64b5889 | L3 agent   | compute02   | :-)   | True           | neutron-l3-agent |
| 6a7d5e2f-f9bc-4623-9614-17b1db06c068 | L3 agent   | controller01| :-)   | True           | neutron-l3-agent |
+--------------------------------------+------------+-------------+-------+----------------+------------------+
```

Figure 9.2

If an agent is not listed in the output as expected, troubleshoot any errors that may be indicated in the `/var/log/neutron/l3-agent.log` log file on the respective node.

Managing distributed virtual routers

With few exceptions, managing a distributed router is no different from its standalone counterpart. Neutron's router management commands were covered in *Chapter 7, Creating Standalone Routers with Neutron*. The exception is covered in the following section.

Creating distributed virtual routers

As an administrator, distributed virtual routers can be created using the following Neutron `router-create` command syntax:

```
usage:    router-create [--tenant-id TENANT_ID] [--admin-state-down]
          --distributed {True,False}
          NAME
```

> As a regular user, the type of router that is created, whether it's a standalone, HA, or distributed virtual router, is determined by the `router_distributed` option in the Neutron configuration file. Users do not have the ability to override the default router type and cannot specify the `--distributed` option.

Routing east-west traffic between instances

In the network world, east-west traffic is traditionally defined as server-to-server traffic. In Neutron, as it relates to distributed virtual routers, east-west traffic is the traffic between instances in different networks owned by the same tenant. In the legacy model, all traffic between different networks traverses a virtual router located on a centralized network node. With DVR, the same traffic bypasses the network node and goes directly between the compute nodes hosting the virtual machine instances.

Reviewing the topology

Logically speaking, a distributed virtual router is a single router object connecting two or more tenant networks, as shown in the following diagram:

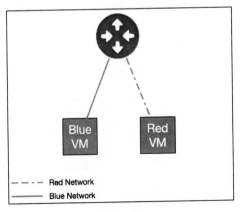

Figure 9.3

In the following example, a distributed virtual router named `MyRouter-DVR` is created and connected to two tenant networks: `TENANT_BLUE` and `TENANT_RED`. Virtual machine instances in each network use their respective default gateways to route traffic to the other network through the same router. The virtual machine instances are unaware of where the router is located.

A look under the hood, however, tells a different story. In the following example, the blue VM pings the red VM:

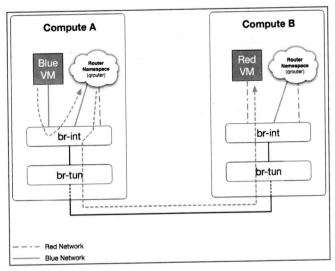

Figure 9.4

As far as the user is concerned, the router connecting the two networks is a single entity known as `MyRouter-DVR`:

```
root@controller01:~# neutron router-list
+--------------------------------------+-------------+---------------------+-------------+-------+
| id                                   | name        | external_gateway_info | distributed | ha    |
+--------------------------------------+-------------+---------------------+-------------+-------+
| cf6230cc-9749-40a6-a15b-ef8b466fe148 | MyRouter-DVR | null               | True        | False |
+--------------------------------------+-------------+---------------------+-------------+-------+
```

Figure 9.5

In reality, each compute node hosts a copy of the router:

```
root@controller01:~# neutron l3-agent-list-hosting-router MyRouter-DVR
+--------------------------------------+--------------+----------------+-------+
| id                                   | host         | admin_state_up | alive |
+--------------------------------------+--------------+----------------+-------+
| 6a7d5e2f-f9bc-4623-9614-17b1db06c068 | controller01 | True           | :-)   |
| 883e73b4-02f0-4d4b-bdb5-6b2dc64b5889 | compute02    | True           | :-)   |
| fbb712cc-4a7f-4d13-a87c-af2bd3a8aa52 | compute01    | True           | :-)   |
+--------------------------------------+--------------+----------------+-------+
```

Figure 9.6

 Until a virtual machine instance is scheduled to a particular compute node, the router will not be scheduled to this node. If a compute node is missing from the list, verify that an instance in the tenant network has been scheduled to it.

Using the `ip netns exec` command, we can see that the `qr` interfaces within the namespaces on each compute node and controller node share the same interface names, IP addresses, and MAC addresses:

```
root@controller01:~# ip netns exec qrouter-cf6230cc-9749-40a6-a15b-ef8b466fe148 ip a
<omit loopback>
18: qr-57d9bd1e-44: <BROADCAST,MULTICAST,UP,LOWER_UP> mtu 1500 qdisc noqueue state UNKNOWN group default
    link/ether fa:16:3e:37:5e:a5 brd ff:ff:ff:ff:ff:ff
    inet 172.16.5.1/24 brd 172.16.5.255 scope global qr-57d9bd1e-44
       valid_lft forever preferred_lft forever
    inet6 fe80::f816:3eff:fe37:5ea5/64 scope link
       valid_lft forever preferred_lft forever
19: qr-29db7422-76: <BROADCAST,MULTICAST,UP,LOWER_UP> mtu 1500 qdisc noqueue state UNKNOWN group default
    link/ether fa:16:3e:95:ad:f9 brd ff:ff:ff:ff:ff:ff
    inet 192.168.1.1/24 brd 192.168.1.255 scope global qr-29db7422-76
       valid_lft forever preferred_lft forever
    inet6 fe80::f816:3eff:fe95:adf9/64 scope link
       valid_lft forever preferred_lft forever
```

Figure 9.7

```
root@compute01:~# ip netns exec qrouter-cf6230cc-9749-40a6-a15b-ef8b466fe148 ip a
<omit loopback>
14: qr-29db7422-76: <BROADCAST,MULTICAST,UP,LOWER_UP> mtu 1500 qdisc noqueue state UNKNOWN group default
    link/ether fa:16:3e:95:ad:f9 brd ff:ff:ff:ff:ff:ff
    inet 192.168.1.1/24 brd 192.168.1.255 scope global qr-29db7422-76
       valid_lft forever preferred_lft forever
    inet6 fe80::f816:3eff:fe95:adf9/64 scope link
       valid_lft forever preferred_lft forever
15: qr-57d9bd1e-44: <BROADCAST,MULTICAST,UP,LOWER_UP> mtu 1500 qdisc noqueue state UNKNOWN group default
    link/ether fa:16:3e:37:5e:a5 brd ff:ff:ff:ff:ff:ff
    inet 172.16.5.1/24 brd 172.16.5.255 scope global qr-57d9bd1e-44
       valid_lft forever preferred_lft forever
    inet6 fe80::f816:3eff:fe37:5ea5/64 scope link
       valid_lft forever preferred_lft forever
```

Figure 9.8

```
root@compute02:~# ip netns exec qrouter-cf6230cc-9749-40a6-a15b-ef8b466fe148 ip a
<omit loopback>
27: qr-29db7422-76: <BROADCAST,MULTICAST,UP,LOWER_UP> mtu 1500 qdisc noqueue state UNKNOWN group default
    link/ether fa:16:3e:95:ad:f9 brd ff:ff:ff:ff:ff:ff
    inet 192.168.1.1/24 brd 192.168.1.255 scope global qr-29db7422-76
       valid_lft forever preferred_lft forever
    inet6 fe80::f816:3eff:fe95:adf9/64 scope link
       valid_lft forever preferred_lft forever
28: qr-57d9bd1e-44: <BROADCAST,MULTICAST,UP,LOWER_UP> mtu 1500 qdisc noqueue state UNKNOWN group default
    link/ether fa:16:3e:37:5e:a5 brd ff:ff:ff:ff:ff:ff
    inet 172.16.5.1/24 brd 172.16.5.255 scope global qr-57d9bd1e-44
       valid_lft forever preferred_lft forever
    inet6 fe80::f816:3eff:fe37:5ea5/64 scope link
       valid_lft forever preferred_lft forever
```

Figure 9.9

In the preceding screenshots, the qrouter namespaces on the controller and compute nodes that correspond to the MyRouter-DVR router contain the same qr-29db7422-76 and qr-57d9db1e-44 interfaces and addresses that correspond to the TENANT_BLUE and TENANT_RED networks. A creative use of routing tables and Open vSwitch flow rules allows traffic between instances behind the same distributed router to be routed directly between compute nodes. The tricks behind this functionality will be discussed in the following sections and throughout the chapter.

Plumbing it up

When a distributed virtual router is connected to a subnet through the router-interface-add command, the router is scheduled to *all* nodes hosting ports on the subnet, including any controller or network node hosting DHCP or load balancer namespaces and any compute node hosting virtual machine instances in the subnet. L3 agents are responsible for creating the respective qrouter network namespace on each node, and the Open vSwitch agent connects the router interfaces to the bridges and configures the appropriate flows.

Distributing router ports

Without precautions, distributing ports with the same IP and MAC addresses across multiple compute nodes presents major issues in the network. Imagine a physical topology that resembles the following diagram:

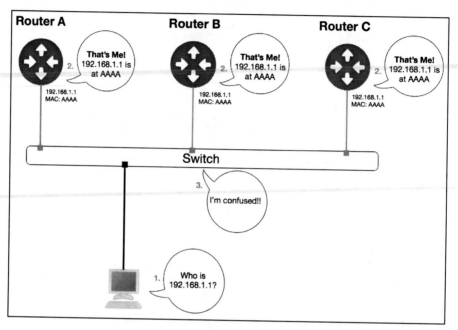

Figure 9.10

In most networks, an environment consisting of multiple routers with the same IP and MAC addresses connected to a switch would result in the switches learning and relearning the location of the MAC addresses across different switch ports. This behavior is often referred to as **MAC flapping** and results in network instability and unreliability.

Virtual switches can exhibit the same behavior regardless of segmentation type as the virtual switch may learn that a MAC address exists both locally on the compute node and remotely, resulting in similar behavior observed on the physical switch.

Making it work

To work around this expected network behavior, Neutron allocates a unique MAC address to each compute node, which is used whenever traffic from a distributed virtual router leaves the node. The following screenshot shows the unique MAC addresses that have been allocated to the nodes in this demonstration:

```
root@controller01:~# mysql -u root -p -e "use neutron; select * from dvr_host_macs;"
Enter password:
+-------------+-------------------+
| host        | mac_address       |
+-------------+-------------------+
| compute01   | fa:16:3f:0e:e0:0a |
| controller01| fa:16:3f:2a:83:a3 |
| compute02   | fa:16:3f:59:c7:ad |
+-------------+-------------------+
```

Figure 9.11

Open vSwitch flow rules are used to rewrite the source MAC address of a packet as it leaves a router interface with the unique MAC address allocated to the source node:

```
root@compute01:~# ovs-ofctl dump-flows br-tun
NXST_FLOW reply (xid=0x4):
                                       Source is non-unique qr MAC address         Modify to unique host MAC address
...
 table=1, n_packets=0, n_bytes=0, idle_age=1353, priority=1,dl_vlan=1,dl_src=fa:16:3e:95:ad:f9 actions=mod_dl_src:fa:16:3f:0e:e0:0a,resubmit(,2)
 table=1, n_packets=1, n_bytes=42, idle_age=1348, priority=1,dl_vlan=2,dl_src=fa:16:3e:37:5e:a5 actions=mod_dl_src:fa:16:3f:0e:e0:0a,resubmit(,2)
 table=1, n_packets=0, n_bytes=0, idle_age=1351, priority=2,dl_vlan=2,dl_dst=fa:16:3e:37:5e:a5 actions=drop
 table=1, n_packets=0, n_bytes=0, idle_age=1353, priority=2,dl_vlan=1,dl_dst=fa:16:3e:95:ad:f9 actions=drop
 table=1, n_packets=0, n_bytes=0, idle_age=1351, priority=3,arp,dl_vlan=2,arp_tpa=172.16.5.1 actions=drop
 table=1, n_packets=1, n_bytes=42, idle_age=1352, priority=3,arp,dl_vlan=1,arp_tpa=192.168.1.1 actions=drop
...
```

Figure 9.12

When traffic comes into a compute node that matches a local virtual machine instance's MAC address and segmentation ID, the source MAC address is rewritten from the unique source node MAC address to the local instance's gateway MAC address:

```
root@compute01:~# ovs-ofctl dump-flows br-int
NXST_FLOW reply (xid=0x4):
                                       When traffic comes over the tunnel from a unique host MAC, go to table 1...
...
 table=0, n_packets=0, n_bytes=0, idle_age=443, priority=2,in_port=3,dl_src=fa:16:3f:2a:83:a3 actions=resubmit(,1)
 table=0, n_packets=0, n_bytes=0, idle_age=579, priority=2,in_port=3,dl_src=fa:16:3f:59:c7:ad actions=resubmit(,1)

 table=1, n_packets=0, n_bytes=0, idle_age=1694, priority=4,dl_vlan=1,dl_dst=fa:16:3e:38:fd:d1 actions=strip_vlan,mod_dl_src:fa:16:3e:95:ad:f9,output:4
...                                     If the dest MAC is that of VM_BLUE...        . change the src MAC to that of the
                                                                                    respective qr gateway interface
```

Figure 9.13

Because the layer 2 header rewrites occur before and after traffic enters or leaves the virtual machine instance, the instance is unaware of the changes made to the frames and operates normally. The following section demonstrates this process in further detail.

Demonstrating traffic between instances

Imagine a scenario where virtual machines in different networks exist on two different compute nodes, as demonstrated in the following diagram:

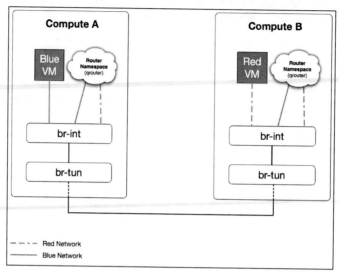

Figure 9.14

Traffic from the blue virtual machine instance on **Compute A** to the red virtual machine instance on **Compute B** will first be forwarded from the instance to its local gateway through the integration bridge and to the router namespace:

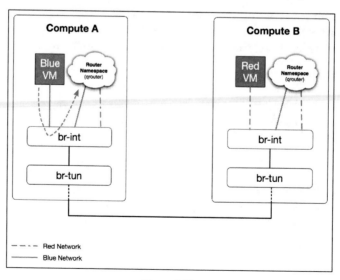

Figure 9.15

Traffic leaves the blue VM and is forwarded to the blue router interface. The original MAC and IP addresses are intact:

Source MAC	Destination MAC	Source IP	Destination IP
Blue VM	Blue router interface	Blue VM	Red VM

The router on **Compute A** routes the traffic from the blue VM to the red VM, replacing the source MAC address with its red interface and the destination MAC address to that of the red VM in the process:

Source MAC	Destination MAC	Source IP	Destination IP
Red router interface	Red VM	Blue VM	Red VM

The router then sends the packet back to the integration bridge, which then forwards it to the tunnel bridge:

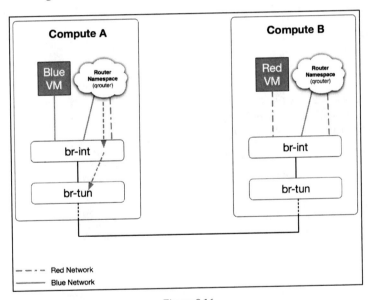

Figure 9.16

As traffic arrives at the tunnel bridge on **Compute A**, a series of flow rules are processed, resulting in the source MAC address being changed from the red interface of the router to the unique MAC address of the host:

Source MAC	Destination MAC	Source IP	Destination IP
Source host (Compute A)	Red VM	Blue VM	Red VM

The traffic is then matched to a flow rule that results in its encapsulation and forwarding out of the appropriate tunnel to **Compute B**:

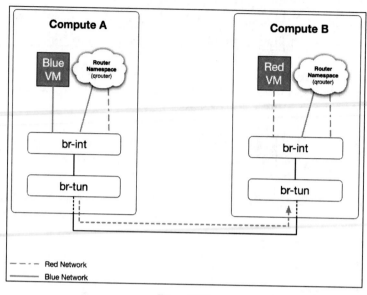

Figure 9.17

When traffic arrives at **Compute B**, it is forwarded through the tunnel bridge and decapsulated. A flow rule adds a local `vlan` header that allows the traffic to be matched when it is forwarded to the integration bridge:

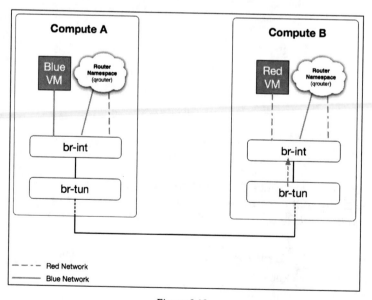

Figure 9.18

Source MAC	Destination MAC	Source IP	Destination IP
Source host (Compute A)	Red VM	Blue VM	Red VM

In the integration bridge, a flow rule strips the local `vlan` tag and changes the source MAC address back to that of the router's red interface. The packet is then forwarded to the red VM:

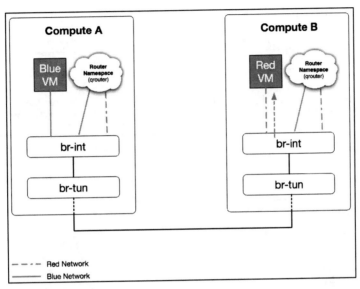

Figure 9.19

Source MAC	Destination MAC	Source IP	Destination IP
Red router interface	Red VM	Blue VM	Red VM

The returning traffic from the red VM to the blue VM undergoes a similar routing path through the respective routers and bridges on each compute node.

Centralized SNAT

Source NAT, or SNAT for short, is the method of changing the source address of a packet as it leaves the interface of a router. When a Neutron router is allocated an IP address from an external network using the `router-gateway-set` command, the IP is used in source NAT operations. The source IP of traffic from virtual machine instances to external networks will be translated as the router's address when the instances do not have 1-to-1 floating IPs configured. All routers in Neutron, whether they are standalone, HA, or distributed, support SNAT.

As of the Kilo release of OpenStack, routers that handle SNAT are centralized on a single node and are not highly available. As a workaround, multiple nodes may be configured in dvr_snat mode.

Reviewing the topology

In this demonstration, the following provider and tenant networks are created:

```
root@controller01:~# neutron net-list
+--------------------------------------+-------------+------------------------------------------------------+
| id                                   | name        | subnets                                              |
+--------------------------------------+-------------+------------------------------------------------------+
| da911578-b8ea-4f03-bd16-5c2593391772 | GATEWAY_NET | e474640e-e6df-4008-9ae6-d5ab3824995a 10.50.0.0/24    |
| 33697943-c693-4f25-9b10-f2617cdb8e19 | TENANT_NET  | 2c6fbf19-1f52-4258-8528-60eed4e7ca64 10.30.0.0/24    |
+--------------------------------------+-------------+------------------------------------------------------+
```

Figure 9.20

Using the --distributed=true option, a distributed virtual router is created:

```
root@controller01:~# neutron router-create --distributed=true MyRouter-DVR
Created a new router:
+-----------------------+--------------------------------------+
| Field                 | Value                                |
+-----------------------+--------------------------------------+
| admin_state_up        | True                                 |
| distributed           | True                                 |
| external_gateway_info |                                      |
| ha                    | False                                |
| id                    | 03788ed7-8687-476a-9fa0-11176bdfa65d |
| name                  | MyRouter-DVR                         |
| routes                |                                      |
| status                | ACTIVE                               |
| tenant_id             | da6c995d9f834090bd7a00d13d40b817     |
+-----------------------+--------------------------------------+
```

Figure 9.21

In this environment, the L3 agent on the controller is in dvr_snat mode and serves as the centralized SNAT node. Attaching the router to the TENANT_NET tenant network results in the router being scheduled to the controller node:

```
root@controller01:~# neutron l3-agent-list-hosting-router MyRouter-DVR
+--------------------------------------+--------------+----------------+-------+
| id                                   | host         | admin_state_up | alive |
+--------------------------------------+--------------+----------------+-------+
| 6a7d5e2f-f9bc-4623-9614-17b1db06c068 | controller01 | True           | :-)   |
+--------------------------------------+--------------+----------------+-------+
```

Figure 9.22

When an instance is spun up in the tenant network, the router is also scheduled to the respective compute node:

```
root@controller01:~# neutron l3-agent-list-hosting-router MyRouter-DVR
+--------------------------------------+--------------+----------------+-------+
| id                                   | host         | admin_state_up | alive |
+--------------------------------------+--------------+----------------+-------+
| 6a7d5e2f-f9bc-4623-9614-17b1db06c068 | controller01 | True           | :-)   |
| fbb712cc-4a7f-4d13-a87c-af2bd3a8aa52 | compute01    | True           | :-)   |
+--------------------------------------+--------------+----------------+-------+
```

Figure 9.23

At this point, both the controller node and compute node each have a `qrouter` namespace that corresponds to the `MyRouter-DVR` router. Attaching the router to the external network using the `router-gateway-set` command results in the creation of a `snat` namespace on the controller node. Now, on the controller node, *two* namespaces exist for the same router — `snat` and `qrouter`:

```
root@controller01:~# ip netns
snat-03788ed7-8687-476a-9fa0-11176bdfa65d
qrouter-03788ed7-8687-476a-9fa0-11176bdfa65d
qdhcp-33697943-c693-4f25-9b10-f2617cdb8e19
```

Figure 9.24

This configuration can be represented by the following diagram:

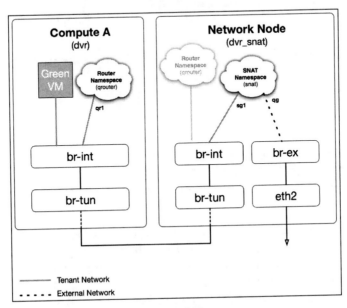

Figure 9.25

The `qrouter` namespace on the controller node is identical to the `qrouter` namespace on the compute node and is used to service DHCP, load balancer, and other traffic that traverses this host. The `snat` namespace is for the centralized SNAT service.

Within the `qrouter` namespace, observe the following interfaces — `lo` (loopback) and `qr`:

```
root@controller01:~# ip netns exec qrouter-03788ed7-8687-476a-9fa0-11176bdfa65d ip a
1: lo: <LOOPBACK,UP,LOWER_UP> mtu 65536 qdisc noqueue state UNKNOWN group default
    link/loopback 00:00:00:00:00:00 brd 00:00:00:00:00:00
    inet 127.0.0.1/8 scope host lo
       valid_lft forever preferred_lft forever
    inet6 ::1/128 scope host
       valid_lft forever preferred_lft forever
21: qr-e8917a97-16: <BROADCAST,MULTICAST,UP,LOWER_UP> mtu 1500 qdisc noqueue state UNKNOWN group default
    link/ether fa:16:3e:ce:da:eb brd ff:ff:ff:ff:ff:ff
    inet 10.30.0.1/24 brd 10.30.0.255 scope global qr-e8917a97-16
       valid_lft forever preferred_lft forever
    inet6 fe80::f816:3eff:fece:daeb/64 scope link
       valid_lft forever preferred_lft forever
```

Figure 9.26

Unlike the `qrouter` namespace of a legacy router, there is no `qg` interface even though the router is attached to the external network.

However, take a look inside the `snat` namespace:

```
root@controller01:~# ip netns exec snat-03788ed7-8687-476a-9fa0-11176bdfa65d ip a
1: lo: <LOOPBACK,UP,LOWER_UP> mtu 65536 qdisc noqueue state UNKNOWN group default
    link/loopback 00:00:00:00:00:00 brd 00:00:00:00:00:00
    inet 127.0.0.1/8 scope host lo
       valid_lft forever preferred_lft forever
    inet6 ::1/128 scope host
       valid_lft forever preferred_lft forever
22: sg-9fd05929-6d: <BROADCAST,MULTICAST,UP,LOWER_UP> mtu 1500 qdisc noqueue state UNKNOWN group default
    link/ether fa:16:3e:3a:a8:b8 brd ff:ff:ff:ff:ff:ff
    inet 10.30.0.4/24 brd 10.30.0.255 scope global sg-9fd05929-6d
       valid_lft forever preferred_lft forever
    inet6 fe80::f816:3eff:fe3a:a8b8/64 scope link
       valid_lft forever preferred_lft forever
23: qg-47ef57fa-7c: <BROADCAST,MULTICAST,UP,LOWER_UP> mtu 1500 qdisc noqueue state UNKNOWN group default
    link/ether fa:16:3e:70:10:91 brd ff:ff:ff:ff:ff:ff
    inet 10.50.0.100/24 brd 10.50.0.255 scope global qg-47ef57fa-7c
       valid_lft forever preferred_lft forever
    inet6 fe80::f816:3eff:fe70:1091/64 scope link
       valid_lft forever preferred_lft forever
```

Figure 9.27

Inside the `snat` namespace, you will find the `qg` interface that is used to handle outgoing traffic from virtual machine instances. In addition to the `qg` interface, there is now a new interface with the prefix `sg`. A virtual router will have a `qr` interface and new `sg` interface for *every* internal network it is connected to. The `sg` interfaces are used as an extra hop when traffic is source NAT'd, and this will be explained in further detail in the following sections.

Using the routing policy database

When a virtual machine instance without a floating IP sends traffic destined to an external network, such as the Internet, it hits the local `qrouter` namespace on the compute node and is routed to the `snat` namespace on the centralized network node. To accomplish this task, special routing rules are put in place within the `qrouter` namespaces.

Linux offers a **routing policy database** made up of multiple routing tables and rules that allow for intelligent routing based on destination and source addresses, IP protocols, ports, and more. There are source routing rules for every subnet that a virtual router is attached to.

In this demonstration, the router is attached to a single tenant network: 10.30.0.0/24. Take a look at the main routing table within the `qrouter` namespace on compute01:

```
root@compute01:~# ip netns exec qrouter-03788ed7-8687-476a-9fa0-11176bdfa65d ip route
10.30.0.0/24 dev qr-e8917a97-16  proto kernel  scope link  src 10.30.0.1
```

Figure 9.28

Note that there is no default route in the main routing table.

On the compute node, use the `ip rule` command from within the `qrouter` namespace to list additional routing tables and rules created by the Neutron agent:

```
root@compute01:~# ip netns exec qrouter-03788ed7-8687-476a-9fa0-11176bdfa65d ip rule
0:   from all lookup local
32766:   from all lookup main
32767:   from all lookup default
169738241:   from 10.30.0.1/24 lookup 169738241
```

Figure 9.29

The table numbered `169738241` is created by Neutron. The additional routing table is consulted and a default route is found:

```
root@compute01:~# ip netns exec qrouter-03788ed7-8687-476a-9fa0-11176bdfa65d ip route show table 169738241
default via 10.30.0.4 dev qr-e8917a97-16
```

Figure 9.30

From this output, we can see that `10.30.0.4` is the default gateway address and corresponds to the `sq` interface within the `snat` namespace on the centralized node. When traffic reaches the `snat` namespace, the source NAT is performed and the traffic is routed out of the `qg` interface.

Tracing a packet through the SNAT namespace

In the following example, the green VM sends traffic to 8.8.8.8, a Google DNS server, as shown in the following diagram:

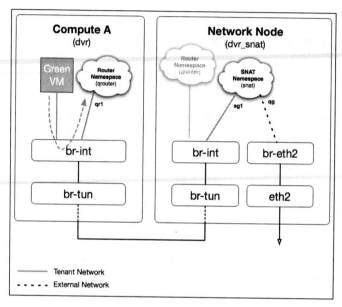

Figure 9.31

Source MAC	Destination MAC	Source IP	Destination IP
Green VM	Green router interface (qr1)	Green VM	8.8.8.8 (Google DNS)

When traffic arrives at the local `qrouter` namespace, the main routing table is consulted. The destination IP, 8.8.8.8, does not match any directly connected subnet and a default route does not exist. Secondary routing tables are then consulted, where a match is found based on the *source interface*. The router then routes the traffic from the green VM to the green interface of the SNAT namespace, `sg1`, through the east-west routing mechanisms covered earlier in this chapter:

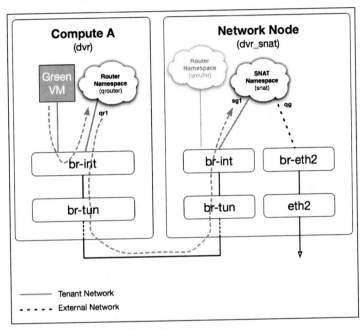

Figure 9.32

Source MAC	Destination MAC	Source IP	Destination IP
Green router interface (`qr1`)	Green SNAT interface (`sg1`)	Green VM	8.8.8.8 (Google DNS)

When traffic enters the snat namespace, it is routed out the qg interface. The iptables rules within the namespace change the source IP and MAC addresses to that of the qg interface to ensure that the traffic is routed back properly:

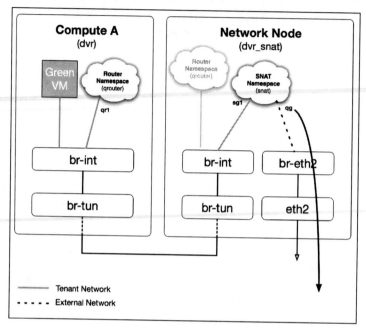

Figure 9.33

Source MAC	Destination MAC	Source IP	Destination IP
External SNAT interface (qg)	Physical default gateway	External SNAT interface (qg)	8.8.8.8 (Google DNS)

When the remote destination responds, a combination of flow rules on the centralized network node and compute node ensures that the response is routed back to the green VM with the proper IP and MAC addresses in place.

Floating IPs through distributed virtual routers

In the network world, north-south traffic is traditionally defined as client-to-server traffic. In Neutron, as it relates to distributed virtual routers, north-south traffic is the traffic that originates from an external network to virtual machine instances using floating IPs, or vice-versa.

In the legacy model, all traffic to or from external clients traverses a centralized network node hosting a router with floating IPs. With DVR, the same traffic bypasses the network node and is routed directly to the compute nodes that host the virtual machine instance. This functionality requires compute nodes to be connected directly to external networks through an external bridge; a configuration that, up until now, has only been seen on nodes hosting legacy or HA routers.

Introducing (yet) another namespace

Unlike SNAT traffic, the traffic through a floating IP is handled on individual compute nodes rather than a centralized node. When a floating IP is attached to a virtual machine instance, the L3 agent on the compute node creates a new `fip` namespace, which corresponds to the external network that the floating IP belongs to if one doesn't already exist:

```
root@compute01:~# ip netns
fip-da911578-b8ea-4f03-bd16-5c2593391772    Network ID
qrouter-03788ed7-8687-476a-9fa0-11176bdfa65d
```

Figure 9.34

Router namespaces on a compute node connected to the *same* external network share a single `fip` namespace and are connected to the namespace using a veth pair. Veth pairs are treated as point-to-point links between the `fip` namespace and individual `qrouter` namespaces and are addressed as /31 networks using a common 169.254/16 link-local address space. As the network connections between namespaces exist only within the nodes themselves and are used as point-to-point links, a Neutron tenant network allocation is not required.

In the `qrouter` namespace, one end of the veth pair has the prefix `rfp`, which means router to FIP:

```
root@compute01:~# ip netns exec qrouter-03788ed7-8687-476a-9fa0-11176bdfa65d ip a
<omit loopback>
2: rfp-03788ed7-8: <BROADCAST,MULTICAST,UP,LOWER_UP> mtu 1500 qdisc pfifo_fast state UP group default qlen 1000
    link/ether d6:fd:c0:b8:44:51 brd ff:ff:ff:ff:ff:ff
    inet 169.254.31.28/31 scope global rfp-03788ed7-8
       valid_lft forever preferred_lft forever
    inet 10.50.0.101/32 brd 10.50.0.101 scope global rfp-03788ed7-8
       valid_lft forever preferred_lft forever
    inet6 fe80::d4fd:c0ff:feb8:4451/64 scope link
       valid_lft forever preferred_lft forever
20: qr-e8917a97-16: <BROADCAST,MULTICAST,UP,LOWER_UP> mtu 1500 qdisc noqueue state UNKNOWN group default
    link/ether fa:16:3e:ce:da:eb brd ff:ff:ff:ff:ff:ff
    inet 10.30.0.1/24 brd 10.30.0.255 scope global qr-e8917a97-16
       valid_lft forever preferred_lft forever
    inet6 fe80::f816:3eff:fece:daeb/64 scope link
       valid_lft forever preferred_lft forever
```

Figure 9.35

Inside the `fip` namespace, the other end of the veth pair has the prefix `fpr`, meaning FIP to router:

```
root@compute01:~# ip netns exec fip-da911578-b8ea-4f03-bd16-5c2593391772 ip a
<omit loopback>
2: fpr-03788ed7-8: <BROADCAST,MULTICAST,UP,LOWER_UP> mtu 1500 qdisc pfifo_fast state UP group default qlen 1000
    link/ether 76:4b:23:ce:cc:ff brd ff:ff:ff:ff:ff:ff
    inet 169.254.31.29/31 scope global fpr-03788ed7-8
       valid_lft forever preferred_lft forever
    inet6 fe80::744b:23ff:fece:ccff/64 scope link
       valid_lft forever preferred_lft forever
21: fg-c6f3b0ad-c1: <BROADCAST,MULTICAST,UP,LOWER_UP> mtu 1500 qdisc noqueue state UNKNOWN group default
    link/ether fa:16:3e:30:25:a3 brd ff:ff:ff:ff:ff:ff
    inet 10.50.0.102/24 brd 10.50.0.255 scope global fg-c6f3b0ad-c1
       valid_lft forever preferred_lft forever
    inet6 fe80::f816:3eff:fe30:25a3/64 scope link
       valid_lft forever preferred_lft forever
```

Figure 9.36

In addition to the `fpr` interface, a new interface with the prefix `fg` can be found inside the FIP namespace. The `rfp`, `fpr`, and `fg` interfaces will be discussed in the following sections.

Tracing a packet through the FIP namespace

When a floating IP is assigned to an instance using the `floatingip-associate` command, a couple of things occur:

- A `fip` namespace for the external network is created on the compute node if one doesn't exist
- The route table within the `qrouter` namespace on the compute node is modified

The following sections demonstrate how traffic to and from floating IPs is processed.

Sending traffic from an instance with a floating IP

Imagine a scenario where a floating IP, `10.50.0.101`, has been assigned to the green VM, as represented in the following diagram:

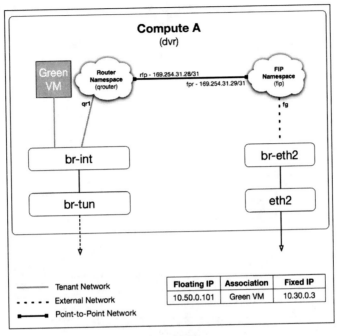

Figure 9.37

When the green virtual machine instance at 10.30.0.3 sends traffic to an external resource, it arrives at the local qrouter namespace, as follows:

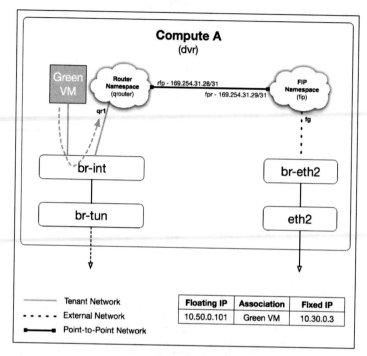

Figure 9.38

Source MAC	Destination MAC	Source IP	Destination IP
Green VM	Green qr interface	Green VM Fixed IP (10.30.0.3)	8.8.8.8 (Google DNS)

When traffic arrives at the local qrouter namespace, the routing policy database is consulted so that traffic may be routed accordingly. Upon association of the floating IP with a port using the Neutron floatingip-associate command, a source routing rule is added to the route table within the qrouter namespace:

```
root@compute01:~# ip netns exec qrouter-03788ed7-8687-476a-9fa0-11176bdfa65d ip rule
0:      from all lookup local
32766:  from all lookup main
32767:  from all lookup default
32768:  from 10.30.0.3 lookup 16  ◄───────
169738241:  from 10.30.0.1/24 lookup 169738241
```

Figure 9.39

The main routing table inside the `qrouter` namespace with a higher priority does not have a default route, so the `32768: from 10.30.0.3 lookup 16` rule is matched instead.

A look at the referenced routing table, table 16, shows that the `fip` namespace's `fpr` interface is the default route for traffic sourced from the fixed IP of the instance `10.30.0.3`:

```
root@compute01:~# ip netns exec qrouter-03788ed7-8687-476a-9fa0-11176bdfa65d ip route show table 16
default via 169.254.31.29 dev rfp-03788ed7-8
```

Figure 9.40

The `qrouter` namespace performs the NAT translation of the fixed IP to the floating IP and sends the traffic to the `fip` namespace, as demonstrated in the following diagram:

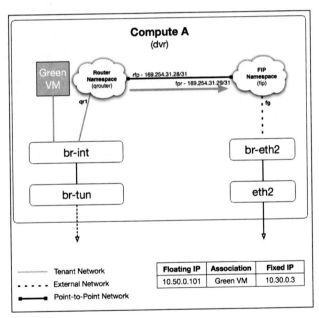

Figure 9.41

Source MAC	Destination MAC	Source IP	Destination IP
`rfp` interface	`fpr` interface	Green VM Floating IP (`10.50.0.101`)	`8.8.8.8` (Google DNS)

Once traffic arrives at the `fip` namespace, it is forwarded out of the `fg` interface to its default gateway:

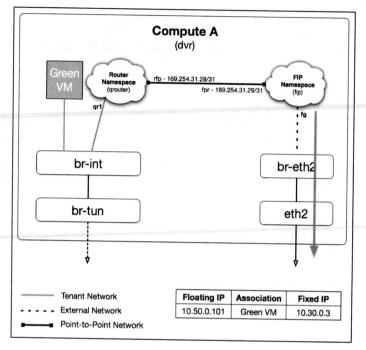

Figure 9.42

Source MAC	Destination MAC	Source IP	Destination IP
`fg` interface	Physical default gateway	Green VM floating IP (`10.50.0.101`)	`8.8.8.8` (Google DNS)

Returning traffic to the floating IP

If you recall from earlier in this chapter, a single `fip` namespace on a compute node is shared by every `qrouter` namespace on this node connected to the external network. Much as a standalone or HA router has an IP address from the external network on its `qg` interface, each `fip` namespace has a single IP address from the external network configured on its `fg` interface.

On `compute01`, the IP address is `10.50.0.102`:

```
root@compute01:~# ip netns exec fip-da911578-b8ea-4f03-bd16-5c2593391772 ip a
<omit loopback>
2: fpr-03788ed7-8: <BROADCAST,MULTICAST,UP,LOWER_UP> mtu 1500 qdisc pfifo_fast state UP group default qlen 1000
    link/ether 76:4b:23:ce:cc:ff brd ff:ff:ff:ff:ff:ff
    inet 169.254.31.29/31 scope global fpr-03788ed7-8
       valid_lft forever preferred_lft forever
    inet6 fe80::744b:23ff:fece:ccff/64 scope link
       valid_lft forever preferred_lft forever
21: fg-c6f3b0ad-c1: <BROADCAST,MULTICAST,UP,LOWER_UP> mtu 1500 qdisc noqueue state UNKNOWN group default
    link/ether fa:16:3e:30:25:a3 brd ff:ff:ff:ff:ff:ff
    inet 10.50.0.102/24 brd 10.50.0.255 scope global fg-c6f3b0ad-c1
       valid_lft forever preferred_lft forever
    inet6 fe80::f816:3eff:fe30:25a3/64 scope link
       valid_lft forever preferred_lft forever
```

Figure 9.43

If a floating IP were assigned to an instance on `compute02`, an `fip` namespace would be created on this node along with a corresponding `fg` interface with its own address from the external network. On `compute02`, the IP address is `10.50.0.104`:

```
root@compute02:/home/jdenton# ip netns exec fip-da911578-b8ea-4f03-bd16-5c2593391772 ip a
<omit loopback>
2: fpr-03788ed7-8: <BROADCAST,MULTICAST,UP,LOWER_UP> mtu 1500 qdisc pfifo_fast state UP group default qlen 1000
    link/ether 6a:3f:50:7e:73:4e brd ff:ff:ff:ff:ff:ff
    inet 169.254.31.29/31 scope global fpr-03788ed7-8
       valid_lft forever preferred_lft forever
    inet6 fe80::683f:50ff:fe7e:734e/64 scope link
       valid_lft forever preferred_lft forever
34: fg-ca5ddd06-38: <BROADCAST,MULTICAST,UP,LOWER_UP> mtu 1500 qdisc noqueue state UNKNOWN group default
    link/ether fa:16:3e:c2:d3:1d brd ff:ff:ff:ff:ff:ff
    inet 10.50.0.104/24 brd 10.50.0.255 scope global fg-ca5ddd06-38
       valid_lft forever preferred_lft forever
    inet6 fe80::f816:3eff:fec2:d31d/64 scope link
       valid_lft forever preferred_lft forever
```

Figure 9.44

Unlike a legacy router, the `qrouter` namespaces of distributed routers do *not* have direct connectivity to the external network. However, the `qrouter` namespace is still responsible for performing the source NAT from the fixed IP to the floating IP. Traffic is then routed to the `fip` namespace and from there out to the external network.

Using proxy ARP

Floating IPs are configured on the `rfp` interface within the `qrouter` namespace, but they are *not* directly reachable from the gateway of the external network as the `fip` namespace sits between the `qrouter` namespace and the external network. To allow the routing of traffic through the `fip` namespace back to the `qrouter` namespace, Neutron relies on the use of **proxy ARP**. By automatically enabling proxy ARP on the `fg` interface, the `fip` namespace can respond to ARP requests for the floating IP, and on behalf of it, from the upstream gateway device.

When traffic is routed from the gateway device to the `fip` namespace, the routing table is consulted and traffic is routed to the respective `qrouter` namespace:

```
root@compute01:~# ip netns exec fip-da911578-b8ea-4f03-bd16-5c2593391772 ip r
default via 10.50.0.1 dev fg-c6f3b0ad-c1
10.50.0.0/24 dev fg-c6f3b0ad-c1  proto kernel  scope link  src 10.50.0.102
10.50.0.101 via 169.254.31.28 dev fpr-03788ed7-8
169.254.31.28/31 dev fpr-03788ed7-8  proto kernel  scope link  src 169.254.31.29
```
Route to fpr interface of qrouter namespace

Figure 9.45

The following diagram demonstrates how proxy ARP works in this scenario:

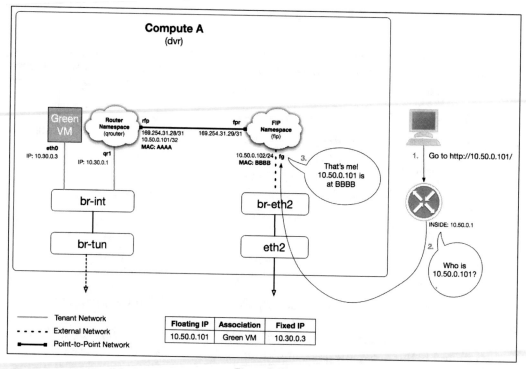

Figure 9.46

The `fg` interface within the `fip` namespace responds on *behalf* of the `rfp` interface within the `qrouter` namespace as this interface is not directly connected to the external network. The use of a single `fip` namespace and proxy ARP eliminates the need to provide each `qrouter` namespace with its own IP address from the external network, which reduces unnecessary IP address consumption and makes more floating IPs available for use by virtual machine instances and other network resources.

Summary

Distributed virtual routers have a positive impact on the network architecture as a whole by pushing east-west traffic between instances and north-south traffic through floating IPs to the compute nodes, removing bottlenecks and single points of failure seen in the legacy model. Traffic from virtual machines without floating IPs must still traverse a centralized network node when routing to external networks. This is seen as a compromise, however, given that a high number of IPv4 addresses would be required if SNAT were handled at the compute node layer.

While distributed virtual routers help provide parity with nova-network's multi-host capabilities, they are not without their limitations. Work is under way to add support to distributed virtual routers for IPv6, advanced services such as LBaaS, FWaaS, and VPNaaS, conversions from legacy to distributed routers, and more. Implementing a distributed virtual router is transparent to the user, but it is operationally complex and considerably more difficult to troubleshoot if things go wrong when compared to a legacy router.

In the next chapter, we will look at the advanced networking service known as LBaaS, or Load Balancing as a Service, and its reference architecture using the HAProxy plugin. LBaaS allows users to create and manage load balancers that can distribute workloads across multiple virtual machine instances. Using the Neutron API, users can quickly scale their application while providing resiliency and high availability.

10
Load Balancing Traffic to Instances

The Neutron **Load Balancing as a Service** extension, known as **LBaaS**, provides users with the ability to load balance traffic to applications running on virtual instances in the cloud. Neutron provides an API to manage virtual IPs, pools, pool members, and health monitors.

In this chapter, we will cover some fundamental load balancing concepts, including:

- Virtual IPs, pools, and pool members
- Load balancing algorithms
- Monitors
- Persistence

Neutron uses drivers to interact with hardware or software load balancers. In Kilo, the reference driver interacts with HAProxy. HAProxy is a free, open source load balancer that is available for most Unix-based operating systems. Third-party drivers are supported by LBaaS but are outside the scope of this book.

In this chapter, we will work through the following:

- Integrating load balancers into the network
- Installing and configuring the LBaaS agent
- Creating a load balancer
- Demonstrating load balanced traffic to instances

The LBaaS API underwent a major overhaul over the last few release cycles, which resulted in version 2 of the API. This chapter, however, focuses on version 1. Most of the concepts described throughout this chapter directly apply to both versions of the API, though the syntax to implement various components may differ.

Fundamentals of load balancing

There are three major components to a load balancer in Neutron:

- Pool members
- Pools
- Virtual IPs

A **pool member** is a layer 4 object that is composed of the IP address and listening port of a service. For example, a pool member might be a web server with a configured IP address of 10.30.0.2 listening on TCP port 80.

A **pool** is a group of pool members that typically serve identical content. A pool composed of web servers, for example, may resemble the following membership:

- **Server A**: 10.30.0.2:80
- **Server B**: 10.30.0.4:80
- **Server C**: 10.30.0.6:80

A **virtual IP**, or VIP, is an IP address that resides on the load balancer and listens for incoming connections. The load balancer then balances client connections among the members of the associated pool. A virtual IP is usually exposed to the Internet and often mapped to a domain name.

 The term *virtual IP* is also used in reference to VRRP, a router redundancy protocol, and should not be confused with its use in the context of load balancing. VRRP and load balancing are unrelated technologies.

Load balancing algorithms

In version 1 of the LBaaS API, the following load balancing algorithms can be applied to a pool:

- Round robin

- Least connections
- Source IP

With the **round robin** algorithm, the load balancer passes each new connection to the next server in line. Over time, all connections are distributed evenly across all machines being load balanced. Round robin is the least resource-intensive algorithm and has no mechanism to determine when a machine is being overwhelmed by connections. To avoid overwhelming a pool member, all members should be equal in terms of processing speed, connection speed, and memory.

With the **least connections** algorithm, the load balancer passes a new connection to a server that has the least number of current connections. It is considered a dynamic algorithm as the system keeps track of the number of connections attached to each server and balances traffic accordingly. Pool members of higher capabilities would likely receive more traffic as they are able to process connections quicker.

With the **source IP** algorithm, all connections originating from the same source IP address are sent to the same pool member. Connections are initially balanced using the round robin algorithm and then tracked in a table for future lookup with subsequent connections from the same IP address. This algorithm is useful in cases where the application requires clients to persist to a particular server for all requests, such as an online shopping cart that stores session information on the local web server.

Monitoring

The LBaaS API supports multiple monitor types, including TCP, HTTP, and HTTPS. The TCP monitor tests connectivity to pool members at layer 4, while the HTTP and HTTPS monitors test the health of pool members based on the layer 7 HTTP status codes.

Session persistence

LBaaS supports session persistence, otherwise known as sticky sessions or session affinity, on virtual IPs. Session persistence is a method of load balancing that forces multiple client requests of the same protocol to be directed to the same node. This feature is commonly used with many web applications that do not share an application state among pool members.

The types of session persistence supported with the HAProxy driver include the following:

- `SOURCE_IP`
- `HTTP_COOKIE`
- `APP_COOKIE`

Using the SOURCE_IP persistence type configures HAProxy with the following settings within the backend pool configuration:

```
stick-table type ip size 10k
stick on src
```

The first time a client connects to the virtual IP, HAProxy creates an entry in a sticky table based on the client's IP address and sends subsequent connections from the same IP address to the same backend pool member. Based on the configuration, up to 10,000 sticky entries can exist in the sticky table. This persistence method can cause a load imbalance among pool members if users connect from behind a proxy server that identifies multiple clients as a single address.

Using the HTTP_COOKIE persistence type configures HAProxy with the following settings within the backend pool configuration:

```
cookie SRV insert indirect nocache
```

The first time a client connects to the virtual IP, HAProxy balances the connection to the next pool member in line. When the pool member sends its response, HAProxy injects a cookie named "SRV" into the response before sending it to the client. The value of the SRV cookie is a unique server identifier. When the client sends subsequent requests to the virtual IP, HAProxy strips the cookie from the request header and sends the traffic directly to the pool member identified in the cookie. This persistence method is recommended over source IP persistence as it is not reliant on the IP address of the client.

Using the APP_COOKIE persistence type configures HAProxy with the following settings within the backend pool configuration:

```
appsession <CookieName> len 56 timeout 3h
```

When an application cookie is defined in a backend, HAProxy checks when the server sets such a cookie, stores its value in a table, and associates it with the server's identifier. Up to 56 characters from the value are retained. On subsequent client connections, HAProxy looks for the cookie. If a known value is found, the client is directed to the pool member associated with the value. Otherwise, the round-robin load balancing algorithm is applied. Cookies are automatically removed from memory when they go unused for longer than three hours.

Integrating load balancers into the network

When using the HAProxy driver, load balancers are implemented in **one-arm** mode. In the one-arm mode, a load balancer is not in the path of normal traffic to the pool members. The load balancer has a single interface for ingress and egress traffic to and from clients and pool members.

A logical diagram of a load balancer in one-arm mode can be seen in *Figure 10.1*:

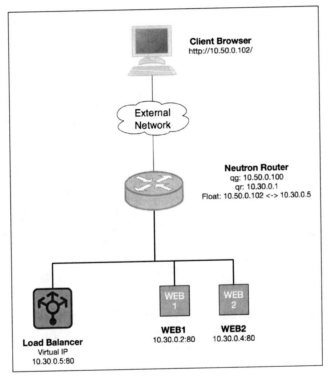

Figure 10.1

In *Figure 10.1*, a load balancer is configured in one-arm mode and resides in the same subnet as the servers that it is balancing traffic to.

As a load balancer in one-arm mode is not the gateway for the pool members that it is sending traffic to, it must rely on the use of source NAT, or SNAT, to ensure that return traffic from the members to the client is sent back through the load balancer. An example of the traffic flow can be seen in *Figure 10.2*:

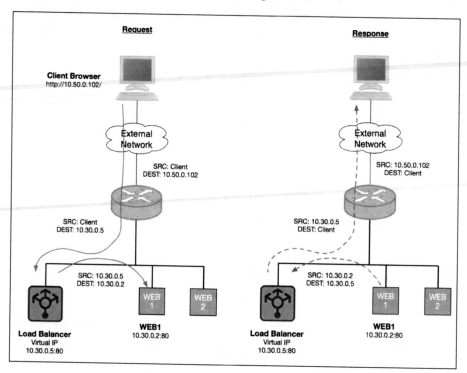

Figure 10.2

In *Figure 10.2*, the load balancer receives a request from the client and forwards it to WEB1. The load balancer then modifies the source IP of the request to its own address, 10.30.0.5, before forwarding the request to the server. This ensures that the server sends the response back to the load balancer, which then rewrites the destination IP as the client address. If the server were to send the response directly to the client, the client would reject the packet.

Neutron configures HAProxy to send an HTTP X-Forwarded-For header to the pool member, which allows the pool member to get the original client address. Without this header, all traffic would be identified as coming from the load balancer.

Alternatives to the one-arm mode include the routed and transparent modes. In **routed mode**, the load balancer acts as a gateway between the client and pool member. The source addresses of packets do not need to be manipulated in most cases as the load balancer servers act as the gateway for pool members.

In **transparent mode**, the load balancer acts as a network bridge between two VLANs configured with the same subnet(s). Using this mode allows users to introduce a load balancer to the network with minimal disruption as pool members do not need to change their gateway.

 There is currently no way to change the way an HAProxy-based load balancer is integrated into the network. Some third-party drivers, however, may not be limited to the one-arm mode and can function in any mode.

Network namespaces

Neutron relies on network namespaces to provide individual load balancers when using the HAProxy plugin. Every VIP has a corresponding network namespace. Load balancers are scheduled to LBaaS agents in the environment, which are responsible for creating a corresponding network namespace and appropriate configuration. Namespaces used for load balancers are prefaced with `qlbaas` in the `ip netns` output.

Installing LBaaS

The `neutron-lbaas-agent` service typically runs on the network node, which in this demonstration is `controller01`.

Issue the following command on the controller node to install the LBaaS agent and its dependencies, including HAProxy:

```
# apt-get install neutron-lbaas-agent
```

Configuring the Neutron LBaaS agent service

Neutron stores the LBaaS agent configuration in the `/etc/neutron/lbaas_agent.ini` file. The most common configuration options will be covered in the upcoming sections.

Defining an interface driver

Like the previously installed agents, the Neutron LBaaS agent must be configured to use an interface driver that corresponds to the chosen networking driver. In this configuration, there are two options:

- LinuxBridge

- Open vSwitch

Update the Neutron LBaaS agent configuration file node at `/etc/neutron/lbaas_agent.ini` on the controller to use one of the following drivers.

For LinuxBridge:

```
[DEFAULT]
...
interface_driver = neutron.agent.linux.interface.BridgeInterfaceDriver
```

For Open vSwitch:

```
[DEFAULT]
...
interface_driver = neutron.agent.linux.interface.OVSInterfaceDriver
```

Defining a device driver

To manage a load balancer, the Neutron LBaaS agent must be configured to use a device driver that provides an interface between the Neutron API and the programming of the load balancer itself.

Update the Neutron LBaaS agent configuration file node at `/etc/neutron/lbaas_agent.ini` on the controller to use the HAProxy device driver:

```
[DEFAULT]
...
device_driver = neutron.services.loadbalancer.drivers.haproxy.
namespace_driver.HaproxyNSDriver
```

Configuring Neutron

In addition to configuring the LBaaS agent, Neutron must be configured to use an LBaaS service plugin and driver before the API can be utilized to create LBaaS objects.

Defining a service plugin

Add the `lbaas` service plugin to the existing `service_plugins` configuration option found in the Neutron configuration file at `/etc/neutron/neutron.conf` on the controller, as follows:

```
[DEFAULT]
...
service_plugins = router,lbaas
```

Defining a service provider

As of the Kilo release of OpenStack, many advanced service configuration options have moved out of the main Neutron configuration file into their own files. On the controller node, update or create the Neutron LBaaS configuration file at /etc/neutron/neutron_lbaas.conf and define the HAProxy service provider driver for LBaaS, as follows:

```
[service_providers]
...
service_provider = LOADBALANCER:Haproxy:neutron_lbaas.services.
loadbalancer.drivers.haproxy.plugin_driver.HaproxyOnHostPluginDriver:
default
```

Restarting the Neutron LBaaS agent and API service

The neutron-lbaas-agent and neutron-server services must be restarted for the changes to take effect. Issue the following commands on the controller node to restart the services:

```
# service neutron-server restart
# service neutron-lbaas-agent restart
```

Verify whether the agent is running through the following command:

```
# service neutron-lbaas-agent status
```

The service should return similar output to the following:

```
root@controller01:/etc/init.d# service neutron-lbaas-agent status
neutron-lbaas-agent start/running, process 12927
```

If you encounter any issues, be sure to check the LBaaS agent log found at /var/log/neutron/neutron-lbaas-agent.log before proceeding.

Load balancer management in the CLI

Neutron offers a number of commands that can be used to create and manage virtual IPs, pools, pool members, and health monitors for load balancing purposes.

In version 1 of the LBaaS API, the pool is the root object to which all other load balancer resources are associated. The workflow to create a functional load balancer starts with creating a pool and then continues with creating and associating pool members, health monitors, and a virtual IP.

Managing pools in the CLI

The following commands are used to manage pools in the CLI:

- `lb-pool-create`
- `lb-pool-delete`
- `lb-pool-list`
- `lb-pool-list-on-agent`
- `lb-pool-show`
- `lb-pool-stats`
- `lb-pool-update`

Creating a pool

A pool is a set of devices, such as web servers, that are grouped together to receive and process traffic. When traffic is sent to a virtual IP, the load balancer sends a request to any of the servers that are members of this pool.

To create a pool, use the Neutron `lb-pool-create` command, as follows:

```
Usage:    lb-pool-create [--tenant-id TENANT_ID]
          [--admin-state-down] [--description DESCRIPTION]
          --lb-method {ROUND_ROBIN,LEAST_CONNECTIONS,SOURCE_IP}
          --name <pool name> --protocol {HTTP,HTTPS,TCP}
          --subnet-id <subnet id>
```

Here, the `--tenant-id` flag is optional and allows you to associate the pool with the specified tenant.

The `--admin-state-down` attribute, when set, does not have any affect on the state of the pool. This is likely a bug or unimplemented feature.

The `--lb-method` attribute is used to specify the load balancing algorithm, which is used to distribute traffic among the pool members. Possible options include ROUND_ROBIN, LEAST_CONNECTIONS, or SOURCE_IP.

The `--name` attribute is used to specify a name for the pool.

The `--protocol` attribute is used to specify the type of traffic that the pool will balance. The HTTP and HTTPS protocols are used to balance nonsecure and secure web traffic, respectively. Use TCP for all other TCP traffic.

The subnet specified using the `--subnet-id` attribute should match the subnet of the pool members to be added to the pool.

Deleting a pool

To delete a load balancer pool, use the Neutron `lb-pool-delete` command, as follows:

Usage: `lb-pool-delete POOL`

Here, the keyword `POOL` represents the ID of the pool. Before a pool can be deleted, any associated virtual IP must be disassociated.

Listing pools

To obtain a list of the configured load balancer pools, use the Neutron `lb-pool-list` command, as follows:

Usage: `lb-pool-list`

In this command, the returned list includes details of the pools in the running tenant, such as the ID, name, load balancing method, protocol, admin state, and status.

Showing pool details

To show the details of a pool, use the Neutron `lb-pool-show` command, as follows:

Usage: `lb-pool-show POOL`

Here, the keyword `POOL` represents the ID of the pool. Details returned include the admin state, description, ID, load balancing method, members, protocol, provider, status, subnet ID, tenant ID, VIP ID, and health monitors associated with the pool.

Showing pool statistics

To display the statistics of a pool, use the Neutron `lb-pool-stats` command, as follows:

Usage: `lb-pool-stats POOL`

In the preceding command, the keyword `POOL` represents the ID of the pool. The statistics returned include the number of active connections, total bytes in, total bytes out, and total connections.

> A pool must be in an ACTIVE state before statistics are collected, and even then connection counters may be inaccurate. Attempting to return statistics on a pool in any other state may result in an error.

Updating a pool

To update the attributes of a pool, use the Neutron `lb-pool-update` command, as follows:

```
Usage:    lb-pool-update POOL [--description DESCRIPTION]
          [--lb-method {ROUND_ROBIN,LEAST_CONNECTIONS,SOURCE_IP}]
```

The `--lb-method` attribute is used to specify the load balancing algorithm used to distribute traffic among pool members. Possible options include ROUND_ROBIN, LEAST_CONNECTIONS, or SOURCE_IP.

Listing pools associated with an agent

When a pool is created, it is scheduled to a load balancer agent. The idea is that multiple LBaaS agents can exist in an environment to provide high availability. To list the pools associated with an agent, use the Neutron `lb-pool-list-on-agent` command, as follows:

```
Usage:    lb-pool-list-on-agent <agent id>
```

To determine the ID or name of the load balancing agents known to Neutron, use the Neutron `agent-list` command.

Managing pool members in the CLI

The following commands are used to manage pool members in the CLI:

* `lb-member-create`
* `lb-member-delete`
* `lb-member-list`
* `lb-member-show`
* `lb-member-update`

Creating pool members

To create a pool member, use the Neutron `lb-member-create` command, as follows:

```
Usage:    lb-member-create [--tenant-id TENANT_ID]
          [--admin-state-down] [--weight WEIGHT]
          --address <IP addr of member>
          --protocol-port <application port number>
          POOL
```

Here, the `--tenant-id` flag is optional and allows you to associate the pool member with the specified tenant.

The `--admin-state-down` attribute is a Boolean that, when set to `true`, places the pool member administratively in a down state. In this state, a pool member is not eligible to receive traffic; they, therefore, default to an administrative up state.

The `--weight` attribute allows you to associate a weight with the pool member. When set, a pool member may receive more or less traffic than other members in the same pool. For example, a pool member with a weight of 2 will receive twice the traffic as a pool member with the weight of 1, a pool member with a weight of 3 will receive three times the traffic, and so on.

The `--address` attribute is required and used to specify the IP address of the pool member.

The `--protocol-port` attribute is required and used to specify the listening port of the application being balanced. For example, if you are balancing HTTP traffic, the listening port specified would be `80`. For SSL traffic, the port specified would be `443`. In most cases, the VIP associated with the pool utilizes the same application port number.

Deleting pool members

To delete a pool member, use the Neutron `lb-member-delete` command, as follows:

Usage: **lb-member-delete MEMBER**

Here, the keyword MEMBER represents the ID of the pool member to be deleted.

Listing pool members

To obtain a list of pool members, use the Neutron `lb-member-list` command, as follows:

Usage: **lb-member-list [--pool-id=<POOL ID>]**

The returned list of pool members includes member details, such as the ID, address, protocol port, admin state, and status. Use `--pool-id` to return pool members in the specified pool only.

Showing pool member details

To show the details of a pool member, use the Neutron `lb-member-show` command, as follows:

```
Usage:    lb-member-show MEMBER
```

In the preceding command, the keyword MEMBER represents the ID of the member to be shown. The returned details include the address, admin state, ID, pool ID, protocol port, status, description, tenant ID, and weight of the member.

Updating a pool member

To update the attributes of a pool member, use the Neutron `lb-member-update` command, as follows:

```
Usage:    lb-member-update MEMBER [--weight WEIGHT]
          [--admin_state_up <true/false>]
```

Here, the keyword MEMBER represents the ID of the pool member.

Managing health monitors in the CLI

LBaaS in Neutron provides the ability to monitor the health of pool members as a method of ensuring the availability of an application. If a pool member is not in a healthy state, Neutron can pull it out of rotation, limiting the impact of the issues between the client and application.

The following commands are used to manage health monitors in the CLI:

- `lb-healthmonitor-create`
- `lb-healthmonitor-delete`
- `lb-healthmonitor-associate`
- `lb-healthmonitor-disassociate`
- `lb-healthmonitor-list`
- `lb-healthmonitor-show`
- `lb-healthmonitor-update`

Creating a health monitor

To create a health monitor, use the Neutron `lb-healthmonitor-create` command, as follows:

```
Usage:    lb-healthmonitor-create [--tenant-id TENANT_ID]
          [--admin-state-down] [--expected-codes EXPECTED_CODES]
          [--http-method HTTP_METHOD] [--url-path URL_PATH]
          --delay DELAY --max-retries MAX_RETRIES
          --timeout TIMEOUT --type {PING,TCP,HTTP,HTTPS}
```

In the preceding command, the `--tenant-id` flag is optional and allows you to associate the monitor with the specified tenant.

The `--expected-codes` attribute is optional, and allows you to specify the HTTP status code(s) that indicate a pool member is working as expected when the monitor sends an HTTP request to the pool member for the specified URL. For example, if a GET request for a URL is sent to a pool member, the server is expected to return a 200 OK status upon the successful retrieval of the page. If 200 is listed as an expected code, the monitor will mark the pool member as UP. As a result, the pool member will be eligible to receive connections. If a 500 status code were returned, it could indicate that the server is not properly processing connections. The health monitor would mark the pool member as DOWN and temporarily remove it from the pool. The default value is 200.

The `--http-method` attribute is optional and used in conjunction with `--expected-codes` and `--url-path`. It is used to specify the type of HTTP request being made. Common types include GET and POST. There is no validation of this attribute, which may allow users to create monitors that don't work as expected. The default value is GET.

The `--url-path` attribute is optional and used in conjunction with `--expected-codes` and `--http-method`. When specified, the system performs an HTTP request defined by `--http-method` for the URL against the pool member. The default value is root or /.

The `--delay` attribute is required and used to specify the period between each health check (in seconds). A common starting value is 5 seconds.

The `--max-retries` attribute is required and used to specify the maximum number of consecutive failures before a pool member is marked as DOWN. A common starting value is 3 retries.

The `--timeout` attribute is required and used to specify the number of seconds for a monitor to wait for a connection to be established. The value must be less than the delay value.

The `--type` attribute is required and used to specify the type of monitor being configured. The four types include:

- **PING**: The simplest of all monitor types, PING uses ICMP to confirm connectivity to pool members.

 The PING type is not supported by the HAProxy driver and results in the same behavior as the TCP monitor type.

- **TCP**: This instructs the load balancer to send a TCP SYN packet to the pool member. Upon receiving a SYN ACK back, the load balancer resets the connection. This type of monitor is commonly referred to as a half-open TCP monitor.
- **HTTP**: This instructs the monitor to initiate an HTTP request to a pool member based on the `expected_codes`, `url_path`, and `http_method` attributes described here.
- **HTTPS**: This instructs the monitor to initiate an HTTPS request to a pool member based on the `expected_codes`, `url_path` and `http_method` attributes described here.

Deleting a health monitor

To delete a health monitor, use the Neutron `lb-healthmonitor-delete` command, as follows:

```
Usage:    lb-healthmonitor-delete HEALTH_MONITOR
```

In the preceding command, the keyword `HEALTH_MONITOR` represents the ID of the health monitor to be deleted.

Associating a health monitor with a pool

To associate a health monitor with a pool, use the Neutron `lb-healthmonitor-associate` command, as follows:

```
Usage:    lb-healthmonitor-associate HEALTH_MONITOR_ID POOL
```

Here, the keyword `POOL` represents the ID of the pool to be associated with the monitor.

More than one health monitor can be associated with a single pool. Also, a single monitor can be leveraged by multiple pools.

Disassociating a health monitor from a pool

To disassociate a health monitor from a pool, use the Neutron `lb-healthmonitor-disassociate` command, as follows:

`Usage:    lb-healthmonitor-disassociate HEALTH_MONITOR_ID POOL`

Here, the keyword `POOL` represents the ID of the pool to be disassociated from the monitor.

Listing health monitors

To obtain a list of health monitors, use the Neutron `lb-healthmonitor-list` command, as follows:

`Usage:    lb-healthmonitor-list`

In this command, the list returned includes the ID, type, and admin status of all health monitors.

Showing health monitor details

To show the details of a health monitor, use the Neutron `lb-healthmonitor-show` command, as shown in the following example:

`Usage:    lb-healthmonitor-show HEALTH_MONITOR`

Here, the details returned include the delay, expected codes, HTTP method, ID, max retries, pools, tenant ID, timeout, type, and URL path.

Updating a health monitor

To update the attributes of a health monitor, use the Neutron `lb-healthmonitor-update` command, as follows:

`Usage:    lb-healthmonitor-update HEALTH_MONITOR_ID`

Here, the updateable attributes include the delay, expected codes, HTTP method, max retries, timeout, and URL path.

Managing virtual IPs in the CLI

The following commands are used to manage virtual IPs in the CLI:

- `lb-vip-create`
- `lb-vip-delete`
- `lb-vip-list`
- `lb-vip-show`
- `lb-vip-update`

Creating a virtual IP

To create a virtual IP, use the Neutron `lb-vip-create` command, as follows:

```
Usage:     lb-vip-create [--tenant-id TENANT_ID]
           [--address ADDRESS] [--admin-state-down]
           [--connection-limit CONNECTION_LIMIT]
           [--description DESCRIPTION] --name NAME
           --protocol-port PROTOCOL_PORT
           --protocol {TCP,HTTP,HTTPS}
           --subnet-id SUBNET
           POOL
           [--session-persistence type=TYPE]
```

Here, the `--tenant-id` flag is optional and allows you to associate the monitor with the specified tenant.

The `--admin-state-down` attribute, when set, does not have any affect on the state of the load balancer.

The `--address` attribute is optional and allows you to specify the IP address of the listener. A Neutron port will be created to reserve the address specified here.

The `--connection-limit` attribute is optional and allows you to define a connection limit on the virtual IP. Once the limit is reached, new client traffic will not be balanced.

The `--name` attribute is required and used to define the name of the virtual IP.

The `--protocol-port` attribute is required and used to specify the listening port of the application being balanced. For example, if you were balancing HTTP traffic, the port specified would be 80. For SSL traffic, the port specified here would be 443. In most cases, the pool associated with the virtual IP utilizes the same application port number.

The `--protocol` attribute is required and used to specify the type of traffic being load balanced. Options include TCP, HTTP, and HTTPS. This value must match the protocol of the associated pool.

The `--subnet-id` attribute is required and used to provide the proper network configuration of the load balancer. Every load balancer exists in its own network namespace, and the subnet specified here is what is used to configure networking within the namespace, including the IP address and default route.

The keyword `POOL` represents the pool to be balanced by this virtual IP.

The `--session-persistence` attribute is optional and allows you to specify a method of persistence for clients connecting to the VIP. The placement of `--session-persistence` within the command structure is important and can result in an error if placed before the pool name.

To enable `SOURCE_IP` or `HTTP_COOKIE` persistence, use the following syntax:

```
lb-vip-create ... POOL --session-persistence type=dict type=HTTP_
COOKIE
lb-vip-create ... POOL --session-persistence type=dict type=SOURCE_IP
```

To enable `APP_COOKIE` persistence, use the following syntax:

```
lb-vip-create ... POOL --session-persistence type=dict type=APP_
COOKIE,cookie_name=<application cookie name>
```

 The preceding `lb-vip-create` examples should be entered as one line, but they may appear line-wrapped in the text. The persistence of `APP_COOKIE` requires the use of a specified cookie name that is unique to your application. A common example is the use of a `JSESSIONID` cookie in a JSP application.

Deleting a virtual IP

To delete a virtual IP, use the Neutron `lb-vip-delete` command, as follows:

Usage: `lb-vip-delete VIP`

In the preceding command, the keyword `VIP` represents the ID of the virtual IP to be deleted.

Listing virtual IPs

To obtain a list of virtual IPs, use the Neutron `lb-vip-list` command, as follows:

Usage: `lb-vip-list`

The returned output includes a list of virtual IPs and details such as the ID, name, address, protocol, and state.

Showing virtual IP details

To show the details of a virtual IP, use the Neutron `lb-vip-show` command, as follows:

Usage: `lb-vip-show VIP`

The keyword `VIP` represents the ID of the virtual IP. Returned details include the address, connection limit, description, ID, name, pool ID, port ID, protocol, protocol port, status, subnet ID, and tenant ID.

Updating a virtual IP

To update the attributes of a virtual IP, use the Neutron `lb-vip-update` command, as follows:

Usage: `lb-vip-update VIP [--connection-limit CONNECTION_LIMIT]`
             `[--session-persistence type=TYPE]`
             `[--pool-id POOL]`

Persistence types include `SOURCE_IP`, `HTTP_COOKIE`, or `APP_COOKIE`.

Building a load balancer

To demonstrate the creation and use of load balancers in Neutron, this next section is dedicated to building a functional load balancer based on the following scenario:

A tenant has a simple Neutron network set up with a router attached to both an external provider network and internal tenant network. The user would like to load balance HTTP traffic between two instances running a web server. Each instance is configured with an index.html page containing a unique server identifier.

To eliminate the installation and configuration of a web server for this example, you can mimic the behavior of one using the `SimpleHTTPServer` Python module on the instances, as follows:

```
ubuntu@web1:~$ echo "This is Web1" > ~/index.html
ubuntu@web1:~$ sudo python -m SimpleHTTPServer 80
Serving HTTP on 0.0.0.0 port 80 ...
```

Repeat the mentioned commands for the second instance, substituting `Web2` for `Web1` in the `index.html` file.

Creating a pool

The first step to building a functional load balancer is to create a pool. Using the Neutron `lb-pool-create` command, create a pool with the following attributes:

- **Name**: `WEB_POOL`

- **Load balancing method**: `Round robin`

- **Protocol**: `HTTP`

- **Subnet ID**: `<Subnet ID of the pool members>`

```
root@controller01:~# neutron lb-pool-create --description "The Web Pool" --lb-method ROUND_ROBIN \
> --name WEB_POOL --protocol HTTP --subnet-id 2c6fbf19-1f52-4258-8528-60eed4e7ca64
Created a new pool:
+-----------------------+--------------------------------------+
| Field                 | Value                                |
+-----------------------+--------------------------------------+
| admin_state_up        | True                                 |
| description           | The Web Pool                         |
| health_monitors       |                                      |
| health_monitors_status|                                      |
| id                    | 3f314bd2-9fdf-4397-8f1c-ee530a1ed134 |
| lb_method             | ROUND_ROBIN                          |
| members               |                                      |
| name                  | WEB_POOL                             |
| protocol              | HTTP                                 |
| provider              | haproxy                              |
| status                | PENDING_CREATE                       |
| status_description    |                                      |
| subnet_id             | 2c6fbf19-1f52-4258-8528-60eed4e7ca64 |
| tenant_id             | da6c995d9f834090bd7a00d13d40b817     |
| vip_id                |                                      |
+-----------------------+--------------------------------------+
```

Figure 10.3

 The state of the pool will remain `PENDING_CREATE` until a virtual IP is associated with it.

Creating pool members

The next step to building a functional load balancer is to create and associate pool members with the pool.

In this environment, there are two instances eligible for use in the pool:

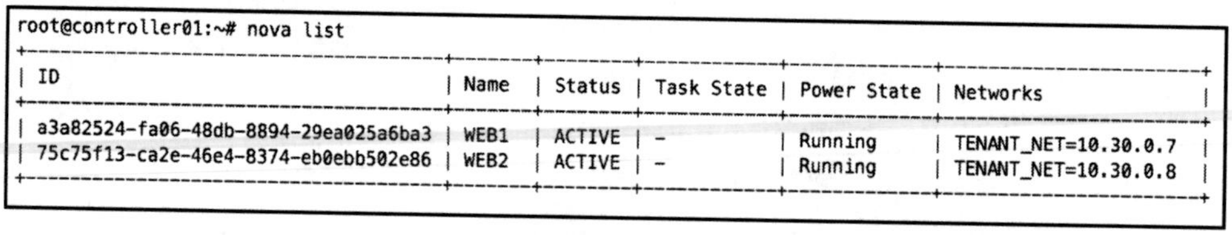

```
root@controller01:~# nova list
+--------------------------------------+------+--------+------------+-------------+------------------------+
| ID                                   | Name | Status | Task State | Power State | Networks               |
+--------------------------------------+------+--------+------------+-------------+------------------------+
| a3a82524-fa06-48db-8894-29ea025a6ba3 | WEB1 | ACTIVE | -          | Running     | TENANT_NET=10.30.0.7   |
| 75c75f13-ca2e-46e4-8374-eb0ebb502e86 | WEB2 | ACTIVE | -          | Running     | TENANT_NET=10.30.0.8   |
+--------------------------------------+------+--------+------------+-------------+------------------------+
```

Figure 10.4

Using the Neutron `lb-member-create` command, create two pool members with the following attributes based on the `nova list` output:

- **Member 1**:
    - **Name**: `WEB1`
    - **Address**: `10.30.0.7`
    - **Protocol port**: `80`
    - **Pool**: `WEB_POOL`

- **Member 2**:
    - **Name**: `WEB2`
    - **Address**: `10.30.0.8`
    - **Protocol port**: `80`
    - **Pool**: `WEB_POOL`

The following screenshot demonstrates the process of creating the first pool member:

```
root@controller01:~# neutron lb-member-create --address 10.30.0.7 --protocol-port 80 WEB_POOL
Created a new member:
+--------------------+--------------------------------------+
| Field              | Value                                |
+--------------------+--------------------------------------+
| address            | 10.30.0.7                            |
| admin_state_up     | True                                 |
| id                 | cb51bd34-0be6-4044-8f89-a61d2d75cb07 |
| pool_id            | 3f314bd2-9fdf-4397-8f1c-ee530a1ed134 |
| protocol_port      | 80                                   |
| status             | PENDING_CREATE                       |
| status_description |                                      |
| tenant_id          | da6c995d9f834090bd7a00d13d40b817     |
| weight             | 1                                    |
+--------------------+--------------------------------------+
```

Figure 10.5

Repeat the process shown in the preceding screenshot to create the second pool member.

The Neutron lb-member-list command returns a list showing the two pool members but does not list their associated pools:

```
root@controller01:~# neutron lb-member-list
+--------------------------------------+------------+---------------+--------+----------------+--------+
| id                                   | address    | protocol_port | weight | admin_state_up | status |
+--------------------------------------+------------+---------------+--------+----------------+--------+
| a0bd5575-3675-4004-9c6f-b9e9d0e3cedd | 10.30.0.8  |            80 |      1 | True           | ACTIVE |
| cb51bd34-0be6-4044-8f89-a61d2d75cb07 | 10.30.0.7  |            80 |      1 | True           | ACTIVE |
+--------------------------------------+------------+---------------+--------+----------------+--------+
```

Figure 10.6

As a workaround, you can include certain columns to be returned, as shown in the following figure:

```
root@controller01:~# neutron lb-member-list -c pool_id -c id -c address -c protocol_port
+--------------------------------------+--------------------------------------+------------+---------------+
| pool_id                              | id                                   | address    | protocol_port |
+--------------------------------------+--------------------------------------+------------+---------------+
| 3f314bd2-9fdf-4397-8f1c-ee530a1ed134 | a0bd5575-3675-4004-9c6f-b9e9d0e3cedd | 10.30.0.8  |            80 |
| 3f314bd2-9fdf-4397-8f1c-ee530a1ed134 | cb51bd34-0be6-4044-8f89-a61d2d75cb07 | 10.30.0.7  |            80 |
+--------------------------------------+--------------------------------------+------------+---------------+
```

Figure 10.7

Creating a health monitor

To provide high availability of an application to clients, it is recommended to create and apply a health monitor to a pool. Without a monitor, the load balancer will continue to send traffic to members that may not be available.

Using the Neutron `lb-healthmonitor-create` command, create a health monitor with the following attributes:

- **Delay**: 5
- **Max retries**: 3
- **Timeout**: 4
- **Type**: TCP

```
root@controller01:~# neutron lb-healthmonitor-create --delay 5 --max-retries 3 --timeout 4 --type TCP
Created a new health_monitor:
+----------------+------------------------------------+
| Field          | Value                              |
+----------------+------------------------------------+
| admin_state_up | True                               |
| delay          | 5                                  |
| id             | 69d357dc-4e82-4556-8486-4bfebde21332 |
| max_retries    | 3                                  |
| pools          |                                    |
| tenant_id      | da6c995d9f834090bd7a00d13d40b817   |
| timeout        | 4                                  |
| type           | TCP                                |
+----------------+------------------------------------+
```

Figure 10.8

To associate the newly created health monitor with the pool, use the `lb-healthmonitor-associate` command, as follows:

```
lb-healthmonitor-associate HEALTH_MONITOR_ID POOL
```

Now, consider the following screenshot:

```
root@controller01:~# neutron lb-healthmonitor-associate 69d357dc-4e82-4556-8486-4bfebde21332 WEB_POOL
Associated health monitor 69d357dc-4e82-4556-8486-4bfebde21332
```

Figure 10.9

Creating a virtual IP

The last step in creating a function load balancer is to create the virtual IP, or VIP, which acts as a listener and balances traffic across pool members. Using the Neutron `lb-vip-create` command, create a virtual IP with the following attributes:

- **Name**: WEB_VIP
- **Protocol port**: 80
- **Protocol**: HTTP
- **Subnet ID**: <Subnet ID of Pool>
- **Pool**: WEB_POOL

```
root@controller01:~# neutron lb-vip-create --description "The Web VIP" --name WEB_VIP \
> --protocol-port 80 --protocol HTTP --subnet-id 2c6fbf19-1f52-4258-8528-60eed4e7ca64 WEB_POOL
Created a new vip:
+---------------------+--------------------------------------+
| Field               | Value                                |
+---------------------+--------------------------------------+
| address             | 10.30.0.9                            |
| admin_state_up      | True                                 |
| connection_limit    | -1                                   |
| description         | The Web VIP                          |
| id                  | ec4df104-403c-4da2-988e-5a6b794290fe |
| name                | WEB_VIP                              |
| pool_id             | 3f314bd2-9fdf-4397-8f1c-ee530a1ed134 |
| port_id             | 5e234421-01a6-47e3-a64d-d814f28e6301 |
| protocol            | HTTP                                 |
| protocol_port       | 80                                   |
| session_persistence |                                      |
| status              | PENDING_CREATE                       |
| status_description  |                                      |
| subnet_id           | 2c6fbf19-1f52-4258-8528-60eed4e7ca64 |
| tenant_id           | da6c995d9f834090bd7a00d13d40b817     |
+---------------------+--------------------------------------+
```

Figure 10.10

Once the virtual IP is created, the state of the VIP and pool will change to ACTIVE:

```
root@controller01:~# neutron lb-vip-list
+--------------------------------------+---------+-----------+----------+----------------+--------+
| id                                   | name    | address   | protocol | admin_state_up | status |
+--------------------------------------+---------+-----------+----------+----------------+--------+
| ec4df104-403c-4da2-988e-5a6b794290fe | WEB_VIP | 10.30.0.9 | HTTP     | True           | ACTIVE |
+--------------------------------------+---------+-----------+----------+----------------+--------+
root@controller01:~# neutron lb-pool-list
+--------------------------------------+----------+----------+-------------+----------+----------------+--------+
| id                                   | name     | provider | lb_method   | protocol | admin_state_up | status |
+--------------------------------------+----------+----------+-------------+----------+----------------+--------+
| 3f314bd2-9fdf-4397-8f1c-ee530a1ed134 | WEB_POOL | haproxy  | ROUND_ROBIN | HTTP     | True           | ACTIVE |
+--------------------------------------+----------+----------+-------------+----------+----------------+--------+
```

Figure 10.11

The LBaaS network namespace

A listing of the network namespaces on the host running the LBaaS agent reveals a network namespace that corresponds to the load balancer just created:

```
root@controller01:~# ip netns
qlbaas-3f314bd2-9fdf-4397-8f1c-ee530a1ed134
qrouter-70705227-a6a2-4681-9445-152676e3d607
qdhcp-33697943-c693-4f25-9b10-f2617cdb8e19
```

Figure 10.12

The IP configuration within the namespace reveals an interface that corresponds to the subnet of the virtual IP:

```
root@controller01:~# ip netns exec qlbaas-3f314bd2-9fdf-4397-8f1c-ee530a1ed134 ip a
<omit loopback>
26: tap5e234421-01: <BROADCAST,MULTICAST,UP,LOWER_UP> mtu 1500 qdisc noqueue state UNKNOWN group default
    link/ether fa:16:3e:b1:e9:25 brd ff:ff:ff:ff:ff:ff
    inet 10.30.0.9/24 brd 10.30.0.255 scope global tap5e234421-01
       valid_lft forever preferred_lft forever
    inet6 fe80::f816:3eff:feb1:e925/64 scope link
       valid_lft forever preferred_lft forever
```

Figure 10.13

Neutron creates an HAProxy configuration file specific to every load balancer created by users. The load balancer configuration files can be found in the `/var/lib/neutron/lbaas/` directory of the host running the LBaaS agent.

The configuration file for this load balancer built by Neutron can be seen in the following screenshot:

```
root@controller01:~# cat /var/lib/neutron/lbaas/3f314bd2-9fdf-4397-8f1c-ee530a1ed134/conf
global
    daemon
    user nobody
    group nogroup
    log /dev/log local0
    log /dev/log local1 notice
    stats socket /var/lib/neutron/lbaas/3f314bd2-9fdf-4397-8f1c-ee530a1ed134/sock mode 0666 level user
defaults
    log global
    retries 3
    option redispatch
    timeout connect 5000
    timeout client 50000
    timeout server 50000
frontend ec4df104-403c-4da2-988e-5a6b794290fe
    option tcplog
    bind 10.30.0.9:80
    mode http
    default_backend 3f314bd2-9fdf-4397-8f1c-ee530a1ed134
    option forwardfor
backend 3f314bd2-9fdf-4397-8f1c-ee530a1ed134
    mode http
    balance roundrobin
    option forwardfor
    timeout check 4s
    server cb51bd34-0be6-4044-8f89-a61d2d75cb07 10.30.0.7:80 weight 1 check inter 5s fall 3
    server a0bd5575-3675-4004-9c6f-b9e9d0e3cedd 10.30.0.8:80 weight 1 check inter 5s fall 3
```

Figure 10.14

Confirming load balancer functionality

From within the router namespace, confirm direct connectivity to WEB1 and WEB2 via their respective addresses over port 80 using curl:

```
root@controller01:~# ip netns exec qrouter-70705227-a6a2-4681-9445-152676e3d607 curl http://10.30.0.7
This is Web1
root@controller01:~# ip netns exec qrouter-70705227-a6a2-4681-9445-152676e3d607 curl http://10.30.0.8
This is Web2
```

Figure 10.15

By opening multiple connections to the virtual IP 10.30.0.9 within the router namespace, you can observe a round robin load balancing in effect:

```
root@controller01:~# ip netns exec qrouter-70705227-a6a2-4681-9445-152676e3d607 curl http://10.30.0.9
This is Web1
root@controller01:~# ip netns exec qrouter-70705227-a6a2-4681-9445-152676e3d607 curl http://10.30.0.9
This is Web2
root@controller01:~# ip netns exec qrouter-70705227-a6a2-4681-9445-152676e3d607 curl http://10.30.0.9
This is Web1
root@controller01:~# ip netns exec qrouter-70705227-a6a2-4681-9445-152676e3d607 curl http://10.30.0.9
This is Web2
```

Figure 10.16

With round robin load balancing, every connection is evenly distributed among the two pool members.

Observing health monitors

A packet capture on WEB1 reveals that the load balancer is performing TCP checks its health every 5 seconds:

```
root@web1:~# tcpdump -i any -n port 80
tcpdump: verbose output suppressed, use -v or -vv for full protocol decode
listening on any, link-type LINUX_SLL (Linux cooked), capture size 65535 bytes
11:02:40 902872 IP 10.30.0.9.43795 > 10.30.0.7.80: Flags [S], seq 1910133662, win 29200, options
11:02:40 902937 IP 10.30.0.7.80 > 10.30.0.9.43795: Flags [S.], seq 2262228566, ack 1910133663, w
11:02:40 903979 IP 10.30.0.9.43795 > 10.30.0.7.80: Flags [R.], seq 1, ack 1, win 229, options [n

11:02:45 904274 IP 10.30.0.9.43797 > 10.30.0.7.80: Flags [S], seq 3823809227, win 29200, options
11:02:45 904317 IP 10.30.0.7.80 > 10.30.0.9.43797: Flags [S.], seq 1588491583, ack 3823809228, w
11:02:45 905370 IP 10.30.0.9.43797 > 10.30.0.7.80: Flags [R.], seq 1, ack 1, win 229, options [n

11:02:50 905388 IP 10.30.0.9.43799 > 10.30.0.7.80: Flags [S], seq 3079898771, win 29200, options
11:02:50 905420 IP 10.30.0.7.80 > 10.30.0.9.43799: Flags [S.], seq 3837093337, ack 3079898772, w
11:02:50 906275 IP 10.30.0.9.43799 > 10.30.0.7.80: Flags [R.], seq 1, ack 1, win 229, options [n
```

Figure 10.17

In the preceding output, the load balancer sends a `TCP SYN` packet every 5 seconds and immediately sends a `RST` upon receiving the `SYN ACK` from the pool member.

To observe the monitor removing a pool member from eligibility, stop the web service on `Web1` and observe the packet captures and logs:

```
root@web1:~# tcpdump -i any -n port 80
tcpdump: verbose output suppressed, use -v or -vv for full protocol decode
listening on any, link-type LINUX_SLL (Linux cooked), capture size 65535 bytes
11:06 35 987740 IP 10.30.0.9.43890 > 10.30.0.7.80: Flags [S], seq 2051332219, win 29200, options [mss 1460,sackOK,TS
11:06 35 987769 IP 10.30.0.7.80 > 10.30.0.9.43890: Flags [R.], seq 0, ack 2051332220, win 0, length 0

11:06 40 989032 IP 10.30.0.9.43892 > 10.30.0.7.80: Flags [S], seq 2849503740, win 29200, options [mss 1460,sackOK,TS
11:06 40 989060 IP 10.30.0.7.80 > 10.30.0.9.43892: Flags [R.], seq 0, ack 2849503741, win 0, length 0

11:06 45 990502 IP 10.30.0.9.43894 > 10.30.0.7.80: Flags [S], seq 2605972483, win 29200, options [mss 1460,sackOK,TS
11:06 45 990541 IP 10.30.0.7.80 > 10.30.0.9.43894: Flags [R.], seq 0, ack 2605972484, win 0, length 0
```

Figure 10.18

In the preceding output, the web service is stopped and connections to port `80` are refused. Immediately following the third failure, the load balancer marks the pool member as `DOWN`:

```
root@controller01:~# tail -f /var/log/syslog | grep haproxy
Oct 20 11:06:46 controller01 haproxy[20618]: Server
3f314bd2-9fdf-4397-8f1c-ee530a1ed134/cb51bd34-0be6-4044-8f89-a61d2d75cb07 is DOWN, reason: Layer4 connection
problem, info: "Connection refused", check duration: 1ms. 0 active and 0 backup servers left. 0 sessions active, 0
requeued, 0 remaining in queue.
```

Figure 10.19

While `WEB1` is down, all subsequent connections to the VIP are sent to `WEB2`:

```
root@controller01:~# ip netns exec qrouter-70705227-a6a2-4681-9445-152676e3d607 curl http://10.30.0.9
This is Web2
root@controller01:~# ip netns exec qrouter-70705227-a6a2-4681-9445-152676e3d607 curl http://10.30.0.9
This is Web2
root@controller01:~# ip netns exec qrouter-70705227-a6a2-4681-9445-152676e3d607 curl http://10.30.0.9
This is Web2
root@controller01:~# ip netns exec qrouter-70705227-a6a2-4681-9445-152676e3d607 curl http://10.30.0.9
This is Web2
```

Figure 10.20

After restarting the web service on `WEB1`, the load balancer places the server back in the pool upon the next successful health check:

```
Oct 20 11:13:21 controller01 haproxy[20618]: Server
3f314bd2-9fdf-4397-8f1c-ee530a1ed134/cb51bd34-0be6-4044-8f89-a61d2d75cb07 is UP, reason: Layer4 check passed, check
duration: 1ms. 2 active and 0 backup servers online. 0 sessions requeued, 0 total in queue.
```

Figure 10.21

Connecting to the virtual IP externally

To connect to a virtual IP externally, a floating IP must be associated with the VIP because the virtual IP exists within a subnet behind the router and is not reachable directly.

Using the Neutron `floatingip-create` command, assign a floating IP to be used with the virtual IP:

```
root@controller01:~# neutron floatingip-create GATEWAY_NET --port-id=$(neutron port-list | grep 10.30.0.9 | awk '{print $2}')
Created a new floatingip:
+---------------------+--------------------------------------+
| Field               | Value                                |
+---------------------+--------------------------------------+
| fixed_ip_address    | 10.30.0.9                            |
| floating_ip_address | 10.50.0.108                          |
| floating_network_id | da911578-b8ea-4f03-bd16-5c2593391772 |
| id                  | 709d34dc-94e5-4f01-bdad-11dca6cfac78 |
| port_id             | 5e234421-01a6-47e3-a64d-d814f28e6301 |
| router_id           | 70705227-a6a2-4681-9445-152676e3d607 |
| status              | DOWN                                 |
| tenant_id           | da6c995d9f834090bd7a00d13d40b817     |
+---------------------+--------------------------------------+
```

Figure 10.22

A test from a workstation to the floating IP confirms external connectivity to the load balancer and its pool members:

```
workstation:~ james.denton$ curl http://10.50.0.108
This is Web2
workstation:~ james.denton$ curl http://10.50.0.108
This is Web1
workstation:~ james.denton$ curl http://10.50.0.108
This is Web2
workstation:~ james.denton$ curl http://10.50.0.108
This is Web1
```

Figure 10.23

Load balancer management in the dashboard

In the Horizon dashboard, load balancers can be managed from the **Project** panel by clicking on **Load Balancers** in the menu on the left-hand side of the screen:

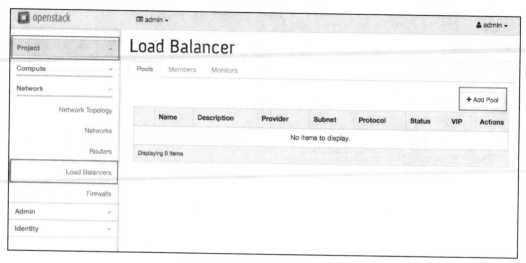

Figure 10.24

From the **Load Balancers** screen, pools, members, and monitors can be managed from their respective tab.

Creating a pool in the dashboard

To create a pool, perform the following steps:

1. Click on the **Add Pool** button within the **Pools** section. A window will pop up that resembles the one shown in the following screenshot:

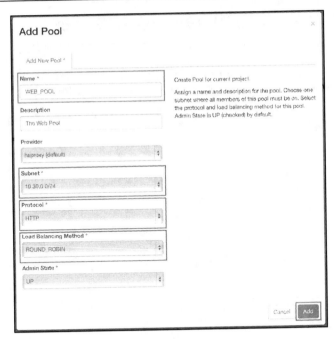

Figure 10.25

2. From the **Add Pool** window, you can specify a name for the pool and choose the subnet, protocol, and load balancing method. To create the pool, click on the blue button labeled **Add**. Once created, the pool will be listed in the **Pools** section, as follows:

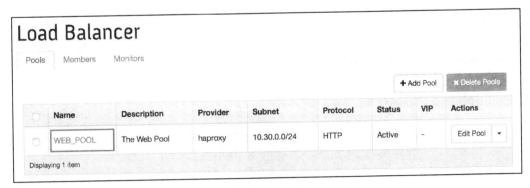

Figure 10.26

Creating pool members in the dashboard

To create a pool member, perform the following steps:

1. Click on the **Add Member** button within the **Members** section. A window will pop up that resembles the one shown in the following screenshot:

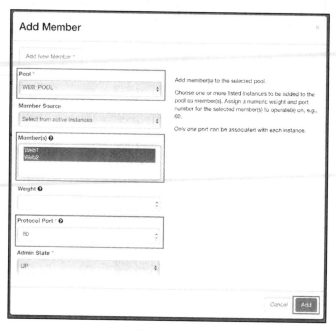

Figure 10.27

2. From the **Add Member** window, you can add multiple members to a pool simultaneously and set a common weight and protocol port for the chosen pool members. To create the pool members, click on the blue button labeled **Add**. The pool members and their pool association will be listed in the **Members** window:

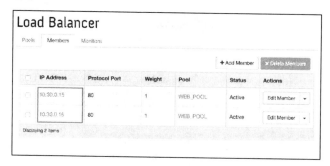

Figure 10.28

3. To edit a particular pool member, click on the **Edit Member** button under the **Actions** column next to the pool member:

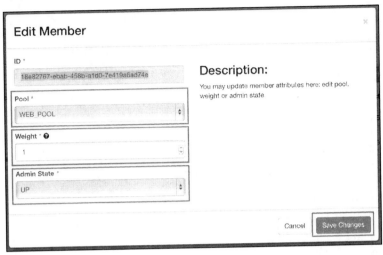

Figure 10.29

4. From the **Edit Member** screen, you can move the member to another pool, change the weight, or mark the member as administratively down. To save your changes, click on the blue **Save Changes** button.

Creating a virtual IP in the dashboard

To create a virtual IP, perform the following steps:

1. Navigate to the list of pools by clicking on the **Pools** tab in the **Load Balancers** section. Choose **Add VIP** from the **More** menu next to the pool:

Figure 10.30

2. A window will pop up similar to the following:

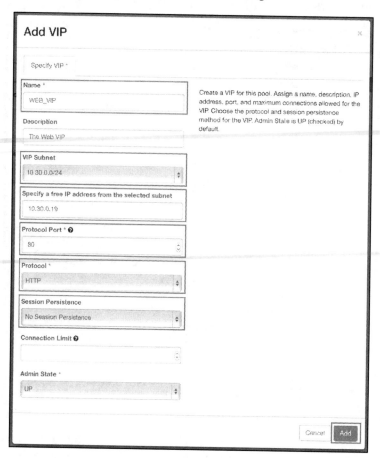

Figure 10.31

3. From the **Add VIP** window, you can assign a name to the VIP, specify an IP address, specify the protocol and listener port, define a type of session persistence, and set the connection limit. Information on session persistence types was discussed earlier in this chapter. Once configured, click on the blue **Add** button to associate the VIP with the pool.

Connecting to the virtual IP externally

In versions of OpenStack as far back as Havana, the ability to assign a floating IP to the virtual IP from the **Add VIP** window is not functional or is removed. Instead, you must perform the following steps:

1. Navigate to the **Instances** pane and select **Associate Floating IP** from any of the instances listed:

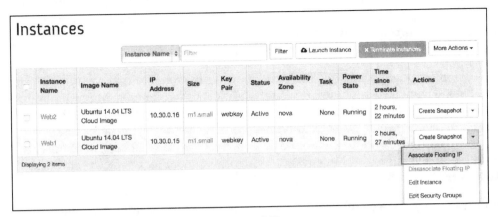

Figure 10.32

2. A window will pop up similar to the one in the following figure:

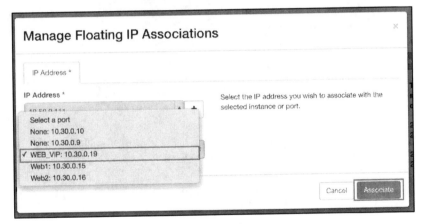

Figure 10.33

3. From the **Manage Floating IP Associations** window, select a floating IP from the **IP Address** menu and select the address utilized by the virtual IP from the **Port To Be Associated** menu. Click on the blue **Associate** button to associate the floating IP with the virtual IP.

Summary

Load Balancing as a Service provides users with the ability to scale their application programmatically through the Neutron API. Users can balance traffic to pools consisting of multiple application servers and provide high availability of their application through the use of intelligent health monitors.

The reference plugin based on HAProxy offers a functionality that can address basic load balancing needs and may be enough for most environments. Major limitations found in version 1 of the LBaaS API, such as the inability to create multiple virtual servers using the same IP address and different layer 4 ports, the lack of SSL offloading support, and the lack of advanced layer 7 load balancing methods, are addressed by version 2 and integration with other OpenStack projects, such as Barbican.

In the next chapter, we will take a look at another advanced service provided by Neutron known as Firewall as a Service, which can be used to implement virtual firewalls at the edge of tenant networks.

11
Firewall as a Service

Neutron includes an advanced service known as **Firewall as a Service**, or **FWaaS**, which enables users to create and manage firewalls that provide layer 3 and layer 4 filtering at the perimeter of the network. Using the reference driver and Neutron API, users can:

- Apply firewall rules to the traffic entering and leaving the tenant networks attached to Neutron routers
- Create and share firewall policies that hold an ordered collection of the firewall rules
- Audit firewall rules and policies

The FWaaS extension introduces the following network resources:

- **Firewall**: A logical firewall resource that a tenant can instantiate and manage. A firewall is associated with a single firewall policy.
- **Firewall policy**: An ordered collection of firewall rules that can be shared across tenants.
- **Firewall rule**: A collection of attributes such as layer 3 addresses and layer 4 ports that are allowed or denied access through an interface.

As with security groups, firewalls in Neutron utilize iptables to perform traffic filtering when an iptables-based reference driver is used. Rather than being configured on every compute node, however, firewall rules are implemented within a Neutron router namespace.

In this chapter, we will cover the following:

- Enabling FWaaS in Neutron
- Creating and managing Neutron firewalls
- Demonstrating traffic flow through a Neutron firewall

Enabling FWaaS

To enable FWaaS, some changes must be made to Neutron configuration files on the network and controller node. In this environment, the controller serves as the network node. There is no dedicated agent needed to implement FWaaS as the existing Neutron L3 agent handles all firewall functionalities.

Configuring the firewall driver

Neutron stores the FWaaS driver configuration in the `/etc/neutron/fwaas_driver.ini` file. The most common configuration options will be covered in the following sections.

Defining a device driver

To manage a firewall, Neutron must be configured to use a device driver that provides the interface between the Neutron API and the programming of the service or device.

On the controller node, enable FWaaS and define the `iptables` device driver in the FWaaS driver configuration file, as follows:

```
[fwaas]
...
enabled = true
driver = neutron_fwaas.services.firewall.drivers.linux.iptables_fwaas.
IptablesFwaasDriver
```

Configuring Neutron

In addition to configuring the firewall driver, Neutron must be configured to use the firewall service plugin before the API can be utilized to create firewall objects.

Defining a service plugin

Update the `service_plugins` configuration option found in the `/etc/neutron/neutron.conf` file on the controller by adding the `firewall` service plugin to the list of enabled plugins:

```
[DEFAULT]
...
service_plugins = router,lbaas,firewall
```

Restart the `neutron-server` and `neutron-13-agent` services with the following commands:

```
# service neutron-server restart
# service neutron-13-agent restart
```

Workarounds

Due to a bug in the release of Kilo available at the time this book is published, it may be necessary to update the Neutron database schema to allow FWaaS to operate properly.

To update the schema, run the following command on the controller node:

```
# neutron-db-manage --service fwaas upgrade head
```

For more information on the bug, refer to the following URL:

```
https://bugs.launchpad.net/neutron/+bug/1463830
```

Firewall Management in the CLI

The primary commands associated with FWaaS in the Neutron CLI include:

- `firewall-create`
- `firewall-delete`
- `firewall-list`
- `firewall-policy-create`
- `firewall-policy-delete`
- `firewall-policy-insert-rule`
- `firewall-policy-list`
- `firewall-policy-remove-rule`
- `firewall-policy-show`
- `firewall-policy-update`
- `firewall-rule-create`
- `firewall-rule-delete`
- `firewall-rule-list`
- `firewall-rule-show`
- `firewall-rule-update`

- `firewall-show`
- `firewall-update`

Like LBaaS, FWaaS requires a specific workflow to properly implement firewall policies. First, firewall rules must be created. Then, a firewall policy can be created that references firewall rules. Lastly, a firewall is created and associated with a firewall policy. Once a firewall policy is applied, the rules are immediately put in place on the routers associated with the firewall.

Firewall policies can be shared among tenants, which means that whenever a policy is updated, it results in the immediate updating of any firewall associated with the policy.

Managing firewall rules

The first step in creating a firewall is to create one or more firewall rules that can be applied to a policy. Firewall rules are limited to layer 3 and layer 4 attributes, such as addresses and ports, and can be configured to allow or deny traffic based on these attributes.

Creating a firewall rule in the CLI

To create a firewall rule in the CLI, use the Neutron `firewall-create` command, as follows:

```
usage:      firewall-rule-create [--tenant-id TENANT_ID]
            [--name NAME] [--description DESCRIPTION]
            [--shared]
            [--source-ip-address SOURCE_IP_ADDRESS]
            [--destination-ip-address DESTINATION_IP_ADDRESS]
            [--source-port SOURCE_PORT]
            [--destination-port DESTINATION_PORT]
            [--enabled {True,False}]
            --protocol {tcp,udp,icmp,any}
            --action {allow,deny}
```

Here, the `--tenant-id` flag is optional and allows you to associate the firewall rule with the specified tenant.

The `--name` flag is optional and allows you to provide a name to the rule.

The `--description` flag is also optional and allows you to provide a description of the firewall rule.

The `--shared` flag is optional and allows the rule to be shared among other tenants.

The `--source-ip-address` flag is optional as well and allows you to specify the source host or network that the rule should apply to.

The `--destination-ip-address` flag is optional and allows you to specify the destination host or network that the rule should apply to.

The `--source-port` flag is optional and allows you to specify a source port or range of the ports that the rule should apply to. If you are specifying a range of ports, use a colon between the start and end ports.

The `--destination-port` flag is optional and allows you to specify a destination port or range of ports that the rule should apply to. If you are specifying a range of ports, use a colon between the start and end ports.

The `--disabled` flag is also optional and allows you to specify whether or not the rule is inserted into the firewall.

The `--protocol` flag is required and used to specify the type of traffic that the rule applies to. Possible options include `tcp`, `udp`, `icmp`, or others.

Finally, the `--action` flag is required and allows you to specify the action that takes place when the traffic matches the rule's criteria. Possible actions are `allow` or `deny`.

Deleting a firewall rule in the CLI

To delete a firewall rule in the CLI, use the Neutron `firewall-rule-delete` command, as follows:

```
usage:    firewall-rule-delete FIREWALL_RULE
```

Here, the keyword `FIREWALL_RULE` is used to represent the ID of the firewall rule to be deleted.

Listing firewall rules in the CLI

To list all firewall rules within the CLI, use the Neutron `firewall-rule-list` command, as follows:

```
usage:    firewall-rule-list
```

Here, the returned output includes the ID, name, summary, associated firewall policy, and status of firewall rules within the tenant.

Showing the details of a firewall rule in the CLI

To show the details of a firewall rule within the CLI, use the Neutron `firewall-rule-show` command, as follows:

```
usage:    firewall-rule-show FIREWALL_RULE
```

The returned output includes the name, description, action, destination IP address, destination port, source IP address, source port, associated firewall policy, position, protocol, and tenant ID of the specified firewall rule.

Updating a firewall rule in the CLI

Many of the attributes of a firewall rule are editable at any time. To update an attribute of a firewall rule in the CLI, use the Neutron `firewall-rule-update` command, as follows:

```
usage:    firewall-rule-update
          [--description DESCRIPTION] [--shared]
          [--source-ip-address SOURCE_IP_ADDRESS]
          [--destination-ip-address DESTINATION_IP_ADDRESS]
          [--source-port SOURCE_PORT]
          [--destination-port DESTINATION_PORT]
          [--protocol {tcp,udp,icmp,any}]
          [--action {allow,deny}]
          FIREWALL_RULE
```

Updating the firewall rules associated with a live firewall may result in an error due to a bug in the Kilo release of FWaaS. To work around this issue, the firewall must be marked DOWN to remove the rules and then UP to reapply them.

For more information on the bug, visit the following URL:

```
https://bugs.launchpad.net/neutron/+bug/1475244
```

Managing firewall policies

The next step in creating a firewall is to create a firewall policy that references one or more firewall rules.

Creating a firewall policy in the CLI

To create a firewall policy, use the Neutron `firewall-policy-create` command, as follows:

```
usage:    firewall-policy-create [--tenant-id TENANT_ID]
          [--description DESCRIPTION] [--shared]
          [--firewall-rules FIREWALL_RULES] [--audited]
          NAME
```

Here, the `--tenant-id` flag is optional, and allows you to associate the firewall rule with the specified tenant.

The `--description` flag is optional and allows you to provide a description of the firewall policy.

The `--shared` flag is optional and allows the policy to be shared among other tenants. Before a policy can be shared, all associated firewall rules must be shared.

The `--firewall-rules` flag is also optional and is used to add firewall rules to the policy during creation. If multiple rules are specified, they should be enclosed in quotes and separated by spaces. In the following example, two firewall rules are added to the policy named `EXAMPLE_POLICY` during its creation:

```
(neutron) firewall-policy-create --firewall-rules "a7a03a5f-ecda-
    4471-92db-7a1c708e20e1 a9dd1195-f6d9-4942-b76a-06ff3bac32e8"
    EXAMPLE_POLICY
```

 Neutron always adds a default "deny all" rule at the lowest precedence of each policy. As a result, a firewall policy with no rules blocks all traffic by default.

Finally, the `--audited` flag is optional and is used to reflect whether or not a policy is audited by an external resource. There are no audit logs or auditing mechanisms within Neutron.

Deleting a firewall policy in the CLI

To delete a firewall policy within the CLI, use the Neutron `firewall-policy-delete` command, as follows:

```
usage:    firewall-policy-delete FIREWALL_POLICY
```

Here, the keyword `FIREWALL_POLICY` is used to represent the ID of the firewall policy to be deleted.

Listing firewall policies in the CLI

To list all firewall policies within a tenant in the CLI, use the Neutron `firewall-policy-list` command, as follows:

```
usage:    firewall-policy-list
```

The returned output includes the ID, name, and firewall rules associated with the policies.

Showing the details of a firewall policy in the CLI

To show the details of a firewall policy in the CLI, use the Neutron `firewall-policy-show` command, as follows:

```
usage:    firewall-policy-show FIREWALL_POLICY
```

The returned output includes the ID, name, description, tenant ID, audited status, and associated firewall rules of the specified policy.

Updating a firewall policy in the CLI

To update the attributes of a firewall policy, use the Neutron `firewall-policy-update` command, as follows:

```
usage:    firewall-policy-update FIREWALL_POLICY
          [--name NAME] [--description DESCRIPTION] [--shared]
          [--firewall-rules RULES]
```

Multiple rules should be enclosed in quotes and separated by a space.

Inserting rules into firewall policies in the CLI

Using the Neutron `firewall-policy-insert-rule` command, it is possible to insert firewall rules into an existing policy before or after the existing rules. The syntax to insert a rule into a policy is as follows:

```
usage:    firewall-policy-insert-rule
          [--insert-before FIREWALL_RULE]
          [--insert-after FIREWALL_RULE]
          FIREWALL_POLICY FIREWALL_RULE
```

Here, the `--insert-before` flag is optional and allows you to insert a new firewall rule before the specified firewall rule.

The `--insert-after` flag is optional and allows you to insert a new firewall rule after the specified firewall rule.

 The `--insert-before` and `--insert-after` flags are mutually exclusive and cannot be used at the same time.

The keyword `FIREWALL_POLICY` is used to represent the ID of the firewall policy to be updated.

Finally, the keyword `FIREWALL_RULE` is used to represent the ID of the firewall rule to be added to the policy.

Removing rules from firewall policies in the CLI

Using the Neutron `firewall-policy-remove-rule` command, it is possible to remove firewall rules from a firewall policy. The syntax to remove a rule from a policy is as follows:

```
usage:     firewall-policy-remove-rule
           FIREWALL_POLICY_ID FIREWALL_RULE_ID
```

The keyword `FIREWALL_POLICY` is used to represent the ID of the firewall policy to be updated.

The keyword `FIREWALL_RULE` is used to represent the ID of the firewall rule to be removed from the policy.

 Updating the firewall policies associated with a live firewall may result in an error due to a bug in the Kilo release of FWaaS. To work around this issue, the firewall must be marked DOWN to remove the rules and then UP to reapply them.

For more information on the bug, visit the following URL:

`https://bugs.launchpad.net/neutron/+bug/1475244`

Managing firewalls

The last step in creating a firewall is to create a firewall object that references a single firewall policy and associate it with one or more routers.

Creating a firewall in the CLI

To create a firewall within the CLI, use the Neutron `firewall-create` command, as follows:

```
usage:    firewall-create [--tenant-id TENANT_ID] [--name NAME]
          [--description DESCRIPTION] [--shared]
          [--admin-state-down]
          POLICY
          [--router-ids list=true ROUTER]
```

Here, the `--tenant-id` flag is optional and allows you to associate the firewall with the specified tenant.

The `--name` flag is optional and allows you to provide a name for the firewall.

The `--description` flag is also optional and allows you to provide a description of the firewall.

The `--admin-state-down` flag is optional and allows you to create the firewall in a DOWN state. In a DOWN state, firewall rules are not applied.

The keyword POLICY is used to represent the ID of the policy that should be applied to the firewall. Firewalls are limited to a single policy.

The `-router-ids` flag is optional and allows you to associate the firewall with one or more routers. Finally, The keyword ROUTER is used to represent the ID of a router that should be associated with the firewall. To specify more than one router, use a space to separate the router IDs.

Deleting a firewall in the CLI

To delete a firewall within the CLI, use the Neutron `firewall-delete` command, as follows:

```
usage:    firewall-delete FIREWALL
```

Here, the keyword FIREWALL is used to represent the ID of the firewall to be deleted.

Listing firewalls in the CLI

To list all firewalls within a tenant in the CLI, use the Neutron `firewall-list` command as follows:

```
usage:    firewall-list
```

The returned output includes a list of firewalls containing the ID, name, and associated firewall policy for each firewall within the tenant.

Showing the details of a firewall in the CLI

To show the details of a firewall within the CLI, use the Neutron `firewall-show` command as follows:

`Syntax:`   `firewall-show FIREWALL`

The output returned includes the ID, admin state, name, description, status, tenant ID, associated firewall policy, and associated routers of the specified firewall.

Updating a firewall in the CLI

To update the attributes of a firewall within the CLI, use the Neutron `firewall-update` command, as follows:

`usage:`   `firewall-update FIREWALL [--name NAME]`

`[--firewall-policy-id FIREWALL_POLICY_ID]`

`[--admin-state-up]`

Here, the keyword `FIREWALL` is required and used to represent the ID of the firewall to be updated.

The `--name` flag is optional and allows you to update the name of the firewall.

The `--firewall-policy-id` flag is also optional and allows you to associate a different policy with the firewall.

The `--admin-state-up` flag is a Boolean that, when set to `FALSE`, puts the firewall in a `DOWN` state. When a firewall is in a `DOWN` state, all rules are removed from the Neutron router.

Firewall management in the dashboard

Within the Horizon dashboard, the firewalls are managed in the **Firewalls** section under the **Network** tab:

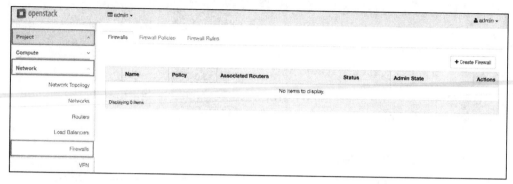

Figure 11.1

In the dashboard, the workflow to create functional firewalls is similar to that in the CLI. First, the firewall rules must be created, then a firewall policy, and lastly, the firewall itself.

Creating a firewall rule

To create a firewall rule, perform the following steps:

1. Click on **Firewalls** under the **Network** menu within the **Project** screen. In the **Firewall Rules** tab, click on the **Add Rule** button in the upper right-hand corner of the screen. A window will appear that allows you to create a firewall rule:

Figure 11.2

2. From within this window, you can specify source and destination addresses, source and destination ports, the protocol, and the desired action—**ALLOW** or **DENY**. To create the rule, click on the blue **Add** button. The rule will be listed on the main **Firewalls** page under **Firewall Rules**, as shown in the following screenshot:

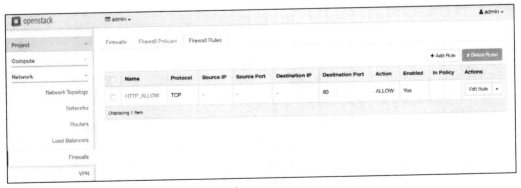

Figure 11.3

Creating a firewall policy

To create a firewall policy, perform the following steps:

1. To create a firewall policy that will contain the rule(s), click on the **Add Policy** button within the **Firewall Policies** tab. A window will appear that allows you to create a firewall policy:

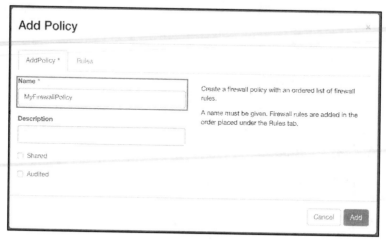

Figure 11.4

2. Click on the **Rules** tab to insert rules into the policy:

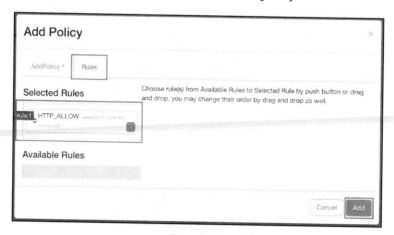

Figure 11.5

3. Use the up and down arrows to order the rules if you are adding more than one. Once the desired rules are moved from the **Available Rules** section to the **Selected Rules** section, click on the blue **Add** button to complete the policy creation process.

4. The resulting policy will be listed on the main **Firewalls** page under **Firewall Policies**, as shown in the following screenshot:

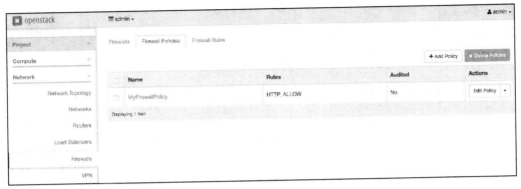

Figure 11.6

Creating a firewall

To create a firewall, perform the following steps:

1. From the **Firewalls** tab, click on the **Create Firewall** button in the upper right-hand corner of the screen. A window will appear that allows you to create a firewall:

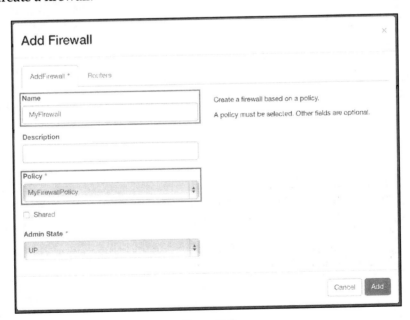

Figure 11.7

2. Click on the **Routers** tab to associate the firewall with a router:

Figure 11.8

3. To associate the firewall with a router, move the router from the **Available Routers** section to the **Selected Routers** section. Click on the blue **Add** button to complete the firewall creation process.

4. The resulting firewall will be listed on the main **Firewalls** page under **Firewall**, as shown in the following screenshot:

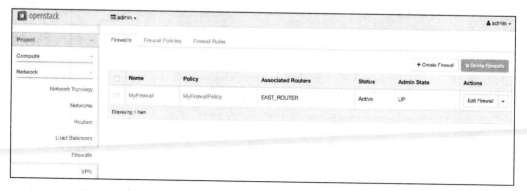

Figure 11.9

 The firewall status will remain PENDING_CREATE until the rules are applied to the associated Neutron routers.

Demonstrating traffic flow through a firewall

To see how firewall policies are applied to a Neutron router, take note of the following firewall rule, which allows HTTP traffic from *any* source to *any* destination on TCP port 80:

```
root@controller01:~# neutron firewall-rule-list
+-------------------------------------+------------+--------------------------------------+----------------------+---------+
| id                                  | name       | firewall_policy_id                   | summary              | enabled |
+-------------------------------------+------------+--------------------------------------+----------------------+---------+
| 086ef656-858e-40c6-82d5-f6522b9cf81c | HTTP_ALLOW | 4d1139fd-c901-4ba1-bf6e-db599647676e | TCP,                 | True    |
|                                     |            |                                      | source: none(none),  |         |
|                                     |            |                                      | dest: none(80),      |         |
|                                     |            |                                      | allow                |         |
+-------------------------------------+------------+--------------------------------------+----------------------+---------+
```

Figure 11.10

The firewall rule was applied to the policy named `MyFirewallPolicy` as shown in the following screenshot:

```
root@controller01:~# neutron firewall-policy-list
+--------------------------------------+------------------+-------------------------------------------------+
| id                                   | name             | firewall_rules                                  |
+--------------------------------------+------------------+-------------------------------------------------+
| 4d1139fd-c901-4ba1-bf6e-db599647676e | MyFirewallPolicy | [086ef656-858e-40c6-82d5-f6522b9cf81c]          |
+--------------------------------------+------------------+-------------------------------------------------+
```

Figure 11.11

As the final step, the policy is associated with a firewall, `MyFirewall`, as shown in the following screenshot:

```
root@controller01:~# neutron firewall-list
+--------------------------------------+------------+--------------------------------------+
| id                                   | name       | firewall_policy_id                   |
+--------------------------------------+------------+--------------------------------------+
| a4040d8b-6d9b-4904-afb6-6c164f55176e | MyFirewall | 4d1139fd-c901-4ba1-bf6e-db599647676e |
+--------------------------------------+------------+--------------------------------------+
```

Figure 11.12

Examining the chains

Once a firewall is created, the rules within the firewall policy are implemented on the associated router. Running `iptables -L -t filter` or `iptables-save` within a router namespace reveals the iptables rules that are implemented by the L3 agent. For readability, only the `filter` table is shown in the following screenshot:

```
# Generated by iptables-save v1.4.21 on Sun Nov  1 19:56:01 2015
*filter
:INPUT ACCEPT [0:0]
:FORWARD ACCEPT [0:0]
:OUTPUT ACCEPT [0:0]
:neutron-filter-top - [0:0]
:neutron-l3-agent-FORWARD - [0:0]
:neutron-l3-agent-INPUT - [0:0]
:neutron-l3-agent-OUTPUT - [0:0]
:neutron-l3-agent-fwaas-defau - [0:0]
:neutron-l3-agent-iv4a4040d8b - [0:0]
:neutron-l3-agent-local - [0:0]
:neutron-l3-agent-ov4a4040d8b - [0:0]
-A INPUT -j neutron-l3-agent-INPUT
-A FORWARD -j neutron-filter-top
-A FORWARD -j neutron-l3-agent-FORWARD
-A OUTPUT -j neutron-filter-top
-A OUTPUT -j neutron-l3-agent-OUTPUT
-A neutron-filter-top -j neutron-l3-agent-local
-A neutron-l3-agent-FORWARD -o qr-+ -j neutron-l3-agent-iv4a4040d8b
-A neutron-l3-agent-FORWARD -i qr-+ -j neutron-l3-agent-ov4a4040d8b
-A neutron-l3-agent-FORWARD -o qr-+ -j neutron-l3-agent-fwaas-defau
-A neutron-l3-agent-FORWARD -i qr-+ -j neutron-l3-agent-fwaas-defau
-A neutron-l3-agent-INPUT -m mark --mark 0x1 -j ACCEPT
-A neutron-l3-agent-INPUT -p tcp -m tcp --dport 9697 -j DROP
-A neutron-l3-agent-fwaas-defau -j DROP
-A neutron-l3-agent-iv4a4040d8b -m state --state INVALID -j DROP
-A neutron-l3-agent-iv4a4040d8b -m state --state RELATED,ESTABLISHED -j ACCEPT
-A neutron-l3-agent-iv4a4040d8b -p tcp -m tcp --dport 80 -j ACCEPT
-A neutron-l3-agent-ov4a4040d8b -m state --state INVALID -j DROP
-A neutron-l3-agent-ov4a4040d8b -m state --state RELATED,ESTABLISHED -j ACCEPT
-A neutron-l3-agent-ov4a4040d8b -p tcp -m tcp --dport 80 -j ACCEPT
COMMIT
# Completed on Sun Nov  1 19:56:01 2015
```

Figure 11.13

As with security groups, the FORWARD chain is used as the traffic is forwarded through the namespace rather than directed at it:

```
-A FORWARD -j neutron-filter-top
-A FORWARD -j neutron-l3-agent-FORWARD
```

A `neutron-filter-top` chain does not exist, so the traffic moves to the `neutron-13-agent-FORWARD` chain, as shown in the following screenshot:

```
-A neutron-l3-agent-FORWARD -o qr-+ -j neutron-l3-agent-iv4a4040d8b
-A neutron-l3-agent-FORWARD -i qr-+ -j neutron-l3-agent-ov4a4040d8b
-A neutron-l3-agent-FORWARD -o qr-+ -j neutron-l3-agent-fwaas-defau
-A neutron-l3-agent-FORWARD -i qr-+ -j neutron-l3-agent-fwaas-defau
```

Figure 11.14

The first rule matches all traffic *exiting* any qr-* interface attached to the router and sends it to the `neutron-13-agent-iv4a4040d8b` chain:

```
-A neutron-l3-agent-iv4a4040d8b -m state --state INVALID -j DROP
-A neutron-l3-agent-iv4a4040d8b -m state --state RELATED,ESTABLISHED -j ACCEPT
-A neutron-l3-agent-iv4a4040d8b -p tcp -m tcp --dport 80 -j ACCEPT
```

Figure 11.15

The packets that are invalid are dropped, while the established connections are accepted without further processing. New connections destined to any destination address on port 80 are allowed.

The next rule in the `neutron-13-agent-FORWARD` chain matches all traffic *entering* any qr-* interface attached to the router and sends it to the `neutron-13-agent-ov4a4040d8b` chain:

```
-A neutron-l3-agent-ov4a4040d8b -m state --state INVALID -j DROP
-A neutron-l3-agent-ov4a4040d8b -m state --state RELATED,ESTABLISHED -j ACCEPT
-A neutron-l3-agent-ov4a4040d8b -p tcp -m tcp --dport 80 -j ACCEPT
```

Figure 11.16

As with the previous chain, the packets that are invalid are dropped, while the established connections are accepted without further processing. New connections destined to any outside network on port 80 are allowed.

The traffic that does not match rules in either of the mentioned chains is *dropped* by the `neutron-13-agent-fwaas-defau` chain via the following command:

```
-A neutron-l3-agent-fwaas-defau -j DROP
```

Unlike security group rules, there is no way to differentiate between the directions of the traffic when we create firewall rules with the FWaaS API. By default, firewall rules are applied to both incoming and outgoing traffic in an identical manner. Work is underway in the FWaaS project to solve this issue and others in future OpenStack releases.

Summary

FWaaS enables users to create and manage firewalls that provide layer 3 and layer 4 filtering at the perimeter of tenant networks connected to Neutron routers. The reference driver uses iptables to implement firewalling within router namespaces. FWaaS is often used as a compliment to security groups as it currently lacks some functionality that security groups provide—most notably, the ability to specify the direction of traffic that should be filtered.

FWaaS saw major improvements in the Kilo release and will continue to improve in releases to come. As of Kilo, FWaaS remains in an experimental status and is not recommended for production use. Be sure to reference the OpenStack Neutron Networking guide found at the following URL for up-to-date changes and examples for topics covered in this chapter and others:

```
http://docs.openstack.org/networking-guide/
```

In the next chapter, we will explore another advanced Neutron service known as Virtual Private Network as a Service, or VPNaaS. VPNaaS provides users with the ability to build site-to-site IPSec tunnels that provide encryption and authentication of tenant traffic behind Neutron routers.

12
Virtual Private Network as a Service

Neutron includes an advanced service known as **Virtual Private Network as a Service**, or **VPNaaS**, which enables users to send and receive data between instances or remote hosts and across secure tunnels. A **virtual private network** enables users to segment data from other traffic so that only the intended recipient has access. VPNs commonly describe secure connections over a public network, such as the Internet, and can be created by establishing a connection between two endpoints, or peers, through the use of dedicated connections, virtual tunneling protocols, or traffic encryption.

The VPNaaS extension introduces the following network resources that allow users to build IPSec-based virtual private networks:

- **IKE policies:** These define the parameters used for phase 1 of an IPSec connection
- **IPSec policies:** These define the parameters used for phase 2 of an IPSec connection
- **VPN services:** These define the local encryption domain
- **IPSec site connections:** These define IKE and IPSec policies, a VPN service, the peer address, and the remote encryption domain

In this chapter, I will discuss the basics of IPSec and the workflow to create site-to-site connections, including:

- Enabling VPNaaS in Neutron
- Managing IKE and IPSec policies
- Managing VPN services
- Managing IPSec site connections
- Demonstrating how VPNs are built by Neutron

An overview of IPSec

IPSec is a standard suite of protocols that provides security at layer 3, or the IP layer, and was designed to provide the following security features when transferring packets across a network:

- **Authentication**: This verifies that the received packet is from the legitimate sender
- **Integrity**: This ensures that the contents of the packet did not change during transit
- **Confidentiality**: This conceals the payload through the use of encryption

IPSec contains many elements, which will be discussed in the following sections.

Encapsulating Security Payload

Encapsulating Security Payload (ESP) provides authentication, integrity, and confidentiality, which help protect against data tampering and provide message content protection. IPSec implements industry standard algorithms, such as SHA and MD5, to produce a unique identifier for each packet that cannot be forged. These "fingerprints" allow the receiver to determine whether a packet has been tampered with. Packets that are not authenticated are discarded and not delivered.

ESP provides encryption services in IPSec and translates readable messages into unreadable formats to hide message content. When the encrypted packet is received, the data is then decrypted from the unreadable format back to a readable message. The use of encryption and decryption allows only the sender and authorized receiver to read the data.

An ESP header is inserted into each packet between the IP header and the rest of the packet, as demonstrated in the following diagram:

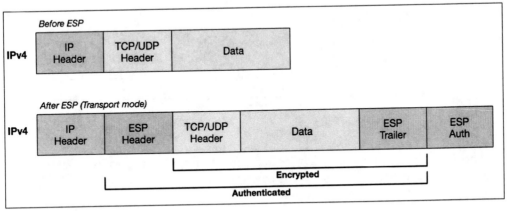

Figure 12.1

ESP operates on top of IP. When building an IPSec tunnel through a firewall, be sure to allow the IP protocol number 50 between the two peer devices.

Authentication Header

Authentication Header (AH) provides authentication and integrity using the same algorithms as ESP. In addition to protecting against data tampering, an AH can provide anti-replay protection, which protects against the unauthorized retransmission of packets. The authentication header is inserted into each packet between the IP header and the rest of the packet. The payload, however, is not encrypted. The AH allows the receiver to verify that the message is intact and unaltered, but the message is potentially vulnerable to snooping.

The following diagram shows the insertion of the authentication header between the IP header and the rest of the packet:

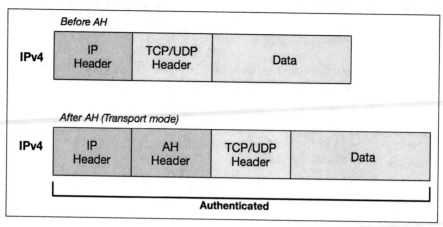

Figure 12.2

AH and ESP can be used separately or in conjunction with one another. Details about when to use one or the other as well as examples of use cases for AH over ESP or vice versa are outside the scope of this book.

 AH operates on top of IP. When building an IPSec tunnel through a firewall, be sure to allow the IP protocol number 51 between the two peer devices.

Security association

A **security association**, or **SA**, is a logical connection between two endpoints transferring data and provides data protection for unidirectional traffic using defined IPSec protocols. An IPSec tunnel usually consists of two unidirectional SAs, one for each direction of traffic, which together provide a protected, full duplex channel to transfer data.

A **security policy**, or **SP**, defines the traffic to which a security association is applied, resulting in its encryption or another action that an SA may prescribe.

Modes

A mode is a method in which the IPSec protocol is applied to a packet. IPSec can be used in tunnel or transport mode.

Tunnel mode

In **tunnel mode**, IPSec encapsulates the entire IP packet, including the original headers. Once encapsulated, the original packet becomes the payload of a new packet with its own set of headers. The new IP header contains two IPSec gateway addresses and hides the internal addresses. The following diagram demonstrates a packet in tunnel mode:

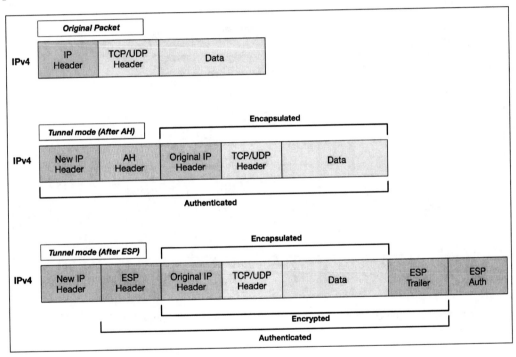

Figure 12.3

Tunnel mode is commonly used for site-to-site and remote access VPN tunnels.

Transport mode

In **transport mode**, IPSec encapsulates *only* the packet payload; the IP header is not changed or concealed. As a result, an attacker can learn where the packet is coming from and where it is headed. The following diagram demonstrates a packet in transport mode:

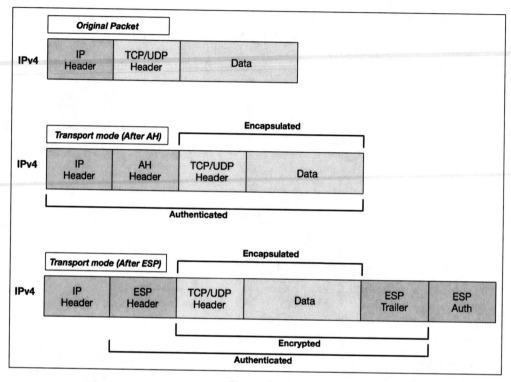

Figure 12.4

Transport mode is used for end-to-end tunnels, such as between a client and server, and is often used when another tunneling protocol, such as GRE, is first used to encapsulate a packet; then, IPSec is used to protect the GRE tunnel.

Internet Security Association and Key Management Protocol

Internet Security Association and Key Management Protocol (ISAKMP) is a protocol to establish security associations and cryptographic keys. The use of keys ensures that only the sender and receiver of a message can access it. ISAKMP only provides a framework for authentication and key exchange and uses the **Internet Key Exchange (IKE)** protocol and others to facilitate the setup of security associations and the exchange of keys between parties that are sending messages. IPSec requires that keys be recreated or refreshed frequently so that parties can continue to communicate securely with one another and uses IKE to manage the process of refreshing keys.

 When building an IPSec tunnel through a firewall, be sure to allow for ISAKMP communication over UDP port 500 between the two peer devices.

Creating a secure tunnel

An IPSec tunnel establishment can be summarized in the following steps: initiation, IKE phase 1, IKE phase 2, data transfer, and termination.

Initiation

As network traffic is matched for protection according to the IPSec security policy configured on an IPSec peer, an IPSec tunnel is initiated.

IKE phase 1

In **IKE phase 1**, the security parameters and keys required to establish an ISAKMP SA are negotiated. The ISAKMP SA is then used to set up a secure channel to negotiating the IKE phase 2 parameters.

IKE phase 2

In **IKE phase 2**, the security parameters and keys required to establish unidirectional IPSec SAs for each direction of traffic are negotiated. The IPSec SAs are used to protect network traffic while it is transferred across the network.

Data transfer

When data is transferred through the tunnel, it is encapsulated according to the security algorithms and parameters provided by the security association.

Termination

A tunnel is closed when its IPSec SAs are deleted or have timed-out. An IPSec SA may time out as a result of being idle for a specified period of time or once a specified amount of traffic has passed through the tunnel.

Neutron provides users with the ability to define many of the IKE, IPSec, and key management parameters through the use of profiles and connection definitions. These profiles and their use in creating secure site-to-site tunnels will be covered later in the following sections.

Installing VPNaaS

The `neutron-vpn-agent` service typically runs on the network node, which in this environment is `controller01`.

Issue the following command on the controller node to install the VPN agent and its dependencies, including the strongSwan VPN software package:

```
# apt-get install neutron-vpn-agent
```

During the installation, you may notice the following message:

```
The following packages will be REMOVED:
    neutron-l3-agent
```

Here, the `neutron-vpn-agent` service replaces `neutron-l3-agent` but inherits all of its functionality and configuration.

 The agents are mutually exclusive and should not be installed simultaneously. Failure to heed this warning will result in unexpected issues.

Configuring the Neutron VPN agent service

Neutron stores the VPN agent configuration in the `/etc/neutron/vpn_agent.ini` file. The most common configuration options will be covered in the upcoming sections.

Defining a device driver

To manage a VPN service or device, the Neutron VPN agent must be configured to use a device driver that provides an interface between the Neutron API and programming of the service or device.

On the controller node, update the VPN agent configuration file and define the `strongswan` device driver, as follows:

```
[vpnagent]
...
vpn_device_driver = neutron_vpnaas.services.vpn.device_drivers.
strongswan_ipsec.StrongSwanDriver
```

Configuring Neutron

In addition to configuring the VPN agent, Neutron must be configured to use a VPN service plugin and driver before the API can be utilized to create VPN objects.

Defining a service plugin

Update the `service_plugins` configuration option found in the `/etc/neutron/neutron.conf` file on the controller by adding the `vpnaas` service plugin to the list of enabled plugins:

```
[DEFAULT]
...
service_plugins = router,lbaas,firewall,vpnaas
```

Defining a service provider

As of the Kilo release of OpenStack, many advanced service configuration options have moved out of the main Neutron configuration file into their own files. On the controller node, update or create the Neutron VPNaaS configuration file at `/etc/neutron/neutron_vpnaas.conf` and define the following generic IPsec service provider driver:

```
[service_providers]
...
service_provider = VPN:vpnaas:neutron_vpnaas.services.vpn.service_
drivers.ipsec.IPsecVPNDriver:default
```

 Be sure to comment out any existing service provider drivers, such as openswan.

Restart the `neutron-server` service as follows:

```
# service neutron-server restart
```

Configuring AppArmor

AppArmor, the Linux kernel security module that confines programs to a particular set of resources, may interfere with the creation of IPSec tunnels when using strongSwan. To work around this, some IPSec-related AppArmor definitions must be removed from the kernel.

Use the following commands on the controller node to configure and restart the AppArmor service:

```
# sudo ln -sf /etc/apparmor.d/usr.lib.ipsec.charon /etc/apparmor.d/disable/
```

```
# sudo ln -sf /etc/apparmor.d/usr.lib.ipsec.stroke /etc/apparmor.d/disable/
```

```
# service apparmor restart
```

Additional workarounds

Due to an Ubuntu bug in the packaging of the Neutron VPN agent, `neutron-vpn-netns-wrapper` may not be included and could result in the failure to build VPN connections. More information on this bug can be found at the following link:

```
https://bugs.launchpad.net/neutron/+bug/1456335
```

To work around this issue, a small program must be created on the controller node. The following text should be entered and terminated with EOF to create the file and populate it accordingly:

```
cat >> /usr/bin/neutron-vpn-netns-wrapper << EOF
#!/usr/bin/python2
import sys
from neutron_vpnaas.services.vpn.common.netns_wrapper import main

if __name__ == "__main__":
    sys.exit(main())
EOF
```

Set the appropriate permissions to allow the file to be executed with the following command:

```
# chmod 755 /usr/bin/neutron-vpn-netns-wrapper
```

Restarting the Neutron VPN agent service

The `neutron-vpn-agent` service must be restarted for the changes to take effect. Issue the following command on the controller node to restart the service:

```
# service neutron-vpn-agent restart
```

Verify whether the agent is running through the following command:

```
# service neutron-vpn-agent status
```

The service should return a similar output to the following:

```
root@lb-controller01:~# service neutron-vpn-agent status
neutron-vpn-agent start/running, process 11308
```

If you encounter any issues, be sure to check the VPN agent log found at `/var/log/neutron/vpn_agent.log` before proceeding.

VPN management in the CLI

The primary commands associated with VPNaaS in the Neutron CLI include:

- `vpn-ikepolicy-create`
- `vpn-ikepolicy-delete`
- `vpn-ikepolicy-list`
- `vpn-ikepolicy-show`
- `vpn-ikepolicy-update`
- `vpn-ipsecpolicy-create`
- `vpn-ipsecpolicy-delete`
- `vpn-ipsecpolicy-list`
- `vpn-ipsecpolicy-show`
- `vpn-ipsecpolicy-update`
- `vpn-service-create`

- `vpn-service-delete`
- `vpn-service-list`
- `vpn-service-show`
- `vpn-service-update`
- `ipsec-site-connection-create`
- `ipsec-site-connection-delete`
- `ipsec-site-connection-list`
- `ipsec-site-connection-show`
- `ipsec-site-connection-update`

Managing IKE policies

IKE policies define the parameters used to establish phase 1 of an IPSec tunnel and are a required component of IPSec site connections.

Creating an IKE policy in the CLI

To create an IKE policy in the CLI, use the Neutron `vpn-ikepolicy-create` command as shown in the following example:

```
usage:    vpn-ikepolicy-create [--tenant-id TENANT_ID]
          [--description DESCRIPTION]
          [--auth-algorithm {sha1}]
          [--encryption-algorithm ENCRYPTION_ALGORITHM]
          [--phase1-negotiation-mode {main}]
          [--ike-version {v1,v2}]
          [--pfs {group2,group5,group14}]
          [--lifetime units=UNITS,value=VALUE]
          NAME
```

Here, the `--tenant-id` flag is optional and allows you to associate the IKE policy with the specified tenant.

The `--description` flag is optional and allows you to provide a description of the IKE policy.

The `--auth-algorithm` flag is also optional and allows you to specify the authentication algorithm. The default and only available option at this time is `sha1`.

The `--encryption-algorithm` flag is optional as well and allows you to specify the encryption algorithm. Available options include `3des`, `aes-128`, `aes-192`, and `aes-256`. The default is `aes-128`.

The `--phase1-negotiation-mode` flag is optional and allows you to specify the IKE Phase 1 negotiation mode. The default and only available option at this time is `main`.

The `--ike-version` flag is optional and allows you to specify the IKE version. Available options include `v1` or `v2`; the default is `v1`.

The `--pfs` flag is optional and allows you to specify the Perfect Forward Secrecy group. Available options include `group2`, `group5`, and `group14`. The default is `group5`.

The `--lifetime` flag is also optional and is used to specify the interval between phase 1 rekeys. The only unit of time available at this time is `seconds`. The default value is `3600` (one hour).

Finally, the `NAME` keyword is used to name the policy.

Deleting an IKE policy in the CLI

To delete an IKE policy in the CLI, use the Neutron `vpn-ikepolicy-delete` command as shown here:

```
usage:    vpn-ikepolicy-delete IKEPOLICY
```

The keyword `IKEPOLICY` is used to represent the ID of the IKE policy to be deleted.

Listing IKE policies in the CLI

To list all IKE policies in the CLI, use the Neutron `vpn-ikepolicy-list` command as shown here:

```
usage:    vpn-ikepolicy-list
```

The returned output includes the ID, name, authentication algorithm, encryption algorithm, IKE version, and PFS group number of the IKE policies within the tenant.

Showing the details of an IKE policy in the CLI

To show the details of an IKE policy within the CLI, use the Neutron `vpn-ikepolicy-show` command, as follows:

```
usage:    vpn-ikepolicy-show IKEPOLICY
```

The returned output includes the name, authentication algorithm, encryption algorithm, IKE version, lifetime, PFS group number, and Phase 1 negotiation mode of the specified IKE policy.

Updating an IKE policy in the CLI

Many of the attributes of an IKE policy are editable *prior* to the IKE policy being applied to an IPSec site connection. To update an attribute of an IKE policy in the CLI, use the Neutron vpn-ikepolicy-update command, as follows:

```
usage:     vpn-ikepolicy-update NAME
           [--description DESCRIPTION]
           [--encryption-algorithm ENCRYPTION_ALGORITHM]
           [--ike-version {v1,v2}]
           [--pfs {group2,group5,group14}]
           [--lifetime units=UNITS,value=VALUE]
           [--name NEWNAME]
```

Once an IKE policy is applied to an IPSec site connection, none of the attributes can be modified.

Managing IPSec policies

IPSec policies define the parameters used to establish Phase 2 of an IPSec tunnel and are a required component of IPSec site connections.

Creating an IPSec policy in the CLI

To create an IPSec policy in the CLI, use the Neutron vpn-ipsecpolicy-create command, as follows:

```
usage:     vpn-ipsecpolicy-create [--tenant-id TENANT_ID]
           [--description DESCRIPTION]
           [--transform-protocol {esp,ah,ah-esp}]
           [--auth-algorithm {sha1}]
           [--encryption-algorithm ENCRYPTION_ALGORITHM]
           [--encapsulation-mode {tunnel,transport}]
           [--pfs {group2,group5,group14}]
           [--lifetime units=UNITS,value=VALUE]
           NAME
```

Here, the `--tenant-id` flag is optional and allows you to associate the IKE policy with the specified tenant.

The `--description` flag is also optional and allows you to provide a description of the IKE policy.

The `--transform-protocol` flag is optional as well and allows you to specify the transform protocol. Available options include `esp`, `ah`, and `ah-esp`. The default is `esp`.

The `--auth-algorithm` flag is optional and allows you to specify the authentication algorithm. The default and only available option at this time is `sha1`.

The `--encryption-algorithm` flag is optional and allows you to specify the encryption algorithm. Available options include `3des`, `aes-128`, `aes-192`, and `aes-256`. The default is `aes-128`.

The `-encapsulation-mode` flag is optional as well and allows you to specify the encapsulation mode. Available options include `tunnel` or `transport`. The default is `tunnel`.

The `--pfs` flag is also optional and allows you to specify the Perfect Forward Secrecy group. Available options include `group2`, `group5`, and `group14`. The default is `group5`.

The `--lifetime` flag is optional, and is used to specify the interval between Phase 2 rekeys. The only unit of time available at this time is `seconds`. The default value is `3600` (one hour).

Finally, the keyword `NAME` is used to name the policy.

Deleting an IPSec policy in the CLI

To delete an IKE policy in the CLI, use the Neutron `vpn-ipsecpolicy-delete` command, as follows:

```
usage:    vpn-ikepolicy-delete IPSECPOLICY
```

Here, the keyword `IPSECPOLICY` is used to represent the ID of the IPSec policy to be deleted.

Listing IPSec policies in the CLI

To list all the IPSec policies in the CLI, use the Neutron vpn-ipsecpolicy-list command, as follows:

```
usage:    vpn-ipsecpolicy-list
```

The returned output includes the ID, name, authentication algorithm, encryption algorithm, and PFS group number of the IPSec policies within the tenant.

Showing the details of an IPSec policy in the CLI

To show the details of an IPSec policy within the CLI, use the Neutron vpn-ipsecpolicy-show command, as follows:

```
usage:    vpn-ipsecpolicy-show IPSECPOLICY
```

The returned output includes the name, authentication algorithm, encapsulation mode, encryption algorithm, lifetime, PFS group number, and transform protocol of the specified IKE policy.

Updating an IPSec policy in the CLI

Many of the attributes of an IPSec policy are editable *prior* to the IPSec policy being applied to an IPSec site connection. To update an attribute of the IPSec policy in the CLI, use the Neutron vpn-ipsecpolicy-update command, as follows:

```
usage:    vpn-ipsecpolicy-update NAME
          [--description DESCRIPTION]
          [--encapsulation-mode {tunnel,transport}]
          [--encryption-algorithm ENCRYPTION_ALGORITHM]
          [--pfs {group2,group5,group14}]
          [--lifetime units=UNITS,value=VALUE]
          [--transform-protocol {esp,ah,ah-esp}]
          [--name NEWNAME]
```

Once an IPSec policy is applied to an IPSec site connection, none of the attributes can be modified.

Managing VPN services

VPN services are profiles that define the local encryption domain in a site-to-site tunnel and are a required component of IPSec site connections.

Creating a VPN service in the CLI

To create a VPN service in the CLI, use the Neutron `vpn-service-create` command, as follows:

```
usage:     vpn-service-create [--tenant-id TENANT_ID]
           [--description DESCRIPTION]
           [--name NAME]
           ROUTER SUBNET
```

Here, the `--tenant-id` flag is optional and allows you to associate the VPN service with the specified tenant.

The `--description` flag is optional and allows you to provide a description of the IKE policy.

The `--name` flag is also optional and allows you to specify a name for the service.

The keyword ROUTER is used to specify the router associated with the service and is a required component.

Finally, the keyword SUBNET is used to specify the subnet in the local encryption domain and is a required component. This must be a tenant subnet connected to the specified router.

Deleting a VPN service in the CLI

To delete a VPN service in the CLI, use the Neutron `vpn-service-delete` command, as follows:

```
usage:     vpn-service-delete VPNSERVICE
```

Here, the keyword VPNSERVICE is used to represent the ID of the VPN service to be deleted.

Listing VPN services in the CLI

To list all the VPN services in the CLI, use the Neutron `vpn-service-list` command, as follows:

```
usage:    vpn-service-list
```

The returned output includes the ID, name, associated router ID, and status of VPN services within the tenant.

Showing the details of a VPN service in the CLI

To show the details of a VPN service within the CLI, use the Neutron `vpn-service-show` command, as follows:

```
usage:    vpn-service-show VPNSERVICE
```

In the preceding command, the returned output includes the name, associated router ID, and status of the specified VPN service.

Updating a VPN service in the CLI

To update an attribute of a VPN service in the CLI, use the Neutron `vpn-service-update` command, as follows:

```
usage:    vpn-service-update NAME
          [--description DESCRIPTION]
```

Managing IPSec connections

An IPSec site connection is a profile that defines the parameters used to construct an IPSec site-to-site connection between a Neutron router and another peer.

Creating a site-to-site connection in the CLI

To create an IPSec site connection in the CLI, use the Neutron `ipsec-site-connection-create` command, as follows:

```
usage:    ipsec-site-connection-create [--tenant-id TENANT_ID]
          [--admin-state-down] [--name NAME]
          [--description DESCRIPTION] [--mtu MTU]
          [--initiator {bi-directional,response-only}]
          [--dpd action=ACTION,interval=INTERVAL,timeout=TIMEOUT]
          --vpnservice-id VPNSERVICE
```

```
--ikepolicy-id IKEPOLICY

--ipsecpolicy-id IPSECPOLICY

--peer-address PEER_ADDRESS

--peer-id PEER_ID

--peer-cidr PEER_CIDRS

--psk PSK
```

Here, the `--tenant-id` flag is optional and allows you to associate the connection with the specified tenant.

The `--description` flag is optional and allows you to provide a description of the connection.

The `--name` flag is also optional and allows you to specify a name for the connection.

The `--initiator` flag is optional as well and allows you to specify whether the local end of the connection can both initiate and respond to connection attempts or only respond. The default is `bi-directional`.

The `--dpd` flag is optional and allows you to specify dead peer detection attributes. Available actions include `hold`, `clear`, `disabled`, `restart`, and `restart-by-peer`. The default action is `hold`. Both interval and timeout values should be nonnegative integers, and the interval should be less than the timeout value. The default interval is `20` seconds and the default timeout is `30` seconds. More information on DPD can be found in RFC 3706, which is available at `https://tools.ietf.org/html/rfc3706`.

The `--vpnservice-id` flag is required and is used to associate a VPN service with the connection.

The `--ikepolicy-id` is required and is used to associate an IKE policy with the connection.

The `--ipsecpolicy-id` flag is also required and is used to associate an IPSEC policy with the connection.

The `--peer-address` flag is required as well and is used to specify the IP address of the peer device.

The `--peer-id` flag is required and is used to specify the identity of the peer device. Available options include an IPv4/IPv6 address, e-mail address, key ID, or FQDN. It is common to specify the peer address as the peer ID for site-to-site connections.

The `--peer-cidr` flag is required and is used to specify the remote encryption domain. One or more remote subnets can be specified in a comma-separated format.

Finally, the `--psk` flag is also required and is used to specify the preshared key. Both ends of the connection must be configured with the same preshared key for the connection to be successful.

Deleting a site-to-site connection in the CLI

To delete an IPSec site connection in the CLI, use the Neutron `ipsec-site-connection-delete` command, as follows:

```
usage:    ipsec-site-connection-delete IPSEC_SITE_CONNECTION
```

The keyword `IPSEC_SITE_CONNECTION` is used to represent the ID of the IPSec site connection to be deleted.

Listing site-to-site connections in the CLI

To list all the IPSec site connections in the CLI, use the Neutron `ipsec-site-connection-list` command, as follows:

```
usage:    ipsec-site-connection-list
```

Here, the returned output includes the ID, name, peer address, peer CIDRs, route mode, authentication mode, and status of the IPSec site connections within the tenant.

Showing the details of a site-to-site connection in the CLI

To show the details of an IPSec site connection within the CLI, use the Neutron `ipsec-site-connection-show` command, as follows:

```
usage:    ipsec-site-connection-show IPSEC_SITE_CONNECTION
```

Here, the returned output includes the authentication mode, description, IKE policy, initiator status, IPSec policy, MTU, name, peer address, peer CIDRs, preshared key, route mode, VPN service, and status of the specified IPSec site connection.

Updating a site-to-site connection in the CLI

To update an attribute of an IPSec site connection in the CLI, use the Neutron `ipsec-site-connection-update` command, as follows:

```
usage:    ipsec-site-connection-update

          [--dpd action=ACTION,interval=INTERVAL,timeout=TIMEOUT]

          IPSEC_SITE_CONNECTION
```

VPN management in the dashboard

In the Horizon dashboard, VPN policies and connections are managed within the **VPN** section under the **Project** tab:

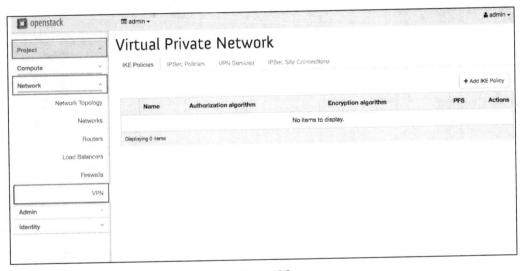

Figure 12.5

In the dashboard, the workflow to create functional site-to-site connections is similar to the CLI. IKE policies, IPSec policies, and VPN services must first be created and then applied to the IPSec site connections, which completes the tunnel configuration.

Creating an IKE policy

To create an IKE policy, perform the following steps:

1. From the **IKE Policies** tab, click on the **Add IKE Policy** button in the upper right-hand corner of the screen. A window will appear that allows you to create an IKE policy:

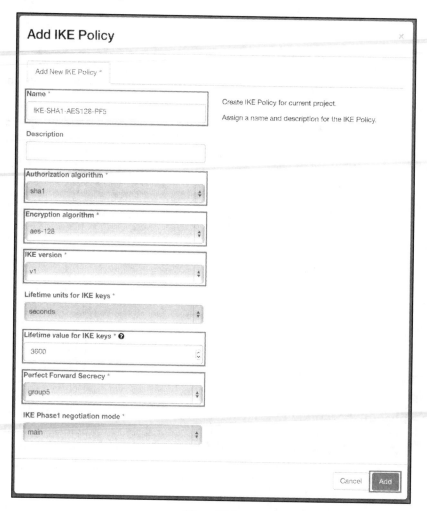

Figure 12.6

2. Once the IKE policy is configured, click on the blue **Add** button to create the policy. The resulting policy will be listed on the main **VPN** page under **IKE Policies**, as shown in the following screenshot:

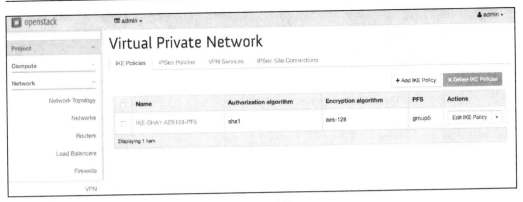

Figure 12.7

Creating an IPSec policy

To create an IPSec policy, perform the following steps:

1. From the **IPSec Policies** tab, click on the **Add IPSec Policy** button in the upper right-hand corner of the screen. A window will appear that allows you to create an IPSec policy:

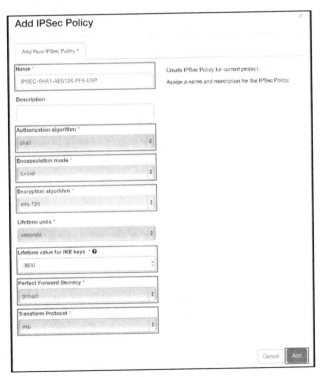

Figure 12.8

2. Once the IPSec policy is configured, click on the blue **Add** button to create the policy. The resulting policy will be listed on the main **VPN** page under **IPSec Policies**, as shown in the following screenshot:

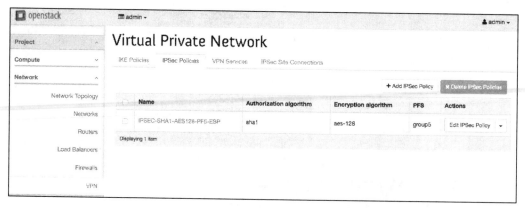

Figure 12.9

Creating a VPN service

To create a VPN service, perform the following steps:

1. From the **VPN Services** tab, click on the **Add VPN Service** button in the upper right-hand corner of the screen. A window will appear that allows you to create a VPN service:

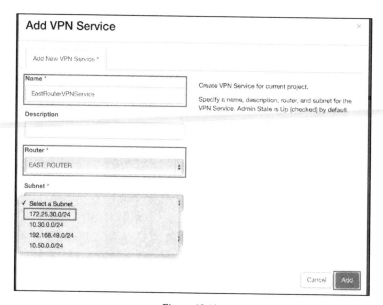

Figure 12.10

2. As part of the VPN configuration, the chosen subnet will be included as the local encryption domain for the IPSec site connection. The subnet should match a tenant network that is directly connected to the chosen router. At this time, only a single local subnet can be associated with the VPN service.

3. Once the VPN service is configured, click on the blue **Add** button to create the policy. The resulting policy will be listed on the main **VPN** page under **VPN Services**, as shown in the following screenshot:

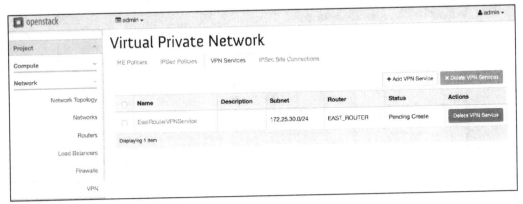

Figure 12.11

4. As they are created, additional VPN services can be observed under **VPN Services**:

Figure 12.12

Creating an IPSec site connection

To create an IPSec site connection, perform the following steps:

1. From the **IPSec Site Connections** tab, click on the **Add IPSec Site Connection** button in the upper right-hand corner of the screen. A window will appear that allows you to create a connection:

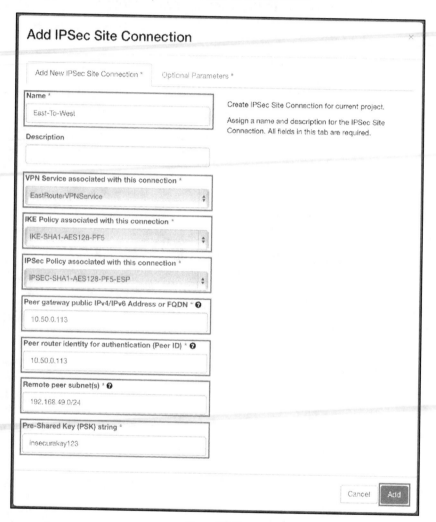

Figure 12.13

2. The IPSec site connection must be associated with previously configured IKE and IPSec policies as well as a VPN service. Subnets that make up the remote encryption domain should be defined in the **Remote peer subnet(s)** field.

3. Once the IPSec site connection is configured, click on the blue **Add** button to create the connection. The resulting connection will be listed on the main **VPN** page under **IPSec Site Connections**, as shown in the following screenshot:

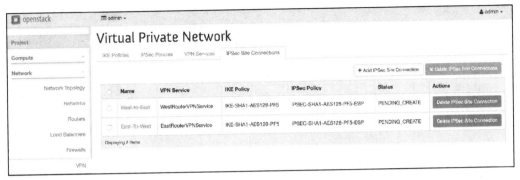

Figure 12.14

4. An IPSec site connection will remain in the **PENDING_CREATE** status until Neutron completes the local VPN configuration.

A tale of two routers

The following diagram represents the tunnel between two Neutron routers that are constructed from the IPSec site connections created in the previous section:

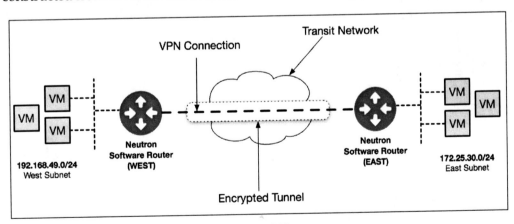

Figure 12.15

Neutron automatically generates an `ipsec.conf` VPN configuration file according to the settings defined by the user. The configuration files can be found on the network node in the `/var/lib/neutron/ipsec/<router_id>/etc/` directory that corresponds to the individual Neutron router. In this demonstration, the controller node is also the network node.

The following configuration files correspond to the EAST and WEST routers, respectively:

```
# Configuration for EastRouterVPNService
config setup

conn %default
        ikelifetime=60m
        keylife=20m
        rekeymargin=3m
        keyingtries=1
        authby=psk
        mobike=no

conn ada99bbe-4e96-4252-8d12-f9c981980942
    keyexchange=ikev1
    left=10.50.0.112
    leftsubnet=172.25.30.0/24
    leftid=10.50.0.112
    leftfirewall=yes
    right=10.50.0.113
    rightsubnet=192.168.49.0/24
    rightid=10.50.0.113
    auto=route



# Configuration for WestRouterVPNService
config setup

conn %default
        ikelifetime=60m
        keylife=20m
        rekeymargin=3m
        keyingtries=1
        authby=psk
        mobike=no
```

```
conn f3d96653-6bef-4f60-95c3-6d1c51853ee9
    keyexchange=ikev1
    left=10.50.0.113
    leftsubnet=192.168.49.0/24
    leftid=10.50.0.113
    leftfirewall=yes
    right=10.50.0.112
    rightsubnet=172.25.30.0/24
    rightid=10.50.0.112
    auto=route
```

Building a tunnel

When traffic routed through a Neutron router matches a route and transform policy, the creation of a site-to-site VPN tunnel is initiated using the defined parameters. In this example, when traffic from a virtual machine behind the EAST router in the 172.25.30.0/24 subnet instance hits the gateway, a route lookup is performed within the router namespace. The following screenshot shows the routing table within the namespace:

```
root@controller01:/var/log/neutron# ip netns exec qrouter-a631ffa9-413b-4bc3-bf51-0bc8f90c30b2 ip rule
0:   from all lookup local
220:     from all lookup 220
32766:   from all lookup main
32767:   from all lookup default
```

Figure 12.16

Table 220 is created by Neutron and contains the route to the remote subnet 192.168.49.0/24 defined in the IPSec site connection, East-to-West:

```
root@controller01:/var/log/neutron# ip netns exec qrouter-a631ffa9-413b-4bc3-bf51-0bc8f90c30b2 ip route show table 220
192.168.49.0/24 via 10.50.0.113 dev qg-c88dbd04-c3  proto static   src 172.25.30.1
```

Figure 12.17

Note how the next hop address is 10.50.0.113, which is the IP address of the WEST router. Once a route is determined, an XFRM lookup is performed. **XFRM** is a framework to transform packets, which includes encrypting their payloads and is used to implement the IPSec protocol suite in Linux. XFRM implements two important concepts in IPSec: security policies and security associations.

If you recall, the security association, or SA, contains the security parameters and keys that are used between peers. An SA is unidirectional, meaning that there should always be two—one for each direction or traffic. The `ip xfrm state` command can be used to determine the security associations in place. The security policy, or SP, defines the traffic to which a security association is applied, resulting in its encryption or any other action an SA may prescribe. The `ip xfrm policy` command can be used to determine the security policies in place.

> The Neutron VPN agent is responsible for programming security associations and security policies into the kernel within router namespaces when the IPSec site connections are configured.

In this example, the XFRM policy table contains three policies that match the traffic:

```
root@controller01:/var/log/neutron# ip netns exec qrouter-a631ffa9-413b-4bc3-bf51-0bc8f90c30b2 ip xfrm policy
src 192.168.49.0/24 dst 172.25.30.0/24
    dir fwd priority 3907
    tmpl src 10.50.0.113 dst 10.50.0.112
        proto esp reqid 2 mode tunnel
src 192.168.49.0/24 dst 172.25.30.0/24
    dir in priority 3907
    tmpl src 10.50.0.113 dst 10.50.0.112
        proto esp reqid 2 mode tunnel
src 172.25.30.0/24 dst 192.168.49.0/24
    dir out priority 3907
    tmpl src 10.50.0.112 dst 10.50.0.113
        proto esp reqid 2 mode tunnel
...
```

Figure 12.18

The first policy listed is known as a **forwarding policy**, and it matches traffic to and from virtual machine instances behind the VPN gateway. In this case, the VPN gateway is the Neutron router. It is a bidirectional policy where source and destination addresses work in both directions. The second and third policies are matched if the destination or source address, respectively, is assigned to one of the local interfaces of the Neutron router.

When a policy is matched, the source and destination addresses are matched against a single security association. Looking at the XFRM state table, we can see that no SA exists by default:

```
root@controller01:/var/log/neutron# ip netns exec qrouter-a631ffa9-413b-4bc3-bf51-0bc8f90c30b2 ip xfrm state
root@controller01:/var/log/neutron#
```

Figure 12.19

As traffic is generated, the kernel builds the appropriate security associations that match this tunnel and forward the traffic to the remote peer through the secure tunnel.

Confirming connectivity

In the following example, the tunnel is in a DOWN state and will be initiated by a ping
from the EAST instance to the WEST instance:

```
root@controller01:~# ip netns exec qdhcp-e441e7a6-a285-4c6e-abf4-2d2dce0668a1 ssh cirros@172.25.30.3
The authenticity of host '172.25.30.3 (172.25.30.3)' can't be established.
RSA key fingerprint is 80:f8:11:6c:bf:53:16:b9:92:12:3d:3f:6d:d2:db:29.
Are you sure you want to continue connecting (yes/no)? yes
Warning: Permanently added '172.25.30.3' (RSA) to the list of known hosts.
cirros@172.25.30.3's password:
$
$ hostname
eastinstance
$
$ ping 192.168.49.3
PING 192.168.49.3 (192.168.49.3): 56 data bytes
64 bytes from 192.168.49.3: seq=1 ttl=62 time=3.090 ms
64 bytes from 192.168.49.3: seq=2 ttl=62 time=1.426 ms
64 bytes from 192.168.49.3: seq=3 ttl=62 time=1.605 ms
64 bytes from 192.168.49.3: seq=4 ttl=62 time=1.980 ms
64 bytes from 192.168.49.3: seq=5 ttl=62 time=1.602 ms
64 bytes from 192.168.49.3: seq=6 ttl=62 time=1.872 ms
64 bytes from 192.168.49.3: seq=7 ttl=62 time=1.476 ms
64 bytes from 192.168.49.3: seq=8 ttl=62 time=1.692 ms
64 bytes from 192.168.49.3: seq=9 ttl=62 time=1.803 ms
64 bytes from 192.168.49.3: seq=10 ttl=62 time=1.576 ms
^C
--- 192.168.49.3 ping statistics ---
11 packets transmitted, 10 packets received, 9% packet loss
round-trip min/avg/max = 1.426/1.812/3.090 ms
```

Figure 12.20

A single packet is lost as the creation of the tunnel is initiated and completed. Using
the `ip xfrm state` command, we can see that the security associations are now
established:

```
root@controller01:~# ip netns exec qrouter-a631ffa9-413b-4bc3-bf51-0bc8f90c30b2 ip xfrm state
src 10.50.0.112 dst 10.50.0.113
    proto esp spi 0xc082f5d4 reqid 2 mode tunnel
    replay-window 32 flag af-unspec
    auth-trunc hmac(sha1) 0x5ccb37cd7c046edaa8c6b3a2c80f0765a98edb25 96
    enc cbc(aes) 0x88520d0aac433660a56b5b1d894ef13e
src 10.50.0.113 dst 10.50.0.112
    proto esp spi 0xcdefc241 reqid 2 mode tunnel
    replay-window 32 flag af-unspec
    auth-trunc hmac(sha1) 0xfbf72de92e5cfa017f65720cd0531cada5b6a0f6 96
    enc cbc(aes) 0x226640c88743db78b254cd31597fc4e6
```

Figure 12.21

A quick look at the IPSec site connection list shows that both connections are ACTIVE:

```
root@controller01:~# neutron ipsec-site-connection-list
+--------------------------------------+--------------+--------------+------------------+------------+-----------+--------+
| id                                   | name         | peer_address | peer_cidrs       | route_mode | auth_mode | status |
+--------------------------------------+--------------+--------------+------------------+------------+-----------+--------+
| 07bdb0bb-ed93-428e-a2c1-d7b01061b4a3 | West-to-East | 10.50.0.112  | "172.25.30.0/24" | static     | psk       | ACTIVE |
| f94b4cac-780c-4964-929b-ef3c532232cb | East-to-West | 10.50.0.113  | "192.168.49.0/24"| static     | psk       | ACTIVE |
+--------------------------------------+--------------+--------------+------------------+------------+-----------+--------+
```

Figure 12.22

Traffic is encrypted according to the parameters of the SA and routed to the remote peer, 10.50.0.113. The remote peer will have a similar configuration that allows for the decryption and forwarding of the packet to the host in the 192.168.49.0/24 network.

Once the tunnel is established, the instances will be able to communicate with one another via their fixed addresses provided the proper security group rules that allow communication between them are in place. The process of establishing the tunnel can take upwards of 5-10 seconds, though this time may vary between environments. Using SSH, we can confirm that access to the fixed IP of the WEST instance from the EAST instance is now possible over the VPN:

```
root@controller01:~# ip netns exec qdhcp-e441e7a6-a285-4c6e-abf4-2d2dce0668a1 ssh cirros@172.25.30.3
cirros@172.25.30.3's password:
$ hostname
eastinstance
$
$ ssh cirros@192.168.49.3
Host '192.168.49.3' is not in the trusted hosts file.
(fingerprint md5 78:9c:3b:1b:09:05:59:68:79:45:59:14:34:d4:4c:ec)
Do you want to continue connecting? (y/n) yes
cirros@192.168.49.3's password:
$
$ hostname
westinstance
```

Figure 12.23

Summary

IPSec is a suite of protocols, standards, and security algorithms that help secure traffic over unsecure and untrusted networks, such as the Internet. RFCs 4301 and 4309 describe IPSec in much more detail than covered here and can be found at the following locations:

- `https://tools.ietf.org/html/rfc4301`
- `https://tools.ietf.org/html/rfc4309`

The use of virtual private networks to securely transfer data among tenant and remote networks is a viable and recommended alternative to exposing the instances directly through the use of floating IPs. In this chapter, I demonstrated creating a VPN between two Neutron routers. Depending on the driver, it is possible to create tunnels between Neutron routers and physical VPN gateways, such as the Cisco ASA, Juniper SRX, and others.

As of Kilo, VPNaaS is no longer considered experimental. However, proposals to change the API to extend functionality are submitted, which may deprecate the methods and commands described here. Be sure to reference the OpenStack Neutron Networking guide found at the following URL for up-to-date changes and examples for topics covered in this chapter and others:

`http://docs.openstack.org/networking-guide/`

You will find brief explanations of the commands and command set not described anywhere else in the book in the upcoming *Appendix A, Additional Neutron Commands.*

A
Additional Neutron Commands

In the book, we covered the core Neutron commands related to building networks, routers, firewalls, load balancers, and virtual private networks. Neutron is capable of much more, provided the appropriate extension or plugin is installed. In this appendix, you will find the Neutron commands that didn't quite have a home in other chapters or are used in network solutions outside the scope of this book. Commands used to manage the following resources are discussed in this appendix:

- Agents
- Quotas
- Cisco 1000V
- VMware NSX
- Nuage VSP
- L3 metering
- The LBaaS v2 API

Neutron extensions

Neutron extensions allow a plugin to extend the Neutron API to provide advanced functionality or expose a capability before it is incorporated into the official API.

Listing the Neutron API extensions

To list the extensions available in Neutron, use the Neutron `ext-list` command, as follows:

```
Usage:   ext-list
```

The returned output includes a list of the available extensions, as shown in the following screenshot:

```
root@controller01:~# neutron ext-list
+-------------------------+---------------------------------------------+
| alias                   | name                                        |
+-------------------------+---------------------------------------------+
| ext-gw-mode             | Neutron L3 Configurable external gateway mode |
| binding                 | Port Binding                                |
| agent                   | agent                                       |
| subnet_allocation       | Subnet Allocation                           |
| l3_agent_scheduler      | L3 Agent Scheduler                          |
| external-net            | Neutron external network                    |
| net-mtu                 | Network MTU                                  |
| quotas                  | Quota management support                    |
| l3-ha                   | HA Router extension                         |
| provider                | Provider Network                            |
| multi-provider          | Multi Provider Network                      |
| vpnaas                  | VPN service                                 |
| lbaas                   | LoadBalancing service                       |
| extraroute              | Neutron Extra Route                         |
| lbaas_agent_scheduler   | Loadbalancer Agent Scheduler                |
| router                  | Neutron L3 Router                           |
| extra_dhcp_opt          | Neutron Extra DHCP opts                     |
| service-type            | Neutron Service Type Management             |
| security-group          | security-group                              |
| dhcp_agent_scheduler    | DHCP Agent Scheduler                        |
| port-security           | Port Security                               |
| allowed-address-pairs   | Allowed Address Pairs                       |
| dvr                     | Distributed Virtual Router                  |
+-------------------------+---------------------------------------------+
```

Figure A.1

Showing the details of an API extension

To show the details of an API extension, use the Neutron `ext-show` command, as follows:

```
Usage:   ext-show EXTENSION_ALIAS
```

Here, the keyword EXTENSION_ALIAS represents the alias of the extension provided in the `ext-list` output. The returned output includes the alias, description, name, namespace, and updated date of the specified extension.

To find more information on creating Neutron API extensions, visit the Neutron development Wikipedia page at the following location:

```
https://wiki.openstack.org/wiki/NeutronDevelopment
```

Neutron agents

Neutron agents are discovered by the `neutron-server` service when they are first activated, and these can be managed with the following commands:

- `agent-delete`
- `agent-list`
- `agent-show`
- `agent-update`

DHCP agents

To schedule or unschedule a network to or from a DHCP agent or to determine a network to DHCP agent association, use the following commands:

- `dhcp-agent-list-hosting-net`
- `dhcp-agent-network-add`
- `dhcp-agent-network-remove`
- `net-list-on-dhcp-agent`

L3 agents

To schedule or unschedule a network to or from an L3 agent or to determine a network to an L3 agent association, use the following commands:

- `l3-agent-list-hosting-router`
- `l3-agent-router-add`
- `l3-agent-router-remove`
- `router-list-on-l3-agent`

LBaaS agents

To determine an LBaaS pool to an LBaaS agent association, use the following command:

- `lb-pool-list-on-agent`

Per-tenant quotas

To prevent system resources from being exhausted, Neutron supports per-tenant quota limits via the `quotas` extension. Every tenant is bound to a default quota that is set by the administrator in the Neutron configuration file, as follows:

```
[quotas]
# Default driver to use for quota checks
# quota_driver = neutron.db.quota_db.DbQuotaDriver


# Resource name(s) that are supported in quota features
# quota_items = network,subnet,port


# Default number of resource allowed per tenant.
# default_quota = -1


# Number of networks allowed per tenant.
# quota_network = 10


# Number of subnets allowed per tenant.
# quota_subnet = 10


# Number of ports allowed per tenant.
# quota_port = 50


# Number of security groups allowed per tenant.
# quota_security_group = 10


# Number of security group rules allowed per tenant.
# quota_security_group_rule = 100


# Number of vips allowed per tenant.
# quota_vip = 10


# Number of pools allowed per tenant.
# quota_pool = 10
```

```
# Number of pool members allowed per tenant.
# quota_member = -1

# Number of health monitors allowed per tenant.
# quota_health_monitor = -1

# Number of loadbalancers allowed per tenant.
# quota_loadbalancer = 10

# Number of listeners allowed per tenant.
# quota_listener = -1

# Number of v2 health monitors allowed per tenant.
# quota_healthmonitor = -1

# Number of routers allowed per tenant. \
# quota_router = 10

# Number of floating IPs allowed per tenant.
# quota_floatingip = 50

# Number of firewalls allowed per tenant.
# quota_firewall = 1

# Number of firewall policies allowed per tenant.
# quota_firewall_policy = 1

# Number of firewall rules allowed per tenant.
# quota_firewall_rule = 100
```

A negative value for a quota means that the tenant may create an unlimited amount of the resource. To change the default, change the value and uncomment the line associated with the quota that you want to change. A restart of the neutron-server service is necessary for the changes to take effect.

The following Neutron commands can be used to manage per-tenant quotas:

- quota-delete
- quota-list

- `quota-show`
- `quota-update`

Listing the current tenant quotas

To get a list of the current quotas, use the Neutron `quota-show` command, as follows:

```
Usage:   quota-show [--tenant-id TENANT_ID]
```

The returned output will contain the current per-tenant Neutron quotas, as shown in the following screenshot:

```
root@controller01:~# neutron quota-show
+-----------------------+-------+
| Field                 | Value |
+-----------------------+-------+
| floatingip            | 50    |
| health_monitor        | -1    |
| ikepolicy             | -1    |
| ipsec_site_connection | -1    |
| ipsecpolicy           | -1    |
| member                | -1    |
| network               | 10    |
| pool                  | 10    |
| port                  | 50    |
| router                | 10    |
| security_group        | 10    |
| security_group_rule   | 100   |
| subnet                | 10    |
| vip                   | 10    |
| vpnservice            | -1    |
+-----------------------+-------+
```

Figure A.2

Updating tenant quotas

To update a quota for a specified tenant, use the Neutron `quota-update` command, as shown here:

```
Usage:    quota-update --tenant-id TENANT_ID
              [--network NUM_OF_NETWORKS]
              [--port NUM_OF_PORTS]
              [--subnet NUM_OF_SUBNETS]
              [--floatingip NUM_OF_FLOATING_IPS]
              [--security-group NUM_OF_SEC_GROUPS]
              [--security-group-rule NUM_OF_SEC_GROUP_RULES]
              [--router NUM_OF_ROUTERS]
```

The attributes in brackets are optional and allow you to specify new values for the respective quota. You can update multiple attributes simultaneously, as shown in the following screenshot:

```
root@controller01:~# openstack project list
+----------------------------------+---------+
| ID                               | Name    |
+----------------------------------+---------+
| 4cc0fdddb2974ac2bad5f1ef2f2c0803 | demo    |
| 8b6c2eee0ef442eeaa0fe3938f92e019 | service |
| da6c995d9f834090bd7a00d13d40b817 | admin   |
+----------------------------------+---------+
root@controller01:~# neutron quota-update --tenant-id=4cc0fdddb2974ac2bad5f1ef2f2c0803 --router 4 —floatingip 10
+-----------------------+-------+
| Field                 | Value |
+-----------------------+-------+
| floatingip            | 10    |
| health_monitor        | -1    |
| ikepolicy             | -1    |
| ipsec_site_connection | -1    |
| ipsecpolicy           | -1    |
| member                | -1    |
| network               | 10    |
| pool                  | 10    |
| port                  | 50    |
| router                | 4     |
| security_group        | 10    |
| security_group_rule   | 100   |
| subnet                | 10    |
| vip                   | 10    |
| vpnservice            | -1    |
+-----------------------+-------+
```

Figure A.3

Listing tenant quotas

To list the quotas of a tenant, use the Neutron `quota-list` command as shown below:

    Usage: quota-list

If a tenant is using the default quotas, no output will be provided. If the quotas are modified, the output will resemble the following screenshot:

Figure A.4

Deleting tenant quotas

To make the tenant quotas revert to their default value, use the Neutron `quota-delete` command, as follows:

    Usage: quota-delete --tenant-id TENANT_ID

The `quota-delete` command results in all per-tenant quotas being reverted to their default values. It is not possible for a single quota to revert.

Cisco Nexus 1000V command reference

OpenStack Networking supports the Cisco Nexus 1000V switch through the use of an API extension and plugin. The following commands enable you to manage network profiles, policy profiles, profile binding, and credentials:

* `cisco-credential-create`
* `cisco-credential-delete`
* `cisco-credential-list`
* `cisco-credential-show`
* `cisco-network-profile-create`
* `cisco-network-profile-delete`
* `cisco-network-profile-list`
* `cisco-network-profile-show`
* `cisco-network-profile-update`
* `cisco-policy-profile-list`
* `cisco-policy-profile-show`
* `cisco-policy-profile-update`

The `cisco-network-profile` commands enable you to create, modify, list, delete, and show details of Cisco Nexus 1000V network profiles.

The `cisco-policy-profile` commands enable you to list and show details of Cisco Nexus 1000V policy profiles as well as associate or disassociate profiles with tenants.

The `cisco-credential` commands enable you to create, update, delete, and show details of Cisco Nexus 1000V credentials.

For more information regarding configuring a Cisco Nexus 1000V with KVM in OpenStack, refer to the official Cisco product page at the following location:

`http://www.cisco.com/c/en/us/products/switches/nexus-1000v-kvm/index.html`

VMware NSX command reference

OpenStack Networking supports VMware NSX through the use of API extensions and plugins. These plugins leverage standard and extended Neutron commands to manage network resources. The following Neutron commands are specific to the NSX extension:

- `net-gateway-connect`
- `net-gateway-create`
- `net-gateway-delete`
- `net-gateway-disconnect`
- `net-gateway-list`
- `net-gateway-show`
- `net-gateway-update`
- `gateway-device-create`
- `gateway-device-delete`
- `gateway-device-list`
- `gateway-device-show`
- `gateway-device-update`
- `queue-create`
- `queue-delete`
- `queue-list`
- `queue-show`

For more information regarding configuring Neutron with the NSX plugin, refer to the *OpenStack Configuration Reference* guide at the following location:

`http://docs.openstack.org/kilo/config-reference/content/networking-plugin-nsx.html`

Nuage VSP command reference

OpenStack Networking supports Nuage Networks **Virtual Service Platform (VSP)** through the use of API extensions and plugins. These plugins leverage standard and extended Neutron commands to manage network resources. The following Neutron commands are specific to the Nuage extension:

- `nuage-netpartition-create`

- nuage-netpartition-delete
- nuage-netpartition-list
- nuage-netpartition-show

For more information regarding the Nuage plugin, refer to the Nuage Networks product documentation at the following location:

http://www.nuagenetworks.net/products/virtualized-services-platform/

L3 metering

The L3 metering extension enables administrators to assign labels to networks to facilitate the metering of the traffic traversing a virtual router. A metering label contains metering rules and is associated with a tenant. The following Neutron commands are specific to the L3 metering extension:

- meter-label-create
- meter-label-delete
- meter-label-list
- meter-label-rule-create
- meter-label-rule-delete
- meter-label-rule-list
- meter-label-rule-show
- meter-label-show

The Neutron metering agent can be installed on the node hosting the Neutron router with the following command:

```
# apt-get install neutron-metering-agent
```

The configuration file can be found at /etc/neutron/metering-agent.ini. The configuration and use of the Neutron metering agent is outside the scope of this book. For more information on the metering agent, refer to the blueprint at the following location:

https://wiki.openstack.org/wiki/Neutron/Metering/Bandwidth

The LBaaS v2 API

The LBaaS v2 extension enables tenants to manage load balancers for their virtual machine instances. The v2 API provides improved object models to support advanced use cases, such as layer 7, TLS, high availability, and more. The following Neutron commands are specific to the LBaaS v2 extension:

- `lbaas-healthmonitor-create`
- `lbaas-healthmonitor-delete`
- `lbaas-healthmonitor-list`
- `lbaas-healthmonitor-show`
- `lbaas-healthmonitor-update`
- `lbaas-listener-create`
- `lbaas-listener-delete`
- `lbaas-listener-list`
- `lbaas-listener-show`
- `lbaas-listener-update`
- `lbaas-loadbalancer-create`
- `lbaas-loadbalancer-delete`
- `lbaas-loadbalancer-list`
- `lbaas-loadbalancer-show`
- `lbaas-loadbalancer-update`
- `lbaas-member-create`
- `lbaas-member-delete`
- `lbaas-member-list`
- `lbaas-member-show`
- `lbaas-member-update`
- `lbaas-pool-create`
- `lbaas-pool-delete`
- `lbaas-pool-list`
- `lbaas-pool-show`
- `lbaas-pool-update`

The LBaaS v2 extension is considered experimental as of the Kilo release of OpenStack; however, its configuration and use is outside the scope of this book.

Summary

As features that extend Neutron's functionality are added to it, most are implemented as extensions to the core API. For more information on how to utilize some of the included extensions, refer to the Neutron API documentation found at `http://developer.openstack.org/api-ref-networking-v2-ext.html`.

Many third-party extensions require the use of additional software or hardware that are often proprietary and may have associated support and operational costs. A production-grade OpenStack cloud does not require the use of third-party extensions and can simply leverage the open-source compute and networking technologies outlined in this book. Proprietary software and hardware may provide additional features, functionality, and stability that are not yet available with open-source alternatives and should be taken into consideration when developing your OpenStack network architecture.

In *Appendix B, Virtualizing the Environment*, we will take a look at the use of the virtualization software known as VirtualBox as an alternative to physical hardware when completing the exercises outlined in this book.

Virtualizing the Environment

Throughout this book, many examples and architectures assume that a physical network and server hardware are used for the OpenStack infrastructure. If you do not have the physical hardware available, it is possible to set up a virtual environment using software such as VMware ESX/ESXi or VirtualBox. This appendix is meant to assist with the setup of a virtual environment using VirtualBox so that many of the examples throughout the book can be followed. This appendix covers the following topics:

- VirtualBox 5.0.x configuration on MacOS X 10.11 (El Capitan)
- Changes to the OpenStack installation process

Configuring VirtualBox networking

When configuring VirtualBox networking, the following networks and types are required:

Network Type	Name	Network	Adapter Address	DHCP
NAT	<default>	<default>	<default>	Yes
Host-only	vboxnet0	10.254.254.0/24	10.254.254.1	No
Host-only	vboxnet1	10.50.0.0/24	10.50.0.1	No
Internal	overlay	172.18.0.0/24	n/a	No

Some of these networks are configured within the **Preferences** window of the VirtualBox application, while others are configured within the virtual machine settings window. The configuration of these networks is covered in the following sections.

Configuring host-only networks

To configure host-only networks within VirtualBox, open up the **Preferences** window. On a MacOS X machine, this can be found under the **VirtualBox** menu; on a Windows machine, this can be found under the **File** menu. By default, the **General** settings window will appear:

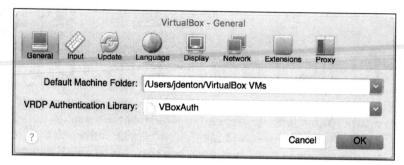

Figure B.1

Perform the following steps to configure the host-only networks:

1. Click on the **Host-only Networks** button to reveal the existing host-only networks:

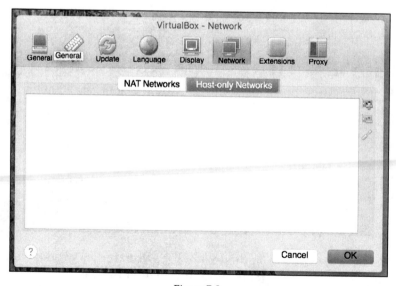

Figure B.2

2. Here, there are no host-only networks defined by default. On the right-hand side of the window, click on the icon shaped like a PCI card with a plus sign to add a new network:

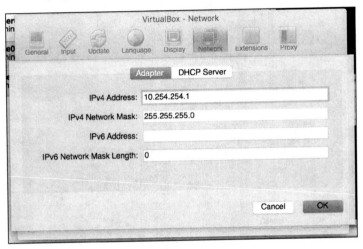

Figure B.3

The first network will correspond to MGMT_NET, which is the OpenStack management and API network. The host machine, in this case the workstation running VirtualBox, needs an IP address from the network in order to communicate with the virtual OpenStack infrastructure nodes. Specify the address as `10.254.254.1` and a netmask of `255.255.255.0`.

3. Be sure to disable DHCP in the **DHCP Server** section and click on the **OK** button to save the changes. Once the changes are saved, the network will appear in the list:

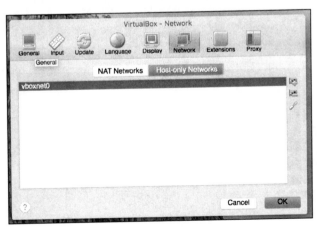

Figure B.4

4. Add an additional network that will be used for external network traffic, specifically the floating IP network `10.50.0.0/24`:

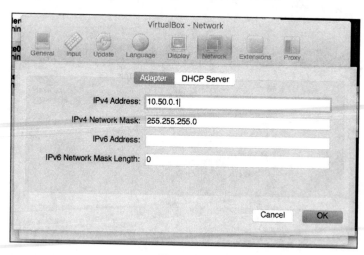

Figure B.5

5. Click on **OK** to save the changes. VirtualBox automatically configures an interface on the host machine with the address `10.50.0.1` and will be able to communicate with the floating IPs that are configured throughout the book. Once the changes are saved, both networks will be listed under **Host-only Networks**:

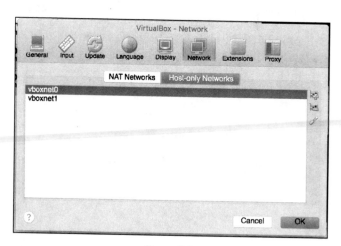

Figure B.6

6. Click on the **OK** button to save the networks.

Creating a virtual machine

To create a virtual machine, perform the following steps:

1. Click on the **New** icon in VirtualBox Manager:

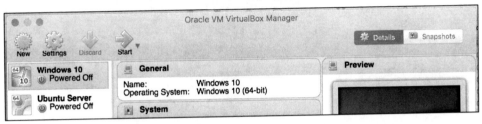

Figure B.7

2. In the wizard, name the virtual machine and specify the operating system version; then, click on **Continue**:

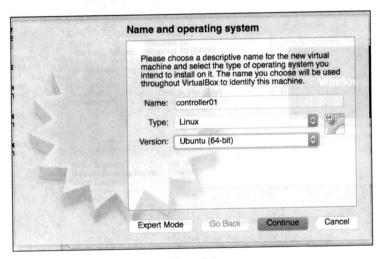

Figure B.8

3. In the next window, specify the amount of memory to be allocated to the virtual machine and click on Continue. A minimum of 4096 MB of RAM is recommended:

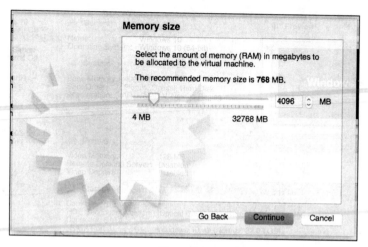

Figure B.9

4. In the next window, click on **Continue** to create a virtual hard disk:

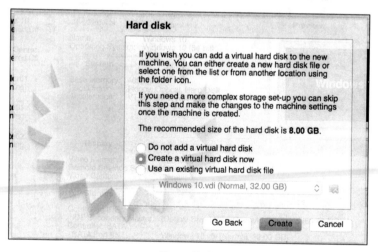

Figure B.10

5. A hard disk wizard will appear that allows you to specify the virtual hard disk type. Choose the default VDI image type and click on **Continue**:

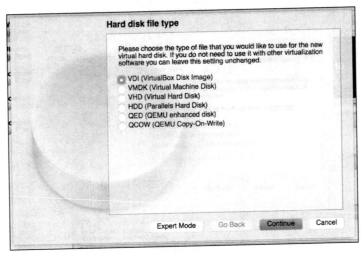

Figure B.11

6. The next step of the wizard allows you to specify whether the disk should grow dynamically as data is added up to the maximum size or be fully allocated at creation. Choose your preference and click on **Continue**:

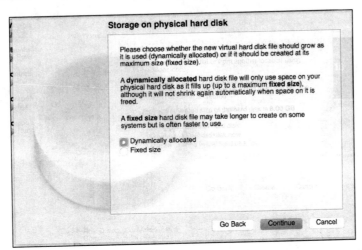

Figure B.12

7. Lastly, provide a name for the virtual hard disk file and the size of the disk to be created. For this book, a minimum of 8 GB is recommended:

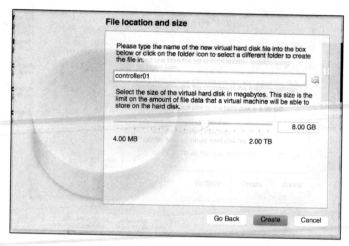

Figure B.13

8. Click on the **Create** button to complete the creation of the virtual machine. The virtual machine will be listed in VirtualBox Manager:

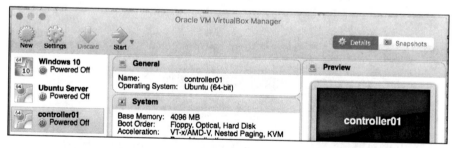

Figure B.14

Repeat these steps as necessary to create additional virtual machines that will serve as compute01 and compute02.

Configuring a virtual machine

Before an operating system is installed on the virtual machine, it is a good idea to configure the virtual network interfaces available to the machine through the following steps:

1. In VirtualBox Manager, choose the virtual machine and click on the **Settings** icon. A window will appear that defaults to the **General** settings:

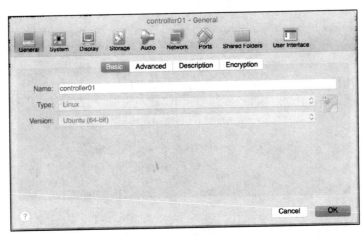

Figure B.15

2. Click on the **Network** icon to modify the network interfaces presented to the virtual machine. The first adapter available, **Adapter 1**, should be enabled and attached to the vboxnet0 host-only network that was created earlier:

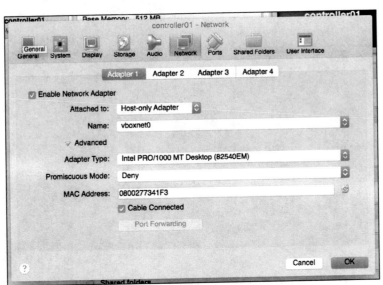

Figure B.16

3. **Adapter 2** should be enabled and attached to the internal network named `overlay`. Internal networks can be specified in the free-form text box labeled **Name:**

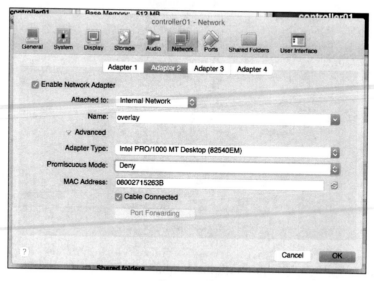

Figure B.17

4. **Adapter 3** should be enabled and attached to the `vboxnet1` host-only network created earlier. The **Promiscuous Mode** setting should be changed to `Allow All` in order to support 802.1q VLAN tagging between the virtual machines:

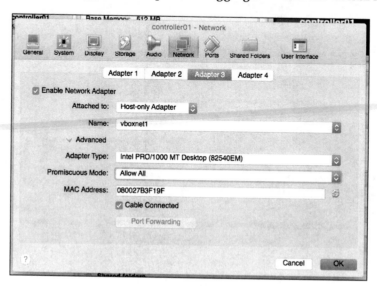

Figure B.18

5. **Adapter 4** should be enabled and attached to the NAT network:

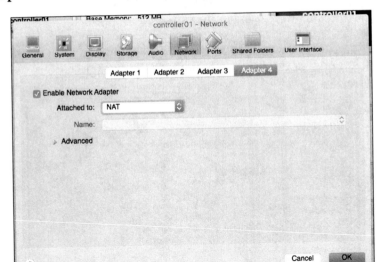

Figure B.19

By default, VirtualBox provides a NAT network that allows virtual machines to use the host machine for outbound network access. This network is required for the virtual OpenStack infrastructure nodes to download the OpenStack software. The NAT network is a DHCP network that provides the virtual machines with an IP address and default route through the host machine.

6. Click on the **OK** button to complete the network adapter configuration process and close the settings window.

Repeat these steps as necessary to configure additional virtual machines.

Installing the Ubuntu operating system

Before an operating system can be installed, an ISO image must be downloaded from the Internet and attached to the virtual machine as a CD. The Ubuntu 14.04 LTS Server operating system can be downloaded from the following location:

```
http://www.ubuntu.com/download/server
```

Attaching the ISO to the virtual machine

Once the ISO is downloaded, perform the following steps:

1. Select the virtual machine in VirtualBox Manager and click on the **Settings** icon. Click on the **Storage** icon to manage the storage options:

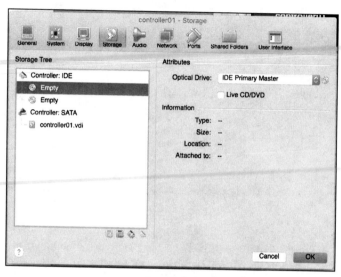

Figure B.20

2. Click on the first CD icon labeled **Empty** to modify the Primary IDE Slave controller. Click on the CD icon to attach the ISO to the virtual machine. When prompted, click on **Choose Virtual Optical Disk File** to find the ISO on the local machine:

Figure B.21

3. Select the ISO and click on **Open** to attach the image. Once attached, the image will be listed under the IDE controller:

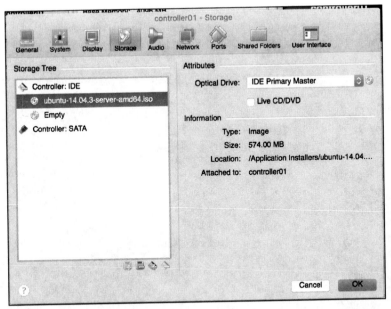

Figure B.22

4. Click on **OK** to close the settings window.

Starting the virtual machine

From VirtualBox Manager, select the virtual machine and click on the **Start** icon:

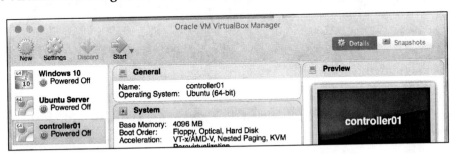

Figure B.23

The virtual machine will boot off the CD image and present you with the installation screen:

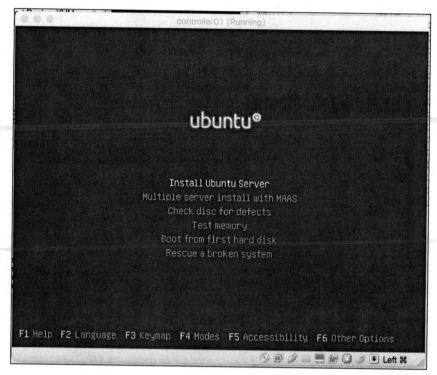

Figure B.24

Installing the guest operating system is outside the scope of this book. However, there are plenty of guides available on the Internet, including the following from Ubuntu:

```
https://help.ubuntu.com/lts/serverguide/installing-from-cd.html
```

It is safe to ignore the prompts to configure networking as these tasks will be completed once the virtual machine is up and running.

Repeat these steps as necessary to install the operating system on additional virtual machines.

Configuring virtual machine networking

Once the guest operating system is installed, it is time to configure the networking within the virtual machine. This includes the setup of the management, overlay, external, and NAT networks.

Accessing the virtual machine

Before networking is configured, access to the virtual machine will be limited to the console. From the virtual machine console, enter the credentials specified during the installation process. A successful login should result in a screen similar to the following:

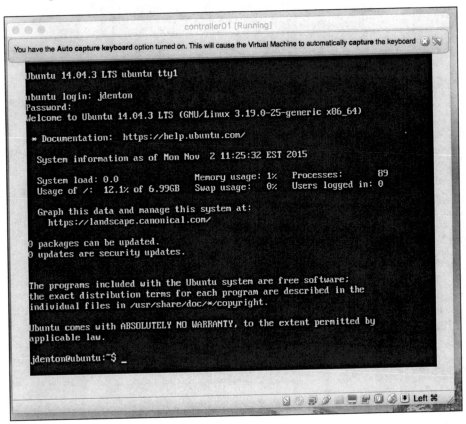

Figure B.25

Use the sudo command to log in as root:

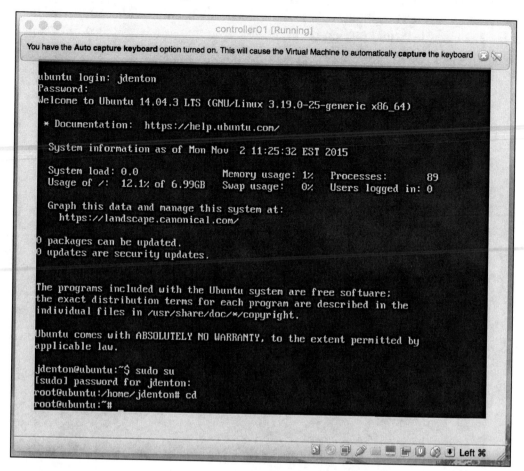

Figure B.26

Configuring network interfaces

Using the `ip a` command to verify that four network interfaces are attached to the virtual machine. The network interfaces will likely be labeled `eth0` through `eth3`:

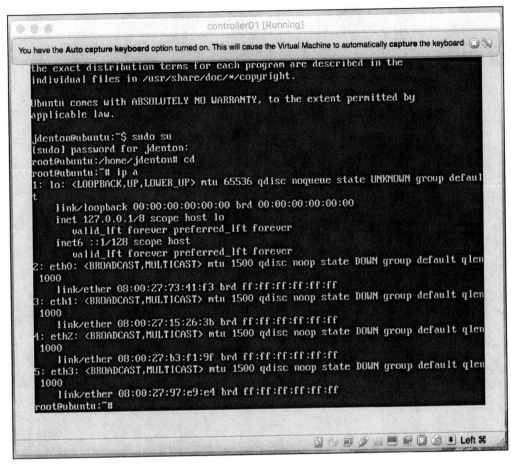

Figure B.27

Using a text editor, edit the network interfaces file found at `/etc/network/`
`interfaces` and add the following interfaces and their respective addresses.
The addresses can be found in *Chapter 2, Installing OpenStack*:

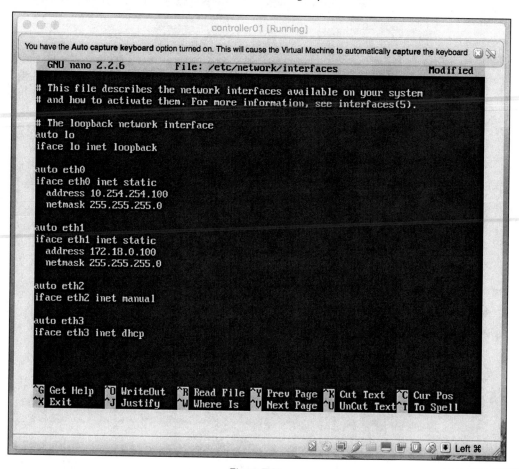

Figure B.28

Close the file and run `ifup --all` to bring up the network interfaces:

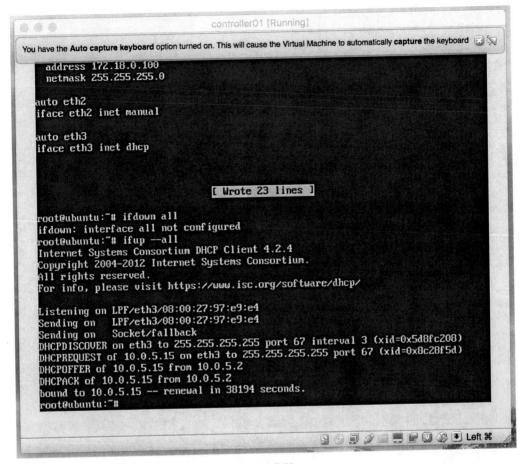

Figure B.29

The output of the `ip a` command shows that the interfaces are UP and configured with the specified addresses:

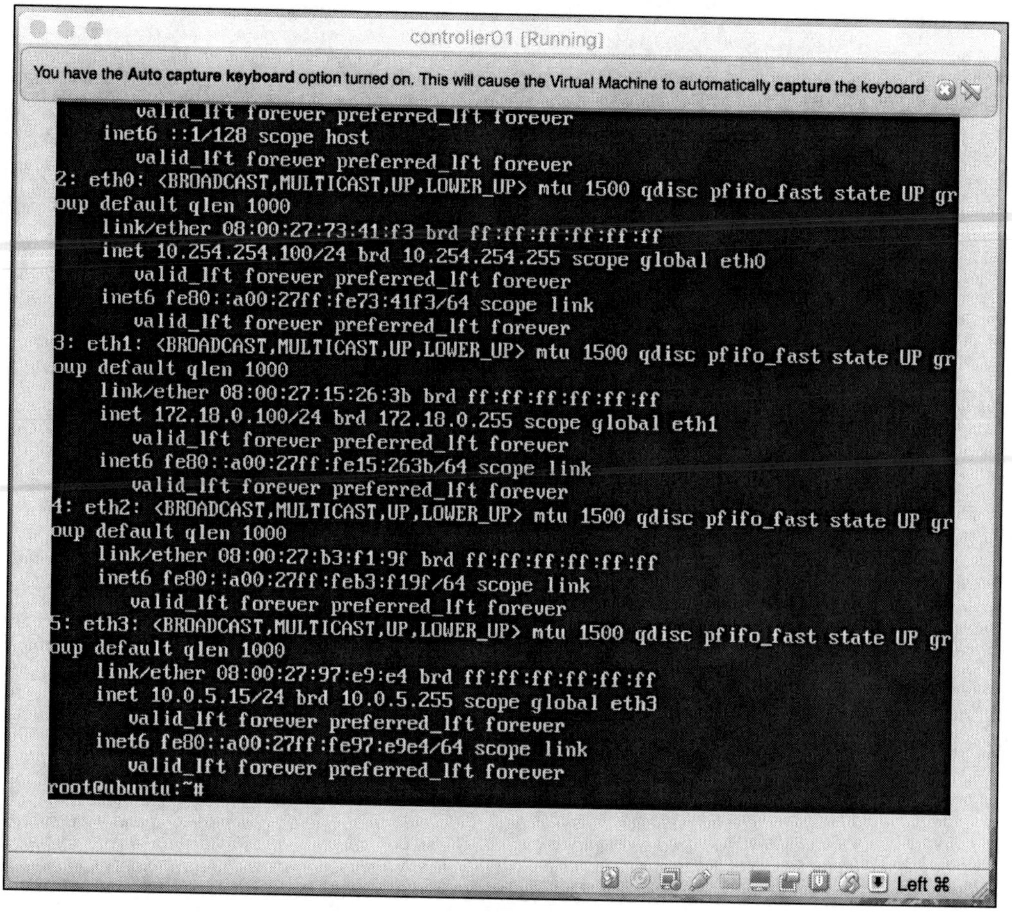

Figure B.30

A quick connectivity test shows that the virtual machine is able to access the Internet:

```
          valid_lft forever preferred_lft forever
3: eth1: <BROADCAST,MULTICAST,UP,LOWER_UP> mtu 1500 qdisc pfifo_fast state UP gr
oup default qlen 1000
    link/ether 08:00:27:15:26:3b brd ff:ff:ff:ff:ff:ff
    inet 172.18.0.100/24 brd 172.18.0.255 scope global eth1
       valid_lft forever preferred_lft forever
    inet6 fe80::a00:27ff:fe15:263b/64 scope link
       valid_lft forever preferred_lft forever
4: eth2: <BROADCAST,MULTICAST,UP,LOWER_UP> mtu 1500 qdisc pfifo_fast state UP gr
oup default qlen 1000
    link/ether 08:00:27:b3:f1:9f brd ff:ff:ff:ff:ff:ff
    inet6 fe80::a00:27ff:feb3:f19f/64 scope link
       valid_lft forever preferred_lft forever
5: eth3: <BROADCAST,MULTICAST,UP,LOWER_UP> mtu 1500 qdisc pfifo_fast state UP gr
oup default qlen 1000
    link/ether 08:00:27:97:e9:e4 brd ff:ff:ff:ff:ff:ff
    inet 10.0.5.15/24 brd 10.0.5.255 scope global eth3
       valid_lft forever preferred_lft forever
    inet6 fe80::a00:27ff:fe97:e9e4/64 scope link
       valid_lft forever preferred_lft forever
root@ubuntu:~# ping 8.8.8.8
PING 8.8.8.8 (8.8.8.8) 56(84) bytes of data.
64 bytes from 8.8.8.8: icmp_seq=1 ttl=63 time=28.4 ms
64 bytes from 8.8.8.8: icmp_seq=2 ttl=63 time=29.6 ms
64 bytes from 8.8.8.8: icmp_seq=3 ttl=63 time=28.4 ms
^C
--- 8.8.8.8 ping statistics ---
3 packets transmitted, 3 received, 0% packet loss, time 2004ms
rtt min/avg/max/mdev = 28.454/28.845/29.621/0.565 ms
root@ubuntu:~#
```

Figure B.31

Repeat these steps as necessary to configure the network interfaces on additional virtual machines using the table provided at the beginning of this appendix.

Accessing a virtual machine over SSH

Once networking is configured on the virtual machines, it should be possible to access them over the management network via SSH from your client workstation. Within a terminal, SSH to the virtual machines using the username and password provided during installation:

```
retina-imac:~ jdenton$ ssh jdenton@10.254.254.100
The authenticity of host '10.254.254.100 (10.254.254.100)' can't be established.
ECDSA key fingerprint is SHA256:iBQym782HQddwZxW8YcxDbzMsOn74mRj03njCLy7yT8.
Are you sure you want to continue connecting (yes/no)? yes
Warning: Permanently added '10.254.254.100' (ECDSA) to the list of known hosts.
jdenton@10.254.254.100's password:
Welcome to Ubuntu 14.04.3 LTS (GNU/Linux 3.19.0-25-generic x86_64)

 * Documentation:  https://help.ubuntu.com/

  System information as of Mon Nov  2 11:40:25 EST 2015

  System load:  0.42               Users logged in:       0
  Usage of /:   12.1% of 6.99GB    IP address for eth0: 10.254.254.100
  Memory usage: 1%                 IP address for eth1: 172.18.0.100
  Swap usage:   0%                 IP address for eth3: 10.0.5.15
  Processes:    85

  Graph this data and manage this system at:
    https://landscape.canonical.com/

0 packages can be updated.
0 updates are security updates.

Last login: Mon Nov  2 11:40:25 2015
jdenton@ubuntu:~$
```

Figure B.32

Verify connectivity to each host over the management network. Once you successfully log in to each host, you may proceed with the installation of OpenStack documented in *Chapter 2, Installing OpenStack*.

 It is safe to ignore any network interface configuration directives during the installation process as network interfaces are configured as part of the process documented in this appendix.

Changes to the OpenStack installation

OpenStack can run in a virtualized environment, but various components must be tuned accordingly. The configuration is not optimal but should provide an experience that is acceptable for demonstration purposes.

Changes to the Nova configuration

After the OpenStack installation is complete, a change must be made to the Nova configuration on the virtual machines running the `nova-compute` service before instances can be booted. Software-based virtualization must be enabled in place of the faster, hardware-based KVM hypervisor.

On the compute node virtual machines, edit the auxiliary Nova configuration file at `/etc/nova/nova-compute.conf` and set `virt_type` to qemu from kvm:

```
[libvirt]
...
virt_type=qemu
```

Restart the `nova-compute` service on both the compute nodes with the following command:

```
# service nova-compute restart
```

Changes to the Neutron configuration

Due to the lack of flexibility in configuring tagged networks with VirtualBox, the external `GATEWAY_NET` provider network that was configured in *Chapter 7, Creating Standalone Routers with Neutron*, must be configured as a flat network. To enable the use of flat networks, the `flat_networks` configuration option in the ML2 configuration file must be updated.

Using a text editor, update the `flat_networks` configuration option within the `[ml2_type_flat]` section of the ML2 configuration file on all hosts with the following:

```
[ml2_type_flat]
...
flat_networks = physnet2
```

For reference, the ML2 plugin configuration file can be found at `/etc/neutron/plugins/ml2/ml2_conf.ini`.

Restart the `neutron-server` service on the controller node for the changes to take effect.

```
# service neutron-server restart
```

When creating the GATEWAY_NET network, be sure to use the `--provider:network_type=flat` and `--provider:physical_network=physnet2` options rather than `vlan`. Your workstation should be able to access floating IPs thanks to the VirtualBox host-only network configuration implemented earlier in this appendix.

Summary

A virtualized environment using VirtualBox provides the ability to demonstrate and test many of the configurations and examples outlined in this book. However, there are limitations that inhibit the usefulness of a virtualized environment, such as the use of software virtualization with qemu and the inability of an instance to access remote networks, including the Internet, without network modifications to the underlying host, which are outside the scope of this book. Whenever possible, the use of physical hardware is recommended to ensure a successful experience.

Index

Thank you for buying
Learning OpenStack Networking (Neutron)
Second Edition

About Packt Publishing

Packt, pronounced 'packed', published its first book, *Mastering phpMyAdmin for Effective MySQL Management*, in April 2004, and subsequently continued to specialize in publishing highly focused books on specific technologies and solutions.

Our books and publications share the experiences of your fellow IT professionals in adapting and customizing today's systems, applications, and frameworks. Our solution-based books give you the knowledge and power to customize the software and technologies you're using to get the job done. Packt books are more specific and less general than the IT books you have seen in the past. Our unique business model allows us to bring you more focused information, giving you more of what you need to know, and less of what you don't.

Packt is a modern yet unique publishing company that focuses on producing quality, cutting-edge books for communities of developers, administrators, and newbies alike. For more information, please visit our website at www.packtpub.com.

About Packt Open Source

In 2010, Packt launched two new brands, Packt Open Source and Packt Enterprise, in order to continue its focus on specialization. This book is part of the Packt Open Source brand, home to books published on software built around open source licenses, and offering information to anybody from advanced developers to budding web designers. The Open Source brand also runs Packt's Open Source Royalty Scheme, by which Packt gives a royalty to each open source project about whose software a book is sold.

Writing for Packt

We welcome all inquiries from people who are interested in authoring. Book proposals should be sent to author@packtpub.com. If your book idea is still at an early stage and you would like to discuss it first before writing a formal book proposal, then please contact us; one of our commissioning editors will get in touch with you.

We're not just looking for published authors; if you have strong technical skills but no writing experience, our experienced editors can help you develop a writing career, or simply get some additional reward for your expertise.

OpenStack Cloud Security

ISBN: 978-1-78217-098-3   Paperback: 160 pages

Build a secure OpenStack cloud to withstand all common attacks

1. Design, implement, and deliver a safe and sound OpenStack cluster using best practices.

2. Create a production-ready environment and make sure your cloud storage and other resources are secure.

3. A step-by-step tutorial packed with real-world solutions that helps you learn easily and quickly.

Production Ready OpenStack - Recipes for Successful Environments

ISBN: 978-1-78398-690-3   Paperback: 210 pages

Over 90 practical and highly applicable recipes to successfully deploy various OpenStack configurations in production

1. Get a deep understanding of OpenStack's internal structure and services.

2. Learn real-world examples on how to build and configure various production grade use cases for each of OpenStack's services.

3. Use a step-by-step approach to install and configure OpenStack's services to provide Compute, Storage, and Networking as a services for cloud workloads.

Please check **www.PacktPub.com** for information on our titles

CPSIA information can be obtained
at www.ICGtesting.com
Printed in the USA
FSOW01n2347220316
18304FS